Psychology in Industrial Organizations

LAURENCE SIEGEL, PH.D.

Chairman, Department of Psychology
Professor of Psychology
Louisiana State University

IRVING M. LANE, PH.D.

Assistant Professor of Psychology
Louisiana State University

1974 · Third Edition

RICHARD D. IRWIN, INC. Homewood, Illinois 60430
IRWIN-DORSEY INTERNATIONAL London, England WC2H 9NJ
IRWIN-DORSEY LIMITED Georgetown, Ontario L7G 4B3

Third Edition

First Printing, April 1974

Previous editions published under the title
Industrial Psychology

ISBN 0-256-01563-5
Library of Congress Catalog Card No. 73–91791

Printed in the United States of America

To those whose smiles light up our worlds

Preface

Successive revisions of a book entail an evolutionary process which at some point generates an offspring qualitatively different in significant ways from its ancestors. Such has occurred with this book as evidenced by the fact of coauthorship, revision of the Table of Contents, and the change in title of this edition from *Industrial Psychology* to *Psychology in Industrial Organizations*. Nevertheless certain assumptions have permeated this endeavor since writing the first word of the first edition about 14 years ago.

First, the book is intended for undergraduate students enrolled in *survey* courses variously designated Business Psychology, Industrial Psychology, or Industrial and Organizational Psychology. Our aim is to provide an overview of the full scope of the field in a text appropriate to a single quarter or single semester course.

Second, a background in introductory psychology will probably prove helpful to the student but is not indispensable. While preparing the manuscript we have attempted to keep in mind the type of student likely to enroll in the course. For a few students, this course will be a first exposure to a study of psychology; many will have had a prior course in introductory psychology. It has been our experience that both groups benefit when certain "bridges" between the content regarded as *general* psychology and that as *industrial and organizational* psychology are provided.

Such bridges appear at various points in the text: the viewpoint and methods of present-day psychology are presented in the first chapters; certain principles of measurement are discussed in the chapter on testing; pertinent concepts of learning are presented in the training chapter; motivation is discussed in the context of job satisfaction; and some rudimentary principles of social psychology, with elaboration of those particularly pertinent to leadership and organizations, precede the consideration of their applications in industry. These bridges are relatively brief and are not intended to duplicate the content of an introductory psychology course. Rather, they were designed to facilitate the transition from discussions of behavior in general to a discussion of industrial behavior.

Granting these assumptions, this revision differs from its immediate predecessor in two major ways. First, through deletions and additions, we have attempted to integrate the recent research literature into our discussions of "traditional" topics carried over from the previous editions. This has led to expanded coverage of such topics as testing and training for disadvantaged employees, job enrichment and job enlargement, alternative work schedules (such as the four-day week), the social implications of work, managerial assessment centers, and laboratory (including sensitivity) training. Second, we have altered the balance of the text by reducing the proportional coverage of topics in personnel psychology (7 of 21 chapters in the second edition versus 5 of 20 chapters here) and increasing the proportional coverage of topics in human relations and organizational psychology (from 5 of 21 chapters in the earlier edition to 7 of 20 chapters here.)

This alteration in balance entailed several major changes in the internal structure of the book. Two of the chapters from the second edition have been dropped entirely: one designated "Job Evaluation" because of feedback from colleagues that they tended to omit discussion of this topic; the other designated "Morale" because we judged it to have outworn its usefulness as a concept in understanding behavior in organizations. Six other chapters from the second edition have been here compressed into three. And one chapter from the previous edition ("Organizational Theories and Structures") has here been elaborated to five.

The five new chapters provide a greatly expanded discussion of the (a) origins of the human relations movement in both the Hawthorne and Tavistock Institute Coal Mining studies, (b) theoretical positions of McGregor, Herzberg, and Likert; (c) methods of studying behavior in organizations; (d) social psychology of organizations; and (e) implementation and evaluation of planned organizational change.

Many other more subtle changes in topical placement and coverage will be apparent to users of the previous editions. These include a revised set of unit designations moving the reader sequentially from an introductory unit to personnel psychology, human factors psychology, human relations psychology, organizational psychology, and finally to consumer psychology.

So much for the changes. We are obliged to point to three features of the earlier edition which we still regard as useful and desirable and therefore have continued in the present one.

1. We still allocate two full chapters to the introductory unit (Scope and Methods) in keeping with our assumption about the academic background of most students taking this course.

2. We still regard consumer psychology as an appropriate topic for inclusion in this text even though some instructors—particularly those teaching a one-quarter course—do not cover it.

3. We have retained as an Appendix a chapter on "Statistical Computation" for use by instructors desiring it.

We are under no delusion that this book will satisfy all psychologists with respect to breadth of coverage, depth of treatment, or topical emphases. However, we hopefully anticipate that the book will contribute effectively to the instructional partnership formed by teacher and author. A textbook, after all, is not a course. It may serve as the skeleton for a course and even provide some of the muscle for it; but the lifeblood of a subject is infused into it by the teacher.

We acknowledge with gratitude the helpful comments volunteered over the years by those of our colleagues who have accepted us as their partner in this way, and by others who have provided systematic critical readings of the manuscript. All of these persons will recognize in the finished work some evidence that certain of their suggestions were implemented.

February 1974   LAURENCE SIEGEL
                                         IRVING M. LANE

Table of Contents

I.

Introduction

In the course of a single day, the psychologist working in an industrial setting may find himself called upon to administer tests, confer with supervisors, attend a training conference, design an experiment to test the effectiveness of a new advertising campaign, perform the statistical analysis of questionnaire data from a morale survey, and counsel an employee who is experiencing some kind of personal difficulty. This list of functions is by no means exhaustive; it represents just a sample of the industrial psychologist's sphere of activity.

The chapters in this section are designed to provide a base for subsequent discussions. These chapters will introduce you to the field of industrial psychology by indicating something of the scope of psychological services available to business and industry, the training and employment of industrial psychologists, and the research methods employed by them. In short, the two chapters which ensue focus upon what the industrial psychologist does and how he goes about doing it.

1. Scope of Industrial Psychology

Psychology is usually defined as the scientific study of behavior. As such it has matured considerably during the past half century. Its maturity is evidenced by its increased reliance upon the appropriate application of scientific methods and its increased devotion to studying "behavior." Thus it is relatively uncommon now for even moderately sophisticated persons to confuse the methods and concerns of scientific psychology with those of such *pseudo*psychologies as physiognomy, phrenology, and palmistry. Whereas the latter attempted to relate personality to facial characteristics (physiognomy), bumps on the head (phrenology), or lines in the palm (palmistry), psychology attempts systematically to understand how and why people act as they do.

One of the consequences of the maturation of scientific psychology is a growing demand for the application of psychological knowledge and the consequent development of psychological *practice*. To the extent that behavior can be scientifically understood, it may be predicted in advance of its occurrence and sometimes may be modified. Such applications of psychological knowledge are clearly relevant to people at work and constitute the subject matter of industrial psychology.

Whereas not all company executives are "sold" on the desirability of consulting with an industrial psychologist, their receptivity seems gradually to be increasing. One survey, taken about 30 years ago (Stagner, 1946), reported 53 percent of a sample of corporate executives as favoring the employment of industrial psychologists. In a more recent survey of another sample of executives (Feinberg

3

& Lefkowitz, 1962), this percentage had increased to 66 percent. Furthermore, among those executives holding favorable attitudes toward employing industrial psychologists, the latter study revealed greater acceptance of the psychologist's potential contribution to solving problems in the areas of personnel selection, personnel training, and morale than to problems in such areas as production efficiency and accident control. Apparently in these latter areas management has not been apprised of some of the significant developments in industrial psychology.

Rather than view this failure of total acceptance pessimistically, it is significant that acceptance is so high in view of the short history of scientific psychology. The first laboratory for studying psychological phenomena was initiated about 90 years ago; and the first major book dealing with *industrial* psychology was written only about 55 years ago.

In spite of this very short history of scientific psychology, people have undoubtedly always evidenced a concern for how and why human beings behave as they do. Until recently this concern was largely speculative. It was based upon opinion and casual observation which gave rise to a considerable body of folklore and "common sense" about behavior.

One needs only to point to the endless series of "psychological" articles appearing in newspapers, magazines, and Sunday supplements offering prescriptions for child care, advice to the lovelorn, and helpful hints for happy homes, to verify that there is yet today considerable confusion between common sense and psychology. One writer maintains that children must never be spanked because in so doing the parent descends to the child's level; another maintains that spanking itself may be beneficial because it establishes the parent as an authority figure. Whereas one writer advises her female readers to take an active interest in their husbands' activities and hobbies in order better to experience "togetherness," another advises wives not to pry into their husbands' activities lest the husband resent the invasion of his sense of privacy. The more he reads such articles, the more confused the reader becomes until he is forced to conclude that it's all just so much hogwash. The problem arises, of course, because most of these articles are based upon idle speculation rather than upon scientific evidence. They are in most cases written by professional writers capitalizing upon man's desire to understand himself.

One of our purposes in this chapter is to distinguish between

THE IRWIN SERIES IN MANAGEMENT
AND
THE BEHAVIORAL SCIENCES

L. L. Cummings and E. Kirby Warren   *Consulting Editors*
John F. Mee   *Advisory Editor*

Psychology in Industrial Organizations

common sense and scientific psychology. We will describe the activities of psychologists in general, regardless of whether they function in clinics, schools, research organizations, government agencies, or industries. Furthermore, within the general field of psychology, we will bring into clear focus the role of the psychologist in business and industry. To do this we must begin with the broad problem of defining the subject matter of psychology.

THE SUBJECT MATTER OF PSYCHOLOGY

Conceptions about psychology held by most of the public fall somewhere in the vast middle ground between two extreme viewpoints. At one of these extremes still a few people confuse psychologists with mystics. These people fail to distinguish between scientific psychology and the pseudopsychologies; they may even naïvely attribute special "mental powers" to psychologists! At the other extreme, still a few people regard "psychology" as merely a fancy way of spelling "common sense."

Although most persons today take a moderate position between these extremes, they have a rather hazy notion about what it is that psychologists study. This notion usually equates psychology with the study of "mental functions" like intelligence, thinking, and attitudes.

Although fundamentally correct, this notion is a gross oversimplification of the psychologist's activities. We must recognize at the outset that such an important psychological concept as "attitude" is not directly observable. A person's attitudes cannot be seen or bottled for laboratory analysis. They are not immediately apparent to anyone else, even though this someone else may be a psychologist.

We become aware of the existence and operation of such factors by inference. We judge from something a person does or says that he feels and thinks in certain ways. Thus, when dealing with psychological phenomena, we must begin with something observable. However, even when our observations are carefully made we may arrive at a number of alternative inferences or explanations, each of which seems reasonable or tenable. These in turn must be further studied in order to reject all but the most promising of them. The psychologist's orientation throughout the process of observation, inference, and subsequent test of the inference is one of rigorous scientific verification.

To illustrate, an industrial psychologist might hypothesize from an employee's record of abnormal absence from work that he may be dissatisfied with the job for some reason, or that he may be experiencing personal difficulties in his home environment, or that the work itself may be either too demanding or too unstimulating for his intellectual abilities. This by no means exhausts the list of possible explanations, but it will serve for the present illustration. Once made, these hypotheses would have to be examined and sifted until the most likely ones are isolated for the particular case in question, and remedial steps would follow.

The observable factor studied by the psychologist in the instance noted above is the employee's *behavior*. First, attention is focused upon this particular employee because of undesirable industrial behavior, that is, high rate of absence and sickness reports. The psychologist formulates possible explanations and verifies or discards each by noting other behavioral indices. The suspicion of a discrepancy between level of ability and level of required job performance may be checked by administering intelligence and aptitude tests. Such tests provide a sample of the employee's behavior in a controlled setting designed to determine the level of his abilities. The employee may be interviewed and his responses evaluated with respect to job attitudes and personal adjustment. Supervisors or fellow workers may be called upon to record their observations of the employee's behavior on the job.

Emergence of Scientific Psychology

Man has, to be sure, speculated about phenomena of a psychological nature for a long, long time. One can almost imagine Eve selecting from her wardrobe of fig leaves the ones she calculated to make the most favorable impression upon Adam. A *scientific* approach as opposed to a speculative approach, however, awaited a definition of psychological phenomena in terms that were amenable to observation and experimentation. The key to the development of a scientific body of information in the area was the realization that the only phenomenon that could be directly studied was behavior. And this delineation of the subject matter of psychology as "the study of behavior" is generally identified with the establishment of the first laboratory for the study of psychological phenomena by Wilhelm Wundt in 1879.

Psychologists in the early 20th century adopted a systematic approach to understanding behavior. Instead of correlating external signs with character traits as the pseudopsychologists did, the early scientific psychologists studied the responses made by organisms to particular environmental conditions. The basic approach of these early psychologists was systematically to vary some aspect of the environment, thereby providing a *stimulus,* and noting corresponding changes in the organism's *response.* This approach is sometimes referred to as *S-R* psychology.

Perhaps the two most outstanding characteristics of the early scientific approach to psychology were first its emphasis upon rigorous scientific methodology rather than speculation and second its preoccupation with the study of stimulus conditions and the physiology of the receptors. Neither of these characteristics is surprising in view of the fact that early psychologists received most of their formal training in physiology and physics. The effect of this training was to cause them to apply the research methods of these disciplines to the investigation of behavior and to seek the explanation of response in terms of physical stimuli and physiological functions.

This approach to understanding behavior contrasted markedly with the unscientific approach of the pseudopsychologies. It removed behavior from the realm of mere speculation and made it accessible for study by investigators grounded in the rigors of verification. Thus, the early psychologists made enormous strides by establishing the legitimacy and feasibility of a science of behavior and developing a methodology appropriate to this science.

Although the *S-R* approach to behavior marked a vigorous beginning for psychology, its long-range utility was somewhat limited. Some of the difficulties inherent in this early approach to psychology stemmed from the fact that it attempted to become scientific by emulating the procedures and approaches of the older sciences. Rigorous laboratory investigation can be both a strength and a weakness. It is unrealistic to assume that data uncovered in a laboratory can always be generalized to an environment outside the laboratory. Our attitude toward work, for example, differs when we are required to produce in an industrial setting and when we are required to produce in a laboratory. In the latter instance, we are participating in an experiment; in the former, we are doing our job and earning our income. The incentives for performance in these two situations may be quite different even though the physical setting in the laboratory may attempt to duplicate the work setting.

In addition, stimulus-response relationships are exceedingly complex. A given stimulus may evoke different responses from different persons, or even from the same person on different occasions. To understand behavior it is necessary to discover and understand the roles of the variables intervening between stimuli and responses.

Modern Psychology

A clue to the subject matter of psychology as viewed by present-day psychologists is the observation that a given stimulus typically evokes quite a range and variety of responses. This can be simply illustrated by word association in which respondents are asked to reply with the first word that they think of in response to a stimulus word like *round*. Some of the responses to this stimulus are cited in Figure 1–1. You can probably think of others.

FIGURE 1–1

Associations to Stimulus Word *Round*

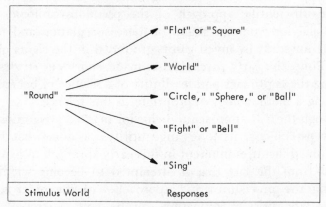

If individual respondents were asked to explain their association between stimulus and response, we might get such varied explanations as "Columbus thought the world was round, not flat"; "I heard the word *round* and thought of its opposite, *square*"; "It made me think of a prizefight"; and so on. Without further laboring the point, it is apparent that the respondents were not replying to a single stimulus word which was uniformly interpreted. Rather, they responded in terms of their personal interpretations of the stimulus word.

An S-I-R *Formulation.*   It is therefore convenient to think of modern psychology as fitting more nearly into an *S-I-R* formulation as opposed to the earlier *S-R* formulation. The response *(R)* is a function of both the stimulus *(S)* and the respondent's interpretation *(I)* of that stimulus. Almost any stimulus, whether it be a word or a more involved stimulus pattern like a memorandum from the supervisor exhorting employees to use safety equipment provided on their machines, may produce a variety of responses depending upon the significance of that stimulus for, and the interpretation of the stimulus by, each individual respondent.

Let us apply the *S-I-R* framework to exploring the range of potential responses employees might make to the aforementioned memorandum regarding safety practices. The stimulus condition *(S)* is identical for all employees; they all receive the same memorandum. This stimulus is evaluated by each employee against the background of his own past experience and attitudes. This evaluation leads each employee to a personal interpretation of the significance of the memorandum for him *(I)* and to a consequent response *(R)*. Several alternative interpretative frameworks and consequent responses are schematically indicated in Figure 1–2.

The relationship between the interpretation of the stimulus condition and the consequent response is considerably oversimplified in the illustration outlined in Figure 1–2. First, many gradations of response other than those indicated in the illustration would be anticipated. And secondly, the memorandum would be interpreted by each employee in the light of other factors in addition to the ones of attitude and past experience. The employee's general satisfaction or dissatisfaction with the job, his physical and mental health, his mood as a result of specific experiences during the day, as well as other variables, may influence his reaction to this apparently simple stimulus condition.

An Elaborated S-I-R *Formulation.*   Thus far we have said that each person's unique interpretation *(I)* of stimulus conditions *(S)* determines how he will respond *(R)* to those conditions. As indicated above, the interpretations made by different people vary with a tremendous number and variety of personal characteristics (like intellectual ability, motivation, emotional state) and previous experiences. Clearly, a person's behavior is flexible. More appropriate

FIGURE 1–2

Multiple Responses to a Uniform Stimulus Condition

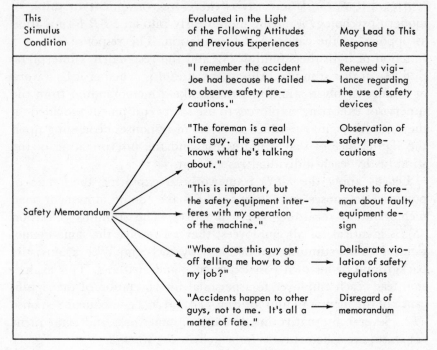

This Stimulus Condition	Evaluated in the Light of the Following Attitudes and Previous Experiences	May Lead to This Response
Safety Memorandum	"I remember the accident Joe had because he failed to observe safety precautions."	Renewed vigilance regarding the use of safety devices
	"The foreman is a real nice guy. He generally knows what he's talking about."	Observation of safety precautions
	"This is important, but the safety equipment interferes with my operation of the machine."	Protest to foreman about faulty equipment design
	"Where does this guy get off telling me how to do my job?"	Deliberate violation of safety regulations
	"Accidents happen to other guys, not to me. It's all a matter of fate."	Disregard of memorandum

responses are substituted for less appropriate ones, implying that the interpretations of stimulus conditions can be modified by experience. In short, people learn.

To indicate something of the influence of past experience upon present behavior requires an elaboration of the *S-I-R* formulation. What occurs after a person behaves in some way? Typically, his behavior is followed by some type of *reinforcement;* that is, an indication of whether his response is appropriate or inappropriate, desirable or undesirable, deserving of praise or reproof, and so on. Such reinforcement may be provided by the responses evoked from other people by his behavior or may be provided by the person himself as he assesses the outcomes of his behavior.

Thus, referring back to Figure 1–2, the employee who disregards the safety memorandum may receive a rebuff from his supervisor for not following instructions. Alternatively, he may suffer an injury which he quite properly attributes to having disregarded the safety

memorandum. In either case the employee's behavior has had consequences. Since these consequences are unfavorable, we refer to them
as *negative* reinforcements. Obviously, praise from a supervisor, a
financial bonus, approval from other workers, or a personal sense of
achievement are all instances of *positive* reinforcements.

An elaborated *S-I-R* formulation showing the influence of reinforcement *(Re)* is given below:

As shown in this scheme, the stimulus condition as interpreted by
the person evokes a response. This response, in turn, is followed by
some kind of reinforcement *(Re)*, the effects of which are "fed
back" into his interpretive framework. If the reinforcement is
positive, the feedback strengthens the existing interpretive framework. However if the reinforcement is negative, the feedback tends
to weaken, and perhaps to modify, the original interpretive framework. Once the *I* is modified, subsequent confrontation by this *S* will
likely generate a modified *R*. This sequence is shown in Figure 1–3
for an employee who learns that accidents can indeed happen to
him.

Of course, the same sequence as outlined in Figure 1–3 can occur
without actual injury as the reinforcement. Hearing about someone
else's injury or experiencing a near-accident can serve the same ends.

Human Systems.   There is an interesting and useful parallel
between the *S-I-R-Re* scheme with a feedback loop as described
above and the concept of a *system* which is further elaborated in the
chapter on engineering psychology. A system, like an electric circuit
to a lamp, has certain inputs (electric current), controls (a switch),
and outputs (glowing bulb). Viewing the human organism as a
system, the stimuli are inputs, the interpretative conditions are
controls, and the responses are outputs.

Furthermore, certain kinds of mechanical systems (that is, closed
loop systems) are self-regulating. Suppose the electric circuit includes a photoelectric cell sensing the daylight outside and activating the control switch only when outside illumination falls below a
twilight level. This cell would then be performing a function similar

FIGURE 1–3

An Illustration of Changed Response Following Reinforcement

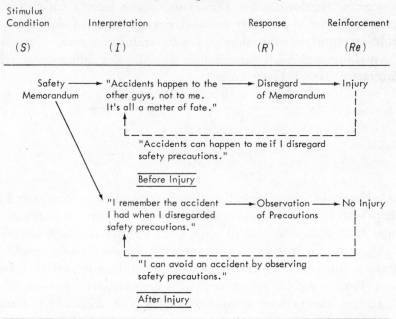

to that of reinforcement in the human system by activating or deactivating the switch through a feedback circuit.

The systems view clarifies the fluid, dynamic, and self-regulatory nature of much human behavior. It also calls attention to the artificiality of designating certain variables as antecedent or causal and others as consequences or effects of these antecedents (Hinrichs, 1970). The interpretive schemes hypothesized in Figure 1–3 can be investigated both as *antecedents* to employee responses to the safety memorandum and as *consequences* of the employee's previous response and associated reinforcement. In the same manner, job satisfaction (discussed in Chapter 16) can and has been investigated both as a consequence of conditions of the job and work environment and as a variable influencing job conditions and the work environment.

PSYCHOLOGY APPLIED TO INDUSTRIAL PROBLEMS

The foregoing discussion has merely hinted at the complexity of human behavior and the challenge of working within the vital and dynamic area of human behavior. Let us now bring the activities of the industrial psychologist, as opposed to specialists in other areas of psychology, into somewhat sharper focus.

We have already defined psychology as "the study of behavior" and have indicated that the industrial psychologist specializes in studying human behavior as it occurs in business and industrial settings. Perhaps the greatest barrier to understanding the functions of the industrial psychologist is the fairly prevalent confusion between industrial psychologists and "efficiency experts." The latter term calls to mind an image of a man more stopwatch than human. The stereotype of an "efficiency expert" is that he equates efficiency with production and regards acceleration or speedup of the activities of each employee as the least expensive road to increased productivity.

Such a stereotype is invalid, bearing no relationship to the activities of the industrial psychologist. He is committed to promoting individual initiative and strengthening personal dignity. The successful realization of these objectives may, of course, be reflected in higher productivity, decreased absenteeism, and other objective criteria of improved performance. The essential point, however, is that the psychologist is interested in maximizing the realization of potential for accomplishment and personal satisfaction. Thus, he has a responsibility to all men, employees as well as employers.

History of Industrial Psychology

It is difficult to date the beginnings of activity that might properly be designated as industrial psychology. The most reasonable date to assign to the formulation of this as an area of specialization within the broader framework of general psychology is 1913 when Hugo Munsterberg's *Psychology and Industrial Efficiency* was published. Efficiency as defined in it involved the dual notions of output or productivity as a function of input or effort.

Although the professional interests of early applied psychologists were rather diverse, American psychologists tended to concentrate most heavily on problems of personnel selection and placement. This emphasis was characteristic of most applied psychological work in the Army during World War I. The successful use of psychological tests for military classification and placement did much to familiarize large segments of the public with the efficacy of psychological testing.

A few years after the end of World War I, the Psychological Corporation was founded to develop and distribute psychological tests and to provide consultative services to industrial and other organizations. In the years since its formation in 1921, the Psychological Corporation has been joined in providing such services by many other such firms both in the United States and abroad.

A noteworthy departure from the early American emphasis upon personnel selection and placement can be dated to 1924 when the Hawthorne studies were undertaken (Roethlisberger & Dickson, 1939). As elaborated in Chapter 11, these studies were designed to determine the relationship between working conditions (like illumination, temperature) and worker efficiency defined by the incidence of fatigue and monotony. While unique in this country, this focus upon the conditions of work had been anticipated somewhat in Great Britain during World War I by the organization of the Industrial Fatigue Research Board.

The significant thing about the Hawthorne studies is that they opened a new era of psychological research in industry. What appeared at first to be a simple problem requiring a brief research program became progressively more involved as the studies continued for the next 15 years. These studies were singularly responsible for bringing the *I* aspects of the *S-I-R* formulation into industrial psychology. They raised questions and provided considerable methodology as well as some solutions to issues concerning attitudes, communication, leadership, and organizational structure. These issues, along with personnel matters, are central to contemporary industrial psychology.

The extensive requirements of the military during World War II for improved personnel assessment and training procedures added further impetus to the development of industrial psychology as we know it today. Enormous methodological advances were made in these areas, including refinements of procedures for personnel classification and performance appraisal. In addition, the rapid rate of technological change during and subsequent to World War II led to the formulation of a new area of specialization within industrial psychology—that of engineering psychology. This area is concerned with designing equipment in accord with the capabilities and limitations of the prospective human operators.

The postwar period has seen a continued development of industrial psychology in all of the areas already mentioned—personnel selection and classification, performance appraisal, working conditions, training, leadership, organizational psychology, and engineering psychology. Of these, the last three have probably captured the attention of recent researchers in the field to a somewhat greater extent than the others.

As industry increasingly accepted psychologists' contributions, the industrial psychologist has come more and more to be consulted on matters affecting all aspects of the industrial enterprise. Whereas the field was initially restricted in scope to studying employee behavior, it has now been extended also to include studies of management and consumer behavior. Whereas early industrial psychologists were limited to studies of behavior within the context of a limited work setting, the field now includes consultations leading to changes in the organizational structures subsuming such settings.

There is every reason to believe that the growth and expansion of activity by industrial psychologists will continue in the future. Most of society's significant problems are at least in part psychological. Likewise many of society's significant goals require for their attainment the kinds of knowledge that psychologists have generated in the past and will generate to an even greater extent in the future. With astronauts, automation, the war on poverty, shorter work-weeks, increased requirements for technical and managerial personnel, increasing populations, the consequent possibility of serious food shortages, and the ever-present issues of ethnic, racial, and international relations, there is no shortage of meaningful problems for the field of industrial psychology.

An Overview of the Field

The specific kinds of problems industrial psychologists are called upon to solve are extensive in scope. It will be convenient to indicate something of the range of industrial problems amenable to psychological analysis by presenting what is in essence an overview of the chapters that follow.

Although a book is of necessity divided into chapters and topics, we all realize that people and problems are not neatly segmented in similar fashion. The industrial complex involves interactions cutting across the specific chapter headings and topical organization of any book. Realizing this, let us preview the major topics with which we will subsequently be concerned.

Part I: Scope and Methods. Before we can plunge into a discussion of the applications of psychological principles and methods to industrial problems, we need to know something about psychologists and the ways in which they work. A statement like: "The importance of salary as a determinant of job satisfaction has been vastly overrated by management" is meaningless if the conclusion is predicated upon incomplete or faulty evidence. Thus, the present chapter and the one following are designed to familiarize you with the psychologist's orientation and discipline. These chapters discuss the subject matter and methodology of psychology in general and industrial psychology in particular.

Industrial psychology is an applied discipline. Its practitioner makes direct applications of sound principles underlying knowledge about human behavior gained both from other areas within the broad field of psychology (for example, clinical, experimental, and social psychology) and such other disciplines as sociology, economics, and physiology. These applications are ultimately directed either toward predicting behavior in advance of its occurrence or toward invoking some kind of change in behavior as presently constituted. These two objectives, prediction and change, are a kind of payoff. They represent a practical test of theory.

The point of view taken in this book is that the science and profession of psychology can contribute positively to all elements of the industrial complex. The organization of the book reflects the point of view (Pervin, 1968) that job performance and satisfaction reflect the interaction of individual factors (abilities, interests, drives, and so on) and environmental factors (the work environment, organizational context, and so on).

Part II. Personnel Psychology. This part focuses upon the job applicant and the new employee. The company is often confronted first by the problem of selecting from a group of job applicants those who will best fulfill certain requirements. Which applicants if hired will most likely prove to be efficient and reasonably well-satisfied employees and which ones will find the job too easy, too difficult, or otherwise unsuited to their particular needs and desires?

This is a prediction problem requiring that the psychologist be familiar with the tools and techniques of personnel selection and placement. It may lead him into studies of the predictive efficiency of tests, inventories, interviews, application blanks, and letters of recommendation. He may have to devise new predictive instruments or to modify already existing devices. He must also develop adequate criteria of the outcomes he is attempting to predict, including industrial efficiency and job satisfaction.

Most companies place considerable emphasis upon training programs of various kinds for both new and experienced employees. The primary purpose of industrial training is to develop certain knowledges, skills, and attitudes and to alter working behaviors demonstrated to be relatively inefficient.

A systematic training program is mandatory when a company is compelled to hire inexperienced employees. New employees with prior job experience also benefit from training with respect to company policies and practices. Psychologists can make important contributions to the conduct of such programs. Problems concerning training methods, simulation of working conditions, and teaching approaches have been of significant concern to psychologists for many years.

Industrial training is by no means restricted to new employees. Management may have a number of problems for which a continual program of training for employees already on the job is the only feasible solution. Among these we may simply list as representative the problems of job enlargement, development of potential supervisory personnel, maintenance and improvement of quality as well as output, management development, and preparing employees to take on new jobs created by an ever-expanding technocracy.

Part III. Human Factors Psychology.   This series of chapters is concerned with a constellation of factors affecting the efficiency of employees on the job.

The physical working environment presents a number of problems concerning such things as optimal ventilation, illumination, machine location, and so on. More recently, psychologists have contributed significantly to problems of machine design and the structure of man-machine systems. This activity is particularly critical whenever the complexity of the equipment is such that careless design would strain or exceed human capability. Consider, for example, some of the design problems in developing high-speed aircraft in which a five-second delay during which the pilot fumbles to find a particular lever, knob, button, or dial may well represent a traveled distance of one mile. Less dramatic perhaps but equally important are engineering psychology studies of the optimal location of controls and dials on automobile dashboards and industrial equipment.

In spite of technological advances, and often because of them, fatigue and boredom are often characteristic of work. The deleterious effect of these conditions upon morale, output, and safety are self-evident as problems for psychological analysis.

Part IV. Human Relations Psychology. Our emphasis shifts in Parts IV and V from consideration of individual workers to the interpersonal context for work. In the history of industrial psychology attention to such interpersonal factors as leadership style, informal work groups, and group norms developed after the literature on such traditional topics as personnel selection, placement, training, and the impact of the physical work environment had become fairly extensive.

The evolution of this more contemporary "human relations" viewpoint and its culmination in the body of research on leadership and management development comprises the substance of Part IV. The fact that a man occupies a leadership position by no means guarantees that he will have a willing group of followers. The selection and training of managerial personnel are generally regarded as critical problems in most companies. This statement is not limited to line supervision. Industrial psychologists are increasingly being called upon to develop programs for appraising and developing mid- and top-management.

Part V. Organizational Psychology. Part V elaborates the viewpoints explicated in the preceding section by considering the company organization *in toto* with particular emphasis upon group functioning, motivation and job satisfaction, and attempts at planned organizational change.

The context of work is a social one for most employees. With the exception of a few solitary jobs, most workers are required to interact with one another. Furthermore, an employee brings a social history to the job with him. Outside of work he has many group affiliations including his family, neighborhood, and church, to name just three. Industrial behavior is often clarified by studying the group affiliations and allegiances of the employees. Union and nonunion employees, for example, may react quite differently to salary and promotion policies. Similarly, subgroups of employees by sex, seniority, and level of skill may be responding from different frames of reference.

These social factors interact with other aspects of the job and home environment as well as with work task characteristics and individual employee characteristics culminating in a sense of job satisfaction or dissatisfaction and in a superior, inferior, or average level of job performance.

Motivation is a complex matter. At any moment in time, the goals toward which a person strives reflect the interaction between the present situation and his entire past history. Thus there are widespread individual differences between employees in their attitudes toward work and the satisfactions they derive from it. Employees who feel secure, enjoy their work, and feel amply rewarded in terms of personal recognition and in terms of salary are predisposed to react favorably to management policies and practices. Thus one of the tasks for the industrial psychologist is to discover principles of motivation transcending individual differences in specific work-related drives.

Highly motivated employees do not, of course, always agree with or endorse decisions by management. As a matter of fact they may feel sufficiently comfortable in their working environment to be quite vociferous in voicing objections or criticisms to particular practices. They do not, however, regard every new decision with the suspicion and mistrust characteristic of employees who are dissatisfied with their jobs. Consequently, industrial psychologists are frequently called upon to investigate the sources of dissatisfaction in a particular working environment and are sometimes consulted in helping effect and evaluate planned organizational change.

Part VI. Consumer Behavior. A company survives because consumers buy its products or services. Thus, all parties to the manufacture, distribution, and sale of products or services have a vital interest in understanding consumer behavior.

One of the psychologist's unique contributions in this general area is his application of rigorous scientific methods of inquiry to such diverse problems as the size and constituency of markets, the effectiveness of advertising campaigns, consumer reactions to the product and the company manufacturing it, and the needs and motives underlying consumer behavior, to list a few.

To the extent that there is a psychology of consumer behavior, it has been significantly bolstered by activities of psychologists in the clinical and experimental areas. Clinical tools have been used by motivation researchers to discover the hidden or unconscious reasons underlying consumer behavior. Advertising has capitalized for years upon well-established findings from traditional laboratory-type research in experimental psychology.

Although psychologists have to the present devoted relatively little attention to studying the process of salesmanship, considerable research has been directed toward the problems of selecting and training salesmen.

INDUSTRIAL PSYCHOLOGY AS A PROFESSION

We have thus far described something of the scope of activities of the industrial psychologist. It is apparent from the foregoing discussion that he must possess general knowledge about human behavior and the factors influencing it. In addition, he must have at his command certain rather specific skills. He is a researcher and consequently must be conversant with techniques of assessment including psychological tests, attitude scales, and performance appraisal. He must know how to design experiments and evaluate the results in the broad area of industrial behavior. He must know how to draw representative samples from a population in order to perform certain kinds of market research and opinion studies. And we could list other skills as well. It is appropriate now to inquire into the development of these skills. How is the industrial psychologist trained, and how may we differentiate between the well-qualified practitioner and the glib but untrained charlatan?

Certification and Licensing

The classified section of the telephone directory for almost any large city contains listings under "psychologist." Unfortunately, it is legal in many states for anyone to represent himself to the public through the classified directory or any other outlet as a psychologist. This unhappy state of affairs is gradually being rectified by legislation. Thus, some states *license* psychologists in the same way as physicians, dentists, and lawyers are licensed. It is a criminal offense in such states for an individual without a license to practice psychology or to offer psychological service to the public. Other states *certify* psychologists. Certification involves less legislative control than licensing since it prohibits unqualified persons merely from representing themselves as psychologists or as certified psychologists. It is perfectly legal in some of the states with certification laws for an untrained and unqualified person to represent himself as a psychologist as long as he makes no claim to certification.

Although the number is growing each year, a few states still do not either license or certify psychologists. This means that if you were seeking the services of a bona fide industrial psychologist solely from the listing in a telephone directory in some communities, you might come up with a totally unqualified person. It is important, then, to know something about the training and professional affiliations of qualified industrial psychologists.

Professional Training

Since the public is not adequately protected against fraudulent psychological practice, the primary responsibility for specifying and maintaining standards rests with the psychological profession itself. Most qualified psychologists in this country are members of the American Psychological Association, which is the professional counterpart of such organizations as the American Medical Association and the American Dental Association. The purpose of the American Psychological Association (Bylaws, Article I.1) is "to advance psychology as a science, as a profession and as a means of promoting human welfare." Although the association does not endorse the professional qualifications of any of its members, it has developed a code of ethical practice to which all of its members are required to adhere. The minimum standard for acceptability as a *member* is roughly the doctorate in psychology from an accredited institution and engagement in work primarily psychological in nature. *Fellows* of the association usually have the Ph.D. degree and a minimum of five years of postdoctoral professional experience. The total of both classes of members is approximately 35,000.

The association is composed of divisions representing specialized fields of interest and activities of the members. One of these, designated the Division of Industrial and Organizational Psychology, has as its stated purposes (Bylaws, Article I.2) :

1. Establishing and maintaining high standards of practice in business, industry, public service, and related fields.
2. Encouraging research and publication in these fields.
3. Facilitating the exchange of information and experience among its members and with the general public.
4. Expediting the development of professional opportunities.
5. Fostering cooperative relations with allied professions.

6. Protecting the public from untrained and/or unethical practitioners.
7. Contributing to the advancement of psychology in general.

An additional kind of professional recognition is the diploma awarded by the American Board of Professional Psychology. This diploma is awarded to psychologists who are judged to be well-trained, highly competent, and very responsible practitioners. The requirements for status as a diplomate in the fields of clinical psychology, counseling, and guidance, or industrial psychology are the Ph.D. and five years of professional experience.

Employment of Industrial Psychologists

Industrial psychologists typically are employed in one of three kinds of settings. They may be employed as full-time staff members of a particular industry; they may be a full-time member of an organization of consulting psychologists; or they may hold an academic position in a university or college. Many industrial psychologists employed in the academic setting also consult on a part-time basis.

Industrial psychologists are employed as full-time staff members of quite a variety of industries, including oil companies, automotive companies, insurance companies, and so on. These psychologists are most often designated by some title other than industrial psychologist. Several are personnel directors, vice presidents, and directors of research.

A number of organizations of psychologists offer consultive service to industry. These organizations typically perform studies under contract to a particular industry, business, or government agency. An industrial corporation may, for example, let a contract to a consulting organization to conduct a morale survey, to develop a personnel selection battery, or to establish a training program. A member or team from the consulting group is then assigned to work on the problem for the contracting agency on a temporary basis. They are reassigned when the project is completed.

An analysis of the job duties reported by a sample of 246 industrial psychologists, including some who were employed full time in industry and some whose primary employment was academic, is summarized in Table 1–1 (Mackinney & Dunnette, 1964). The

TABLE 1–1

Job Duties Performed by a Sample of Industrial Psychologists

Job Duty	*Percent*
Consulting with management	67
Personnel (management) development	47
Training	40
Test interpretation	38
Test validation	35
Personnel counseling	34
Organization planning	33
Criterion development	31
Research on personnel policies and practices	31
Attitude research and measurement	30
Personnel administration	30
Recruiting and employment	26
Test development and construction	24
Job studies and job analysis	24
Test administration	21
Wage and salary administration	14
Human engineering	14
Marketing and consumer research	13
Collective bargaining	5
Other specified duties	27

primary work roles of these respondents were subsumed under four major headings:

1. Personnel administration (including recruiting, and wage and salary administration);
2. Test research;
3. Working with people (including personnel counseling, test administration, test interpretation, and management development);
4. Organizational analysis (including attitude measurement, and advising management concerning personnel policy). Other important areas of activity were human engineering and training.

Although the primary emphasis in the employment of industrial psychologists is an *applied* emphasis involving a service commitment, this does not imply the absence of theoretical or pure research in this area. Industrial psychologists, whether employed by industry, a consulting organization, or a university have a commitment to further the development of psychology as a science. Thus, they continuously maintain a research orientation toward such basic problems in the field as improving the techniques of test construction and evaluation procedures, furthering scientific knowledge about human motivation, gaining a more comprehensive understanding of the learning process and, in fact, toward the entire vista of human behavior.

SUMMARY

Industrial and organizational psychology is the study of behavior as it occurs in business and industrial settings. Thus, it is concerned with the behavior of three broad classifications of individuals: workers, management, and consumers. It is a technology and an applied science, both using the findings of the behavioral sciences in general to improve organizational effectiveness and contributing in its own right to furthering the understanding of human behavior.

The application of sound psychological principles differs from both the pseudopsychologies and the stereotype of the efficiency expert. Pseudopsychologies are founded upon a presumed relationship between character traits and external signs like lines in the palm or size of the ears. This presumption is entirely unfounded.

Modern industrial psychology studies behavior with a view to maximizing the realization of potential for accomplishment and personal satisfaction. Thus, it has a responsibility to employees as well as to employers. The psychologist views behavior as a function of precipitating factors (the stimulus conditions) and of intervening variables which determine the way in which particular individuals will perceive and interpret the stimulus.

Some states have no legislation designed to protect the public from fraudulent psychological practice. Consequently, the primary responsibility for specifying and maintaining standards rests with the profession of psychology itself. Most qualified psychologists in this country are members of the American Psychological Association. Membership in this organization is predicated upon satisfactory completion of certain minimum requirements of graduate training and experience.

An industrial psychologist may be employed as a full-time staff member of a particular industrial organization, as a full-time consultant, or as a faculty member in a university or college.

2. Methodology of Industrial Psychology

Frequent reference was made in the previous chapter to the fact that psychology is the *scientific* study of behavior. Some persons find it difficult to conceive of a science without the trappings of a laboratory, including sparkling glassware, bunsen burners, microscopes, and perhaps a cyclotron or two. Reference to a scientific study of behavior is regarded by them as a basic contradiction in terms. They argue that the complexity and variability of human behavior precludes its study in scientific fashion.

Reasoning like this is erroneous because it rests upon an incorrect definition of *science*. A science is characterized by the methods it employs rather than by the phenomena it studies or the physical setting in which it operates. The complexity of human behavior creates special problems for the psychologist to be sure, but it does not itself dictate the application of methods that are unscientific. In essence, the methods employed by psychologists are identical with those employed by researchers in such disciplines as chemistry and physics.

It will be helpful to know something about the characteristics of scientific method in general before considering the specific ways in which the industrial psychologist employs these methods.

ESSENTIALS OF SCIENTIFIC METHOD

You will recall that the pseudopsychologies were primarily based upon speculation rather than upon observation. There is nothing inherently wrong with speculation in itself. Many brilliant ideas originate as figments of someone's vivid imagination. So, too, do many ideas that are not so brilliant! Consider, for example, some of the delusions experienced by certain mental patients who believe they have discovered the secret of perpetual life or have proven that the world is flat after all.

Scientific method requires that we go one step beyond speculation. The investigator's educated guess about relationships between phenomena must be cast into the form of an hypothesis. The hypothesis is a statement of possible relationship that is amenable to investigation by observation.

Objectivity

Scientific observations for the purpose of substantiating or refuting hypotheses must be made in objective rather than subjective fashion. The investigator does not have an axe to grind. He attempts to discover whether or not a hypothesized relationship exists. He is not committed to proving the existence of the relationship.

During the course of everyday living, most of us make observations that are quite subjective in nature and hence are unscientific. We hold certain biases and preconceived notions which color our observations. If, for example, you fear airplane travel, you may find support for your fear in newspaper accounts of airplane accidents. In so doing, however, you are failing to consider all of the data. What about the vast majority of flights which are successful and hence are not newsworthy?

Subjectivity may influence our observations in yet another way. The observer's biases and misconceptions may actually cause him to misinterpret what he sees and hears. Suppose that an employee is convinced that his supervisor is unfair and guilty of favoritism. The fact that this supervisor recommends pay raises for certain of his subordinates and not for others may be incorrectly interpreted by this employee as another sign of favoritism rather than as a reflection of the fact that some employees are truly more deserving of salary increases than others.

Controlled Observation

In addition to objectivity, scientific methods require the exertion of careful controls. It is insufficient, for example, merely to speculate that older employees are more safety-conscious than younger ones. And casual observations of a few older employees at work would not contribute to the scientific validity of this speculative conclusion.

Instead, what is required is a systematic investigation of the injury records of employees of different ages. The influence of factors other than the critical one of age would have to be *controlled* (eliminated or held constant) if the investigation were to have meaning. Such "control variables" might include length of job experience, nature of the work with respect to exposure to potential hazards, and so on.

The Independent Variable. The elements of scientific method—observation, objectivity, and control—are translated by the researcher into an investigation of the relationship between two basic kinds of variables. One of these, the independent variable, is the factor whose effects are being investigated.

The range of independent variables of interest to the industrial psychologist is quite extensive. He may, for example, be interested in studying the effects of changes in the physical working environment, a new safety program, or a training program for supervisors. Any factor that is systematically controlled so that it operates under certain circumstances and not under others (or is operative for certain groups and not for others) may be investigated as an independent variable.

The Dependent Variable. The behaviors studied as possible functions of the independent variable are referred to as dependent variables. The investigator is interested in determining whether certain aspects of behavior can be shown to depend upon manipulation of the independent variable.

The dependent variables of greatest concern to industrial psychologists are (a) performance and (b) satisfaction. The importance of performance measures as dependent variables is almost self-evident. In investigating the effect of some change in the working environment or some new job practice it is logical to inquire whether performance is improved, diminished, or unaffected as a consequence of the change. The kinds of performance measures used for this purpose are exceedingly diverse, including such things as productivity, absenteeism, turnover, spoilage, suspensions, and accidents.

The importance of satisfaction as a dependent variable may not be quite as obvious unless we recognize that management and workers do not always share similar objectives. Although increased output may be regarded by management as a desirable consequence of altered working conditions, such alterations sometimes lead to considerable worker dissatisfaction. Dissatisfaction can be fertile soil for low morale, increased turnover, and absenteeism. Hence, it often is imperative to ascertain the impact of independent variable manipulations upon criteria of both satisfaction and output.

Causality?

The scientist is acutely aware of the fact that he may demonstrate a relationship between two variables but can never actually prove that one *causes* the other. Cause-effect relationships are, to be sure, frequently inferred from a set of observations. Quite often, however, we can demonstrate a relationship between variables without having any indication of which one is cause and which is effect.

Suppose, for example, that the psychologist makes the observation that, in general, insurance salesmen who have been with a company for more than one year sell more insurance (that is, are more productive) than salesmen who have been with the company for less than a year. The factors of length of time with the company and productivity are thus related, but which is cause and which is effect? Does experience with the company improve selling technique? Perhaps. It is just as plausible, however, to hypothesize that highly productive salesmen are rewarded both in terms of salary and job satisfaction, causing them to remain with the company for a relatively long period of time. Unproductive salesmen, on the other hand, may receive lower commissions and become sufficiently discouraged with the job to seek employment elsewhere within a year or less. Finally, we cannot discount the possibility that *neither* experience nor productivity is a causal factor since both may themselves be caused by some third factor held in common.

The foregoing discussion has been offered in the nature of a hasty overview of some of the essentials of scientific methodology. Let us now see how the industrial psychologist applies scientific methods to the study of human behavior in three basic ways: naturalistic observation, experimental observation, and clinical observation.

NATURALISTIC OBSERVATION

We have already stated that the scientist attempts to discover relationships between independent and dependent variables. This requires that the independent variable be so manipulated as to reveal corresponding variations in the dependent variable.

Some kinds of independent variables, however, are not amenable to manipulation by the investigator. This situation is perhaps most apparent in astronomy where the observer cannot alter the course of the stars and planets to fulfill the needs of his experimentation. The independent variables of interest to the astronomer are manipulated, so to speak, by nature. The scientist makes his observations whenever conditions existing in their natural state are favorable to the study of the particular phenomenon that he wishes to investigate. Naturalistic observation, then, is characterized by the fact that the researcher does not control the independent variable. Rather, he is compelled to study it as and when it occurs in its natural state.

An Illustration of Naturalistic Observation

Naturalistic observations are frequently made by psychologists. One investigation of this type (Hummel & Schmeidler, 1955) was concerned with studying the relative effectiveness of a stop sign and a red blinker light at an intersection. State law required that a driver bring his car to a full stop at or before such a sign or blinker light.

The independent variable in this study was the signal to stop (sign or light); the dependent variable was the action of the driver in adhering to or disobeying these signals. It would have been extremely difficult for the investigators to study the relationship between these variables in any setting other than the natural environment. Consequently, observations were made at two intersections in the same neighborhood: one intersection had a stop sign while the other had a red blinker light. The observations were made from a sheltered doorway, and the responses of the drivers were classified and tabulated as illustrated in Table 2–1.

The investigators drew the following conclusions: (1) Only about one half of the drivers in the neighborhood studied stopped their cars completely when required to do so by the stop sign or blinker light. (2) A significantly greater percentage of drivers stopped too late (past the intersection) at the stop sign than at the blinker light. (This is interpreted as meaning that the blinker is more readily visible from a distance.) (3) The percentage of drivers who stopped or slowed down for a newly erected sign was about

TABLE 2-1

Stops and Slowdowns of Cars at Intersections with a Stop Sign and with a Blinker Light

Category of Response	Stop Sign 3–4 Weeks after Erection	Stop Sign 3–4 Months after Erection	Red Blinker Light
Full stop with no more than half the car past the intersection line...............	22%	29%	44%
Full stop with more than half the car past the intersection line....................	30	19	9
Slowing down but not a full stop...........	31	35	25
No perceptible slowing down.............	17	17	22
Total...........................	100%	100%	100%

the same as the percentage stopping or slowing down for a sign that had been standing for several months.

The fact that investigators employing naturalistic observation do not themselves manipulate the independent variable does not make the method or the findings unscientific. As long as observations are made systematically and objectively and as long as extraneous factors are controlled, the results of naturalistic investigations can be both meaningful and useful.

Extraneous factors are those potentially affecting the dependent variable but not currently the subject of investigation. Hence, the control of these factors is extremely important and sometimes difficult to achieve in natural situations. The investigators comparing the relative effectiveness of the stop sign and blinker light had to control at least four such factors which might have influenced driver behavior. First, they had to take reasonable precautions to prevent drivers from knowing that their behavior was being studied. It is likely that a higher percentage of drivers would have complied with the law had they known that they were being observed. Secondly, the neighborhood was controlled by making observations at two intersections in the same vicinity. There are undoubtedly differences between neighborhoods in the extent to which drivers adhere to the letter of the law. A third controlled variable was the factor of restraints apart from the stop sign and blinker light. Obviously the experimenters would have contaminated their findings if they had selected one intersection that was regularly patrolled by a policeman (in addition to having a stop sign) and another intersection not similarly patrolled. Finally, the investigators observed that some drivers were compelled to slow down or to stop at the intersection in order to avoid a collision with the car in front. Since it was impossible to determine whether these drivers would have stopped or slowed down for the sign or blinker light, these cases were eliminated from the data analysis.

Evaluation of the Naturalistic Method

The psychologist has certain reservations about using the naturalistic method. Since he has not directly manipulated the independent variable, it is difficult to repeat a set of naturalistic observations under exactly the same conditions as prevailed the first time. What would happen, for example, if we wished to verify the findings cited in Table 2–1? Even if we followed a procedure identical with that originally used and made our observations at the same two intersections, we might obtain different results because of changes in the natural situation. A series of accidents, for example, at the stop sign intersection might have led to the posting of a policeman at this intersection for several weeks. Even though he were no longer present when we recorded driver behavior, his former presence there may have encouraged better driving habits. Furthermore, the sign itself will have been up for a longer time when we repeat our observations. The time of the year at which observations are made may influence our findings. Many high school students take part-time jobs requiring that they drive a car or truck during the summer. Their behavior may be quite different from that of older, more experienced drivers. You can undoubtedly think of other subtle variations that may creep into the natural situation, making it difficult or even impossible to repeat and verify a set of naturalistic observations.

There are nevertheless situations in which the naturalistic method is the best method available to the industrial psychologist. Persons who know that they are being observed in an experimental situation will sometimes deliberately behave in a way calculated to impress the investigator. Such alterations of behavior might be noted, for example, if we were to conduct a study of the kinds of programs TV viewers prefer to watch. We could administer a questionnaire dealing with viewing habits, but the obtained responses might not be trustworthy. An alternative procedure would be to develop an experimental situation in which viewers have access to several TV channels under controlled circumstances and to tabulate the percentage of viewers watching each kind of program. Here again, though, the investigator could not be certain that the viewers had not altered their behavior because they knew they were being observed. Consequently, naturalistic observation would be the method of choice for the study of this problem. Persons might be interviewed in their homes to determine whether or not they were watching TV at the moment and, if so, the particular program being viewed.

THE EXPERIMENTAL METHOD

The primary difference between the experimental and naturalistic methods is that the former places the investigator in charge of the situation. He manipulates the independent variable and controls extraneous factors. This kind of regulation by the experimenter makes it possible to repeat observations under identical conditions in order to verify the findings. It also means that the investigator is in a somewhat stronger position to infer cause-effect relationships because he may systematically vary one factor at a time and note corresponding changes, if any, in other factors that he suspects might be affected.

Experimental Design

The experimental method may be employed in either a laboratory setting or in a real-life setting like an office or industrial plant. The advantage of doing research in a laboratory is that the investigator can arrange his materials and experimental conditions with precision. Since the laboratory is, however, an artificial environment, generalizations from laboratory findings to the industrial setting may be erroneous. Therefore, the industrial psychologist most often accepts laboratory findings as suggestive and attempts to verify them in the plant, office, or other work setting before attempting to apply the results of his experimentation.

The simplest kind of experimental design requires a study of two groups of *subjects* (persons being investigated). One of these groups, the *control group*, serves as a standard for comparative purposes. The *experimental group,* on the other hand, is the one in which the independent variable is manipulated. A simple illustration will serve to clarify the difference between these groups.

Let us assume that we wish to investigate the effect of increased illumination upon the typewriting proficiency of secretaries. The independent variable is level of illumination. Hence, secretaries working under the changed level of illumination would constitute the experimental group. The effectiveness of this variable would be investigated by comparing the typing proficiency of subjects in the experimental group with the performance of secretaries working under normal illumination. Consequently a second group of subjects working under normal illumination conditions would constitute the control group.

The dependent variable in this investigation would be some criterion of typing proficiency like the number of words typed per unit of time and corrected for errors or erasures. It is apparent, however, that many factors aside from the specific independent variable under investigation (illumination) may affect typing speed. Such factors as finger dexterity, length of experience as a typist, and kind of copy being typed may be reflected in speed and accuracy of secretarial performance but are really extraneous to the specific problem under investigation. It would therefore be necessary to insure the similarity of the experimental and control groups with respect to all such extraneous factors before we could attribute any observed differences in typing speed solely to the independent variable.

Matched Group Design.   One procedure for eliminating the effects of extraneous factors is to match or equate the groups of subjects on the basis of such factors. For example, if we wish to investigate only the effects of illumination, it would be necessary somehow to eliminate the potential effect of differences in finger dexterity. This would be accomplished in a matched-groups design by administering a finger dexterity test to a pool of available subjects before assigning anyone to the experimental or control group. Pairs of persons with identical scores would be identified, and one member of the pair would be assigned to the experimental group while her counterpart would be assigned to the control group.

It is exceedingly difficult to implement a matched-groups design for a number of reasons. First, it is necessary to have a large pool of potential subjects available in order to identify pairs that match.

Second, the process of constructing equated groups becomes increasingly difficult as the number of extraneous variables to be controlled increases. You will recall that our hypothetical investigation requires that we eliminate from consideration both the factors of finger dexterity and length of experience. Thus, we would have to identify pairs of subjects who not only have the same scores on a finger dexterity test but also are identical in length of secretarial experience. As we attempt to match for still more variables, the process becomes unmanageable. Third, we have been considering a design involving only two groups of subjects. If, however, our design required more than two groups (and many *do*), the task of matching is still further complicated. Finally, even when a matched-groups design is feasible, it would be erroneous to assume that matching has really accomplished what we set out to do; that is, to eliminate the effects of potentially contaminating factors. There is always the possibility that factors other than the ones on which we equated our groups will exert some consistent and uncontrolled effect upon the dependent variable.

It is for these reasons that most experimental investigations utilize a random group design rather than a matched group design.

Random Group Design.   In this procedure, subjects are randomly assigned to the experimental and control groups. Randomization requires that every subject have an equal chance for assignment to each of the groups required for an experiment. Since no biases of any kind are permitted into the assignment of subjects to groups, we may assume that each randomly constructed group is essentially like every other randomly constructed group drawn from the same original pool of subjects.

Once the subjects are randomly assigned to groups, there remains only the decision about which should be treated experimentally and which should serve as a control. This again should be decided without bias, perhaps by flipping a coin.

An Illustrative Laboratory Experiment

A considerable amount of research in the general area of improving machine design has, as you might suspect, been directed toward facilitating aircraft pilot efficiency. As aircraft become increasingly complex and as their speed increases, the pilot must make correct decisions with increased rapidity. This in turn means that new techniques must be discovered for relaying information about the functioning of aircraft components to the pilot in a way that is readily comprehensible.

The location of various kinds of dials and the normal position of the pointers has been shown to be a critical factor affecting the speed and accuracy with which the dials are read. The best configuration of 16 dials in multiengined aircraft has been demonstrated to be four banks of four dials each, with the normal position of each pointer at the "nine o'clock" position as indicated in Figure 2–1.

FIGURE 2–1

Optimal Arrangement of 16 Aircraft Dials, Each Pointing
to the Normal Condition

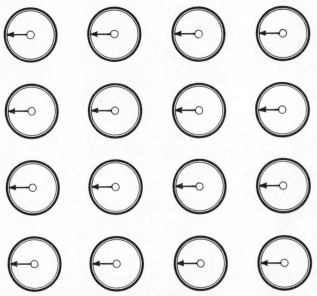

Source: M. J. Warrick & W. F. Grether. The effect of pointer alignment on check reading of instrument panels. Aero Medical Laboratory, *AMCMCREXD 694–17* (June 1948).

Starting with this arrangement of dials, an experiment was performed to determine whether or not speed and accuracy of dial reading could be further improved by combining a deviating pointer (indicating some kind of malfunction or condition that must be corrected) with a change in illumination of the specific dial in question (Bartz, 1957).

The independent variable, then, was change in illumination accompanying a deviating dial pointer. Cockpit dials are normally illuminated in red. The illuminant of deviating dials changed from red to green.

One of the dependent variables was the speed with which the subjects could identify the number of deviating dials (which was varied by the investigator between 1 and 8) in each cluster of 16.

The control condition consisted of presenting the clusters of 16

FIGURE 2–2

Average Response Times to Configurations Containing
One through Eight Error Dials

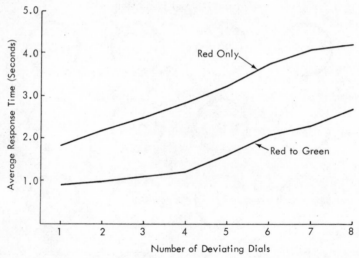

dials with varying numbers and configurations of discrepancies but without changing the illuminant. The experimental condition consisted of the presentation of the same configuration of discrepancies with a red-to-green illuminant for discrepant dials. The same subjects were used under the two conditions, making it unnecessary to equate the experimental and control groups on extraneous factors.

The average times required to count the number of deviating dials under the experimental and control conditions are graphed in Figure 2–2.

Two conclusions follow from these data. First, the time required to count deviant dials increases as a function of the number of such dials. Secondly, this time is considerably reduced when deviation of the pointer is accompanied by changing the illuminant from red to green. The implication of these findings for the design of aircraft instrument panels is obvious.

Speed of discrepancy identification was not the only dependent variable investigated. The experimenter was interested also in comparing the *accuracy* of identification under the experimental and control conditions. He noted that the subjects averaged 1.05 errors (in identifying a total of 36 discrepant dials) with constant red illumination, while they only averaged 0.38 errors with the red-to-green illuminant shift. The interpretation of the average number of errors under these two conditions required a statistical analysis in order to determine that the difference between them was attributable to the experimental conditions rather than to chance. The types and applications of statistics are discussed later in this chapter.

CLINICAL OBSERVATION

Several procedures for gathering and interpreting data are derived from techniques more usually associated with clinical than with industrial psychology. This is most evident in certain studies seeking to relate personality to employee, management, and consumer behavior using depth interviews, projective tests, and the clinical case history. Such procedures have been used for such diverse projects as morale assessments, investigations of personality patterns associated with accident-proneness, and analysis of the impact of advertising appeals and product design upon consumers' unconscious needs.

A distinguishing characteristic of clinical observation as a method is its emphasis upon gathering information in depth about one person at a time. This focus upon the dynamics of an individual's behavior does not preclude generalizations about groups of persons. In order to make such generalizations, clinical observations must be collated across people.

Although clinical observation can be a useful supplement to the naturalistic and experimental methods, it suffers certain limitations when applied to problems in industrial psychology.

First, there is the matter of the appropriateness in industry of procedures developed for application in treatment settings. This may impinge upon the employee's right to privacy. A person seeking psychological treatment voluntarily places himself in the role of patient and accepts the fact that it is in his own best interest to aid the clinical diagnostician by revealing his needs, fears, and wishes—both conscious and unconscious. However, there is a legitimate question about the propriety of requiring employees to be similarly revealing.

Second, some of the tools of clinical observation lack refinement by the standards imposed upon scientific methods in general. This is a somewhat less serious problem when these techniques are used for their intended diagnostic purpose by experienced clinical psychologists than when they are used by relatively untrained or inexperienced researchers. This is a less serious problem also when these clinical tools are used to generate leads for further investigation than when they alone provide the data for generalizing about industrial behavior.

The foregoing paragraphs do not deny the usefulness of some kinds of clinical observation in industrial settings. Indeed, two essentially clinical procedures—the personal interview and the life history—are extensively and profitably used in industrial psychology. However, other clinical procedures which seek to probe personality in depth must be used cautiously both in industrial research and practice.

STATISTICS

Statistics of various kinds are used in conjunction with almost any experiment performed by the industrial psychologist. The investigator typically measures change in the dependent variable associated with manipulation of the independent variable. Hence, the outcome of an experiment is usually expressed in numerical form, that is, test scores, production records, accident rates, numbers of persons answering yes to a questionnaire item, and so on. The summary and interpretation of numerical results is facilitated by statistical analysis.

Statistical techniques fall generally into three classes: descriptive statistics, statistical inference, and correlation.

Descriptive statistics provide a kind of shorthand description of a mass of data. This is a kind of statistic with which you are most familiar. When we speak of an average score or a range of scores, we are really summarizing a mass of data in a simple and convenient way.

A second kind of statistic is required to facilitate the interpretation of obtained averages or ranges of scores. You will recall that the results of the dial reading experiment indicated that subjects made fewer errors when the illuminant was changed than when it remained constant. Before interpreting these findings as indicative of the superiority of illuminant change, however, we must be certain that the difference between the number of errors under the two conditions did not arise solely as a function of chance. *Statistical inference* provides us with an indication of the likelihood that our experimental findings are merely chance findings. As the likelihood of attributing obtained findings to chance is reduced, we may have increased confidence in the conclusion that these findings resulted from the manipulation of the independent variable.

A third statistical procedure is that of *correlation*. Correlational analysis reveals the magnitude and direction of the relationship between variables. If measures of these variables parallel each other closely, they are strongly correlated. However, when there is little or no parallelism between these measures, correlation is weak or absent. Thus, correlational analysis could be used, for example, to determine whether there is a relationship between seniority and supervisory ratings of employee proficiency, between preemployment test scores and a subsequently obtained performance measure, between age and accident frequency, and so on.

The ensuing discussion concerns some of the simpler statistics. The computation of these statistics is not considered in this chapter. Rather, we will illustrate some of the ways in which descriptive and inferential statistics and correlation are applied. The reader interested in computational procedures is referred to Appendix A.

Descriptive Statistics

Many kinds of data may be conveniently summarized by counting the number of persons (or computing the percentage of persons) obtaining each score. This summary may be visually presented by plotting a *frequency polygon* or a *histogram* as illustrated in Figure 2–3.

Both of the plots in Figure 2–3 were derived from the same set of IQ data. They show the percentage of youngsters earning IQs within each 10-point interval starting with the interval 40 to 49.

The Normal Distribution Curve. As the number of observations

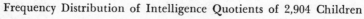

FIGURE 2–3

Frequency Distribution of Intelligence Quotients of 2,904 Children

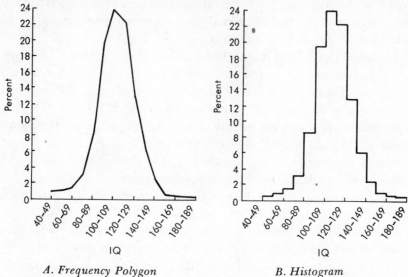

A. *Frequency Polygon*   B. *Histogram*

Source: L. M. Terman & M. A. Merrill. *Measuring intelligence.* Cambridge: Riverside Press, 1937. P. 37.

plotted on a graph is increased, the resultant distribution tends more and more to approximate a curve rather than a polygon. When we have made a substantial number of observations free of biasing factors, the obtained curve often has the characteristics of the normal distribution. Such a normal distribution curve is illustrated in Figure 2–4. You will note that very few persons have IQs as low as 40 or as high as 160. The highest percentage of persons have IQs which cluster closely about 100.

Graphed data do not always take the form of a normal distribution. Some characteristics are not normally distributed even when data are plotted for the entire population. In addition, when the sample of persons is not randomly selected (that is, is somehow biased), the resultant distribution of data is usually asymmetrical.

Suppose, for example, we administered a 180-point test of blueprint reading knowledge to a group of job applicants and separated these applicants into two subgroups: one with previous work experience entailing some sort of blueprint reading, and the other without such experience. The resultant test score distributions would look

FIGURE 2–4

A Normal Distribution Curve Obtained
from Measurement of IQ

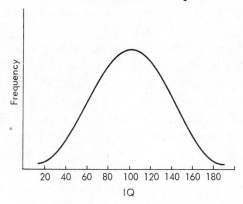

like those in Figure 2–5. These distributions are *skewed* (unsymmetrical) because we have plotted measurements for selected groups of persons. We expect the distribution to be normal only when selective factors are absent.

The curve for inexperienced applicants shows that whereas most earned relatively low scores, a few earned atypically high scores, perhaps because of formal training in blueprint reading or hobbies requiring such knowledge. This curve is *positively* skewed. In con-

FIGURE 2–5

Skewed Distributions

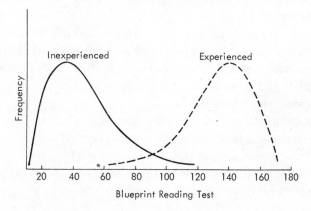

trast, the curve for experienced applicants is *negatively* skewed. In spite of previous work experience which ought to be helpful to performance on this test, some of these applicants apparently know relatively little about reading a blueprint. This is probably the reason they are seeking another job!

Although it is possible to summarize a set of data by graphing the distribution, this kind of summary can be rather inconvenient. Alternatively, we can pretty well summarize the data presented in Figure 2–4, for example, in terms of two critical features: the average IQ, and the spread of IQs away from this average. The typical or average score is statistically expressed by a measure of *central tendency*. The spread of scores is expressed by a measure of *variability*.

Central Tendency. The three primary measures of central tendency are the mean, median, and mode.

The *mean* ($\bar{X}$) is the measure with which you are probably most familiar. It is simply the arithmetic average computed by adding the scores and dividing by the number of cases or observations. The computational formula for the mean is written

$$\bar{X} = \frac{\Sigma X}{N},$$

where X is used to denote a score, Σ is the process of summing, and N is the number of cases.

The *median (Med)* is the score falling precisely at the middle of the distribution. If a distribution of IQs earned by 501 employees were arranged in order from lowest to highest, the median IQ would be the one earned by the 251st worker. Two hundred fifty employees will have earned IQs below the median and 250 would have earned IQs above the median.

The *mode (Mo)* is simply the score that occurs most frequently within a distribution. It is little used as a measure of central tendency except under special circumstances. A shoe buyer, for example, would find it useful to know the modal shoe size worn by men in order to place his orders wisely.

The mean, median, and mode are identical when the distribution of data is normal. These three measures of central tendency diverge, however, when the distribution is skewed. The relationships between mean, median, and mode in normal and skewed distributions are illustrated in Figure 2–6.

FIGURE 2–6

Measures of Central Tendency in Normal and in Skewed Distributions

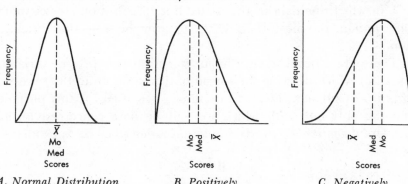

A. Normal Distribution   *B. Positively Skewed Distribution*   *C. Negatively Skewed Distribution*

You will note that the mean is more sensitive to the "tail" of the distribution than is the median. The fact that the mean is highly influenced by extreme or unusual cases in a distribution implies that its use should be limited to situations in which the distribution of data is not seriously skewed. You can readily see that the median, which is less influenced by extreme cases in a distribution, is a more representative measure of central tendency than the mean when distributions are skewed.

Consider, for example, the interpretation of the statement that the average annual income of 10 secretaries in a company is $5,550. The first question we might raise concerns the type of average computed. Was it a mean, median, or mode? Secondly, the interpretation of this average would depend upon the shape of the distribution. Is it normal or skewed? Suppose $5,550 represents the mean income derived from the following set of figures: $4,000, $4,200, $4,300, $4,500, $5,000, $5,000, $5,500, $6,500, $6,500, and $10,000. The fact that one of these 10 women (the president's personal secretary) is receiving an atypically high salary has acted to increase the mean for the group to a figure that does not truly reflect typical earnings. A more realistic kind of average under such circumstances would be the median, here computed as $5,000.

A Measure of Variability. An indication of central tendency does not by itself provide an adequate description of a distribution of scores. It is perfectly possible, for example, for the means of two normal distributions to be identical even though these distributions may be quite different with respect to variability (or spread of scores away from the mean). This kind of situation is illustrated in Figure 2–7, in which the data in the dotted-line distribution cluster more closely about the mean than do the data in the solid line distribution.

There are a number of different statistical measures of variability, all of which describe the spread of data away from the measure of central tendency. The statistic most often used for this purpose and the only one with which we will be here concerned is the *standard deviation* (σ). Its computation is described in Appendix A.

FIGURE 2–7

Two Normal Distributions with Identical
Means but Different Variabilities

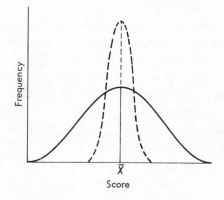

Approximately 68 percent (actually 68.26 percent) of the scores in a normal distribution fall within the scores delimited by one standard deviation on either side of the mean. This percentage is constant regardless of the type of score that is plotted and of the computed mean, *provided that the distribution of data is normal.*

Suppose we have calculated the mean of a set of mechanical aptitude test scores as 50 and the standard deviation of the distribution of scores as 10. The limits defined by $\pm 1\sigma$ (one standard deviation on either side of the mean) are thus 40 and 60, and approximately 68 percent of the obtained scores fall between these limits. The remaining 32 percent of the scores is equally divided, with 16 percent falling below the score corresponding to -1σ (40) and 16 percent falling above the score corresponding to $+ 1\sigma$ (60). The distribution of scores obtained on this test of mechanical aptitude is schematically represented in Figure 2–8.

If we administered the same test to another group of persons and found here that the mean was still 50 but that the standard deviation was only 5, the middle 68 percent of the scores would fall between the limits of 45 to 55. Similarly, if we had a third distribution of data also with a mean of 50 but with a standard deviation of 15, the middle 68 percent of the cases would fall between scores of 35 and 65. Thus, the larger the standard deviation the greater is the

FIGURE 2–8

A Distribution of Test Scores in Which the Mean Is 50 and the Standard Deviation Is 10

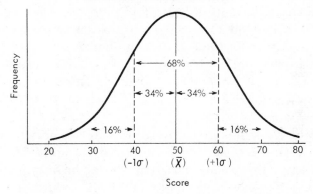

spread of scores away from the mean. Conversely, as the size of the standard deviation decreases, the scores cluster more tightly about the mean.

Just as the percentage of cases between the limits of $\pm 1\sigma$ is constant for normal distributions, so too is the percentage of cases between the limits defined by two and three standard deviations on either side of the mean. The scores between -2σ and $+2\sigma$ include 95.44 percent of the cases, while virtually all of the cases in normal distributions (99.74 percent) are included between the score limits defined by three standard deviations on either side of the mean.

Knowledge about the standard deviation of a distribution of data is useful in a number of ways. One application of this statistic relates to the interpretation of test scores. Let us assume that we have administered two tests to an individual, a test of mechanical aptitude and a test of manual dexterity. We will further assume that this person earned a score of 80 on the mechanical aptitude test and a score of 115 on the dexterity test. Did he score better on the mechanical or manual test? It is obvious that the information thus far presented is insufficient to make a judgment.

A partial answer to this question is provided by comparing his performance with the mean performance of large groups of persons who have previously taken both tests. Suppose the mean mechanical aptitude score earned by such groups was 60 and the mean manual dexterity score was 105. It is apparent now that this person scored somewhat better than average both on the mechanical aptitude and on the dexterity test. In order to find out *how much* better than average he scored on these tests we might want to examine the standard deviations of the two distributions of test scores. We will assume that the standard deviation as computed for the mechanical aptitude test is 20 while the standard deviation for the manual dexterity test is 30. The distributions of scores for these two tests are shown in Figure 2–9.

When the test scores are converted to standard deviation units as shown in Figure 2–9, this person's mechanical aptitude score converts to $+1\sigma$ (1 standard deviation above the mean) while his manual dexterity score converts to $+0.33\sigma$ (one third of a standard deviation above the mean) . Since a standard deviation is uniformly interpreted regardless of the test or the unit of measurement, provided that the distributions are normal, it is apparent that this person scored better on the mechanical test than on the manual test. In addition, we can see how much better he scored on mechanical aptitude by comparing the percentage of persons scoring below $+1\sigma$ (84 percent) with the percentage scoring below $+0.33\sigma$ (62 percent) .

By way of summary to the present point, then, we can completely describe any set of normally distributed data by indicating the mean and standard deviation of the distribution and the number of subjects upon whom observations were made. The typical experiment yields at least two distributions of data: one for the experimental group and one for the control group. These distributions must be evaluated by the investigator in order to determine whether they are

FIGURE 2-9

Distributions of Scores on a Test of Mechanical Aptitude and
a Test of Manual Dexterity Showing the Relative Position
of Individual X in Each Distribution

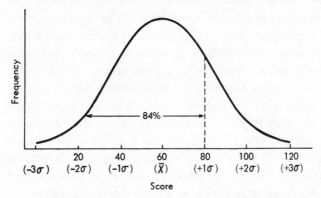

A. Mechanical Aptitude: $\bar{X} = 60$ $\sigma = 20$ $X = 80 = +1\sigma$

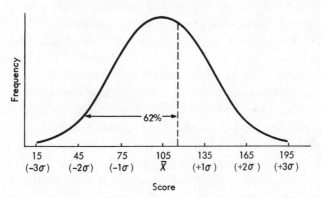

B. Manual Dexterity: $\bar{X} = 105$ $\sigma = 30$ $X = 115 = +0.33\sigma$

similar or dissimilar. It is to this matter of interpreting the outcomes of experimentation that we next turn our attention.

Statistical Inference

The usual control-group experiment illustrates the need for statistical inference. Here, the investigator has made two sets of observations: one in the experimental group and one in the control group.

He wishes to determine whether differences between the distributions of data in these two groups can be attributed to the influence of the independent variable.

The Difference between Means.   One way in which to evaluate the effectiveness of an industrial training program is periodically to test the employees' knowledge as the training progresses. This is quite comparable to the usual practice in colleges and universities of testing students' knowledge during the course of the academic year.

Suppose we were interested in comparing the effectiveness of two kinds of industrial training programs. The first kind, which we will refer to as "distributed training," requires that employees attend training sessions two hours a day for five days. The second kind of program, "massed training," also offers a total of 10 hours of instruction. Employees under this program, however, attend class five hours a day for two consecutive days. The trainees are randomly assigned to the two groups to control extraneous factors, and a test of their knowledge at the end of 10 hours of training yields a mean score in the distributed group of 52.5 while the mean for the massed group is only 50.0. Although it appears upon superficial examination that distributed training is superior to massed training, it is impossible to interpret these data properly until we apply a test of statistical significance to the obtained difference between means.

The fundamental problem underlying statistical inference stems from the fact that experimental data are accumulated over a finite period of time and from limited numbers of experimental subjects. In the illustrative training program experiment we are dealing with *samples* of employees receiving massed and distributed training rather than with the *population* (all employees to whom such training might be given) . Furthermore, the criterion measure of knowledge after 10 hours of training must, of necessity, sample this knowledge rather than measure all of its components. Thus, the criterion instrument itself samples from the population of information and skills constituting "job knowledge."

However, our interest in experimental findings is not limited to the performance of samples of persons upon samples of possible test questions. We wish instead to make inferences of a more general nature from our data. We want to be able, for example, to formulate generalizations about the performance on the *population* of test questions measuring job knowledge by the *population* of employees.

The extent to which we can confidently make such generalizations is largely dependent upon the magnitude of our sampling errors. The smaller such errors, the more confidence we may place in generalizations about the population. When we statistically test the significance of the difference between means, we are in effect asking: "What is the probability of obtaining a difference between means as great or greater than the one we have noted for our samples *when there is actually no difference between the population means?*" In other words, what is the likelihood that we have obtained a chance rather than a statistically significant difference?

In addition to the magnitude of sampling errors influencing the

FIGURE 2–10

Distributions of Test Scores after Massed and Distributed Training Sessions: The Effect of Large Standard Deviations

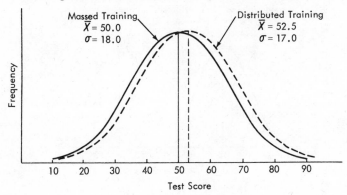

means, the answer to this question is dependent upon the errors of measurement itself (which are usually small) and the size of the obtained difference between sample means. Sampling and measurement errors affect the accuracy of the mean, and their influence can be estimated by formula from the standard deviation of the scores in the distribution and the number of subjects in the group.

Let us assume that there were 100 trainees in each group, that the standard deviation as computed for the distributed group was 17.0, and that the standard deviation as computed for the massed group was 18.0. The distributions of data for the two groups are shown in Figure 2–10.

The two distributions shown in Figure 2–10 overlap to a considerable extent. A statistic for estimating *percentage overlap* between two such distributions is described in Appendix A. Applying this statistic, the actual amount of overlap is estimated as 94 percent. This means that virtually every test score was earned by some persons from both training groups. Only 6 percent of the cases were clearly distinguishable on the basis of the training they had received. Since the distributions overlap to such a great extent, it is evident in this instance that performance was not affected by the nature of the training program.

What can we say about the obtained difference between the

FIGURE 2–11

Distributions of Test Scores after Massed and Distributed
Training Sessions: The Effect of Relatively Small
Standard Deviations

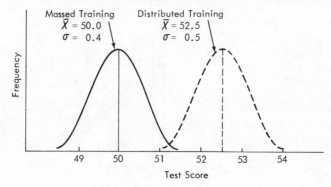

means of the massed and distributed training groups? Since the distributions are so much alike (94 percent overlap), we cannot be at all confident that the 2.5-point difference between means would be obtained again if the experiment were repeated.

By way of contrast, however, if the standard deviations were smaller, say 0.5 for the distributed group and 0.4 for the massed group, the plotted distributions of scores would look like those illustrated in Figure 2–11. You notice in this instance that the distributions of scores are quite independent of one another. Little overlap (less than 1 percent) exists, indicating that most of the scores were obtained either by trainees in the distributed group or the massed group, but not by trainees in both groups. Such data indicate that the two distributions of scores are independent. In this instance we would conclude that distributed training is really superior to massed training.

Statistical Significance.   Let us probe this matter of testing the difference between means in somewhat greater depth.

Suppose we drew two random samples from the same population and subjected each group to the *identical condition.* Under such circumstances we would expect the mean scores in the two groups to be very similar. These means would not be identical because of chance factors operating when individuals are assigned to groups. Sometimes the mean of one group would be higher, and vice versa.

Thus, if we assume the operation only of chance factors, we would anticipate a certain amount of fluctuation between sample means and as a consequence a certain amount of fluctuation in the size of the difference between pairs of sample means. If the samples are randomly drawn from the same population, the differences between pairs of means should be distributed closely about a value of zero.

Expectations about the fluctuation of mean differences attributable *solely to chance* can be determined statistically. The "standard error of the difference" tells us how much chance variation to anticipate in a distribution of differences between pairs of means for groups randomly drawn from the same population. The standard error of the difference is in effect a standard deviation of a distribution of mean differences attributable to chance when groups are randomly drawn from the same population.

In actual experimentation, we begin with random groups and subject them to *different* conditions. What would happen if these conditions had no effect at all upon performance? The obtained difference between the group means would fall within the range of differences anticipated solely on the basis of chance. However, if the obtained difference exceeds differences attributable to chance fluctuations, we have evidence for a "statistically significant" difference.

In practice, the investigator applies a statistical test to his obtained difference between means in order to determine whether this difference is a real or chance finding. This statistic, the *t ratio,* involves a comparison between the obtained mean difference and the standard error of the difference (that is, the amount of mean fluctuation attributable to chance variation) .

The *t* ratio indicates the likelihood that the mean difference for samples drawn from a single population is *smaller* than the one ac-

tually obtained from the experimental samples. Convention dictates that when this probability exceeds 5 percent, we regard the obtained difference as not significant. We must, in other words, have evidence that a difference as great or greater than the one we obtained would occur by chance only five times in a hundred before attributing this difference to manipulation of the independent variable rather than to chance. Although a probability of 0.05 is generally accepted as indicating a statistically significant difference, lower probabilities on the order of 0.01 or 0.001 often are obtained and give cause for still greater confidence in the experimental conclusion.

Statistical versus Practical Significance. The distinction between statistical and practical significance is of great importance in applied research. To illustrate, consider again the hypothetical investigation of the effects of increased illumination upon typing speed. Even if the mean performance in the experimental group (with increased illumination) was statistically superior to that in the control group, we still must inquire whether the amount of improvement justifies the expense of rewiring and installing new fixtures in the office.

A relatively small difference between means may be statistically significant when the groups are large but may lack statistical significance when the groups are small. If very large groups are required to demonstrate statistical significance, the practical utility of the finding may be questionable.

Correlation

As we have previously said, correlation is a statistical procedure for determining the strength and direction of relationship between variables. This relationship is statistically expressed by the coefficient of correlation (r).

Although the ensuing discussion of correlation is limited to its application when two variables are involved, correlational studies need not be limited in this way. The usual predictive study, for example, involves an attempt to maximize the efficiency with which the criterion (say, job performance) is predicted from combined scores on several preemployment measures (tests, interviews, personal history data, and so on), each weighted optimally. The statistical technique appropriate to this kind of problem is *multiple correlation*.

It must be emphasized that although correlation implies a relationship between scores or events, it does not provide evidence regarding causation. Assuming the existence of a correlation between two variables, either one may be cause and the other effect. Furthermore, it is quite possible to obtain a correlation when *neither* of them is cause or effect. This occurs whenever the correlated variables

FIGURE 2–12

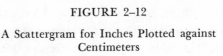

A Scattergram for Inches Plotted against
Centimeters

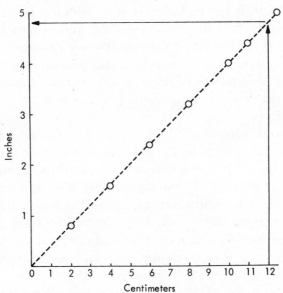

are themselves dependent upon some third or fourth variable underlying the two particular ones correlated by the investigator.

A Perfect Positive Correlation. Two sets of observations made under comparable circumstances may be conveniently presented in the form of a crossplot or *scattergram*. Such a scattergram showing the relationship between inches and centimeters is illustrated in Figure 2–12. Measurement of distance in inches is shown on the *Y*-axis; corresponding distances in centimeters show on *X*-axis.

This scattergram shows eight pairs of observations, each indicated by a dot. Each of these points shows the distance on a centimeter scale corresponding to a particular distance on an inch scale.

You will note that all of the plotted points in this scattergram can be joined by a straight line. The fact that all pairs of observations fall on this line indicates the existence of a perfect correlation between the two variables under consideration. When computed, the numerical value of the coefficient of correlation would be 1.00, which is the maximum value that this statistic may attain.

What does a correlation coefficient of 1.00 tell us? It indicates in the first place that there is a complete and inflexible relationship between the two variables. One centimeter, for example, always corresponds to 0.3937 inch, two centimeters to 0.7874 inch, and so on. Secondly, differences between pairs of measurements of one variable are reflected in proportional differences between pairs of measurements of the second variable. In our illustration, every increase or decrease of 1 centimeter corresponds to an increase or decrease of 0.3937 inch. The effect of proportional change in the two variables is to produce the straight line relationship illustrated in Figure 2–12.

A perfect relationship, like the one illustrated, enables us to predict one variable from the other without error. Suppose, for example, that we lost the ruler that measures in inches and had only the one that measures in centimeters. We could transform a measured distance of 12 centimeters to 4.72 inches simply by inspection of the scattergram. We could, in other words, predict what the measurement would have been if we had used a scale calibrated in inches. As long as the correlation between the variables is perfect (1.00), such predictions will be entirely free of error.

In addition to being perfect, the correlation for data like those presented in Figure 2–12 is positive; the computed value of the coefficient will be +1.00. The fact that the obtained correlation carries a + sign indicates that there is a *direct* relationship between the two variables. Increases in score on either of the variables are paralleled by increases in score on the other variable. Similarly, a decrease in score on one variable is paralleled by a corresponding decrease on the other variable.

A Perfect Negative Correlation. Correlation coefficients are not always positive. An illustration of a scattergram yielding a perfect negative correlation (−1.00) is presented in Figure 2–13.

Again, all pairs of observations fall on a straight line indicating a perfect relationship between variables X and Y and hence errorless predictability of one variable from the other. Knowing, for example,

FIGURE 2–13

Scattergram Indicating a Perfect Negative Correlation

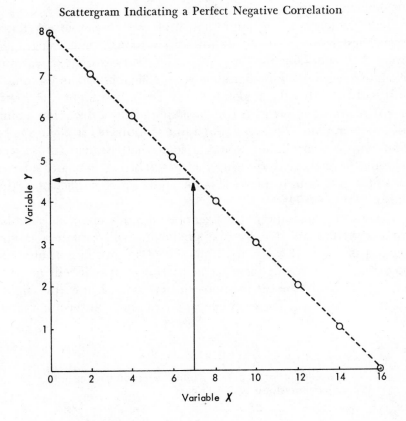

Variable **X**

that an individual scored 7.0 on variable X we would predict that his score on variable Y would be 4.5.

The variables in this illustration are, however, inversely rather than directly related. An increase in scores on variable X is paralleled by a corresponding decrease in Y-scores; and a decrease in X-scores is paralleled by a corresponding increase in Y-scores. This inverse relationship would be reflected in the computation of r by the assignment of a negative sign to the correlation coefficient.

A High Correlation. Perfect correlations do not occur when we deal with psychological phenomena. Let us assume that we have constructed a test for selecting personnel and wish to validate it against the criterion of supervisor's rating of efficiency at the end of six months of employment. We would administer the test to all new employees and correlate the scores with the supervisor's ratings which would be available six months later. Figure 2–14 shows a hypothetical scattergram of such data.

This scattergram indicates that 4 of the 36 employees tested earned test scores of 60; their ratings six months later ranged between 5.50 and 7.00. Similarly, five employees earned test scores of 50 and received ratings ranging between 4.30 and 6.50 and so on.

It is obvious that the 36 points do not fall on a straight line; hence the correlation between the two variables is not perfect. The points do, however, tend to cluster about a line as indicated in Figure 2–14. The computed correlation would be somewhat less than perfect, and it would be positive, indicating that as test scores increase, supervisor's ratings tend to be more favorable. The actual coefficient in this illustration is +0.74.

Can we use an imperfect correlation like this one as a basis for making predictions? Yes, but our predictions will contain a certain amount of error. If a job applicant scored 55 on the test, our best point prediction about his efficiency rating is that it will be 5.70. The more closely the observations cluster about a line (the higher the correlation), the more confidence we can have in the accuracy of

FIGURE 2–14

A Crossplot of Scores on a Personnel Selection Test against Supervisory Ratings of Efficiency

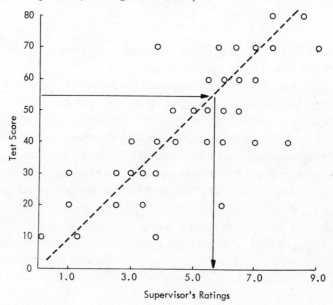

this prediction. Conversely, the more dispersed are the observations from a line (the lower the correlation), the less confident we will be of the accuracy of this prediction.

What would happen to the obtained correlation coefficient if we had plotted the test scores in terms of the number of items answered incorrectly instead of in terms of the number of correct answers. The strength of the relationship between the test and criterion would be unaffected. The direction of this relationship would, however, be reversed. In other words, as error scores increased, efficiency ratings would decrease. The resultant value of r would be negative, although the numerical value of the coefficient would be unchanged. Thus, the coefficient computed under these circumstances would be −0.74.

A Zero Correlation. Suppose we wish to determine the extent of relationship between the heights of college students and their grade-point averages. We could plot these variables against each other and would obtain results approximating those displayed in Figure 2–15. This scattergram indicates that there is no relationship between the two variables in question. The grade-point averages of tall students

FIGURE 2–15

Heights of College Students Plotted against Grade-Point Averages Indicating a Correlation Coefficient of 0.00

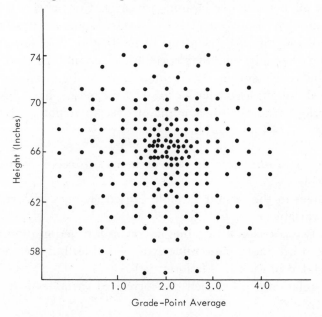

are no different from those of short students, and in consequence, the computed r is 0.00. This minimum value of the correlation coefficient indicates that it is impossible to fit any line to the data. As a result, predictions of one variable from the other will have only chance accuracy.

Interpretation of Correlation Coefficients. A correlation coefficient is most properly interpreted in the light of the purpose for which it was computed. When estimating the validity of a test, coefficients in the vicinity of 0.40 are generally acceptable. Reliability studies, however, must demonstrate the existence of a more substantial correlation. The manuals for most published tests generally report reliability coefficients within the range 0.80–0.95.

As indicated earlier, correlational analysis has numerous applications aside from those related to the reliability and validity of tests. One such application utilizes the coefficient to provide an index of the amount of overlapping variance. The higher the correlation, the greater is the amount of overlap between variables. When the obtained correlation is 1.00, the variances overlap completely; when the correlation is 0.00, the variables do not overlap at all.

It is unfortunate that correlation coefficients look like percentages. The resemblance is entirely superficial. The percentage of overlapping variance is given by the *coefficient of determination* (r^2) rather than by the r itself. A correlation of 0.60, for example, indicates 36 percent overlapping variance. Conversely, the *coefficient of nondetermination* ($1 - r^2$) in this instance indicates that 64 percent of the variance is independent (that is, does not overlap).

We have already said that correlations do not imply causality. Thus, the coefficient of determination must be interpreted cautiously. Although, a correlation of 0.60 means we have 36 percent overlapping variance, this amount of overlap might have resulted from any one of four conditions:

1. Changes in one variable caused changes to occur in the second variable.
2. Changes in the second variable caused changes to occur in the first variable.
3. The two correlated variables covary as a function of changes in some third, more basic underlying variable, but are themselves unrelated in causative fashion.
4. The relationship between the correlated variables is interactive

in nature. An obtained correlation between productivity of piece-rate workers and their job satisfaction might reflect such an interaction. High productivity results in higher pay and may therefore lead to increased job satisfaction. Dissatisfaction with the job, however, may be responsible for diminished interest in the work and hence for lowered output.

Regardless of the conditions responsible for correlation, covariation enables us to predict scores on one variable from knowledge about scores on the other variable. The accuracy of these predictions is a function of the magnitude of r. As the numerical value of r decreases, our predictions become less and less accurate until with a correlation of 0.00 all predictions have chance accuracy.

Assume, for example, we find a 0.00 correlation between students' heights and their grade-point averages. This means that 50 percent of the students who are taller than average earn above-average grade points, and 50 percent of the shorter than average students also earn above-average grade points. Clearly, then, knowledge about height will not aid us in predicting grade point.

If, however, we used a test of academic ability as a predictor of scholastic performance we could make predictions with better than chance accuracy. Suppose we obtain a correlation between the test and grade point of 0.40. It has been shown that with such a correlation 63 percent of the students earning above-average predictor scores also earn above-average criterion scores. If the correlation were 0.60, 70 percent of the students earning above-average test scores also earn above-average grade points.

We will mention just one other application of the correlation coefficient. Sometimes the investigator merely wishes to determine whether the relationship between variables exceeds expectations on the basis of chance. Any r in excess of what would be expected as a chance deviation from a correlation of 0.00 would be statistically significant under such circumstances. As is the case with the t ratio discussed earlier, convention requires a probability level of 5 percent or better. In other words, for an obtained correlation to be regarded as statistically significant from 0.00, the probability of its occurrence as a chance variation from a true value of 0.00 must be 5 percent or less. Table 2–2 shows the value of r required for statistical significance at both the 5 and 1 percent levels for selected N's (number of pairs of observations) .

TABLE 2–2

Values of *r* Required for Significance at the
5 and 1 Percent Levels*

N	5 Percent Level	1 Percent Level
10	0.63	0.77
25	0.40	0.51
50	0.28	0.36
75	0.23	0.30
100	0.20	0.26
500	0.09	0.12
1,000	0.06	0.08

* After L. D. Edmison in J. E. Wert, C. O. Neidt, & J. S. Ahmann. *Statistical methods in educational and psychological research.* New York: Appleton-Century-Crofts, Inc., 1954.

Note that the size of *r* required for *statistical significance* decreases as the number of pairs of observations from which *r* is computed increases. Thus when the correlation is calculated from 1,000 pairs of observations, a value of only 0.06 is statistically significant at the 5 percent level.

In this regard it is important to recall the distinction made earlier between statistical and practical significance. A relatively low correlation may be statistically different from a correlation of 0.00 but lack practical significance for predictive applications.

SUMMARY

The basic approaches to the study of behavior utilized by the industrial psychologist are identical to the methodological approaches utilized in any of the other sciences. These methods are characterized by observation rather than by speculation, by objectivity rather than subjectivity, and by controls making it possible to repeat a set of observations and to draw meaningful conclusions. These elements of scientific method are translated by the researcher into an investigation of the relationship between two basic kinds of variables. One of these, the independent variable, is the factor whose effects are being investigated. The behaviors studied as possible functions of the independent variable are referred to as dependent variables. Thus, in an experiment concerning the effects of illumination upon industrial productivity, illumination is the independent variable and productivity is the dependent variable.

The relationship between independent and dependent variables may be studied by means of the naturalistic method, by the experimental method, and by clinical observation. Naturalistic observations are made whenever the independent variable is not amenable to manipulation by the investigator. Under these circumstances the effects of the independent variable must be studied in natural surroundings without interference by the researcher. The experimental method, on the other hand, requires that the investigator manipulate the independent variable and control extraneous factors. The simplest kind of experimental design utilizes two groups of subjects: a control group, which serves as a standard for comparative purposes; and an experimental group, in which the independent variable is manipulated. Clinical observation emphasizes studies in depth of the subject's personality and motivation.

The summary and interpretation of research data requires that they be submitted to a statistical analysis. Data may be statistically summarized by measures of central tendency and variability. Measures of central tendency indicate the typical or average score; measures of variability indicate the spread of scores away from this average. The primary measures of central tendency are the mean (the arithmetic average), the median (the middle score in the distribution), and the mode (the score that occurs most frequently). The only measure of variability discussed in the chapter is the standard deviation.

The *t* ratio is a statistical technique aiding data interpretation. It is a test of the likelihood that an obtained difference between means is attributable to chance rather than to the independent variable. The rationale for making this test is that the investigator initiates his study (before application of the independent variable) by establishing experimental and control groups which are random samples from the same population. Hence, any difference in performance at the inception of the study is attributable solely to chance. The object of the study is to provide different treatments (by manipulating the independent variable) to these groups in an attempt to determine whether the independent variable manipulations generate corresponding changes in the dependent variable(s). If the independent variable *does* have this effect, the groups which were originally drawn as random samples from the same population will be shown at the conclusion of the study to exhibit statistically significant performance differences. Conversely, if the independent variable does *not* have this effect these groups will be shown at the conclusion of the study to exhibit performance differences within the range of variation expected by chance whenever random samples from the same population are compared.

This chapter concludes with a discussion of correlation. Correlational analysis reveals the magnitude and direction of the relationship between two or more variables.

II.

Personnel Psychology

This group of chapters concerns employee selection, placement, and training. The fundamental objective of personnel programs in industry is to best utilize the specific capabilities and interests of employees. Every individual has a unique pattern of abilities and history of past experiences. Such individual differences result from the interaction of inherited predispositions and environmental influences, in turn influencing the kinds of satisfactions we seek from work and from life in general.

Employers generally consider several factors when hiring a new worker. First, there must be some evidence that the applicant has the capabilities and knowledges required for satisfactory job performance and completion of the company's training program. Second, employers seek workers who will be interested in and stimulated by their work to the maximum extent possible. A third consideration in many instances is the applicant's potential for advancement to positions of greater responsibility within the company.

The reasons for regarding both ability and satisfaction as important elements in personnel selection and placement are fairly obvious. Employees who lack the required abilities, regardless of whether these requisites are intellectual or personal, simply cannot work efficiently. The salesman who cannot converse easily, the supervisor who cannot direct the activities of subordinates, the laborer who lacks the necessary physical stamina, and the teacher who does not know her subject matter are all relatively ineffectual as employees. Similarly, employees who are capable but do not regard their work as enjoyable or stimulating may reflect their dissatisfaction in lowered productivity and high absenteeism and turnover.

Thus, the primary problem in selecting and placing personnel is predictive in nature. The employer needs to know, in advance, which of several applicants will, if hired, be most efficient as an employee. Furthermore, he must be guided in placing employees in order to best utilize their abilities, skills, knowledge, and personal characteristics. The logical place to begin our consideration of issues and procedures in personnel psychology is with an elaboration of the criteria of "employee efficiency" which the employer seeks to predict. Chapter 3 discusses both such objective forms of performance appraisal as output, spoilage, and turnover and such subjective criteria as those derived from supervisory ratings.

Chapters 4, 5, and 6 describe the major selection and placement techniques including interviews, application forms, letters of recommendation, and psychological tests. We are specifically concerned in those chapters with the ways in which these techniques are developed, used, and improved.

The relationship between selection-placement programs and training programs (Chapter 7) is almost self-evident. A fundamental purpose of training is to develop job-related knowledges, skills, and attitudes. In addition, in-service training programs often provide educational experiences of a more-or-less formal nature and are designed to provide employees with opportunities for job enlargement and intracompany promotion.

Sound selection, placement, and training programs yield substantial financial dividends. Every new employee represents a monetary investment by management. In addition to the direct costs of recruitment and training programs, a number of other expenses are incidental to hiring procedures. Every time an employee voluntarily terminates employment or must be fired, this investment is lost.

3. Prediction and Performance Criteria

Virtually everything the industrial psychologist does necessitates his concern with some sort of criterion of job performance. Whether he is engaged in developing techniques for selecting or training personnel, improving the work environment, developing promotional procedures, doing research on conditions contributing to job satisfaction, or anything else, he must come to grips with criterion definition and development. It is insufficient from a research standpoint to speak of improving efficiency or job performance. These can be variously defined; the ways in which they are measured are functions of their definitions; and conditions leading to improvement judged by one criterion may prove ineffective when judged by some other criterion.

The discussion of criteria in this chapter is specifically oriented toward developing measures of job performance suitable for personnel selection and training programs. However, the issues raised in this discussion are sufficiently general to apply to the broader problem of assessing organizational efficiency for any purpose. Specific criterion problems encountered in evaluating training programs, appraising workers on the job, and measuring job satisfaction are described in context throughout subsequent chapters.

PRELIMINARY CONSIDERATIONS

The discussion of descriptive statistics in Chapter 2 concerned procedures for summarizing sets of data like test scores, performance measures, and so on. You will recall that when such data are graphed or arranged in a frequency distribution, some of the persons in the sample are seen to perform at higher levels than others. Thus, some employees are more efficient than others; some job applicants earn higher preemployment test scores than others; some students are brighter than others; some persons are taller than others; and so on.

These differences between individuals reflect the interaction between hereditary predispositions and environmental influences. We need not be concerned here with the relative contributions of these two sets of factors in generating individual differences. It is sufficient here to note that whereas the influence of heredity is particularly strong in generating certain kinds of individual differences (like those of height and weight), environmental factors are primary determinants of others (for example, interests). Furthermore, the interaction between these two general determinants of individual differences is inescapable. Thus, whereas genetic factors may be the primary determinants of height, environmental conditions like climate and nutrition also cause variations in this characteristic. Likewise, whereas environmental factors may be the primary determinants of interests, it is unlikely that an interest will develop in the absence of a genetic predisposition to perform satisfactorily in the interest area. Students with low aptitude for learning mathematics, for example, are unlikely to become interested in graduate training in this area.

The purpose of any criterion is to make evident the differences between individuals. In industry, criteria of job performance are designed to clarify and display the differences between employees who do well and those who do poorly—for example, those who are highly productive and those who are relatively unproductive. Criteria effectively making this distinction are obviously useful as guides to promotion, salary determination, identification of training needs, and related personnel actions. Such criteria also are the dependent variables in research programs designed to determine the effects of altered work environments and training programs.

Since the primary focus in Part II is on personnel selection and placement, this chapter emphasizes yet another application of performance criteria. These measures are what we wish to predict whenever personnel selection devices are administered. The purpose of personnel selection procedures is to identify individual differences between job applicants on measures associated with individual differences between employees on performance criteria. If, for example, the performance criterion that interests us is some measure of productivity, we will wish to use preemployment devices that allow us to identify those persons who if hired will be most likely to rank high in the distribution of productivity.

Reliability and Validity of Criteria

A criterion is a standard against which we evaluate something. The effectiveness of a test battery for selecting workers, for example, is judged by the accuracy of hiring decisions following its use. If the battery is effective, the personnel manager basing his decisions upon it will hire mostly persons who subsequently prove to be efficient workers; most of those he rejects would subsequently have proven to be inefficient workers. In this instance the criterion would have to be some measure of "efficiency."

Particular criteria are often chosen merely because they are readily available, or have been used by other investigators confronted by a similar problem, or are thought by management to be relevant to the problem at hand (Weitz, 1961). Without minimizing the importance of these considerations, they are insufficient by themselves to insure adequacy of the criterion.

Whenever anything is measured, the investigator needs assurance that his yardstick is both reliable and valid. We have already given one definition of reliability, that is, the consistency of measurement. Validity has been defined as the relevance of measurement to whatever it is we intend to measure.

The significance of these concepts for test development will be discussed at some length in Chapter 5. The important point here is that the criteria we expect our tests to predict must themselves be reliable and valid. It is not possible accurately to predict an unstable criterion. Furthermore, there is not much wisdom in predicting a criterion of something other than the thing we really wish to predict.

Kinds of Criteria

The "ultimate" criterion of job success would have to reflect an individual's productive efficiency throughout his working life (Albright, Glennon, & Smith, 1963). It clearly is infeasible to attempt to develop such an ultimate criterion. People change jobs during their lifetimes, and productive efficiency means different things for different jobs. Even for a single job, the definition of productive efficiency may change over a period of time. The components of productive efficiency for any job are typically beyond comprehensive identification in terms amenable to evaluation. And if the foregoing were not enough to discourage a search for ultimate criteria, the simple fact that by definition they are unavailable until the end of an employee's productive lifetime would itself prove discouraging.

Characteristically, then, industrial psychologists develop some sort of intermediate criteria of performance which have components in common with (and therefore are presumed to correlate with) the ultimate criterion. These intermediate criteria are more immediately available and are restricted to performance on the employee's present or prospective job.

The diversity of available criteria of job performance is tremendous. One listing of such criteria includes items bearing upon (*a*) output per unit of time; (*b*) quality of production; (*c*) time lost by personnel because of sickness, accidents, and so on; (*d*) personnel turnover; (*e*) training time; (*f*) promotability; and (*g*) employee satisfaction (Wherry, 1950). Data germane to these criteria are often available in one form or another in already existing company records. The problem from a research standpoint is that often the form in which they have been collected precludes reliability and/or validity.

Certain kinds of criterion data are objectively verifiable. This is the case, for example, with counts of time lost because of accidents or length of job tenure. Other criteria, like promotability, depend upon judgments—typically made by the supervisor—and hence are subjective. We will consider each type of criterion separately.

OBJECTIVE CRITERIA

Undoubtedly some sort of production index is one of the most widely used objective criteria for industrial research. This is so in part because of expediency; most companies maintain production records, and thus they are immediately available to the researcher. Also management generally considers high productivity to be synonymous with efficiency. Thus, we will direct our attention first in this section to criteria of productivity. Whereas we will be considering objective measures of productivity, it should be evident that there are many jobs for which such measures are unobtainable. What production measure should be counted, for example, to appraise supervisory or managerial proficiency? And what can be objectively counted adequately to reflect the performance of an employee rendering a service rather than participating in production of a product? In such instances performance must either be appraised from objective criteria other than a measure of productivity or by some kind of subjective criterion measure.

Productivity

Criteria of productivity ordinarily combine two elements: quantity and quality of output. The quantitative aspects of production records can often be readily tabulated and statistically analyzed; for example, the number of armatures wound by assembly line workers during a shift, the number of words per minute typed by a secretary, or the monthly sales record of an insurance salesman.

However output records are often invalid in their raw form. Productivity may be a meaningless criterion unless it is corrected for spoilage. Some adjustment is necessary when comparing a secretary averaging 70 words per minute but with three errors with one averaging 60 errorless words per minute. Similarly, in evaluating monthly insurance sales records, it is necessary to include some indication of policy cancellations.

Contamination.   Even a measure of output corrected for spoilage and obtained for employees doing what superficially appears to be the same kind of work may not be a satisfactory criterion of job performance because of contamination. *Contamination* refers to the effect upon the criterion of factors which are really extraneous to the measure being sought.

One source of criterion contamination may be the working environment itself. Typing speed and accuracy, for example, are affected by the amount of noise and other distractions in the office. Likewise, for assembly tasks, output may be limited by such things as the output rate of fellow workers, maximum machine speed, and availability of raw materials. Output for salesmen undoubtedly reflects the size of the sales territory and the socioeconomic status of the residents as contaminating factors.

A second source of criterion contamination is subtle differences in the nature of the job itself. A secretary typing a technical manuscript is not doing the same kind of work as one typing letters; an insurance salesman is not doing the same type of work as an automobile salesman. In both instances it would be erroneous to attempt direct comparisons of productivity.

Finally, criteria may be contaminated by variations in job experience. Since there often is a correlation between length of experience and productivity, output measures obtained for relatively new employees cannot be directly compared with those for more experienced employees.

Sampling Errors.   Another possible source of error in developing production criteria results from the fact that production records are not used in their entirety. Instead, these criteria ordinarily are derived from samples of job performance. Samples of output will not accurately reflect fluctuations in performance unless they are drawn from periods representative of the entire shift or in the case of sales positions, from periods representative of the entire year. If each output sample spans only a brief time period, or if too few samples are drawn to insure representativeness, the criterion may lack reliability.

Interpreting Productivity.   Another kind of problem is encountered when the attempt is made to convert performance records to a criterion of goodness or efficiency. This is somewhat analogous to the evaluative problem faced by a teacher when he attempts to judge student performance on an examination. He may be able to convert the student's answers to a numerical score (that is, an output record), but he still must decide whether the score is good enough to merit a grade of A or whether it really deserves only a B or C. The standards for such a judgment, whether it be made for a class or a group of workers, may be relativistic (median output is defined as average) or absolutistic (anyone performing better than some specified level, like 90 percent of capacity, is superior). The latter kind of industrial output evaluation often uses time study results for defining capacity.

Miscellaneous Objective Criteria

Still another type of criterion measure may be derived from the *job sample*. This is a test of job performance under very carefully controlled conditions. It is designed to get at very much the same type of behavior as a production criterion, but without the danger of contamination sometimes present for the latter.

Criterion measures are intended to reflect performance differences between employees attributable to differences in their abilities, motivation, level of experience, and other personal characteristics. As was indicated earlier, measures of performance may be contaminated by factors other than the ones specifically under consideration. Such potentially contaminating factors can often be more easily controlled in a job sample than in the actual work situation.

Productivity, objectively or subjectively appraised, is neither the only nor always the most desirable indication of job performance. Consider, for example, a job requiring a very lengthy initial training period at considerable expense to the company. No company likes to contemplate the prospect of an employee accepting a job offered by a competitor shortly after completing such a training program. Job tenure may actually be a more meaningful criterion than productivity in this instance.

There are a number of jobs in which the range of productivity is so narrow that the difference in output between the best and worst producer is relatively insignificant. This is particularly true of highly repetitive work paid on a piece rate for departments in which the workers have established a "gentleman's agreement" among themselves about how much they will produce. Under these circumstances management may be more interested in predicting such criteria as absenteeism, tardiness, and turnover than output.

There is a relative dearth of research using the latter criterion in spite of the obvious importance of employee tenure to the organization. A greater understanding of the conditions generating turnover would be useful both to the organization in reducing its manpower costs and to individual employees by reducing the disruption often associated with job changes (Hinrichs, 1970). Furthermore, unlike measures of productivity, turnover data do not suffer unreliability. Those studies of turnover that have been reported tend to indicate that employee interests, background, and job satisfaction tend better to predict job tenure than do the most typically used preemployment tests of intelligence, aptitude, and personality (Schuh, 1967).

SUBJECTIVE CRITERIA

The point was made earlier that objective indices of performance sometimes are unobtainable or insufficient. There are some jobs for which it is impossible to count units of production or for which the units when counted reveal relatively little about job performance. In such instances the assessment of performance must rest upon some kind of subjectively made estimate of employee proficiency. These opinions may be rendered by supervisors, managers, or co-workers, and take the form of some kind of rating. Such ratings order employees along subjective continua of overall performance or of selected aspects of overall performance. When the results of a performance rating are properly interpreted to and discussed with the employee, he can be materially aided in improving his performance.

The element of subjectivity is at once the peculiar weakness and strength of rating techniques. Rating procedures tend to be much less reliable than psychological tests or objective performance criteria. Thus, if a supervisor wished to obtain a meaningful index of efficiency for factory assemblers, he might do better to utilize an output measure involving a count of production per unit of time adjusted for spoilage than to trust his personal opinion about employee efficiency.

There are circumstances, however, when a reliable criterion measure is not available. The decision must be made in such instances either to measure with a relatively subjective device or to forego measurement entirely. What can the office supervisor count, for example, when she wishes to appraise the overall efficiency of a statistical clerk in her section? Similarly, what objective measures can be applied to assessing the efficiency of office receptionists or Army officers? The diversity and nature of tasks performed by such workers prevents their assessment by objective indicators. Rating procedures must of necessity be used to provide assessments of performance.

However having said this, we must also be aware that the bases upon which supervisory ratings are made may be unrelated to the actual quality of work performed by the ratee. Judgments about performance are notoriously susceptible to bias; hence, subjectively derived criteria are often relatively invalid. Because of the potential for both unreliability and invalidity of performance ratings, it is clear that these should be supplemented with objective measures whenever possible (Bray & Moses, 1972).

Rating Procedures

All of us constantly evaluate the persons with whom we come in contact. We form first impressions often based upon physical appearance, dress, personal mannerisms, and speech. Subsequent contacts may either reinforce our original impression or cause us to change it. In any event, we continually appraise others and are in turn ourselves appraised in a highly subjective and uncontrolled fashion.

In contrast, performance rating procedures attempt to impose a degree of uniformity on the judgmental process. To the extent that they are successful in accomplishing this end, the rater is provided with a yardstick for appraisal that is appropriate to the particular characteristics he is attempting to describe. In short, effective rating procedures encourage an increased degree of objectivity, reliability, and validity in appraising behavior. We briefly consider five of the most commonly used procedures in the following sections, indicating something of the strengths and weaknesses of each.

The Ranking Method. The rater using this technique merely orders the ratees from best to worst, generally assigning a rank of 1 to the person he judges to be highest or best, a rank of 2 to the second best, and so on. The method is a simple one and may be applied either by assigning "man-as-a-whole" ratings or "trait" ratings. In the former case, the employee is assigned a rank on the basis of the supervisor's overall impression about his efficiency. Ratings of traits, on the other hand, may require the supervisor to rank his employees on several specific characteristics like cooperativeness, initiative, or versatility. Such trait ratings are sometimes averaged to yield a composite index of the supervisor's opinions.

The ranking method is susceptible to two deficiencies that may have deleterious effects upon the validity of the resultant information: (1) the hair splitting necessitated by differentiating between adjacent ranks in the middle of the continuum and (2) the fallacious appearance of equal intervals along a scale of ranks. Thus, if 50 employees are to be ranked, the supervisor very likely will experience difficulty in differentiating between the one who should be ranked 23 and the one who should be ranked 24. Furthermore, it is unlikely that the magnitude of the difference between employees ranked 2 and 3 is of the same order as the difference between the employees ranked 26 and 27, even though only one rank separates each of these pairs.

Certain procedures for minimizing these deficiencies have been suggested. It often is desirable, for instance, to differentiate ranks only for persons in the upper and lower quarter of the total group, assigning a common middle rank to the remaining 50 percent of the group. This modification of the ranking procedure obviates the necessity for making impossibly fine discriminations between persons in the middle of the range.

It should be apparent, however, that the ranking method is a crude one. Its usefulness is limited to situations in which relatively few employees are to be rated. Furthermore, it is applicable only when rating is intended to order employees from best to worst without providing an indication of *how much* better or worse one employee is than another.

Paired Comparisons Method. This procedure for making and summarizing judgments has numerous psychological applications. Fundamentally, the procedure requires the evaluator to compare two objects or events and to judge which is the heavier, rounder, sharper, louder, and so on. The paired comparisons method has enjoyed extensive use in studies of sensation and perception.

The application of the paired comparisons method to rating leads to a certain degree of systematization in the assignment of ranks to employees (Lawshe, Kephart, & McCormick, 1949). Every employee to be rated is compared with every other employee, and the rater judges which member of the pair is the better. The supervisor generally predicates this judgment upon his overall impression of the employees' efficiency, but the method may be used also in a more analytical fashion by requiring the rater to consider specific traits one at a time.

The fundamental advantage of this method over the ranking procedure is that it simplifies the kind of judgment required of the rater. Instead of necessitating simultaneous consideration of all members of the group, the paired comparisons method narrows the field for consideration by the supervisor to just two workers at a time.

A very important practical objection to the procedure, however, is that it is quite unwieldy. The number of pairs of employees to be considered is given by the general formula $N(N-1)/2$, where N is the number of workers included in the evaluation. Thus, if a supervisor applies the paired comparisons method to 20 employees, he must make $20(19)/2$, or 190 comparisons. It is not surprising that the use of this procedure is generally limited to assignment of man-as-a-whole ratings rather than analytical or trait ratings. The latter application in a 20-man department would, of course, require the supervisor to make 190 comparisons for each of the several traits or dimensions of behavior being appraised.

Graphic Rating Scales. This approach to merit rating is very widely used in one form or another. The procedure for constructing graphic rating scales requires that levels or degrees of trait possession be established and defined as unambiguously as possible.

There are so many variations of this procedure now in use that it is possible only to indicate something of the diversity of graphic formats. These formats can be conveniently grouped into two classes: continuous scales and discontinuous scales. *Continuous scales* require the supervisor to inspect a rating continuum and to indicate his evaluation of the employee by making a mark somewhere along that continuum. *Discontinuous scales* require the rater to consider only selected points on the rating continuum. A few illustrations of each type of format are shown in Table 3–1.

All rating procedures, including graphic scales, have certain deficiencies. In spite of these deficiencies, the graphic scale approach to rating has much to recommend it. Its use entails consideration of scale units that can be made more or less comparable across raters if the supervisors are adequately trained. Furthermore, graphic rating scales are easily understood by all persons within the company.

A major source of unreliability in graphic ratings is *halo effect:* that is, the tendency for a ratee to receive consistently high or low ratings as a result of generalization by the rater. This phenomenon operates in many kinds of situations requiring subjective appraisal (for example, job interviews, grading essay examinations, and so on). Since halo effects may operate on any kind of rating scheme including, but not limited to graphic procedures, we will reserve a more extensive discussion of this source of unreliability for a later section wherein we will consider the shortcomings of merit rating procedures in general.

The accuracy of judgments in this most typical and widely used form of criterion measurement is also suspect. The general tendency with graphic ratings is in the direction of leniency; a disproportionate percentage of ratees are assigned favorable ratings. This tendency toward leniency is even more pronounced when graphic rating scales are used for personnel evaluations than when they are used for research purposes (Sharon & Bartlett, 1969).

The Weighted Checklist. It has been suggested that the Thur-

TABLE 3-1

Illustrative Formats for Graphic Scales Requiring Ratings of Dependability

Instructions to the rater: Consider the manner and extent to which the employee is "dependable," using the definition given below, and place a check mark indicating your opinion at the appropriate point (or in the appropriate box) of the scale. *Dependability* is evidenced by the following behaviors: (1) follows instructions, (2) completes job on time, (3) is punctual and regular in attendance, (4) does not require excessive supervision.

Illustrative Continuous Scales

```
0          5          10
|----------|----------|
A          F          K

Extremely    About      Extremely
dependable   average    undependable
```

Illustrative Discontinuous Scales

In the highest 10% of workers.	In the next 20% of workers.	In the middle 40% of workers.	In the next 20% of workers.	In the lowest 10% of workers.
□	□	□	□	□

Exceedingly dependable; follows instructions with only minimal supervision.	Generally dependable but sometimes needs supervision.	About average.	Usually undependable. Needs more than average supervision.	Exceedingly undependable, requires continual supervision.

stone scaling procedure for measuring attitudes can be adapted to provide a scheme for rating (Richardson & Kuder, 1933). This scaling procedure assigns differential weights to statements of opinion. The respondent's attitude is converted to a numerical value by averaging or summing the weights of the statements with which he agrees (Thurstone & Chave, 1928).

The procedure for deriving weights requires that a large number of statements describing work behavior be prepared and submitted to "expert" judges. Illustrative statements used in one such study for rating bake shop managers included: "he seldom forgets what he has once been told"; "his weekly and monthly reports are sometimes inaccurate"; "he often has vermin and insects in his shop" (Knauft, 1948).

Each judge independently places every statement somewhere along a continuum (usually of 7, 9, or 11 categories) ranging from extremely desirable (or favorable) behavior to extremely undesirable (or unfavorable) behavior. The summarized pattern of judgments permits identification and rejection of those statements which are "ambiguous"; that is, yielding considerable variability in the distribution of judgments indicating that the judges failed to agree on the relative desirability or undesirability of the behavior described in the statement.

The remaining statements are assigned weights reflecting the "average" judgment of their positions on the desirability-undesirability scale. The statement's weight may be the median of the distribution of judgments assigned to it, or some transformation of this value.

After the appropriate weights for relatively unambiguous statements are calculated, the statements are arranged as a checklist. The rater, of course, sees only the statements; he is not informed of the weights to be used in scoring. The rater is instructed merely to check those statements most descriptive of the employee's behavior. The weighted checklist is scored by summing or averaging the weights of the checked statements.

A checklist was developed using this procedure, for example, to rate salesmen (Richardson & Kuder, 1933). The scale underlying the assignment of weights to each descriptive statement was based upon a seven-point continuum ranging from "extremely undesirable" at 1 to "extremely desirable" at 7. A few of the items included in this checklist are reproduced below. The weights in parentheses are median values with the decimal eliminated for convenience.

Is weak on planning (29)

Is a good worker (46)

Is making exceptional progress (69)

More recently, a comprehensive set of 2,000 statements concerning worker behavior has been scaled in this fashion (Uhrbrock, 1961). It is possible from these 2,000 items to select a number at various points on the judgmental continuum and appropriate to many different kinds of jobs.

Forced-Choice Ratings. This procedure evolved in the main from research conducted for the military services during World War II. The forced-choice procedure was specifically designed to overcome a major deficiency inherent in all of the other rating techniques, that is, the fact that the rater knows whether he is giving either a high or low rating. This kind of awareness permits the rater to slant his recorded judgment in any direction he chooses. The effects of personal biases and favoritism can be only partly eliminated from rating procedures by a training program for supervisors. The forced-choice procedure is an attempt to increase the objectivity of ratings by preventing the rater from knowing whether he is assigning a favorable or an unfavorable rating.

In its simplest form, a forced-choice format requires the rater to select the one statement from a pair that is either most or least descriptive of the person he is rating. A supervisor might, for example, be required to select the statement from each of the following pairs that he feels best describes the employee he is rating.

1. *a.* Is punctual.
   b. Is careful.
2. *a.* Hard worker.
   b. Cooperative worker.

Similarly, he may be required to select the least descriptive statements from pairs of undesirable behaviors like the following:

3. *a.* Is dishonest.
   b. Is disloyal.
4. *a.* Is overbearing.
   b. Is disinterested in his work.

Alternative arrangements for forced-choice items may consist of groupings of three or four statements with instructions to the rater to mark the one least descriptive and the one most descriptive statement from each triad or tetrad.

The key to the development of forced-choice scales is that the statements within any item are equally attractive or unattractive but differ in discriminative power. In the preceding illustrations, for example, the two statements constituting each pair are grouped together partly because the results of a preliminary investigation have indicated that these statements have similar *preference values,* that is, raters tend to interpret these behaviors as being about equally desirable or undesirable. A second basis for pairing alternatives is that they have been demonstrated to have different *discriminative power,* that is, only one of the alternatives differentiates between efficient and inefficient employees. Each of the alternatives in a forced-choice scale is weighted in terms of its discriminative power, and the entire rating form can thus be scored by summing the weights of the statements marked by the supervisor.

The supervisor who deliberately attempts to overrate or underrate an employee is likely to find that it is very difficult to display intentional bias on a forced-choice scale. The format compels him to choose between alternatives that look equally attractive or unattractive; the rater does not, of course, know which of the alternatives contribute positively or negatively to the scale score. Thus, in theory at least, it would be quite possible for a supervisor to mark only desirable behaviors for a ratee without assigning a favorable rating to him.

The rationale underlying forced-choice procedures is rather ingenious. The available evidence supports the particular usefulness of this technique for developing personality inventories. Studies conducted by the Personnel Research Section of the Adjutant General's Office indicate also that the application of forced-choice procedures to merit rating tends to reduce halo and bias and to yield improved validity and reliability.

The forced-choice method has been used for rating in many different occupations and professions including highway patrolmen, engineers, teachers, and physicians (Zavala, 1965). Nevertheless, it is not as extensively used in industry as the methods described earlier in this chapter. A primary reason for some reluctance to use this procedure is that the development of forced-choice scales is relatively time consuming and costly.

Raters sometimes express objections to the procedure because it compels them to select a descriptive statement from a limited number of alternatives. The supervisor responding to such a scale sometimes feels that he is being forced to choose between alternatives, none of which are applicable. This kind of objection is a relatively superficial one. It can usually be overcome by care in pairing alternatives and training raters.

It has been suggested that one of the major limitations of forced-choice rating is its failure to provide the kind of information that can be used for diagnostic feedback to the employee. This can be a serious objection to the procedure if the rating is to be used for informing individual employees about their own particular strengths and weaknesses.

Forced-choice rating should not be regarded as a panacea. The primary advantages of the technique involve possible reductions in the influence of rater bias and halo. The operation of these undesirable factors can, however, be reduced also for the more usual and less expensive graphic rating procedures. Thus, it is appropriate to consider some of the major sources of unreliability in rating procedures, with particular reference to graphic scales, and some of the steps leading to improved reliability.

Sources of Error in Performance Rating

Rating procedures are subjective and hence unreliable by the standards applied to psychological tests. The reliability of a composite rating derived for a 12-item scale completed by different raters, for example, was estimated at 0.55 (Tiffin & McCormick, 1965). This value is far different from the reliability coefficients usually required for standardized tests and suggests that different raters really use different subjective yardsticks for appraising human behavior. A fundamental problem, then, in improving rating procedures is to increase the uniformity with which subjective evaluations are made. To the extent that this is accomplished, the agreement between raters (reliability) will be increased and the correlations between ratings and other industrial criteria will be improved. We will focus in this section upon the major sources of unreliability in rating and suggest the importance both of training raters and of modifying the techniques themselves to overcome this difficulty.

Format of the Rating Scale. In appraising each of the performance rating procedures, we have observed that some procedures tend to be more reliable than others. This is partly a function of the format employed for rating (Madden & Bourdon, 1964). The paired comparisons method, for example, was found in one study to yield an average reliability coefficient across three pairs of raters of 0.83. Whereas this value compares favorably with those obtained with more objective assessment procedures, it is unusually high for rating procedures.

One aspect of format clearly influencing the reliability of ratings is ambiguity in the scale itself. If the trait descriptions or guideposts along the continuum are ambiguous, various raters cannot possibly respond to them uniformly. A trait designation like cooperativeness, for example, may mean quite different things to different raters. Hence, it is imperative that the characteristics to be rated be defined with extreme care and that the raters themselves be trained to interpret these definitions in the intended manner.

Halo Effect. You are well aware of the lasting consequences of first impressions because of the halo effect. We tend to generalize from our present experiences to our subsequent experiences. This kind of generalization may exert a pronounced effect upon performance ratings. Thus, although a rating form may contain 10 or 15 separate scales, the supervisor may respond carefully only to the first one or two of these, marking the remaining ones on the basis of the impressions he has recorded earlier.

Reversal of the Poles. One solution to this problem is to randomize the location of the favorable and unfavorable ends of each scale. By designating the left end of some scales as the "high" or "favorable" pole and of others as the "low" or "unfavorable" pole, the rater is at least compelled to examine each scale carefully enough to determine which end is favorable.

Horizontal Rating. Although reversal of the poles probably reduces the operation of halo effects somewhat, it is not as effective as horizontal rating. Horizontal rating requires that all employees be rated on a single trait or characteristic at a time. Thus, if employees were to be rated on 10 different graphic scales, the supervisor would be asked to rate every one of the employees on the first scale before moving on to the subsequent ones. This procedure is superior to "vertical rating" in which all trait ratings are assigned in immediate succession to one employee, then to a second employee, and so on.

Systematic Bias. Specific raters sometimes exhibit consistently favorable or unfavorable biases in appraising the performance of virtually all of their subordinates. Such a predilection for using either the high or the low end of the rating continuum defeats the fundamental purpose of performance rating by making it virtually impossible to differentiate between the ratees.

Forcing the Distribution. If a relatively large number of persons are to be rated by a particular supervisor, we might expect the distribution of the ratings he assigns to approximate a normal distribution. If a five-point graphic scale is used, for example, rather few employees ought to be assigned ratings at either the top or bottom pole. Assuming a perfectly normal distribution, we would anticipate that about 7 percent would receive ratings at each of the poles, 38 percent in the middle or average category, and 24 percent in each of the remaining categories.

Supervisors can be forced to adhere to a normal distribution when making their ratings. Such forcing will, of course, overcome any systematic rating bias that the supervisor may have. There is the danger, however, that forced distributions of ratings may actually produce some unfairly harsh appraisals when the department as a whole is better than average. Similarly, a forced distribution will produce a number of overly lenient ratings in departments with a large number of inefficient employees.

The dilemma of forced distributions for ratings is quite analogous to "curved" grades. It is advisable to make a study of the legitimacy of requiring a normal distribution before deciding to force either merit ratings or course grades to such a distribution. How can we know whether or not it is legitimate to impose a normal distribution upon merit ratings? We would have to examine both the personnel selection program and the training program before answering this question. If employees were carefully selected through the application of rather rigorous standards and if they were carefully trained, it would be erroneous to require the supervisor's appraisals of their performance to conform to a normal distribution. The anticipated distribution under these circumstances should contain a relatively large proportion of favorable ratings. Conversely, if the selection and training programs were relatively weak, we should anticipate a skew in the opposite direction.

Ratings Based upon Inadequate Information. Supervisors often feel compelled to assign ratings even though they have not had an adequate opportunity to observe the employee relative to the particular characteristic in question. In many instances, this feeling probably reflects the supervisor's own insecurity. He may be concerned lest an admission that he is not sufficiently familiar with one of his subordinates be interpreted by management as an indication of his inadequacy as a supervisor.

Ratings made on the basis of inadequate information are relatively valueless to management and may do considerable harm to the employee so rated. Thus, it is advisable for the rating scheme to embody a provision whereby the supervisor can refuse to rate any subordinate if he feels that he possesses insufficient or inadequate information to make a valid rating. This provision must be accompanied by a program of management education and supervisory training, however, if it is to work effectively. Management must not impose the impossible demand that supervisors know enough about every salient characteristic of every employee to rate him; supervisors must be informed about the deleterious effects of assigning ratings predicated upon inadequate information and reassured that their unwillingness to rate under such circumstances will not reflect unfavorably upon them.

Ratings Reflecting Uncontrolled Factors

Assuming that the rating procedures have been developed to maximize their reliability and validity and that the raters are carefully trained to make their ratings as objective and useful as possible, the interpretation of the ratings may be confounded by a variety of uncontrolled factors. The rater is required to appraise certain of the employee's behaviors. Unfortunately, this appraisal may reflect the influence of factors that really are unrelated to the dimensions supposedly under consideration. The supervisor may be unduly influenced, for example, by such things as the employee's job level or classification, the department within which he works, his age and seniority, and even by the employee's sex.

It is generally desirable, therefore, to interpret the merit ratings received by an employee in relation to those received by others in his own reference group, that is, other employees in similar departments, on similar jobs who are of about the same age, and so on.

CRITERION COMBINATION

Which of the criteria described above is the "best" or "most useful" index of job performance? Obviously, this question is not answered easily. Whereas productivity or output somehow corrected for spoilage is extremely relevant for some positions, it is irrelevant for others. Furthermore, even when relevant, a measure of productivity may not tell the whole story. A highly productive employee who has a record of excessive absenteeism or who lacks the necessary skills for eventual promotion to a supervisory position may be less valuable to the company than one who, although less productive, is hardly ever absent and is trainable for a supervisory position.

Thus most jobs are not unidimensional. Instead, they have various dimensions each reflecting one of the several goals of "satisfactory" job performance (Ronan & Prien, 1966). One analysis of supervisory behavior, for example, identified the following six dimensions of effective supervision: (a) establishment of an effective climate for work, (b) ethics in managing subordinates, (c) self-development, (d) personal maturity and sensitivity, (e) knowledge and execution of corporate policies and procedures, and (f) technical job knowledge (Peres, 1962). All of these dimensions of effective supervisory behavior must somehow be included in a criterion for supervisors. Evidence of this sort raises two alternative possibilities for criterion development: one is to develop multiple criteria for each job; the other is somehow to combine such multiple criteria into a single index of overall employee effectiveness.

Multiple Criteria

The development of multiple criteria of job success implicitly assumes that a search for *the* criterion is futile. Instead, what is required is the development and utilization of several criteria each reflecting a particular dimension of job performance. According to this line of reasoning, the combination of several criteria into a single measure of "overall effectiveness" obscures important information (Dunnette, 1963). Thus, referring to the dimensions of supervisory behavior, two supervisors judged to be about equal by a composite criterion of overall effectiveness might really function quite differently. One, for example, might have a high level of technical job knowledge but be relatively immature and insensitive; the other may be relatively mature and sensitive but know little about the technical aspects of job performance.

The Single Overall Criterion

The other alternative for criterion development is, of course, somehow to evolve a single overall index of job performance. The practical importance of deriving a single overall criterion is undeniable in certain circumstances; for example, as an aid to making personnel decisions including those related to promotion and salary increase.

A single criterion can be developed in two ways: by combining the several dimensional criterion measures into a single index or by developing some new criterion index underlying a number of separate performance subcriteria.

Combining Subcriteria. When several subcriteria are to be combined into a single overall performance index, each of the subcriteria must somehow be weighted in terms of its contribution to the composite. Such weights are often subjectively assigned by having judges assess the importance of each subcriterion as a partial determinant of overall job performance.

Alternatively, such weights may be statistically determined either by weighting more heavily the more reliable subcriteria or by weighting more heavily those subcriteria which correlate most highly with some overall assessment of job performance.

In either case, the combination of subcriteria into a single criterion index cannot be effected routinely without regard for the intercorrelations between the subcriteria themselves (Guion, 1961). Such combination makes the most sense when the subcriteria are somewhat intercorrelated, indicating that they share a common underlying behavioral core. Subcriterion combination makes less sense when the components are relatively uncorrelated with each other. In this case, without evidence for a common behavioral core underlying the various subcriteria, their combination into a single index would be illogical.

Deriving a New Overall Criterion. The issue of subcriterion intercorrelation is circumvented in a proposed single overall criterion evolved from cost accounting procedures (Brogden & Taylor,

1950). Instead of seeking a common *behavioral* core underlying the subcriteria, this procedure assumes that there is another type of common element reflected in all subcriteria; that is, that of dollar worth to the company.

In these terms, the purpose of a criterion is to reflect the employee's dollar value to the company. Since this value can be viewed as the employee's contribution to helping the company make money, the proponents of the "dollar criterion" suggest that the effect of each subcriterion can be traced out by cost accounting procedures to determine its monetary impact. Those subcriteria related to production of goods or services would thus be positively weighted because they yield a monetary gain. Conversely, errors, spoilage, and so on that result in a dollar loss for the company would be negatively weighted.

PREDICTIVE VALIDITY

When making hiring decisions, the responsible company officer will wish to select from the pool of job applicants those who are most likely to perform satisfactorily. The problem is that of predicting job behavior in advance of its occurrence. Criterion scores related to personnel selection are those performance measures which are to be predicted by the tests, interviews, and so on that are administered to job applicants.

The strength of the relationship between predictor and criterion is termed *predictive validity*. (Other kinds of validity are discussed in Chapter 5.) In its simplest form, predictive validity is determined by correlating the scores on some preemployment measure administered to job applicants with the criterion scores earned by these same people some time later. If this correlation is high, the predictor instrument may be used for personnel selection with some degree of confidence; persons who are high scorers on the predictor are the ones most likely to maintain satisfactory job performance. Conversely, if the predictor-criterion correlation is low, the predictor cannot be included in the preemployment selection program.

How high a predictor-criterion correlation is needed in order for the preemployment measure to be useful in a practical sense? Such correlations rarely exceed 0.55 or 0.60. In order to determine whether a validity coefficient of, say, 0.30 or 0.35 signifies that the predictor ought to be included in or excluded from the preemployment selection program, we must take into account two other considerations: (*a*) the proportion of workers selected without the predictor in question who are regarded as superior employees and (*b*) the selection ratio.

Present Proportion of Superior Employees

Suppose of the present group of employees selected without the predictor in question, only 30 percent is regarded as superior, that is, in the high criterion group. The remaining employees (70 percent) are in the low criterion group. There clearly is room for improvement of the selection process. And some improvement can be anticipated even by adding a selection device with only moderately high predictive validity.

However, the situation is quite different when a high proportion (say, 80 percent) of the present employees are in the high criterion group. With the existing selection program the chances are only 2 in 10 of making an incorrect hiring decision. To reduce this chance of an erroneous hiring decision even further requires insertion into the selection program of a test with very high predictive validity.

Selection Ratio

The selection ratio is simply:

$$\frac{\text{Number of applicants hired}}{\text{Number of applicants available for hiring}}.$$

A company that must hire 80 of each 100 applicants in order to fill its vacant positions cannot afford to be as discriminating as one that hires only 20 of each 100 applicants. The latter company is in the advantageous position of having a low selection ratio. Therefore, it can afford to be stringent in setting the passing score for any new test considered for inclusion in the preemployment program. When the selection ratio is high, the company is compelled by its need to fill vacant positions to hire most applicants—even those with relatively low preemployment test scores.

Relationship between Selection Ratio and Proportion of Successful Employees

The relationship between the selection ratio, proportion of successful employees, and passing score on a preemployment test is clarified in Figure 3–1.

FIGURE 3–1

The Relationship between Selection Ratio and the Proportion of Successful Employees

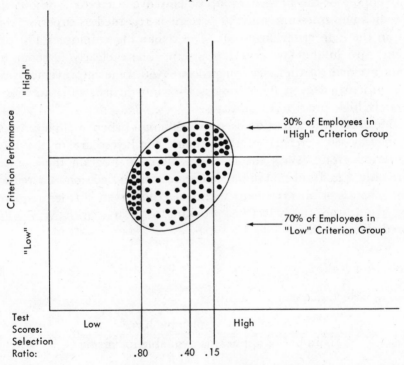

This figure shows a scatterplot of test scores against criterion performance for 100 employees in a company wherein 30 percent of the employees are regarded as successful (in the high criterion group). If we disregarded the new test and selected on the old basis, it is likely that we would continue to find that 30 percent of our newly hired employees would prove to be in the high criterion group.

Note what happens to the proportions of high and low criterion employees as a function of establishing various passing scores on this test. A high selection ratio (say, 0.80) signifies proportionately few applicants relative to the number of vacant positions. As shown in Figure 3–1, of each 80 applicants thus selected, we will obtain 30 who will eventually be in the high criterion group and 50 who will eventually be in the low criterion group. Given this selection ratio, the new test will improve the proportion of high criterion employees selected from the present level of 30 percent to 37.5 percent (30/80) .

Predictive efficiency is improved further as the passing score can be set for a lower selection ratio. Suppose we had a sufficient number of applicants relative to position vacancies to select only 40 of each 100 applicants. As shown in Figure 3–1, this will have two effects. First, a number of applicants will be rejected who would have proven to be high criterion employees. However, the number of such potentially high criterion rejects will be much lower than the number of potentially low criterion employees simultaneously rejected. Thus the second effect of this more stringent passing score will be to improve the selection program still further. In this case we would obtain 20 employees who will eventually be in the high criterion group and 20 who will eventually be in the low criterion group. The selective efficiency is here improved from its present level of 30 percent to 50 percent.

Finally, if the labor market permits, a still greater gain in predictive efficiency will come from setting the passing score still higher. Figure 3–1 shows what will happen if the selection ratio can be reduced to 0.15. For every 15 applicants selected, 10 will be high criterion employees and only 5 will be low criterion employees. Predictive efficiency under these circumstances has risen to 10/15, or 67 percent.

GROUP PREDICTIONS

Returning to the question raised at the beginning of the discussion of predictive validity, what is the practical importance of a validity coefficient of, say, 0.30 compared with one of, say, 0.50? One helpful way in which to rephrase this question is to ask: "Given present conditions in terms of selection ratio and proportion of successful employees, what improvement in selection accuracy can be anticipated from expanding the battery to include a test with a given predictive validity coefficient?" To make the question specific, let us assume that by whatever means employees are now selected, we have a 70 percent batting average; that is, 70 percent of the applicants we select prove after a period of employment to be high criterion employees. Suppose further that our selection ratio is 0.60. Finally, suppose we are considering inclusion in the selection program of a new test with a predictive validity of 0.55. To what extent will inclusion of this test improve the selection program?

The answer to this kind of question is provided by referring to the *Taylor-Russell tables* (1939). These tables are reproduced in Appendix B. The Taylor-Russell tables indicate the proportion of applicants likely to be in the high criterion group under various conditions. Thus these tables facilitate so-called institutional, or group, prediction.

Note that there is one such table for each decile (unit of 10 percentage points) of high criterion employees selected by present methods. Thus, the answer to the illustrative question above is provided in the table headed by 0.70 as the proportion of employees considered satisfactory. Portions of this table are reproduced as Table 3–2.

Entering this table for the appropriate column (a selection ratio of 0.60) and row (predictive validity of 0.55), we see that by add-

TABLE 3–2

Portions of the Taylor-Russell Table Where Proportion
of Employees Considered Satisfactory Is 0.70

	Selection Ratio										
r	0.05	0.10	0.20	0.30	0.40	0.50	0.60	0.70	0.80	0.90	0.95
0.00	0.70	0.70	0.70	0.70	0.70	0.70	0.70	0.70	0.70	0.70	0.70
0.05	0.73	0.73	0.72	0.72	0.72	0.71	0.71	0.71	0.71	0.70	0.70
0.10	0.77	0.76	0.75	0.74	0.73	0.73	0.72	0.72	0.71	0.71	0.70
0.15	0.80	0.79	0.77	0.76	0.75	0.74	0.73	0.73	0.72	0.71	0.71
. . .	. . .	. . .	. . .	. . .	. . .	. . .	. . .	. . .	. . .	. . .	. . .
0.45	0.94	0.93	0.90	0.87	0.85	0.83	0.81	0.78	0.76	0.73	0.72
0.50	0.96	0.94	0.91	0.89	0.88	0.86	0.83	0.81	0.78	0.74	0.72
0.55	0.97	0.96	0.93	0.91	0.90	0.87	0.85	0.82	0.79	0.75	0.73
0.60	0.98	0.97	0.95	0.92	0.92	0.89	0.86	0.83	0.80	0.75	0.73
. . .	. . .	. . .	. . .	. . .	. . .	. . .	. . .	. . .	. . .	. . .	. . .
0.90	1.00	1.00	1.00	1.00	0.99	0.98	0.95	0.91	0.85	0.78	0.74
0.95	1.00	1.00	1.00	1.00	1.00	0.99	0.98	0.94	0.86	0.78	0.74
1.00	1.00	1.00	1.00	1.00	1.00	1.00	1.00	1.00	0.88	0.78	0.74

ing this new test to the existing selection program, our predictive efficiency will be 85 percent. According to the information provided for this illustration, 70 percent of the employees selected *without* this new test now prove to be in the high criterion group. Therefore, since inclusion of this new test in the selection program would increase this proportion to 85 percent, we would have a 21 percent improvement in predictive efficiency (0.15/0.70).

Examine the entries in Table 3–2 for other combinations of selection ratio and predictive validity.

A validity coefficient of 0.00 means that there is no correlation between the test and criterion scores. A test yielding this validity coefficient canot increase the proportion of employees considered satisfactory irrespective of the selection ratio.

Holding the selection ratio constant, the proportion of successful employees increases as a function of the magnitude of the validity coefficient. Note, for example, that with a selection ratio of 0.60, the proportion of satisfactory employees increases from 70 percent to 73 percent by adding a test with a validity of 0.15. However, with the same selection ratio but with a validity coefficient of 0.60 instead of 0.15, this proportion increases from 70 percent to 86 percent. Thus the magnitude of the validity coefficient is one of the determinants of selective efficiency.

The selection ratio is another determinant of predictive efficiency. For a particular validity coefficient, the proportion of successful identification of high criterion employees increases and management can exercise greater selectivity in choosing employees. For example, when the test-criterion correlation is 0.55, the proportion of high criterion employees selected is 97 percent with a selection ratio of 0.05, but only 73 percent with a selection ratio of 0.95.

One final point about predicting employee success needs elaboration. By examining the full set of Taylor-Russell tables in Appendix B, you will note that it is easier to obtain gains in predictive efficiency when the present selection program is relatively ineffective than when it is relatively effective for selecting high criterion employees.

INDIVIDUAL PREDICTION

The Taylor-Russell tables permit predictions about the proportion of successful employees from a *group* of applicants. It is possible also to predict the likelihood of success of an *individual* job applicant from theoretical charts developed for this purpose by Lawshe, Bolda, Brune, and Auclair (1958). These charts are exhibited in Appendix C.

The use of the tables for individual prediction requires much the same information as required for the Taylor-Russell tables. Both sets of tables are entered with (*a*) the proportion of present employees considered satisfactory and (*b*) the validity of the test. The third piece of required information is slightly different for the two sets of tables. Whereas the tables for group prediction require information about the selection ratio, the tables for individual prediction require information about the applicant's test score.

To illustrate the use of the tables for individual prediction, let us assume we are dealing with a situation wherein 30 percent of the employees are considered satisfactory, and further assume we are using a test with a predictive validity of 0.65. Referring to the appropriate table in Appendix C (30 percent of employees considered satisfactory) and checking the entries for the appropriate row ($r = 0.65$), we find the following: An applicant scoring in the upper fifth on the selection test has 68 chances in 100 of being a successful employee, whereas an applicant scoring in the bottom fifth on this test has only 4 chances in 100 of being a successful employee. Intermediate degrees of probable success are associated with intermediate test score categories.

Individual and group predictions are not interchangeable; they serve different purposes for the company. When a decision must be made about whether or not to include a new test in the preemployment program, the answer is given in part by group predictions. These provide information about the probable improvement in efficiency of the selection program to be anticipated with the test in question. In contrast, when the company needs information about the probable success of a particular job applicant, tables for individual prediction will prove useful.

SUMMARY

Criteria make explicit the differences between individuals. Thus they define what is meant by employee success. It is insufficient to select criteria solely on the basis of expediency or perceived relevance by management. Criterion measures must meet acceptable standards of reliability and validity.

An ever-present danger in criterion development is the possibility of criterion contamination. Such contamination results whenever the criterion measure reflects the influence of factors which are really extraneous to the particular measure being sought. Such contamination may be a function of the working environment, subtle differences in the nature of work, and variations in job experience of the employees.

Another possible source of error in criterion development is that associated with an inadequate or inappropriate sampling of production records.

Although output is most frequently used as a performance criterion, it must often be supplemented by or replaced with such criteria as quality, turnover, lost time, and worker satisfaction. Such behavior cannot always be objectively assessed. There are many occasions when the criteria of job performance rest upon supervisory judgments of employee effectiveness.

Several different rating techniques were described in this chapter, which emphasized subjectively derived performance appraisals. The weighted checklist and the forced-choice approach to rating have special advantages, but these are often offset by the relatively high cost involved in developing such scales.

The fundamental problem in improving rating procedures is to effect a higher level of reliability. Various sources of unreliability including halo effect, bias, ambiguity, and others were discussed. It is imperative that the scales be properly structured and the raters trained in their use of the reliability of rating procedures in order to approach satisfactory levels.

It is unrealistic to think of a single best or most appropriate criterion of employee effectiveness for any job. This is so because virtually all jobs are multidimensional. Hence employee effectiveness must be assessed by developing criteria for each of the job's most important dimensions. Such multiple criteria may either be used without combination or may be combined to provide a single index of the employee's overall job performance.

Since Chapter 3 was particularly oriented toward the use of criteria for personnel selection and placement, considerable attention was given to predicting criterion performance from preemployment selection programs. Three factors determine the magnitude of improvements in the efficiency of a selection program: (*a*) the selection ratio, (*b*) the proportion of superior employees selected by the existing program, and (*c*) the predictive validity of new tests considered for inclusion in the program. The interaction of these three factors as summarized in the Taylor-Russell tables permit predictions about the probable increase in selective efficiency to be obtained under specific conditions. Using essentially the same three factors, Lawshe et al. (1958) developed charts permitting predictions about the probable success of individual job applicants.

4. Job Analysis

As we saw in Chapter 1, industrial psychology is concerned with the human side of work. It seeks to improve the conditions and outcomes of work, and to increase the satisfactions afforded by the job. The pursuit of these goals may involve the psychologist in studies of employee selection and training, the physical and social conditions of work, performance appraisal, and organizational management.

Job analysis is an indispensable starting place for many such studies. Its purpose is to provide information about the duties entailed in performing the job and the surroundings in which these duties are performed. Such an analysis involves a comprehensive description of the job and in turn leads to an understanding of the characteristics required of an employee if he is to perform satisfactorily.

WAYS IN WHICH JOB ANALYSIS IS USED

It will be useful to know something about the range of applications for the kind of thorough description of job duties provided by job analyses. The following discussion of some of these applications previews much of the topical content of the remainder of the book.

Personnel Selection and Placement

It would be utterly impossible to fit men to jobs unless we knew a good deal about the jobs we were attempting to fill. The specific duties to be performed by an employee and the circumstances under which these duties are to be performed lead to the specification of necessary employee characteristics. Such specifications dictate the utilization of certain kinds of selection devices and criteria rather than others. Thus, a job involving the use of an electronic computer can be satisfactorily filled only by an employee who either knows how to operate such a computer or has demonstrated the abilities prerequisite to learning the job. A job, like paint mixing, that requires employees to make very fine color discriminations cannot be satisfactorily filled by a color-blind job applicant.

Job analysis sometimes reveals that existent criteria for personnel selection and placement are quite inappropriate. A personnel director may, for example, automatically reject applicants who have not graduated from high school while analysis of the job may reveal that it only requires an eighth-grade education. Conversely, in the absence of a thoroughgoing job analysis, the personnel director may place his requirements for selection and placement at an unrealistically low level.

Training Programs

New employees frequently receive some kind of training during the initial period of their employment. The nature of training programs varies extensively from one industry to another and even between jobs within the same industry. Such training may be a highly formalized program consisting of several hours a week of classroom-type instruction. It may, on the other hand, be a relatively informal program in which new employees work "under the wing" of more experienced employees for a period.

The object of any training program may be to teach certain skills required to do a job, to develop certain attitudes (perhaps with respect to safety practices), or to provide other kinds of information of value to new employees. In any event, it is apparent that the structure and objectives of a training program must depend to a large extent upon a thoroughgoing job analysis. It is necessary to know what a job entails before employees can be properly trained for satisfactory job performance.

Job Evaluation

The purpose of job evaluation is to determine the relative worth of each job in an industrial organization. One of the primary applications of such an evaluation is the establishment of equitable salary ranges for various jobs within a company. By way of simple illustration, some jobs may expose employees to hazardous working conditions but may not require much in the way of formal education. Other jobs may require graduate training of some sort but do not expose employees to undue hazards. A job evaluation under such circumstances would lead to a weighting of the factors of working conditions and educational requirements in order to establish an equitable basis for paying employees on both kinds of jobs.

The determination of the worth of each job within an industrial organization is dependent upon a comparative study of the job duties and the working conditions. Thus, job evaluation must be preceded by an analysis of every job to be evaluated.

Efficient Work Methods

A job analysis may be performed as a preliminary to motion studies designed to develop more efficient methods of work. An analysis for such purposes may reveal, for example, that a particular job requires employees to do considerable walking or an excessive amount of heavy lifting. Rearrangement of the working environment or of materials may reduce the extent of such nonproductive physical activity, leading to a consequent reduction in fatigue and an increase in productivity.

Health, Safety, and Equipment Design

Certain jobs, by their very nature, expose employees to personal danger. Unnecessary exposure to noxious fumes or radiation, for example, may be discovered by the job analyst and the working conditions revised in order to reduce or eliminate such conditions. Similarly, job analysis may reveal that certain features of machine operation are unduly hazardous, leading thereby to redesign of the equipment.

Performance Appraisal

Performance appraisals entail assessments of the employee's job proficiency. Such appraisals are used both as partial determinants of personnel actions (salary increase, promotion, and so on) and in the development of criteria for psychological investigations of such things as working conditions and predictor effectiveness. Data for performance appraisals come from several sources including production and personnel records, proficiency tests, job simulator performance, and supervisory ratings, to name a few.

The development and utiliaztion of any criterion of job proficiency must, of course, be preceded by a job analysis in order to identify those aspects of job performance that are critical to employee success. Consider, for example, the unfortunate practice sometimes followed of administering generalized rating scales wherein the supervisor evaluates each employee in shotgun fashion on various characteristics ranging from *initiative* to *personal appearance*. Such rating scales may have little or no bearing upon the specific job being performed by a particular employee. It is doubtful, for example, that a rating of a lathe operator's personal appearance will indicate anything about his proficiency as a lathe operator.

Delimitation of Functions

Even small businesses and offices employing relatively few workers may utilize job analyses. A major source of bickering and discontent in such organizations results from the lack of clarification of duties of individual employees and delimitation of authority. An analysis leading to the definition of duties of each position may serve to eliminate this source of discontent.

The delimitation of personnel functions may likewise be helpful to larger industrial organizations by suggesting changes in current administrative patterns. Over the years, the areas of responsibility assumed by a manager are likely to reflect his personal interests and strengths. This is particularly true of companies at the forefront of technological change. Such companies are continually creating new jobs not even conceptualized several months or years earlier. Once created, the job is usually subsumed under some existing administrative unit of the company. Hence a periodic reasssessment of all jobs in a company with a view toward their most appropriate administrative allocations may suggest needed changes in present management patterns.

The foregoing descriptions of applications of job analysis is not exhaustive. It is sufficient, however, to indicate the diversity of uses for information of the type provided by such analyses. The specific emphasis in any given job analysis will, of course, reflect the purpose for which the analysis has been performed. Job analyses written to provide clues to more efficient industrial operation will highlight different aspects of the job than will analyses prepared for the purpose of evaluating the relative worth of jobs within an industrial organization. However, aside from minor differences in emphasis as a function of intended application, all job analyses are basically alike in that they are designed to provide a detailed description of the analyzed jobs.

SOURCES OF INFORMATION FOR JOB ANALYSIS

The analyst is frequently required to study jobs with which he is initially unfamiliar, in industries about which he may have relatively little prior knowledge. Thus he must utilize many different sources of information in order to insure the accuracy and meaningfulness of his findings, including questionnaires, checklists, individual and group interviews, observations, technical conferences, daily diaries, work participation, and critical incidents (Morsh, 1962). Although we will discuss many of these methods separately, it should be recognized that they are typically combined to provide information for the job analysis.

Preliminaries to Job Analysis

The Dictionary of Occupational Titles. A useful preliminary to almost any job analysis is to consult analyses of similar jobs prepared in other industries and to review pertinent job descriptions prepared on a national basis. A comprehensive reference for the latter type of job description is the *Dictionary of Occupational Titles (D.O.T.)* which is published in two volumes (United States Employment Service, 1965). Volume I alphabetically lists almost 22,000 job titles and defines each in a brief paragraph. An additional 14,000 alternate titles are listed and cross-indexed.

All titles are assigned a six-digit code number wherein the first digit designates the major occupational category, the second and third digits designate subgroups within that category, and the last three digits designate specific occupations within the subgroups. For example, the code number 633.281 refers to *office-machine serviceman apprentice.* The "6" designates the general category "machine trades occupations"; the second and third digits, "33," indicate the subgroup "business and commercial machine repair-man"; and the last three digits are specific to the title "office-machine serviceman apprentice."

Volume II of the D.O.T. lists all titles according to their code numbers whereas Volume I lists the titles alphabetically.

The descriptions in the D.O.T. are rather terse and somewhat general in nature. They represent a synthesis of the duties encompassed by a particular job title as performed by employees in a number of different industries. However, these descriptions may serve to familiarize the analyst with some of the vocabulary he is likely to encounter from employees and supervisors. Here, for example, is the description of an educational placement officer as presented in the D.O.T. (p. 537).

> PLACEMENT OFFICER (education) 166.268. manager, student employment; placement counselor; placement interviewer; student-employment officer. Provides job placement service for students and graduates: Interviews applicants for full- or part-time employment to determine their qualifications on basis of education, ability, interest, and other employment factors, and eligibility for employment in accordance with school and municipal policies. Matches qualifications to job requirements as indicated by employer and refers applicant to job opening. Gives information to students regarding job opportunities, vocational choice, and desirable qualifications. Maintains file of applicants and record of placement and counseling activities. Develops job openings through employer contact. May arrange for administration and scoring of selected psychological tests. Assembles and maintains current labor market information and assists in developing library of occupational information. May specialize in placing specific groups, such as law students or undergraduates seeking part-time employment.

Previous Job Analyses. The job analyst occasionally finds that the job he is asked to study has previously been submitted to analysis in the same industry, plant, or business in which he is working. Plant modernization and equipment changes may make it necessary to revise and update job analyses performed several years earlier. Furthermore, an analysis originally written for one purpose (for example, improving safety practices) is not always useful for other purposes. Nevertheless the job analyst may profitably study these written analyses as a preliminary to preparing his own analysis.

As was indicated earlier, the job analyst may follow these preliminaries by applying many different methods for assembling the data he needs. We will discuss three of these methods in particular: observation and/or work participation, questionnaire and/ or interview, and critical incidents. These approaches are best regarded as supplemental to one another rather than as mutually exclusive. Specific elements of the job not detected by one method may be revealed by another.

Observation and Work Participation

It is clearly useful for the analyst to watch employees as they work. While so doing he must be careful to be as unobtrusive as possible. Generally he restricts notetaking to a minimum while making the observation, expanding his notes immediately after the observation is completed. The observer must be constantly aware of the fact that he is to note characteristics of the job and not characteristics of individual employees. Personal idiosyncrasies will cause subtle discrepancies in the ways in which individual workers perform the same job.

Whereas observations over a relatively brief period of time will serve to clarify the duties of a repetitive or routine job for an analyst, the same cannot be said for jobs entailing considerable variety of duties and responsibilities. In order more accurately to reflect such variety in, for example, managerial jobs the analyst frequently samples job behavior over a period of time. In one such study (Carroll & Taylor, 1968) the overhead lights were flicked as a cue for employees to record their work activity. In another (Stewart, 1967) a management group participating in the job analysis maintained diaries for a four-week period.

In addition to sampling the diversity of tasks required by any particular job, the analyst must observe an adequate sample of employees holding that job. Obviously if he is to generalize about the job's requirements, the analyst must guard against observing only the best or worst workers, or limiting his observations to periods when workers are performing at their maximum or minimum levels.

The observations will suggest many questions to the analyst about what is being done, why it is done in a particular way, and about the skills, past training, and other prerequisites to satis-

factory job performance. The purpose of interviews and questionnaires is both to elicit new information about the job as suggested
by such questions and to verify the observations.

Questionnaires and Interviews

In gathering information for a job analysis, various persons may
be interviewed and asked to complete questionnaires. These may
include the workers, their subordinates (if any), their immediate
supervisors, higher level management, service personnel, and so
on. The employees themselves are often aware of small details of
job performance that may pass unnoticed by their supervisors or
by the job analyst. The supervisor, on the other hand, is in a somewhat better position by virtue of his responsibility for several employees to separate out job characteristics from worker characteristics.

The use of a job analysis questionnaire can be illustrated by a
study of the work done by production foremen (Kay & Meyer,
1962). The questionnaire consisted of four parts: one concerned
the frequency with which the respondent influenced what went
into the production (for example, "An employee asks me for a
work assignment"); a second concerned the frequency with which
the respondent influenced job *output* (for example, "I check
quality standards with the quality control people"); a third concerned job activities involving *communication;* and the fourth required the respondent to rank such areas of *job responsibility* as
production planning, cost control, and so on, with respect both to
the time devoted to each and the importance of each.

The primary advantage of utilization of a questionnaire rather
than an interview for eliciting job information is that the former is
more economical of time. Persons completing a questionnaire may
do so at their leisure and, if the accompanying directions are self-
explanatory, without the guidance of the job analyst. This advantage is more than offset, however, by two potential deficiencies
in the questionnaire approach. First, it may be difficult to motivate respondents to fill out the questionnaire with the necessary
accuracy and care. Secondly, responses to questionnaire items may
be lacking in the essential detail needed by the job analyst. Consequently, wherever possible, the personal interview either by itself
or in combination with administration of a questionnaire is a

more desirable method for eliciting information of value to the job analyst.

The conduct of an interview is not a simple matter. The completeness of the information elicited during an interview depends in large measure upon the care with which the interviewer phrases his questions and upon the rapport (mutual respect and understanding) developed between interviewer and interviewee. Certain fundamental rules for the conduct of the job analysis interview have been suggested as follows (United States Employment Service, 1944) :

1. Make sure the interviewee knows whom you represent, what your name is, and what you are there for, so he will have a broad idea of what is required of him.
2. Show that his cooperation in giving information is helping to find facts.
3. Carefully think out and word questions before asking them.
4. Be interested in the information which you are receiving.
5. Secure specific and full information as directly as possible.
6. Respect the judgment of the interviewee since he, not the analyst, is the expert.
7. Close the interview promptly.
8. Express appreciation to the one who has granted the interview.

Critical Incidents

This technique emphasizes the specific factors critical to job success or failure. The technique has numerous applications in psychological evaluation and is particularly well suited to job analysis (Flanagan, 1949) .

Almost any job analysis will reveal something about the factors differentiating between efficient and inefficient workers, and hence will suggest specifications for satisfactory job performance. However the critical incidents technique was developed in order to overcome the relatively slipshod way in which some of this information is obtained. It focuses the observer's attention specifically upon the critical behaviors differentiating between satisfactory and unsatisfactory job performance.

In essence the critical incidents technique requires that the supervisor and others familiar with a job carefully observe and record employees' behaviors which are critical to satisfactory job performance. The respondent also records specific incidents in which workers have performed unsatisfactorily.

The critical incidents report usually includes a description of the conditions leading up to the incident, the exact nature of the incident, and its consequences. The unique advantage of this approach to characterizing the duties involved in successful job performance is that it is based upon reports of *actual behavior* rather than upon opinions or other subjective impressions about how the job ought to be done. Typically, after a large number of critical incidents are collected, these serve as the basis for developing a checklist which can be completed by each incumbent and his supervisor.

One illustrative application of the critical incidents procedure identified the behavior associated with successful salesmanship (Kirchner & Dunnette, 1957). The investigators collected over 100 critical incidents in selling as reported by sales managers. These incidents were summarized by classifying them into 13 behavioral categories like being truthful with customers and managers, persisting with tough customers, keeping up with new sales techniques and methods, calling on all accounts, and so on.

ASSEMBLING JOB ANALYSIS INFORMATION

The job information obtained from all sources is assembled to provide a verbal summary of the job duties and requirements. The organization of this summary varies somewhat with the nature of the job being analyzed and the purpose for which the analysis is made. Essentially, though, all job analyses include certain basic elements. The format for assembling job analysis information used by the U.S. Employment Service emphasizes the following items:

1. *Work Performed—Physical and Mental*
    a. *What* the worker does, including physical and mental responses made in work situation.
    b. *How* he does it. What tools, machinery, equipment, and so on does the worker use? What kinds of calculations, formulas, judgments, and so on must the worker make?
    c. *Why* is the job done? What is its overall purpose and how does each task performed relate to this purpose?
2. *Skill Involved*
    a. *Responsibility.* What is the extent of the worker's super-

FIGURE 4–1

Job Analysis Schedule Used by the U.S. Employment Office

Form USES-544 (2–44)

U. S. DEPARTMENT OF LABOR
BUREAU OF EMPLOYMENT SECURITY
UNITED STATES EMPLOYMENT SERVICE

Budget Bureau No. 44-R577.3

JOB ANALYSIS SCHEDULE

1. Job title .... Bank Clerk's Wife

2. Number 102

3. Number employed M ....0.... F ....1....

4. Establishment No. ....

6. Alternate titles ....

5. Date ....1944....

    Spouse

Number of sheets ....

    Darling

8. Industry ....Family

    Battleaxe

9. Branch ....Local

7. Dictionary title and code ....

10. Department ....Uxorial

11. WORK PERFORMED:

    Under supervision of Husband (101) and/or Children (104, 105, 106) maintains household. Allocates funds. Purchases supplies. Contrives, invents means and methods of making Bank Clerk's (101) salary support family. (This is considered impossible, or at least improbable, by careful statisticians.) Entertains intelligentsia (friends and own family) and Morons (husband's friends and family). Supervises Dog (103) and other livestock including Husband (101) and Children (104, 105, 106).

    Daily Duties:

    1. Awakes Clerk (101). Selects suit (selection limited to one). Selects shirt (selection limited to one clean, one soiled and two frayed). Searches for shoes, keys, handkerchiefs, studs. Gives detailed instructions for day's program.

    2. Prepares meal. Disburses carfare and/or lunch funds.

    3. Dresses children (104, 105, 106).

    4. Washes dishes. Scrubs floors, windows, paintwork. Polishes silver, brass, furniture.

    5. Plans day's marketing. Calculates expenditures. Compares calculations with available funds. Recalculates. Goes to market with Children (104, 105, 106). Destroys market list as impractical. Improvises new menu according to availability of materials.

    6. Arbitrates differences of opinion expressed vociferously and belligerently by Children (104, 105, 106).

    7. Washes and irons sheets, shirts, blankets, rugs, underwear.

    8. Mends and repairs sheets, shirts, blankets, rugs, underwear, tables, chairs, beds, radio.

    9. Compromises differences of opinion. Accepts her own opinion. Rejects Husband's.

    10. Exercises Dog (103). Wards off seasonal acquaintances. Takes Dog out when Dog prefers to stay in. Takes Dog in when Dog insists upon staying out. Separates Dog from fights and other turmoils. Relegates Husband (101) to dog-house.

(CONTINUE ON SUPPLEMENTARY SHEETS)

Analyst ....A. Clurk....

Reviewer ....

FIGURE 4–1—*Continued*

SOURCES OF WORKERS

12. Experience: None .... Acceptable ...Charm, poise, amatory efficiency -- past........
...........experience not divulged. Complete knowledge of French, piano, ballet, opera,
...........literature. Ability to handle butlers, personal servants etc............................

13. Training data: Minimum training time—(a) Inexperienced workers.   Varies
                                        (b) Experienced workers.   Varies

Training	Specific Job Skills Acquired Through Training
In-plant (on job) training Continual during the period of employment.	Ability to render first aid, medical advice and treatment and minor surgical assistance. Veterinarian ability. Ability to haggle, wash diapers, iron shirts etc.
Vocational training Continual prior to employment.	twelve hours a day and still look lovely in the evening. Ability to do the work of carpenter, painter, electrician, plumber, cleaning woman, dishwasher, chef, CPA,
Technical training Varies	arbitrator, fashion designer, advisor.
SRW Eng. General education Ability to please, charm and fascinate.	
Activities and hobbies	

14. Apprenticeship: Formal __No__ Informal __No__ Length required ....
15. Relation to other jobs:
    (a) Promotions from and to, transfers, etc.: ...Promotion from 'Teen. Eventual promotion to....
    .....mother-in-law......................................
    ....

    (b) Supervision received: General .... Close __X__ By Husband (101)...........
                                                          (Title)

    (c) Supervision given: None .... Number supervised .....5..... Titles __Husband (101), Children__
    .....(104, 105, 106) and Dog (103)..................................
The following items must be cov-red on supplementary sheets.

PERFORMANCE REQUIREMENTS

16. Responsibility (consider material or product, safety of others, equipment or process, cooperation with others, instruction of others, public contacts, and the like).
17. Job knowledge (consider pre-employment and on-the-job knowledge of equipment, materials, working procedures, techniques, and processes).
18. Mental application (consider initiative, adaptability, independent judgment, and mental alertness).
19. Dexterity and accuracy (consider speed and degree of precision, dexterity, accuracy, coordination, expertness, care, and deftness of manipulation, operation, or processing of materials, tools, instruments, or gages used).

COMMENTS

20. Equipment, materials, and supplies. : Electrical equipment, vacuum cleaner, duster, mop, broom,
21. Definition of terms.   sewing machine, rolling pin, pressure cooker, snow shovel,
22. General comments.   ash cans, washing machine, black lace and other deceptive
                                           devices, eyelashes, girdles, sweaters, lipstick and
                                           perfumes.

GPO 883463

visory responsibility for the activities of other employees? What is the extent of his nonsupervisory responsibility for preventing damage to equipment and materials, for making personal contacts (of the type made by salesmen), and for cooperating with other employees?

b. *Job knowledge.* This factor includes knowledge of equipment, materials, techniques, and processes. The amount of job knowledge required is inversely related to the degree of supervision and guidance received by the employee.

c. *Mental application.* This general designation includes such factors as versatility, judgment, and intellectual alertness.

d. *Dexterity and accuracy.* What kind of manual or manipulative ability is required to perform the work to the degree of accuracy and precision required by the job?

3. *Selection Factors*

a. *Experience and training,* including prior job experience, or experience on related jobs, or educational requirements.

b. *Physical demands.* The physical activities required by the job, the environmental conditions in which the job is performed, and exposure to hazards and dangers.

c. *Worker characteristics* of any kind (both physical and mental) that are related to satisfactory job performance.

This format has been used to provide the analysis of the job of bank clerk's wife shown in Figure 4–1 (pp. 105–106) using a description anonymously prepared (1948) after World War II.

JOB SPECIFICATION

The information obtained from a job analysis is rarely used in its original form. The data as recorded on the job analysis schedule are generally too cumbersome for practical purposes. They must be organized and edited in order to make pertinent information readily accessible to the reader. The resultant statement of duties, qualifications, and other information developed from a job analysis is referred to as a *job description.* When the job description is primarily prepared for specifying worker characteristics to be considered when hiring and placing employees, it is called a *job specification.* A sample job specification presenting a brief job description followed by detailed information about worker characteristics

FIGURE 4–2

Job Specification for Hand Burner; John Doe Shipbuilding Company

---

PAYROLL TITLE ___Hand Burner_____   CLASSIFICATION TITLE _____

_____   Acetylene Burner Operator

DEPARTMENT _____   OCCUPATIONAL CODE _____

___Plate Shop_____   6-85.219

FOREMAN ___John Jones_____   TELEPHONE ___158_____

JOB SUMMARY: Cuts mild steel plates into various shapes with an oxyacetylene cutting torch guided by layout markings on the material. With an oxyacetylene cutting torch, cuts steel plates and shapes to various dimensions and sizes as marked and laid out by LAYOUT MAN, manually moving the cutting torch along prescribed lines so that flame will cut plates squarely or with a specified bevel, as indicated by layout symbols; occasionally heats metal to dry surface, or preheats metal for cutting, bending or shaping, or to burn off paint, rust or scale, preparatory to Arc Welding,

Works under supervision of LEADERMAN (BURNING).

EDUCATIONAL STATUS ___Speak, read, write English_____

EXPERIENCE REQUIRED ___3 months as hand burner helper_____

KNOWLEDGE AND SKILLS: Must know oxyacetylene cutting and heating procedure and how to adjust fuel pressure; must be able to select proper burning tips, to clean and adjust torch and torch tips.

PHYSICAL REQUIREMENTS ___Standard physical examination_____

PERSONAL REQUIREMENTS ___None_____   MARITAL STATUS ___Open_____

SEX ___Male_____   AGE RANGE ___18 and over____   CITIZENSHIP ___Open_____

REFERENCES REQUIRED: WORK ___Yes_____   CHARACTER ___None_____

WORKER MUST FURNISH ___8" pliers; 10" crescent wrench; gloves; helmet._____

WAGE CODE ___3a_____

HOURS ___8_____   DAYS ___6_____   SHIFT ___Day; swing; graveyard_____

TESTS: APTITUDE ___None_____   TRADE ___Performance burning test_____

Source: C. L. Shartle. *Occupational information.* New York: Prentice-Hall, 1952. P. 66.

required for satisfactory job performance is shown in Figure 4–2. The purpose of specifications, like those shown in this figure, is to delineate personnel characteristics differentiating between satisfactory and unsatisfactory employees. Such information contributes to selection and placement by clarifying the nature of the demands imposed by the work. For example, if the job requires a high level of motor coordination, assessment of this ability ought to be included in the personnel selection program.

There are two basic procedures for extrapolating information about worker requirements from the job analysis: (1) estimation and (2) measurement.

Estimation

The earliest approaches were based simply upon the analyst's estimate of the job's requirements derived from his observations and interviews. The characteristics thus delimited tended to be rather vague and ambiguous. Furthermore, it was virtually impossible to arrange the worker characteristics identified in this fashion into a hierarchy of relative importance.

More recent attempts subjectively to delineate worker specifications use more systematic procedures. In general, these begin with a list of job skills, abilities, and traits that might be important for *any* job. Each item in the list is carefully defined and accompanied by a rating scale on which the analyst estimates the degree of importance of each characteristic for the job in question. The pattern of ratings for a given job constitutes its "profile," and a comparison of profiles for various jobs indicates the relative importance of the various worker characteristics across jobs.

One such analysis of generalized job variables cutting across specific jobs identified activities engaged in to a greater or lesser degree by workers at about 400 jobs relatively representative of the range of jobs in general (Cunningham & McCormick, 1964). Some of the variables identified were: (*a*) varied intellectual activities versus structured, repetitive activities; (*b*) decisions directly affecting people; (*c*) gross muscular activities; (*d*) public contact activities; (*e*) persuasive communication activities; and so on. This type of analysis is useful in directing the job analyst's attention to a common core of possible worker activities. By considering these activities as they relate to each job under consideration, his judgments concerning worker specification are given direction.

Another approach to guiding the analyst in extrapolating worker specifications from job analyses is that taken by the U.S. Employment Service. Here the analyst uses a uniform checklist in describing all jobs under consideration. The breadth of this checklist, and hence its appropriateness to a wide range of jobs, is illus-

FIGURE 4-3

Form ES-267 (Reverse)
(Rev. 2-44)

PHYSICAL DEMANDS FORM

Job Title_____Occupational Code_____
Dictionary Title_____
Firm Name & Address_____
Industry_____Industrial Code_____
Branch_____ Department _____
Company Officer_____Analyst_____ Date_____

PHYSICAL ACTIVITIES		WORKING CONDITIONS	
1 Walking	16 Throwing	51 Inside	66 Mechanical Hazards
2 Jumping	17 Pushing	52 Outside	67 Moving Objects
3 Running	18 Pulling	53 Hot	68 Cramped Quarters
4 Balancing	19 Handling	54 Cold	69 High Places
5 Climbing	20 Fingering	55 Sudden Temp. Changes	70 Exposure to Burns
6 Crawling	21 Feeling	56 Humid	71 Electrical Hazards
7 Standing	22 Talking	57 Dry	72 Explosives
8 Turning	23 Hearing	58 Wet	73 Radiant Energy
9 Stooping	24 Seeing	59 Dusty	74 Toxic Conditions
10 Crouching	25 Color Vision	60 Dirty	75 Working With Others
11 Kneeling	26 Depth Perception	61 Odors	76 Working Around Others
12 Sitting	27 Working Speed	62 Noisy	77 Working Alone
13 Reaching	28	63 Adequate Lighting	78
14 Lifting	29	64 Adequate Ventilation	79
15 Carrying	30	65 Vibration	80

DETAILS OF PHYSICAL ACTIVITIES:

7-6307 bu-Final

trated by the form for noting "physical demands" reproduced in
Figure 4-3.

Such generalized lists of work activities and forms for rating job
requirements are distinct improvements upon more subjective approaches to estimating requisite worker characteristics. The former

eliminate some of the ambiguity from these estimates and facilitate the placement of the requirements in a hierarchy of relative importance.

Measurement

All estimates of worker requirements suffer one major shortcoming. Whenever a procedure rests upon estimates made by human beings it is susceptible to subjective errors in judgment. The suggestion was made about 50 years ago (Link, 1920) that job profiles could be objectively developed by relying upon the results of measurement instead of judgment. Instead of requiring analysts to estimate worker requirements, a battery of psychological tests could be administered to workers on different jobs and the resultant scores used to develop profiles of the abilities and traits associated with job performance. This procedure, or some variant of it, is designated the "measurement" approach to worker specification.

A number of difficulties are inherent in the measurement approach to job specification. Foremost among these is the matter of deciding which tests ought to be included in the battery. In attempting to strike a reasonable balance between cost of the program, time available for test administration, and comprehensive coverage of the psychological characteristics measured, there is always the danger that tests measuring important characteristics will not be included in the battery. Thus, although the measurement approach is more objective than the estimating approach to job specification, the latter may provide increased breadth of trait coverage.

The utilization of test scores for constructing job profiles presents another problem. One technique develops the profile from the average scores earned by groups of workers on a given job. This average is presumed to indicate the relative importance of each trait or characteristic: when it is high, the trait is important; when it is low, the trait is unimportant. However, it has been shown that groups of workers may average relatively high scores on tests that are quite unrelated to job performance (Stead & Shartle, 1940).

An alternative to using average scores as indications of relative importance is to weight the abilities or characteristics measured by the tests in terms of their validities. Validity is indicated by the correlation between predictor scores and a performance criterion. Tests correlating substantially with a criterion of job performance may be presumed to be measuring more important characteristics than those measured by tests yielding low validity coefficients. Although the validity approach holds promise, it is limited on the one hand by the scope of the test battery and on the other by the adequacy of the criterion of job success.

SUMMARY

Studies of employee selection and training, the conditions of work, and organizational management typically begin with pertinent job analyses. The purpose of job analysis is to provide information about the duties entailed in job performance and the surroundings in which these duties are performed. Job analysis ultimately leads to specification of worker skills, abilities, and characteristics prerequisite to satisfactory job performance.

The job analyst obtains his information from several sources. Those discussed in this chapter include the *Dictionary of Occupational Titles,* observation, work participation, questionnaire administration, interview, and application of the critical incidents procedure.

The information obtained from a job analysis usually suggests worker characteristics associated with effective personnel selection. The analyst sometimes *estimates* the personnel requirements on the basis of his familiarity with the activities entailed in efficient job performance. Alternatively, he may administer psychological tests to *measure* personnel characteristics differentiating between effective and ineffective employees.

5. Principles of Psychological Testing

The purpose of testing is to provide an *objective* assessment of various kinds of psychological characteristics. When such tests are used for personnel selection, the measured characteristics are those known to be related to success on the job. Thus, a personnel testing program involves first a preliminary study designed to identify measurable characteristics thought to be associated with job success; second, the identification (or sometimes, construction) of a test or *battery* (group) of tests designed to measure these characteristics; and finally, a follow-up study to determine the extent to which the measured characteristics are, in fact, related to employee efficiency. The present chapter is specifically concerned with the kinds of research implied in these three phases of testing for personnel selection.

Psychological tests are used in two general ways: as devices for *predicting* subsequent job performance, and as bases for *evaluating* the employee's present level of job performance and the abilities, knowledge, and personality characteristics related to such performance.

The predictive application is most apparent in the case of pre-employment testing for personnel selection. Here, the test and other data contribute to the decision about whether or not to employ a job applicant. Another application also involving predictions from test scores is personnel placement. The placement function requires that test and other data contribute to the decision about *where* within a company the applicant is most likely to demonstrate satisfactory job performance.

113

On occasion the potential contribution of testing to placement decisions may be even more important than its contribution to selection decisions. This would clearly be the case when a company has an urgent need to fill a variety of job openings and has only relatively few applicants. In such instances the urgency of the need for personnel may reduce the value of tests for *selection;* virtually all applicants must be hired. But correspondingly, the need for proper *placement* is thereby enhanced.

Aside from their contributions to the efficiency of selection and placement programs, psychological tests provide evaluative information needed for other personnel decisions. When administered to present employees rather than job applicants, tests may be used diagnostically to facilitate decisions about employee reassignment, training, or counseling.

Given the broad applicability and usefulness of psychological tests, two points need emphasis at the outset of this discussion.

First, psychological tests are fallible. In regarding them as valuable aids to making personnel decisions, we mean merely that the appropriate use of well-designed tests makes possible more accurate decisions than those made without such test data. We do not mean to imply that these decisions will be faultless, or that the test results upon which they are based are entirely free from error.

Second, psychological tests provide only one source of information pertinent to decisions about personnel. As discussed in Chapter 6, additional useful information can be assembled from the pre-employment interview, application blank, references, and previous job history, in addition to other sources. Furthermore, personnel decisions once made are not irrevocable. Employee performance ought continuously to be monitored by means of periodic performance reviews in order to insure that the most effective use is being made of each person's capabilities, needs, and interests.

THE NATURE OF PSYCHOLOGICAL TESTS

A psychological test is much more than an assemblage of questions, the answers to which are interpreted on the basis of common sense or informal observation.

In essence, a test is a yardstick uniformly and systematically applied in the same way to all persons being assessed. This assessment is made in terms of a common scale on which these persons are ordered along a continuum of the trait or characteristic measured by the test.

However, it is not enough merely to order persons from high to low with reference to some trait or characteristic. When we refer to personnel tests, we imply yardsticks with certain other well-defined qualities. These qualities include: (*a*) assessment of those specific characteristics shown clearly to be related to criteria of job success and (*b*) systems for interpreting test scores in ways calculated to improve the ratio of successful to unsuccessful employees.

Pseudotests

The notion of psychological testing has caught the public fancy to a rather considerable extent. Although this kind of popularity has made it somewhat easier for management to introduce testing programs in industry, it has also had certain rather unfortunate consequences. It has, for example, led to the dissemination of so-called tests purporting to measure virtually everything ranging from *Your Suitability as a Marriage Partner* to *Your Susceptibility to Advertising Appeals* in Sunday supplements and pulp magazines. The questions contained in them and the suggested interpretations of responses make interesting reading. They are, however, relatively valueless as a basis for personal evaluation.

The surprising thing about such popularized pseudotests is that they appeal to and hoodwink so many otherwise hardheaded and sophisticated persons. The typical businessman, for example, tends to consider expenditures associated with engineering and raw materials supply very carefully. He may, however, be amazingly naive in the purchase of an expensive employee selection program that is not properly justified by an accumulation of scientific evidence supportive of its worth. The following study (Stagner, 1958) of the gullibility of personnel managers will serve to illustrate the point.

A legitimately published personality inventory was administered to a group of personnel managers attending a conference. They each then received a fake personality analysis ostensibly based upon their responses to the inventory but actually consisting of 13 glittering generalities. These generalities had been collected from dream books and astrology charts. The 13 general statements were interspersed with other more specific statements about personality.

Both kinds of statement, the general ones and the specific ones, were duplicated; the personnel manager's name was written at the top of the sheet; the 13 general statements were encircled on every sheet; and the sheets were passed out to the respondents. Thus, every personnel manager labored under the delusion that he was receiving a personality analysis based upon the results of the inventory. Furthermore, without knowing it, every personnel manager received the identical "analysis" of his personality.

TABLE 5–1

Evaluations of 13 Glittering Generalities by Personnel Managers Who Thought They Were Receiving a Personality Analysis

| Item | Judgment on Accuracy of Item* | | | | |
	a	b	c	d	e
1. You have a great need for other people to like and admire you	39%	46%	13%	1%	1%
4. You have a tendency to be critical of yourself	46	36	15	3	0
5. You have a great deal of unused capacity which you have not turned to your advantage	37	36	18	4	1
7. While you have some personality weaknesses, you are generally able to compensate for them	34	55	9	0	0
9. Your sexual adjustment has presented problems for you	15	16	16	33	19
10. Disciplined and self-controlled outside, you tend to be worrisome and insecure inside	40	21	22	10	4
12. At times you have serious doubts as to whether you have made the right decision or done the right thing	27	31	19	18	4
15. You prefer a certain amount of change and variety and become dissatisfied when hemmed in by restrictions and limitations	63	28	7	1	1
16. You pride yourself as an independent thinker and do not accept others' statements without satisfactory proof	49	31	12	4	4
18. You have found it unwise to be too frank in revealing yourself to others	31	37	22	6	4
20. At times you are extroverted, affable, sociable, while at other times you are introverted, wary, reserved	43	25	18	9	5
21. Some of your aspirations tend to be pretty unrealistic	12	16	22	43	7
23. Security is one of your major goals in life	40	31	15	9	5

* Definitions of scale steps as follows: (*a*) amazingly accurate, (*b*) rather good, (*c*) about half and half, (*d*) more wrong than right, and (*e*) almost entirely wrong.

The 13 encircled statements received by each manager are shown in Table 5–1. The data in this table following each statement summarize the judgments with respect to the accuracy of each statement. Each man was asked to read the items marked for him and to rate it with respect to accuracy on the following five-step scale: (*a*) amazingly accurate, (*b*) rather good, (*c*) about half and half, (*d*) more wrong than right, and (*e*) almost entirely wrong.

In addition, the personnel managers were asked to make an overall evaluation of the fake analysis. Fifty percent said that the overall description was amazingly accurate, 40 percent thought it was rather good, and only 10 percent rated it as about half and half.

Since the purpose of this demonstration was to educate rather than dupe the personnel men involved, the participants were then asked to compare the personality reports they had received. The author reports, "Upon discovering that all were identical they set up a terrific noise apparently compounded of resentment at being duped and amazement at themselves for being tricked."

The demonstration proved to be extremely valuable for convincing the participants to investigate a test or testing program thoroughly before buying it. In this instance the "test" yielded glittering generalities which apply to virtually everyone and are distinctive for no one. Such generalities do not, of course, have differential value for selection, placement, or any other personnel function.

Characteristics of Useful Tests

Useful tests can be distinguished from pseudotests by the qualities of the former as devices for measurement. These qualities include, as we have already said, the requirements that tests (*a*) be uniformly and systematically applied, (*b*) assess characteristics specifically related to job success, (*c*) permit a meaningful ordering of test performances along some kind of yardstick or scale, and (*d*) provide a system for translating the person's placement on the test score continuum into a prediction about job performance.

These qualities influence the procedures for test construction. In order to insure their presence, all psychological tests have certain well-defined characteristics. It will be helpful to outline these characteristics briefly before discussing the specifics of test construction.

Objectivity. As we will discuss in Chapter 6, the primary objection to the use of both the uncontrolled interview and the application blank for selecting personnel is that these techniques are highly subjective in nature. The usefulness of these techniques is improved when they are made more objective.

The distinction between subjective and objective appraisal is apparent also in the area of testing. A test requiring that the scorer exercise his judgment in appraising the quality of response (for example, an essay test) is subjective in nature. A test that may be scored independently of such judgment (for example, a multiple-choice test) is objective in nature.

Regardless of the merits of subjective tests for enabling the respondent to express himself and to display a sequence of thinking, such tests do suffer from one marked deficiency. The score assigned to the person being tested may reflect an assortment of factors totally unrelated to his qualifications. Bias, halo effect, mood of the reader, as well as other subjective factors may enter into the appraisal of essay responses.

In consequence, industrial tests tend for the most part to be objective. The score earned on such tests by the job applicant is unrelated to mood fluctuations and the personal opinions of the person scoring the test. An additional advantage of objective testing is that these tests may be scored easily and rapidly by clerks with minimal training. This factor materially reduces the cost of administering the testing program compared to what the cost would be if subjective tests were used.

Reliability and Validity. The notions of reliability and validity were introduced earlier, and they are elaborated in detail later in this chapter. At this point it is necessary to make just two general observations about these characteristics of tests:

First, it is perfectly possible for a test to be reliable without being valid. A yardstick, for example, is an extremely reliable measuring device. When applied several times to the same object it will yield about the same score or reading in inches. However, it is totally invalid as a measure of employee efficiency except in very special circumstances (for example, professional basketball) where there is a relationship between height and employee success.

Second, a test may be valid for certain circumstances but not for others. The yardstick which is extremely valid as a measure of height is not at all valid as a measure of muscular coordination.

Uniformity of Interpretation. Suppose we have developed a test and demonstrated that it is both reliable and valid for selecting personnel. We now administer this test to a job applicant and determine that his score on this test is 57. Such a score derived either from the number of correctly answered items or the number right less a correction for guessing is referred to as a *raw score*. It cannot be interpreted properly without reference to test *norms* which summarize the raw scores earned on the test by a large number of persons. Knowledge about the raw score does not in itself enable us to make a decision about whether or not the job applicant ought to be hired.

What kinds of additional information do we need before properly interpreting this score of 57? It might help, for example, to know the maximum possible score on the test. A score of 57 out of a possible 58 points probably means something quite different than does a score of 57 out of a possible 200 points.

A detailed statistical analysis of the distribution of scores earned on this test by persons previously tested would be even more helpful. This might involve the calculation of the mean and standard deviation of the distribution in order to provide an indication of whether the score of 57 is better or worse than average. In addition, the interpretation of this score is greatly facilitated when the data are prepared in such a way as to make possible a statement about the probability that an applicant with a score of 57 will if hired be a successful rather than an unsuccessful employee.

Standardization of Testing Conditions. It is apparent that whenever a number of persons are to be compared with respect to test score, they must either take the same test or different forms of the same test. One cannot hope, for example, to compare the arithmetic test scores of two applicants, one of whom has taken a test requiring that he be familiar with concepts no more complex than long division, while the other has taken a test requiring mastery of fractions and decimals.

It is perhaps less obvious, however, that the mere fact that identical questions are presented to two applicants does not in itself guarantee that they are taking the same test! A test really consists of a set of questions administered under certain conditions of illumination, ventilation, working space, assistance from the proctors, and preliminary directions to the person tested, to name just a few. Test scores may be markedly affected by the conditions under which the test is given. Thus, one of the characteristics of good psychological tests is that the testing conditions are *standardized*. This means that the directions for administering and scoring the test are prescribed and specified so that they may be held relatively constant from one testing session to another. A departure from the standardized testing conditions may well invalidate the test norms. The manual of directions for administering a test will most often specify the specific wording of instructions and will indicate something about the amount of assistance (if any) to be given by the proctors, the kind of physical facilities to be used for testing, the time limit if there is one, and the way in which the test should be scored and interpreted.

TEST CONSTRUCTION

The foregoing description of the required characteristics of psychological tests implies that there is considerably more to construcing a test than merely putting pen to paper and writing questions. We will be concerned in the remainder of this chapter with the implementation of these characteristics.

Job Analysis and Item Development

Nothing concrete can be done in the way of writing test questions until a clear notion of the behavior or personal characteristics to be measured is formulated. This is only possible after a thoroughgoing job analysis designed to clarify the differences between efficient and inefficient employees has been performed. The job analysis will provide the clues about the critical psychological functions, including specific kinds of knowledges, abilities, and personal characteristics that ought to be measured in the selection test.

Once the behavior or personal characteristic to be measured has been identified and defined, the test's architect formulates a *test plan*. By analogy with building construction, the test plan serves as the blueprint for the entire structure. The plan specifies the ultimate nature of the test being formulated with particular reference to the weight to be assigned to various kinds of tested behavior.

Suppose, for example, that we wish to assess arithmetic proficiency as an aid to selecting department store sales clerks. Obviously, the number of arithmetic questions that could be asked is limitless. Equally apparent is the fact that there are practical limits to the length of a test in order to optimize the efficiency of measurement.

Although we could easily write a large number of test items presenting combinations of two three-digit numbers for addition, there is little point to using all of the possible items in this universe. Instead, it makes sense to sample from the total universe of such combinations. If this sample of items is sufficiently large and is representative of the kinds of functions required to handle this type of addition problem, we will be able to generalize from test behavior to behavior with all other problems of this type. The

TABLE 5–2

A Test Plan for Measuring Arithmetic Proficiency
(entries indicate percent of items of each type required)

| | Operations | | | | Content |
Content Combinations	Addition	Subtraction	Multiplication	Division	Weight
Decimals with decimals...	3%	8%	5%	9%	25%
Fractions with fractions...	10	—	—	—	10
Digits with digits........	3	8	6	8	25
Decimals with digits.......	2	9	6	8	25
Fractions with digits......	7	—	8	—	15
Operations weight..	25%	25%	25%	25%	100%

rationale underlying test items as samples of behavior is clearly similar to that underlying sampling procedures in, for example, public opinion polling.

Thus, the plan for our arithmetic proficiency test requires that we consider three kinds of issues before beginning test construction. First, how do we wish to define arithmetic proficiency? What kinds of arithmetic *operations* are included in our definition? Second, upon what kinds of *content* must these operations be performed? Third, how do we wish to *weight* the various kinds of operations and contents?

Such a plan is shown in Table 5–2. This plan reflects the decision that the test will assess four different operations with five different contents (numerical combinations). The plan further indicates that certain operations-contents combinations were judged inappropriate to the purpose of the test and therefore need not be assessed. Finally, it shows the relative weights to be assigned to the several operation and content combinations, and translates these into specifications for the test items. Thus, 3 percent of the test items will require addition of pairs of decimals; 10 percent will require addition of pairs of fractions; and so on.

Item Analysis

An item analysis provides data enabling the test constructor to evaluate the worth of each of the preliminary items he has developed. The item analysis serves as the basis for selecting those items from the preliminary item pool which are to be included in the final version of the test. The typical item analysis provides two kinds of information about each item: (1) information about the discriminatory power of the item and (2) information about the relative ease or difficulty of the item.

Item Discrimination. Every item in a test should make its contribution to the test's power to differentiate between persons on the function the test is measuring. Item discrimination (or item validity) is an indication of the extent to which the test item differentiates between persons who rank at opposite ends of the continuum with respect to the particular characteristic being measured.

This phase of the item analysis requires that the preliminary set of items be administered to a sample of persons like those who will eventually be taking the test in its final form. The persons in this item analysis group are then subdivided into high and low criterion subgroups. In practice this assignment is most often based upon the criterion of total score on the test. Thus, the objective of this phase of the analysis is to determine the extent to which each test item is measuring the function measured by the total test.

It has been determined (Kelley, 1939) that the optimal split for constituting the criterion subgroups is obtained by assigning the 27 percent of the persons with the highest scores to the high criterion group and the 27 percent of the persons with the lowest scores to the low criterion group. Thus, if a test to be item analyzed is administered to a total group of 185 persons, each of the criterion subgroups would contain 50 persons.

It is apparent from the foregoing discussion that an item which has good discriminating power is one that differentiates between the high and low criterion subgroups. So a perfectly valid item is one that is answered correctly by everyone in the high criterion group and answered incorrectly by everyone in the low criterion group. The correlation between item response (correct or incorrect) and criterion subgroup (high or low) for such an item would, of course, be +1.00.

Item analysis data indicative of various degrees of discrimination power are shown in Table 5–3. The entries for the five items

TABLE 5–3

Percentages within Each Criterion Subgroup Correctly and
Incorrectly Answering Items at Various Levels
of Item Discrimination

Item Number	Item Response	Criterion Subgroup		Correlation*
		Low	High	
1.	Right	—	100%	+1.00
	Wrong	100%	—	
2.	Right	15	90	+0.73
	Wrong	85	10	
3.	Right	20	70	+0.50
	Wrong	80	30	
4.	Right	30	60	+0.31
	Wrong	70	40	
5.	Right	40	40	0.00
	Wrong	60	60	

* Correlational values from J. C. Flanagan. A table of the value of the product moment coefficient of correlation in a normal bivariate population corresponding to given proportions of successes. Pittsburgh: American Institute for Research, 1950.

in the table show the percentage of respondents within each criterion subgroup answering the item correctly and incorrectly. The correlational values represent the strength of relationship between item-response and criterion subgroup assignment.

Note particularly that the correlation between item response and total test score (as reflected in criterion subgroup assignment) decreases as the percentage of respondents from each of the subgroups answering correctly becomes increasingly similar. Finally, in item 5, in which the percentage of correct responses is identical for the two criterion subgroups, the correlational value is 0.00.

This item does not differentiate at all between the high and low criterion groups.

This discussion of item discrimination has been limited to item analyses against the internal criterion of total test score. It is quite possible, however, to establish the criterion groups on some basis that is external to the test itself. A measure of productivity, a rating of employee efficiency, or any other external index may serve as a basis for separating high and low criterion groups and hence for item analysis. The use of external criteria for item analysis is much less frequent than is the use of total test score as the criterion.

Item Difficulty.   Questions from the preliminary pool of items are considered for inclusion in the final version of the test only if they have demonstrated discriminative power. The items that have survived this phase of the analysis are further screened on the basis of their relative ease or difficulty before the ultimate selection of items for the final form of the test is made.

What would be the effect, for example, if a test of numerical ability contained items, all of which were extremely easy? Since most persons would be able to answer every item, the test scores would tend to run rather high. The effect of this would be to make it difficult to separate out from the total group of persons tested those who possess a moderately high degree of numerical ability from those who possess a very high degree of such ability. The test would not have enough "top."

Conversely, a test consisting entirely of very difficult items would have too much top. Most persons would receive low scores, making it impossible to separate out the persons of moderately low ability from those of very low ability.

To avoid either of these extreme conditions, tests are generally structured so that they contain items distributed throughout the range of difficulty. The test as finally constituted will contain some rather easy items, some rather difficult items, and a considerable number of items that are in the midrange of difficulty.

Data regarding item difficulty are obtained by computing the percentage of persons in the total item analysis group answering each item correctly. Thus, the test in its final form will contain only those items that have been demonstrated to possess satisfactory discriminative power and a range of relative ease and difficulty. Several things remain to be done with this test, however, before it can be used for personnel selection.

RELIABILITY

From previous discussions it should now be apparent that demonstrated reliability is an essential requirement for psychological tests.

Broadly speaking, a reliable test is one providing a *consistent* yardstick. Thus, a fundamental objective of reliability studies is to demonstrate that the test scores do not fluctuate unduly over time as a result of something inherent in the test itself (including scorer subjectivity), the transitory nature of the function being assessed, or by factors extraneous to the particular behavior the test is designed to evaluate.

On occasion, the concept of reliability as "consistency of measurement" is given a somewhat different but related meaning. Here the reliability study focuses particularly upon the homogeneity of the test—its *internal* consistency—rather than upon consistency in the sense of stability of scores over time. If a test is not homogeneous, then it really is comprised of subsets of items each measuring a different human function.

These different definitions of reliability are reflected in the procedures whereby a test's reliability is estimated. Three such procedures are described below.

Test-Retest Method

A reliable test is one in which an individual will rank in about the same position on successive testings regardless of who administers the test. This definition of reliability suggests a simple method for determining the relative degree of consistency of measurement; that is, give the test twice to the same group of persons and correlate the scores earned on the two administrations. Ideally, the person who earned the highest score (ranked highest) when originally tested should also earn the highest score when retested. Similarly, the person who earned the lowest score for the first time (ranked lowest) should earn the lowest score on the retest, and persons with intermediate scores the first time should maintain their same relative score positions the second time they take the test.

Such a perfect relationship between rankings on the original test and the retest would, of course, yield a correlation coefficient of

+1.00. Although this perfect relationship is never achieved in practice, the requirement for test-retest estimates of reliability is generally set in the vicinity of +0.90.

Numerous objections have been raised to the test-retest method of estimating reliability. It is, in the first place, an uneconomical procedure since it requires that employees be excused from their work for experimental purposes on two separate occasions. Secondly, the period between original test and retest is not vacuous. New learning may occur during this time interval, causing relative rankings on the retest to be somewhat different from the rank position on the original test. Thirdly, employees may remember items from the original session when they are retested. This memory factor will enable them to respond rapidly to the remembered items and to devote proportionately more time to the items which caused them difficulty during the original testing.

The Equivalent Forms Method

This method overcomes some of the objections to the test-retest procedure, particularly those related to the possible operation of learning and memory factors. As the name implies, this method involves the administration of an equivalent form of the original test after a time interval rather than readministration of the original test itself.

Equivalent forms of a test are alike with respect to statistical characteristics (the distribution of item difficulty and item validity indices) and general content, although the specific items in the forms are different. The fact that the specific content of the items in equivalent forms of a test are different means that neither the memory factor nor the learning factor can operate when reliability is estimated by correlating the scores earned on the two forms.

Perhaps the primary objection to this procedure is that the expense of developing equivalent forms of a test is not justified when they are developed solely for a reliability study. There are, however, other reasons for which two or more forms of a test may be developed. It is advantageous, for example, to have multiple test forms for administration when one wishes to measure growth as a result of a formal training program or as a result of job experience. One of the forms can be given as a pretest to new employees while the other form can be given as a posttest after completion of the training program or after a certain period of time on the job. Furthermore, multiple forms of a test are extremely useful whenever a large group of persons is to be tested in a room that does not permit for adequate spacing between seats in order to prevent copying.

Split-Halves Method

A fundamental objection to both the test-retest and the equivalent forms method of estimating reliability is that these procedures require two testing sessions. The split-halves method makes it possible to estimate reliability from a single administration of a test and hence is widely used in the industrial setting.

This method requires that the total test be divided into halves in such a way that the items in each half constitute a miniature representation of the entire test. In practice, this is often accomplished by assigning the odd-numbered items to one half and the even numbered items to the other half, although any other procedure for splitting the test is acceptable provided that it yields halves that are comparable. The halves are scored separately, and the estimate of reliability is derived by correlating the scores earned by a group of persons on the halves of the test.

There are certain parallels between the split-halves method and the equivalent forms method for estimating reliability. Both procedures require the correlation of scores earned on two forms of a test. The equivalent forms method involves the correlation between two full-length forms while the split-halves method involves the correlation between two half-length forms. A fundamental difference between these procedures is the fact that while the forms are deliberately equated for the equivalent forms method the split-halves method correlates two forms that are, at best, crudely comparable.

In appraising the split-halves method, it must be remembered that there is no time interval between administration of halves of a test and that the correlation coefficient resulting from this procedure is based upon only half the number of items in the total test. Each of these unique aspects of the split-halves method has certain implications. The absence of a time interval has the desirable effect of eliminating the possible influences of memory and learning. It also, however, eliminates the possible effects of day-to-day fluctuations in mood, attentiveness, and attitude of the respondents. This latter factor is one that should be included in estimates of test reliability. The effect of eliminating the potential influence of these daily fluctuations is to spuriously increase the reliability coefficient.

A special problem arises when the split-halves method is used to estimate the reliability of speeded tests in which the imposed time limit prevents subjects from completing all questions. Computation of an odd-even reliability under such circumstances tends to over-estimate the test's reliability. This is so because the unanswered questions are distributed evenly between the two halves of the test, thereby exerting a uniform effect upon the individual's relative rank position for each half. This problem is generally resolved either by application of correction formulas estimating the lower limit of reliability for speeded tests or by a rather simple experimental expedient. The latter requires that each half of the total test be separately administered with its own time limit.

The fact that this method yields an estimate of reliability based upon the correlation of scores on two halves of the test means that the resultant coefficient is an estimate of the reliability of a test only half as long as the one actually under consideration. Since reliability is in part a function of test length, estimates of reliability based upon the split-halves method must be adjusted upwards by means of a formula designed to indicate what the reliability would have been for the full-length test. The Spearman-Brown prophecy formula for a test doubled in length is:

$$R = \frac{2r_{11}}{1 + r_{11}}$$

where R is the reliability of the test doubled in length and r_{11} is the reliability of the half-length test. Thus, if the correlation between scores on the halves of a test is 0.80, the estimate of reliability for the total test would be 1.60/1.80, or 0.89.

Comparison between Methods

In the preceding sections we have described three methods for estimating the reliability of a test loosely defined as the consistency of measurement. It is evident that each method is based upon a somewhat different concept of consistency. Hence the methods do not yield comparable estimates of reliability.

For the test-retest procedure, consistency means *stability of scores* over a period of time. A low test-retest coefficient is evidence either for the fact that the function measured by the test is unstable over time, or that test performance is influenced by extraneous factors of an unstable nature.

The split-halves method utilizes quite a different concept of consistency. This method does not consider fluctuations over time; instead it estimates *internal consistency* or homogeneity of the test. As we have described this procedure, it indicates the extent to which one half of the test measures whatever it is that the other half measures. Variations of the general method may split the test into smaller fragments than halves. Thus it is possible when a test is fragmented into single items to inquire whether each item is measuring whatever is measured by each of the other items.

The equivalent forms method involves elements of both the stability and internal consistency concepts. The longer the time interval between the administration of the forms, the heavier is the emphasis upon stability over time. Conversely, with progressively shorter time intervals between test administrations, the coefficient tends increasingly to reflect internal consistency.

It is impossible, in the light of these differences, to single out a particular procedure as best under all circumstances. If we wish the reliability coefficient to reflect score stability over time, the split-halves method is clearly inappropriate. Since this method estimates consistency without a time interval, it overestimates stability. However, the practical consideration of available testing time may overshadow other factors and dictate the use of the split-halves method. Furthermore, there are occasions when the test constructor is more interested in estimating the internal consistency of his test than the stability of the resultant scores. When this is the case, the test-retest method and the equivalent forms method with a relatively long time interval may underestimate the kind of reliability he seeks.

Relationship of Reliability and Validity

When is reliability sufficiently high for practical purposes?

Clearly, the higher the test's reliability, the greater the confidence we can place in the stability of the scores it yields. On this basis, then, we must conclude that the higher the reliability, the better.

And from this standpoint, tests yielding reliability coefficients in the range between 0.85–0.99 are usually regarded as being satisfactorily reliable.

Having stated this as a rule of thumb, we must note an exceptional circumstance where lower reliability coefficients are tolerated. When the testing program requires an assessment of many different functions in a brief time period, the tests comprising the battery will obviously have to be short ones. Since, as we have already discussed, there is a relationship between test length and reliability, it is to be expected that these short tests will each be relatively unreliable. Their use is justified only when the components of the battery are measuring sufficiently independent and important functions that it is worth finding out *something* about each rather than assessing just a few of them more comprehensively and accurately. This is a compromise. When possible, it is far preferable to use tests with higher reliabilities.

Aside from confidence in the relative stability of the scores, there is another reason for ordinarily preferring to use tests with high (above 0.85) reliability. This follows from the relationship between reliability and validity. If test scores are unstable, the value of that test for predicting a criterion is thereby diminished. If the test produces predictor scores which fluctuate unduly for each person, then the correlation between these scores and a performance criterion is adversely affected. The predictor scores for some persons will be higher than they should be, and those for others will be lower than they should be. In the extreme case, where a test's reliability coefficient is estimated as 0.00, the relationship between test and criterion measures must be random; here the validity coefficient will have to be 0.00 also.

Theoretically, a test's maximum potential validity is given by the square root of its reliability. This means, for example, that a test for which reliability is estimated as 0.49 cannot generate a validity coefficient above 0.70. Likewise, if the test's reliability is 0.81, its validity cannot exceed 0.90.

This is *not* to say that a test with a reliability of 0.81 will have a validity of 0.90. In this instance, 0.90 is only the theoretical maximum limit upon the validity coefficient. How closely this theoretically maximum validity is approximated depends upon two characteristics of the *criterion:* relevance and criterion reliability.

No matter how reliable the predictor, it clearly cannot correlate highly with an irrelevant criterion. Thus, although we can measure people's heights with great reliability, these height scores are not valid for predicting, say, job tenure as a criterion. This criterion is irrelevant for this predictor.

Likewise, even a very reliable test cannot efficiently predict an unreliable criterion. Unless the behavior to be predicted is itself relatively stable, there is little point to attempting further to increase the validity coefficient by revising the predictor test to improve *its* reliability.

Since these two criterion conditions, perfect relevance and perfect reliability, can never be satisfied, obtained validity coefficients are always somewhat below the maximum theoretically possible. However, a point to remember is that the *possibility* of a high validity coefficient increases as the reliability of the test increases.

VALIDITY

Our discussions of validity thus far in this chapter and the related discussion in Chapter 3 have all been concerned with one particular definition of validity, that is, the correlation between a predictor test and a criterion of job performance. This definition is really only one of five different ones applicable to validity (American Psychological Association, 1954). Of these five definitions, the first two require the availability of some kind of useful, relevant, and reliable criterion of job performance against which the test can be validated; the three remaining definitions of validity do not depend upon the availability of such criteria.

Involving Criteria of Job Performance

The two types of validity most pertinent to personnel selection tests are "predictive" and "concurrent" validity. These two types of validity are similar in that they are based upon the demonstration of a satisfactory correlation between test scores and job performance criterion measures.

Of the two, *predictive validity* is the more convincing. In order to demonstrate predictive validity, the test must be administered to job applicants, all of whom are hired regardless of test score. The scores are filed until some subsequent time when a criterion job performance measure becomes available. The scores earned on the test by the employees when they were applicants are then correlated with this criterion, thereby indicating the power of the test to predict subsequent performance.

The meaning of predictive validity is graphically shown in Figure 5–1. The data in this graph show the relationship between pilot

FIGURE 5–1

Relation between Elimination Rate and Pilot Aptitude Score

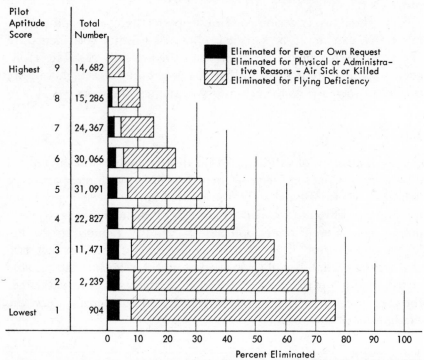

Source: Psychological activities in training command AAF. *Psychological Bulletin,* 1945, *42, 46.*

aptitude score and elimination rate during pilot training in the U.S. Army Air Force. It is apparent that the psychological aptitude test predicted fitness for flight training.

In spite of the desirability of obtaining evidence of predictive validity, resistance to the necessary procedure is often encountered in industry. Management may raise certain obvious objections to hiring all applicants regardless of their performance on the test being validated and in spite of the results of all other selection techniques including the interview and application form. Consequently, industrial tests are often validated by administering them to employees on the job and correlating the scores with an immediately available criterion of efficiency. This procedure establishes *concurrent* rather than predictive validity because the test and criterion measures are available simultaneously.

Not Involving Criteria of Job Performance

Three other kinds of validity do not require test-criterion correlations: "face" validity, content validity, and construct validity.

When a test has the *appearance* of measuring factors germane to the job, it is said to have *face validity*. A pilot selection test, for example, possesses face validity when the item phraseology makes reference to aircraft and flight.

Such an appearance of validity is entirely independent of the statistical characteristics of a test. It is a matter solely of item content. Although conceptually independent of statistical validity, face validity is generally regarded as a desirable characteristic for industrial tests. Such tests look meaningful and therefore facilitate companywide acceptance of the testing program, and they heighten the motivation of persons tested.

Since they are somewhat irrelevant in the context of this discussion of personnel selection and placement, content and construct validity are described only briefly.

Content validity requires an assessment of the test's content to assure that the sample of questions comprising the test is representative of the universe of questions that might have been asked. It is, in short, an assessment of the adequacy of the plan underlying the construction of the test. This nonstatistical assessment is usually dependent upon the judgment of presumed experts and is most appropriate when developing achievement tests.

Construct validity procedures enable us to label the psychological functions measured by a new test. Suppose, for example, that we have developed a test we think measures intelligence. One way to determine whether this new test does in fact measure the psychological construct intelligence is to correlate scores from it with scores obtained by the same people on other, generally accepted, intelligence tests.

Multiple Predictors

We now return to considering validity defined in predictive and concurrent terms. Although the preceding discussion of these kinds of validity was limited to the relationship between a single test and a single criterion of job performance, this is an oversimplification. In practice, the usual selection program uses applicant's scores on a battery, or group, of tests. Furthermore, as described in Chapter 3, this multiple predictor is often correlated with a multiple criterion; that is, one composed of several measures of employee performance.

There are two primary ways in which multiple predictors can be jointly used. By combining several separate tests each of which has moderate predictive validity, both methods attempt to make more accurate predictions than would be possible using any one of the predictors alone.

Successive Hurdles.   This procedure, sometimes designated "multiple cutoff," combines economy with multiple prediction. Given several tests, each of which has predictive validity, applicants are required successively to pass the tests sequentially administered. Those applicants failing the first test in the battery are terminated at that point; the surviving applicants are given the second test, and again those failing it are terminated; the survivors are given the third test; and so on. After administration of the last test in the battery, the only remaining applicants are those who have passed every subtest.

Although useful, this procedure suffers two shortcomings. First, it does not allow for the circumstance where weakness in some tested function may be offset by strength in some other tested function. In presenting subtests as a series of successive hurdles, the assumption is made that job performance depends upon a summation of tested functions. This assumption is untenable where job performance really reflects the *interaction* of tested functions. Thus, successful secretarial performance may be possible both when moderate skill as a typist is combined with superior skill as a stenographer and when moderate stenographic skills are combined with superior typing skills.

Second, whereas the successive hurdles procedure identifies a group of survivors for employment, it provides no single index of the relative predictor standing of each one.

Multiple Correlation.   This is a statistical technique indicating the maximum predictive validity obtainable from the optimal combination of scores on subtests comprising the battery. (The procedures for calculating multiple correlation are beyond the scope of this discussion.) To arrive at the optimal combination of subtest scores, multiple correlation procedures weight the subtests in terms of (*a*) the validity of each separately considered and (*b*) the magnitude of the intercorrelations between these predictors.

Moderator Variables

The general model for predictive or concurrent validity which has thus far been described and which most often serves as the basis for validation studies rests upon the supposition of a simple relationship between predictors and criteria. Starting with this supposition, personnel selection research requires the demonstration that predictor (or battery) *X* correlates with criterion (or criteria) *Y*. Selection practices proceed from such evidence to use scores on test (or battery) *X* to identify potentially successful employees.

This traditional model has recently been questioned and elaborated.

On the predictor side, it is clear that test performance varies between people only partly as a function of differences in whatever the test measures. In other words, only part of the variation in scores on, say, a mathematics test can be attributed to individual differences in mathematical ability. At least some of the variation is attributable to factors extraneous to mathematical ability, like motivation, anxiety over taking a test, and so on.

Variations in criterion performance can be similarly interpreted. In addition to reflecting job proficiency, criteria often reflect such extraneous factors as the employee's sex, age, education, job experience, and assorted personality characteristics.

Thus, validity studies never involve correlations between pure predictor and criterion measures. These measures are always contaminated by experience, attitudes, and so on, which intervene between performance on the predictor and the criterion. These intervening effects moderate the correlation between predictor and criterion, that is, they reduce it. In fact, validity coefficients above

0.50 are rarely obtained; typically, they range between 0.35–0.45 (Ghiselli, 1955).

A "moderator variable" validity design differs from the classical model in that the former requires separate test-criterion correlations for each moderator variable subgroup. By thus controlling for (that is, eliminating the effects of) unwanted variation, such designs seek to increase the power of the predictor. In this way, for example, sex has been found to be a useful moderator variable when predicting scholastic grades. Irrespective of the predictor, grades can pretty much be more accurately predicted for women than for men (Seashore, 1961).

The use of moderator variables is not alone going to be a panacea for increasing predictive validity coefficients. There is some ambiguity in the professional literature in the meaning of the term itself. Furthermore, regardless of how it is used, many studies employing moderator variables have failed to demonstrate that validity is thereby increased (Guion, 1967).

However, the introduction of the moderator variable concept and the consequent embellishment of the classical model for validating tests will have far-reaching effects, indeed. It now seems less important to inquire whether on not a particular test or procedure is any good and more important to inquire into the *circumstances* optimizing the usefulness of predictive tests and other procedures (Dunnette, 1963).

INTERPRETING TEST SCORES

Raw test scores are not very useful in the practical situation because they cannot be interpreted meaningfully. The industrial psychologist who has developed a test for selection purposes must perform statistical analyses designed to answer two general types of questions about every applicant's score. First, how did his score compare to the scores of other applicants who have taken the test? Secondly, did he pass the test; that is, should he be hired? The first of these questions requires that the raw score be transformed to another kind of score reflecting the performance of the specific applicant under consideration in relation to the performance of other applicants who have taken the same test. It involves the development of test *norms*. The second question requires that a passing score be determined for the test.

Test Norms

Norms make possible the expression of an individual's raw test score relative to the distribution of scores earned by a group of persons known as the *standardization* or *norms* group. The development of test norms thus requires that the test first be administered to a sizable group of persons as nearly as possible like the applicants for whom the test is intended. Certain of the statistical operations required to effect the raw score transformations described below are discussed in Appendix A.

The distribution of scores earned by persons in the norms group may serve as the basis for converting raw scores to *percentiles*. A percentile value indicates the percentage of persons who earned a raw score at or below the specific raw score in question. Thus, if it has been determined that a raw score of 35 corresponds to the sixty-second percentile, this would mean that 62 percent of the standardization group scored 35 or less on the test.

FIGURE 5–2

Relationship between Raw Scores, Percentiles, and Standard Scores

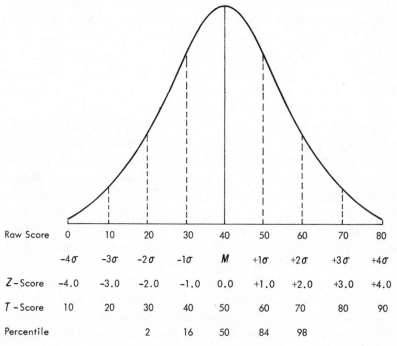

Raw Score	0	10	20	30	40	50	60	70	80
	-4σ	-3σ	-2σ	-1σ	M	$+1\sigma$	$+2\sigma$	$+3\sigma$	$+4\sigma$
Z-Score	-4.0	-3.0	-2.0	-1.0	0.0	+1.0	+2.0	+3.0	+4.0
T-Score	10	20	30	40	50	60	70	80	90
Percentile			2	16	50	84	98		

The interpretation of raw scores may also be facilitated by converting them to some kind of standard scores. Standard scores express test performance as a function of the central tendency and variability of the distribution of scores obtained in the norm group. The most obvious kind of standard score involves the transformation of raw scores to standard deviation units. Suppose, for example, that the mean score in the norms group is 40 and the standard deviation is 10. It follows then that a raw score of 50 would correspond to a transformed score of +1 standard deviation, a score of 30 to −1 standard deviation, and so on.

The relationships between raw scores, percentiles, and two kinds of standard scores (Z scores and T scores) are illustrated in Figure 5–2. You will note one of the major advantages of standard scores in comparison with percentiles: the former are spaced equidistantly along the measurement continuum. Hence, they are amenable to the usual kinds of arithmetic manipulations.

ETHICAL-MORAL-LEGAL CONSIDERATIONS

Granted that psychological tests are valuable aids in selecting and placing personnel, there remains the question of the fairness of selection tests to members of disadvantaged groups. The Civil Rights Act of 1964 makes it illegal when hiring to discriminate on the basis of ethnic background or sex. In consequence, the Equal Employment Opportunity Commission and the Office of Federal Contract Compliance are empowered to exercise legal and economic sanctions against employers using biased tests.

Although tests are not the only predictors challenged on the basis of fairness, they have received the greatest attention (Bray & Moses, 1972). Any preemployment screening technique has the potential for discrimination against culturally and educationally deprived groups whenever such procedures assign unequal probabilities of being hired for the job to persons with equal probabilities of success on the job (Guion, 1966). Hence, test discrimination refers to the way tests are used in making personnel decisions rather than to a property of the test itself (Dunnette, 1970).

The charge of test discrimination is, of course, most often made for black and Chicano applicants. As groups, their absolute educational levels and relative educational attainment levels are below those of white Americans. In consequence of this history of deprivation and discrimination, minority applicants tend to earn lower scores than whites on preemployment tests (Bennett, 1969).

The intent of the EEOC guidelines (1970) is to provide equal employment opportunities for all groups—minority and majority. If an employer uses a test which rejects a higher percentage of minority than majority group applicants, he is suspected of being guilty of discrimination unless he can demonstrate that prediction of job performance was equal for both groups of applicants.

One potential solution to this problem, now largely discarded (Bray & Moses, 1972) is the development of *culture-fair* tests: tests on which performance is relatively independent of environmental background. Theoretically, such a test would have to satisfy one of two conditions: (*a*) all people of all cultures must have had equal opportunities and equal motivation for learning all items on the test; or (*b*) all of the test items must be completely novel for all persons of all cultures (Krug, 1966). It has thus far proven impossible to develop such an instrument even with a nonverbal format.

An alternative solution (Kirkpatrick, Ewen, Barrett, & Katzell, 1968) is to use different selection standards in order to compensate for socially imposed deprivation. In essence, the effective use of differential selection standards rests upon a moderator variable analysis as described earlier in this chapter. To make such an analysis, the test under investigation must be separately validated for each racial subgroup. The typical finding is one of dissimilar validity coefficients, indicating that the probability of job success is an interactive function of the applicant's predictor test score and his moderator group (for example, white or black).

Utilization of moderator variable analysis is not to be confused with lowering standards; furthermore, it is indefensible in the absence of supporting data. The objective of such analysis was stated earlier. Its purpose is simply to assure that persons with equal probabilities of job success will have equal probabilities of being hired.

Although our discussion of fairness in hiring has emphasized test interpretation, two additional factors—recruitment and training— also bear upon this issue. The federal government and the military services have obviously recognized the importance of recruiting for attracting qualified but reluctant job applicants. Companies seriously interested in hiring qualified minority group members must be similarly active in recruiting them. Furthermore, the concept of discrimination embodied in this discussion contains within it, at least implicitly, the moral responsibility to provide opportunities for *all* persons to develop those abilities and skills contributing to probable job success. Accordingly, industry must continue to develop and implement training programs to help compensate for heretofore socially imposed educational deprivation.

SUMMARY

A psychological test is a yardstick uniformly and systematically applied in the same way to all persons being assessed. This assessment is made in terms of a common scale on which all persons are ordered along a continuum of the trait or characteristic measured by the test. This chapter was concerned specifically with the development and application of preemployment tests for selecting and placing personnel.

The point of departure for constructing a preemployment test is the job analysis. This analysis provides clues about the critical psychological functions distinguishing between satisfactory and unsatisfactory employees. Once such a function is identified for assessment, the test constructor develops his test plan to guide item writing. The purpose of the test plan is to insure that the questions comprising the test are a truly representative sample of all such questions that *could* have been written.

The preliminary set of items written for the test is refined by item analysis. This analysis identifies items for inclusion in the final version of the test on the basis of their utility for discriminating effectively between high and low criterion groups and their levels of item difficulty.

Before this collection of items can be considered suitable for preemployment testing, the test must be shown to be both reliable and valid.

Reliability studies supporting use of the test demonstrate that the scores on it do not fluctuate unduly over time as a result of something inherent in the test itself, the transitory nature of the function it assesses, or factors extraneous to the particular behavior the test is designed to evaluate.

Validity studies for preemployment tests are designed to demonstrate that the test scores do in fact correlate with a subsequently obtained performance criterion (predictive validity) or a criterion measure available simultaneously with the test score (concurrent validity).

Finally, before the test can be effectively used, norms must be developed for it. Normative studies provide a basis for interpreting raw test scores and permit determination of a satisfactory or passing score.

This chapter considered the general issue of the fairness of selection tests to members of disadvantaged groups. Moderator variable analysis was discussed as an approach to compliance with the provisions of the Civil Rights Act of 1964. Tests per se cannot be considered fair or unfair; fairness is a property of test interpretation and utilization. Hence, the appropriate application of preemployment testing requires that applicants with equal probabilities of job success have equal probabilities of being hired.

6. Preemployment Evaluation Techniques

The specific procedures used for selecting and placing personnel vary from one industrial organization to another as a function of the specific job to be filled and of the selection ratio. Virtually all preemployment decisions are partly based upon the use of at least two of the devices discussed in this chapter: an application form and some kind of interview. The rationale is that job success depends upon certain critical background factors (like past experience and education) and interpersonal factors (like the ability to create and maintain a favorable impression and to converse easily) and that these are reflected respectively in application blank and interview responses.

The third type of preemployment evaluation—psychological testing—supplements the information obtained from the other two with indications of the applicant's job proficiency, aptitudes, and so on. The principles of psychological testing were clarified in the preceding chapter. The same general principles hold for application forms and interviews in spite of the relative subjectivity inherent in their interpretation. The efforts of industrial psychologists to improve these procedures have been directed toward reducing this subjectivity. This is accomplished by (1) relating interview questions and items on the application blank to the results of a thoroughgoing job analysis suggesting critical items of information to be elicited by these devices; and (2) research demonstrating that such information does, in fact, correlate with a meaningful criterion of job success, that is, that it has predictive validity.

APPLICATION FORMS

Letters of application and responses to formalized application blanks are generally used as preliminary hurdles in the selection process. If, for example, the job specification indicates that a tenth-grade education is prerequisite to satisfactory job performance and the letter of application is written by someone who is virtually illiterate or the schooling section of the application form indicates that the applicant possesses a lesser degree of education, further investigation of the applicant's qualifications is unwarranted. The typical application blank contains items pertaining to the applicant's age, marital status, dependents, schooling, past experience, and references.

The Weighted Application Blank

There is considerable evidence that careful evaluation of the kind of information elicited by the application blank can result in the selection of better qualified employees and the reduction of employee turnover. The application blank is most useful when it is developed and analyzed in accordance with standard research procedures.

This implies that the investigator must determine the extent, if any, of the relationship between responses to the items on the application blank and some criterion of the employee's success. Items which are shown to be related to a criterion, for example, industrial productivity, are weighted to reflect the extent of this relationship, and the total blank is scored by summing the weights of responses to the items.

You will note, from the above description of the various procedures for constructing a standardized application blank, the essential similarity of the steps involved in developing these forms and many other kinds of psychological tests and inventories in this area (as elaborated in Chapter 5). Once the criterion-related application blank items are identified and weighted for scoring purposes, the entire form must be validated against an external criterion.

The usefulness of this general technique has been demonstrated for predicting various criteria of success for a wide range of positions, including sales personnel (Scollay, 1957), seasonally employed production workers (Dunnette & Maetzold, 1955), and office-clerical personnel (Fleishman & Berniger, 1960).

In the latter investigation a weighted application blank was devised to predict turnover of clerical and secretarial employees in a university setting. The replies to each item on an application form completed by employees hired several years earlier were studied. Although all of these employees had been hired on a permanent basis, it was possible to identify "long-tenure" and "short-tenure" subgroups. Persons in the former subgroup had been working from two to four years and were still on the job. Those in the short-tenure group had terminated employment within two years. Each of the items on the application blank was analyzed to determine the extent to which it differentiated between the long- and short-tenure subgroups.

The responses for each group were classified, tallied, and converted to percentages. For some items the percentage of response within each classification was virtually identical for both groups. Since such items did not discriminate, they were weighted zero and hence did not contribute to the score. When it was evident that an item *did* discriminate between the long- and short-tenure groups, it was weighted to reflect both the magnitude and direction of its discrimination. Illustrative data for some discriminatory and non-

TABLE 6–1

Comparison of Item Responses of Long- and Short-Tenure Office Employees

Application Blank Items	Short-Tenure Group	Long-Tenure Group	Weight Assigned to Response
Local address:			
Within city	39%	62%	+2
Outlying suburbs	50	36	−2
Age:			
Under 20	35	8	−3
21–25	38	32	−1
26–30	8	2	−1
31–35	7	10	0
35 and over	11	48	+3
Previous salary:			
Under $2,000	31	30	0
$2,000–$3,000	41	38	0
$3,000–$4,000	13	12	0
Over $4,000	4	4	0
Age of children:			
Preschool	12	4	−3
Public school	53	33	−3
High school or older	35	63	+3

discriminatory items are shown in Table 6–1. As the table shows, local address differentiated effectively between the groups but previous salary was an ineffective differentiator.

The application blanks of a second sample of long- and short-tenure employees were then scored, utilizing the weights derived from this analysis. The total score was obtained simply by adding or subtracting the weights assigned to categories of response for the items. The correlation between application blank scores and subse-

FIGURE 6–1

Percentages of Correct and Incorrect Hiring Decisions that
Would Have Been Obtained for Office Employees

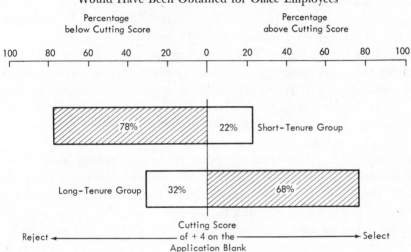

quent tenure for this sample was 0.57. If a critical (passing) score of 4 had been used as the basis for hiring or rejecting these women when they were job applicants, it would have been possible to reduce office turnover considerably (see Figure 6–1).

It is not possible to structure a weighted application blank that will be usable for all jobs in all organizations or even for very similar jobs in different organizations. Every selection program presents a unique problem both with respect to the phrasing of items for inclusion in the blank and the weighting of responses to these items. Consequently, to be most effective, application forms should be tailored to the needs of the specific business or industry desiring to use such a device.

Biographical Information Blank

The usual weighted application blank yields a single overall score which has some predictive usefulness. However, the meaning of this score is uncertain; it does not contribute to understanding the relationship between personal history and job performance (Guion, 1967).

The biographical information blank (BIB) is a refinement of the weighted application blank. It is uniquely suited both to prediction and to research on the relationship between factors in the employee's past history and his level of job performance.

In appearance, the BIB looks like a psychological inventory. It typically consists of a series of items pertaining to the respondent's personal background and present status. For the most part these items concern matters of fact (for example, age, schooling, number of dependents), although some may require expressions of interest or attitude. The BIB usually uses a multiple choice answer format.

By correlating each alternative for every BIB item with the criterion, it is possible to eliminate the invalid items and to develop a scoring key using only the valid items. This process is similar to the one discussed earlier for identifying those application blank items which are to be weighted. Although it is possible similarly to weight BIB items, this is not ordinarily done. Instead, most biographical information blanks are scored by assigning unit weights to the valid items: $+1$ if the item correlates positively with the criterion and -1 if the item correlates negatively with the criterion. The evidence of the desirability of differentially weighting BIB items is conflictual. Some studies have demonstrated that differential weighting permits the inclusion of fewer items in the scoring key (Ehrle, 1964). Others support the use of unit weights.

In addition to correlating BIB items with a criterion in an effort to develop a scorable predictive instrument, the interrelationships between the BIB items themselves may be analyzed. By means of statistical procedures beyond the scope of the present discussion, it is possible to group these items into subsets, or clusters, based upon certain traits, or factors, common to all of the items in a subset. Each of these factors, consisting of *homogeneous* (that is, with a common element) items, may then be scored as a biographical subtest and correlated with the criterion.

The common element defining a cluster of biographical items

may be the type of activity common to all items in that cluster. This was the case, for example, with items administered to high school seniors and clustered into subsets concerned with social activities, religious activities, economic independence, and so on (Siegel, 1956). Alternatively, it has been suggested that our understanding of the personal backgrounds contributing to employee effectiveness can be enhanced by developing clusters of biographical items about such traits as level of maturity, rate of maturation, social adaptability, job interest, and energy level (Henry, 1965).

A special value of this kind of analysis is that it permits additional understanding of the relationship between personal history and job success. Instead of merely contributing to improved prediction, this analysis facilitates the discovery of answers to *why,* in terms of personal history, some persons are more satisfactory employees than others. Further, by comparing biographical factor scores earned by employees in different positions, it becomes possible to hypothesize about the relationship between differences in personal histories and success or failure in various kinds of positions.

THE EMPLOYMENT INTERVIEW

The primary function of the employment interview is to allow the interviewer to meet the applicant in a face-to-face relationship, thereby better permitting the interviewer to evaluate certain of the applicant's qualifications. The interview may be justified as a selection device when personal characteristics, physical appearance, and social factors are critical job requirements. Even under such circumstances, however, the subjectivity of employment interviewing seriously limits its usefulness. The interview should never be considered a substitute for psychological tests specifically designed to measure such factors as intelligence or job knowledge.

When placed in proper perspective, the employment interview serves two functions in addition to the primary one of accepting or rejecting the applicant. Besides securing information bearing upon the applicant's status, the interviewer gives certain information to the applicant about the job and the company and he establishes a friendly relationship with the interviewee. The latter function of employment interviewing is particularly important in situations in which rejected job applicants are potential customers.

Many personnel directors pride themselves on what they consider to be their unique and uncanny ability to select employees by means of an interview. Most generally, however, the validity of their interviewing procedures has never been ascertained (Dunnette & Bass, 1963). A validity study would require data on the number of rejected applicants who would have been successful if they had been hired and the number of accepted applicants who later prove to be unsuccessful employees. When attempted, the results of such studies sometimes indicate that the well-meaning but untrained interviewer might better make his selections on the basis of revelations from a ouija board or crystal ball (Hinrichs, 1960).

Another disturbing feature of the employment interview as usually conducted is its unreliability. Several interviewers may differ

TABLE 6–2

Ranks Assigned to Job Applicants by 12 Sales Managers Who Interviewed Them*

					Interviewer								
Applicant	I	II	III	IV	V	VI	VII	VIII	IX	X	XI	XII	Range
A.........	33	46	6	56	26	32	12	38	23	22	22	9	6–56
B.........	36	50	43	17	51	47	38	20	38	55	39	9	9–55
C.........	53	10	6	21	16	9	20	2	57	28	1	26	1–57

* A rank of 1 signifies that the interviewer believed the applicant to be the most suitable for the position; a rank of 57 means that the applicant was rated as the least suitable for the position.

markedly in their appraisal of the same job applicant. One of the early studies of the reliability of employment interviews compared the ratings assigned to 57 applicants by 12 different interviewers. The interviewers were sales managers, each of whom was allowed to conduct the interview in whatever manner he wished. Each interviewer's ratings were transformed to numerical ranks ranging from 1 to 57 in terms of the suitability of the applicant for the job of salesman. The ranks assigned by the 12 interviewers to several of the applicants are shown in Table 6–2 (Hollingsworth, 1923). Note particularly the spread or range of ranks assigned to each interviewee. In spite of the fact that the interviewers were sales managers, each with considerable interviewing experience, they disagreed extensively in their appraisal of each applicant.

Although evidence like this is disquieting, it must be remembered that the interviewers were not restricted either with respect to procedure or to the bases upon which their evaluations were to be made. The importance of the latter factor was demonstrated by comparing interviewer agreement in evaluating job candidates under two conditions: (*a*) when the interviewers were provided with detailed descriptions of the job to be filled; and (*b*) when the interviewers were provided with nonspecific job descriptions. The reliability coefficients under these circumstances were 0.87 and 0.35, respectively (Langdale & Weitz, 1973). As we will discuss later, standardization of interviewing techniques, structuring the interview, and training of interviewers with respect to the proper criteria for evaluating job applicants does much to improve both the reliability and validity of employment interviews.

There are two general kinds of conditions acting to lower the reliability and validity of interviews, hence limiting their usefulness. These conditions are those associated with the interviewing procedure itself, and with the kind of perceptual distortion that may occur in any interpersonal situation. It will be convenient to separate these two limiting conditions for the purpose of our discussion and to indicate for each the appropriate remedial steps.

Procedure as a Limiting Factor

The unstructured interview is one in which the pattern of questions, the circumstances under which these questions are asked, and the bases for evaluation of replies to these questions are not standardized. These factors vary from one interviewer to another and from one applicant to another. In short, the unstructured interview is subjective in the extreme. This subjectivity may lead different interviewers to disagree quite markedly about the suitability of a particular applicant. Such disagreement adversely affects both the reliability and validity of unstructured interviews.

Reliability and Validity of the Unstructured Interview. Reliability has been defined as consistency of measurement. When applied to the interview, high reliability requires a high degree of interrater agreement. In other words, different interviewers independently interviewing the same candidate would have to agree substantially about that candidate's suitability for employment. As has been previously indicated, interrater *dis*agreement is more common than agreement in interpreting interview performance.

Of the several conditions responsible for the low reliability of the unstructured interview, an important one is the fact that different interviewers are free to cover different material. The simple fact is that different interviewers are interested in different features of the applicant's background and attitudes. And the unstructured interview does not guide the procedure in any way to insure that common questions are asked and that the interviewers are thereby provided with a common basis for assessment (Webster, 1962).

A related condition contributing to the low interrater reliability of the unstructured interview is the fact that such procedures fail to standardize the way in which the information obtained is to be weighted by the interviewers. Even experienced interviewers evaluating candidates for a relatively uncomplicated position from unambiguously presented cues have been found to weight their cues differently. In a demonstration of this, experienced interviewers were required to evaluate the credentials of each of 243 hypothetical job applicants for a secretarial position (Valenzi & Andrews, 1973). These resumes were constructed by compiling all possible combinations of five different cues (typing proficiency, shorthand proficiency, previous experience, formal education, social skills) each at three different levels (low, middle, high). Not only did the interviewers disagree among themselves in the subjective weighting they assigned to the five cues but, not surprisingly, their consequent evaluations of the likelihood of candidate success also differed appreciably.

Even in the unusual circumstance where high reliability can be demonstrated, this cannot be construed as evidence for satisfactory *validity*. The fact that raters agree among themselves in assessing a candidate does not insure that their assessment will permit satisfactory predictions of performance. Furthermore, we have already indicated that the reliability of the unstructured interview tends to be low. Given low reliability, it is impossible to demonstrate high validity. An assessment instrument simply cannot accurately predict a subsequently obtained criterion (that is, cannot be valid) when it measures inconsistently.

In view of the statement above, it is not surprising to note little evidence supporting the validity of the unstructured interview. One source of invalidity is that the interviewers tend to form their judgments about interviewees early, and on the basis of such often irrelevant characteristics as personal dress. Furthermore, their judgments are more easily influenced by unfavorable than by favorable information (Bolster & Springbett, 1961).

The Structured Interview: An Improvement. As discussed above, the basic objection to the unstructured interview is its low reliability and validity. In the absence of standardization of the questions asked, the sequence in which they are asked, and the way in which replies are interpreted, the relative qualifications of the various applicants cannot be compared. The interview must be *structured* (that is, controlled or standardized) with respect to these factors in order to obtain meaningful comparisons across interviewers and between interviewees (Mayfield, 1964). Thus it is clear that structured interviews tend to be more reliable than unstructured interviews and therefore to have greater *potential* (although not always *actual*) validity (Wright, 1969).

Structured interviews most typically are developed for specific jobs in particular companies. In addition, two types of structured interview forms have been devised for use across companies and jobs: the patterned interview and the diagnostic interviewer's guide. Both techniques were designed to overcome some of the deficiencies of uncontrolled interviewing.

The *patterned interview* consists of special interview schedules (lists of questions) which were developed as guides to the interviewer in his search for relevant information about the applicant and his previous work history. This procedure focuses upon such character traits as stability, industry, perseverance, and leadership. It does not attempt to provide information about the applicant's level of job skill; this can be better appraised by methods other than the interview.

The specific advantage of the patterned interview procedure is that it provides the interviewer with a set of carefully worded questions and a sequence in which these questions are to be asked. This eliminates some of the variability of procedure between interviewers. In addition, the interview schedule contains questions designed to guide the interviewer in making his appraisal of the applicant's qualifications. The effect of this is to direct the interviewer's attention to the critical factors to be considered in making his judgment, thereby reducing the effects of personal bias and halo effect.

One indication of the validity of the patterned interview was obtained from a study of the usefulness of the technique for predicting the probable success of truck drivers (McMurry, 1947). One hundred and eight applicants were interviewed, and all were hired regardless of the rating assigned by the interviewers. The data comparing the initial rating by the interviewer and a criterion of employee success determined after 11 weeks are shown in Table 6–3. It is apparent that the patterned interview was quite effective in predicting the ultimate success or failure of the applicants.

The Diagnostic Interviewer's Guide (D.I.G.). The D.I.G. (Hovland & Wonderlic, 1939) is a device which, like the patterned interview, provides a set of standardized questions to be asked of job applicants. In addition, the guide contains a scoring system which enables the interviewer to quantify his impressions of each applicant.

TABLE 6–3

Comparison of Ratings from the Patterned Interview and Success on the Job

	Patterned Interview Rating			
Success on the Job	*1* *Outstanding*	*2* *Good*	*3* *Average*	*4* *Poor*
Successful: Still in service......	75%	38.5%	26.1%	13.3%
Failure: Left service for any reason....................	25	61.5	73.9	86.7

The D.I.G. questions are arranged into four areas covering the applicant's work, family, social, and personal history. The questions in the work history section seek information about the applicant's ability to analyze tasks assigned to him and his ability to profit from his work experience. Family history items relate to his social, economic, and educational background for the job. The section on social history seeks to determine level of sociability and interest in people. Motivational factors like ambition and persistence are covered in the section on personal history.

At the end of each section, there is a series of questions to be answered by the interviewer. One such question in the work history section, for example, is: "Has the applicant indicated a serious and sincere attitude toward the work he has been doing?" The interviewer answers either yes or no; and this answer is transformed to a + or − weight. The algebraic sum of the weights of all of the interviewer's answers to the summary questions constitutes the applicant's score.

An indication of the validity of the D.I.G. is given by a study conducted at the Household Finance Corporation. The guide was completed and scored for 300 applicants, all of whom were hired. The percentages of employees who were still on the job, who had resigned, and who had been dismissed during the course of their employment are summarized in Table 6–4. These data clearly indicate that the percentage of persons still on the job is greater, the higher the D.I.G. score. Note also the marked decrease in the percentage of persons dismissed as the D.I.G. score increases.

The question has been raised whether the relative success of

TABLE 6–4

Percentage of Employees Still on the Job, Resigned, or Dismissed by Category of Score on the D.I.G.

Criterion	D.I.G. Score Category				
	0–10	*12–16*	*18–22*	*24–28*	*30–34*
Still on job.........	38.9%	42.9%	47.2%	48.6%	59.2%
Resigned...........	22.2	25.7	29.2	29.4	34.7
Dismissed..........	38.9	31.4	23.6	22.0	6.1

techniques like the patterned interview and the D.I.G. is attributable primarily to control over the sequence and phraseology of questions or simply to the fact that they focus attention upon specific well-defined traits. It has been suggested that undue control over sequence and phraseology may obscure important characteristics that might become evident in a somewhat freer and more dynamic interaction between interviewer and interviewee. In a pilot study utilizing a standardized but less static format than the typical patterned interview, interviewer ratings of small groups of pharmaceutical employees were correlated with composite supervisors' ratings of job performance. The obtained validity coefficients were statistically significant for three of the five groups and positive though not significant for two of the groups. The investigator concludes that a properly used interview can play a reliable part in overall assessment of an individual's qualities. (Yonge, 1956)

Distorted Interpersonal Perception

The implications of subjectivity were outlined earlier in conjunction with the discussion of the *S-I-R* concept. You will recall from that discussion that responses are functions not only of the precipitating stimuli but also of the interpretation of those stimuli by the respondent. This interpretative factor is the subjective element. The employment interview involves two sets of psychologically significant responses: those made by the interviewer and those made by the job applicant. The stimuli for the interviewer's responses are provided by the applicant's replies to questions, his physical appearance, and personal mannerisms. The ways in which the applicant replies to the questions (the applicant's responses) are in turn a function of stimuli provided by the interviewer—the questions he asks, *his* physical appearance, and *his* personal mannerisms.

The interview, then, involves a very dynamic interpersonal relationship (Hakel & Dunnette, 1968). The two parties react in terms of their perceptions of one another. The factors influencing these perceptions may be quite subtle and not always deliberate, but their effects are manifest in the relatively low reliability and validity of the interview. The human factors operative on both sides of the interviewer's desk which will concern us here are (*a*) lack of rapport, (*b*) bias, (*c*) halo effect, and (*d*) contrast effect.

Lack of Rapport. Virtually every job applicant experiences some degree of anxiety and tension during the employment interview. His nervousness is well founded! The decision about whether or not he is employed rests at least in part upon the impression he makes upon the interviewer. Thus, a normally fluent individual may be quite lost for words during an interview; and a normally calm person may temporarily become a finger drummer, toe tapper, or ear scratcher. The extent to which these behaviors are excused by the interviewer as being atypical and a result of an unusually tense situation varies considerably from one interviewer to another. Similarly, there is considerable variation in the extent to which different interviewers attempt to establish *rapport*—a feeling of warmth, understanding, and relaxation—at the beginning of the interview.

The behavior of any job applicant may be quite different under circumstances in which he is interviewed by a personnel director who is himself calm, relaxed, unhurried, and gives the impression that he truly understands the kind of tension engendered by the situation, from what it is under circumstances in which the interviewer is obviously rushed, tense, and either too busy, disinclined, or personally unable to establish rapport.

Bias. We all have certain biases or preconceptions about people. There are certain characteristics that immediately rub us the wrong way. These may be physical characteristics such as overweight, red hair, dimunitive height, or a physical infirmity of some kind, or some mannerism like gum chewing or smoking. These biases vary from one interviewer to another, influencing their appraisal of the applicant in an uncontrolled fashion. Indeed, recruiters often consider the applicant's personal appearance as the most important aspect of the interview despite the lack of data that this relates to success (Carroll, 1969).

Like the rest of us, interviewers may respond in biased fashion because they identify the applicant with some group about which they have certain preconceptions or *stereotypes*. The interviewer who rejects the blonde applicant for a secretarial position because "blondes are dumb" and the student who knows that "professors are absent-minded" are both victims of stereotyped thinking. They subscribe to rather sweeping generalizations about groups of people which have no basis in fact. Stereotpyed judgments about persons are, of course, most dangerous when any individual's qualifications are evaluated on the basis of ill-conceived generalizations about his particular ethnic or religious group.

The effect of personal bias is to introduce into the employment interview a highly subjective basis for the selection or rejection of particular applicants. The criteria employed by a particular interviewer may be totally unrelated to the abilities required for satisfactory job performance.

Another source of bias is the form in which the questions are asked. Quite different replies may be anticipated to the following questions, each of which is phrased to determine the reasons for which the applicant left his previous employment:

Why did you leave your previous job?
Did you leave your previous job voluntarily or were you fired?
You weren't fired from your last job, were you?

Halo Effect. The tendency to generalize from some specific characteristic or trait to an overall evaluation of the suitability of a job applicant is referred to as the "halo effect." Halo may be positive or negative. The interviewee who is neatly dressed, knocks on the door before entering the office, does not sit down until invited to do so, and is relatively free from nervous mannerisms creates a favorable initial impression. This impression may color the interviewer's perception of the entire interview, leading him to a positive evaluation of the applicant in spite of the fact that he may really be rather poorly qualified for the job in question.

Conversely, the applicant who gives the impression of being overly cocky may create negative halo. The interviewer may fail to perceive such an applicant's strengths of training and past experience because the entire proceedings are unfavorably colored by his perception of the interviewee as a "brash young man."

Certain traits are, to be sure, sufficiently important by themselves to be used as a basis for rejecting a candidate for the job. Some jobs, for example, require that the employee be tactful. An applicant who demonstrates a noticeable lack of tact could legitimately be rejected for this reason alone. An undesirable negative halo effect would be operating, however, when a tactless applicant is rejected for this reason alone in spite of the fact that he is being interviewed for a job in which personal diplomacy is not a critical requirement.

Contrast Effect. Interviews typically evaluate several applicants rather than a single applicant for a given position. This raises the possibility that evaluations of a particular interviewee may be influenced either positively or negatively by the interview performance of the immediately preceding applicant. Such a contrast effect would presumably benefit those interviewees who follow a particularly weak candidate and be detrimental to those following a particularly strong one. This possibility has been experimentally tested in a very limited way and with the general finding that although *statistically* significant contrast effects can be demonstrated, these effects have only limited *practical* significance for applicants who are either clearly qualified or clearly not qualified.

The typical research procedure requires interviewers to read and to evaluate a target resume after examining other resumes which, unknown to the interviewer, are designed to establish an "expectation level." The level of qualifications presented in both the target and preceding resumes is systematically varied to establish whether contrast effects exist at all and, if so, to help delimit the conditions under which they operate.

Minor contrast effects accounting for less than 2 percent of the variance of ratings of target resumes have been demonstrated with written resumes as the stimulus material (Hakel, Ohnesorge, & Dunnette, 1970). Even with videotapes of role-played interviews as the stimulus material, the contrast effect was still quite trivial for target applicants who were either very well qualified or very poorly qualified, although a marked contrast effect was obtained for target applicants who had intermediate qualifications (Wexley, Yukl, Kovacs, & Sanders, 1972).

The research on contrast effects is open to criticism because of its dependence upon artificial rather than real life interview situations (Landry & Bates, 1973). Nevertheless, the data thus far available indicates that contrast effects may unintentionally lead interviewers to overestimate or underestimate the qualifications of those applicants who, by objective standards, have an average level of qualification. By one estimate (Wexley et al., 1972), contrast effect may account for as much as 80 percent of the variation in criterion ratings of average applicants when their interview follow those of several poorly qualified or several well-qualified applicants.

TESTING

Let us assume that the decision has been made to incorporate a psychological testing program into a company's personnel selection and appraisal procedures. Job analyses have been performed, and some of the critical functions to be measured have been identified. There are now two courses of action to be considered. Either tests specifically designed to measure these functions can be custom-built for the company, or already existent tests available from commercial test publishers may be purchased. There is, as a matter of fact, quite a sizable pool of commercially available tests. A primary reference summarizing and reviewing virtually all developments in the field of testing is the series of *Mental Measurements Yearbooks* edited by Buros. The most recent volume in this series appeared in 1972.

Several factors enter into the decision about whether to custom-build tests or to use commercially available standardized tests. Outstanding among the advantages of published instruments is the matter of economy. It is undoubtedly less expensive, particularly when the group is not too large, to purchase testing materials from a publisher than it is to engage in a program of test construction. Furthermore, the process of test development requires considerable time, thereby necessitating a delay in the actual introduction of the testing program. Commercially published tests, on the other hand, are available for virtually immediate use. Finally, many standardized tests have been administered to norms groups of various kinds, thereby facilitating the comparison between the employees now being tested with others who have previously taken the test.

In spite of these virtues, there are certain limitations to the use of commercially available tests. The fact that a test has proven valid in one industrial setting does not guarantee that it will be equally valid even for similar jobs in other settings. It is necessary, therefore, for any test to be validated under the particular circumstances in which it is to be used. Thus, a certain amount of research must be done within the company even when the decision is made to purchase standardized tests.

Secondly, an expanding technocracy implies the creation of new jobs with novel requirements. Testing programs for such jobs may necessitate the development of unique instruments simply because the commercially available tests are not appropriate. Increasingly complex organizational structures necessitate predictions of interpersonal and administrative as well as technical performance. Such predictions usually require assessment methods other than those available as standardized paper-and-pencil tests (Grant, 1970).

Finally, standardized tests may lack face validity for a particular job within particular company.

The choice between utilization of published tests and the development of special tests is one that must be made in each individual case. It is the purpose of the present chapter to indicate something of the range of standardized tests currently available.

Test Formats

Psychological tests differ from one another in the way in which they are structured, administered, and scored. Every kind of format tends to have its own peculiar strengths and weaknesses, although some are more appropriate than others for industrial testing.

Subjective versus Objective Scoring. The primary advantages and disadvantages of subjective as opposed to objective testing were discussed in some detail earlier. Industrial tests are almost exclusively objective in nature because of considerations of reliability and ease of scoring. The skills needed to score an objective test are minimal. The scores obtained from such tests are free from scorer bias and halo effect and are rapidly obtainable after the testing session is terminated.

Speed versus Power Tests. A *speed* test is one with a fixed time limit beyond which the respondents are not permitted to work even though they may not have attempted all of the questions, while a *power* test is administered without a time limit.

The conduct of a large-scale testing program is facilitated somewhat by the administration of time-limit tests. All of the papers are due back within a fixed period of time, thereby permitting the simultaneous scoring and processing of all of the answer sheets.

There are, in addition, certain circumstances in which speed is an essential aspect of the function being measured. Various tests of manual dexterity, for example, are designed to measure both the accuracy and speed of motor activities. These tests are administered with a time limit. Clerical speed is another function measured by means of time-limit tests. The items contained in tests of clerical speed are relatively simple, typically requiring that the respondent examine pairs of names or numbers like those illustrated below and indicate whether they are the same or different.

149278_____149228
192278_____192278
Mary L. Jones_____Mary L. Jones
John R. Smith_____John R. Smyth

The critical function such items measure is not solely the number of pairs that the respondent can answer correctly. Given enough time, most persons would answer almost all such items correctly. The key factor here is the number that can be answered correctly within a limited period of time.

It has been shown that older persons are placed in a somewhat disadvantageous position on speed tests when compared with younger persons, although the performance of these age groups on power tests is quite comparable (Lorge, 1936). Aside from this finding, however, the available evidence supports the use of time-limit tests in the industrial setting.

Group versus Individual Tests. Group tests may be administered simultaneously to a large number of persons while individual tests require that an administrator be present for each person being tested. Group tests are by far the more economical to administer, provided that adequate facilities for seating and proctoring the groups being tested are available.

The unique advantages of individual testing are of greater import in clinical and vocational guidance testing than they are in industrial testing. It is easier to establish a relaxed atmosphere and to note the examinee's behavior during an individual test. It is possible to ask the kind of probing question that may be necessary during certain kinds of personality appraisals only in the individual testing situation. Most industrial testing, however, is the type that lends itself as readily to group as to individual testing.

Performance versus Paper-and-Pencil Tests.   *Paper-and-pencil* tests require the respondent to reply by marking or writing an answer to written questions, while *performance* tests require him to manipulate apparatus or equipment. The apparatus involved in a performance test may duplicate a real-life situation. This is the case, for example, with flight simulators used for training and evaluating aircrews. A performance test may, on the other hand, require the manipulation of apparatus designed solely to measure some psychological function involving motor activity or manual dexterity.

The fact that performance tests require some kind of equipment means that such tests are generally more expensive to administer than are paper-and-pencil tests. Performance tests, furthermore, do not lend themselves readily to large-group testing. Thus, if a psychological function can be measured with equal effectiveness by means of a paper-and-pencil test and a performance test, the former will be the preferred method of measurement.

It should be apparent, however, that certain aspects of behavior can only be measured effectively by performance tests. How, for example, could a skill like typing proficiency be appraised otherwise? The only way in which to determine a typist's skill is to ask her to type a standardized passage under controlled conditions.

Characteristics Measured by Tests

In addition to differences in format, psychological tests are differentiated from one another on the basis of the personal characteristics they measure. These functions are identified as intelligence, aptitude, achievement, interest, and personality. Literally thousands of tests have been reported in the professional literature, reviewed in comprehensive test bibliographies, and are available to qualified users from test publishers. It is possible here to present only a cursory overview of some of the standardized tests most often used in industry.

Intelligence. The definition of intelligence is complicated by the diversity of concepts included in this broad classification. Intelligence is regarded as a general kind of mental alertness. This may involve the ability to learn quickly, to solve problems not encountered previously, and to remember information learned sometime in the past. It certainly involves the ability to think in abstract as well as in concrete terms and to manipulate symbols such as mathematical and verbal concepts. The most outstanding feature of any definition of intelligence is that it involves the *general capacity* for learning and problem solving. Such potential is inferred by comparing a person's present level of cognitive attainment with the level achieved by other persons presumed to have experienced similar opportunities for such attainment.

The fact that intelligence tests purport to measure capacity rather than knowledge means that a high score on such tests is no guarantee of the possession of the specific skills necessary for satisfactory job performance. An applicant who scores high enough on an intelligence test to be considered for the position of bookkeeper or accountant, for example, may actually know very little about bookkeeping or accounting procedures. He has merely demonstrated that he has the capability for learning these skills provided that the appropriate opportunities for training are presented to him.

The notion of minimal intellectual requirements for various kinds of work is fairly obvious. It is not so obvious, however, that certain kinds of work may be performed best by employees below some specified maximum level of intelligence. The concept of optimal intellectual levels for certain kinds of work does not imply that the ability to do the work declines as a function of increased intelligence. Rather, the job may be insufficiently demanding of the employee's intellectual capabilities. This lack of total utilization of capability may be reflected in boredom, job dissatisfaction, absenteeism, and even in increased accident rate.

The *Otis Quick-Scoring Mental Ability Tests* (1937, 1939) is a rapidly administered, paper-and-pencil group measure which although relatively old is still widely used. It may be administered with a 20- or a 30-minute time limit, and an even briefer version has been developed by Wonderlic (1945). This test has demonstrated validity for selecting employees for quite a variety of occupations not requiring a really high level of intelligence. The *Otis* does not have sufficient top, for example, for administration to college students.

The *Wechsler Adult Intelligence Scales* (1955) is an individually administered intelligence test sometimes used for industrial purposes. The advantages of this test are related more to clinical than to industrial applications. The fact that the examiner can probably elicit a higher level of motivation from the respondent and can better observe his behavior while he responds in the individual than in the group testing situation probably leads to a more accurate appraisal of intelligence. Most industrial requirements can, however, be satisfied by more economical procedure of group testing.

Aptitude. Aptitudes are specific capacities for acquiring particular knowledges or skills. One way of viewing the relationship between intelligence and aptitude is that the former is a kind of general aptitude. A number of studies have attempted to fragment general intelligence into component aptitudes. An early study of this type by Thurstone (1938) identified seven primary mental abilities (aptitudes): memory, number, perceptual, reasoning, spatial, verbal, and word fluency. The identification of these aptitudes was accomplished by the statistical procedure known as *factor analysis* whereby the intercorrelations between test scores are examined in order to identify measured functions which cluster or hang together. These seven primary mental abilities cannot be regarded as the ultimate in aptitude identification. As greater variety is introduced into the battery of tests submitted to factor analysis, more and more specific aptitudes are identified. Thus, Guilford (1956) suggested that as many as 40 dimensions of intellect have now been discovered.

Again, as is the case with intelligence, aptitude tests measure capacity but not necessarily knowledge. Tests of general mechanical aptitude attempt to measure capacity for learning to deal with mechanical devices and to perceive mechanical relationships. The person who earns a high mechanical aptitude score may not have had any experience that will qualify him for an industrial position. Similarly, a person who earns a high musical aptitude score may not know how to play a musical instrument or how to compose music.

His test score reveals only a capability for learning in this area, provided that the opportunities are presented to him.

Various standardized aptitude batteries are available from test publishers. One such battery, representative of those published, is the *Flanagan Aptitude Classification Tests* (1959) *(FACT)*. The subtests comprising this battery are cited and defined in Figure 6–2.

FIGURE 6–2

Description of the Flanagan Aptitude Classification Tests

FACT NO.	NAME OF TEST	DESCRIPTION
1	INSPECTION	This test measures ability to spot flaws or imperfections in a series of articles quickly and accurately. The test was designed to measure the type of ability required in inspecting finished or semi-finished manufactured items.
2	CODING	This test measures speed and accuracy of coding typical office information. A high score can be obtained either by learning the codes quickly or by speed in performing a simple clerical task.
3	MEMORY	This test measures ability to remember the codes learned in test 2.
4	PRECISION	This test measures speed and accuracy in making very small circular finger movements with one hand and with both hands working together. The test samples ability to do precision work with small objects.
5	ASSEMBLY	This test measures ability to "see" how an object would look when put together according to instructions, without having an actual model to work with. The test samples ability to visualize the appearance of an object from a number of separate parts.
6	SCALES	This test measures speed and accuracy in reading scales, graphs, and charts. The test samples scale-reading of the type required in engineering and similar technical occupations.
7	COORDINATION	This test measures ability to coordinate hand and arm movements. It involves the ability to control movements in a smooth and accurate manner when these movements must be continually guided and readjusted in accordance with observations of their results.
8	JUDGMENT AND COMPREHENSION	This test measures ability to read with understanding, to reason logically, and to use good judgment in practical situations.
9	ARITHMETIC	This test measures skill in working with numbers—adding, subtracting, multiplying, and dividing.
10	PATTERNS	This test measures ability to reproduce simple pattern outlines in a precise and accurate way. Part of the test requires the ability to sketch a pattern as it would look if it were turned over.
11	COMPONENTS	This test measures ability to identify important component parts. The samples used are line drawings and blueprint sketches. It is believed this performance should be representative of ability to identify components in other types of complex situations.
12	TABLES	This test measures performance in reading two types of tables. The first consists entirely of numbers; the second contains only words and letters of the alphabet.
13	MECHANICS	This test measures understanding of mechanical principles and ability to analyze mechanical movements.
14	EXPRESSION	This test measures feeling for and knowledge of correct English. The test samples certain communication tasks involved in getting ideas across in writing and talking.

Flanagan aptitude classification tests. *Examiner manual.* P. 5.

In was not intended that substantial importance be given to any single test score in the FACT battery. Rather, various combinations of the subtests in the battery have been shown to measure the significant job elements associated with specific occupations. The combination of measures related to the job of accountant, for example, are coding, memory, judgment and comprehension, arithmetic, and tables. Similar patterns of aptitude based upon the signifi-

FIGURE 6–3

Sample Item from Form B of the Bennett,
Seashore, and Wesman Mechanical
Reasoning Test

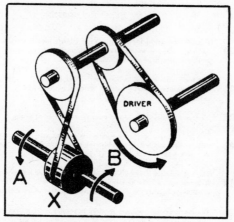

The subject marks *A* or *B* in response to the
question: "If the driver turns in the direction
shown, which way will the pulley at 'X' turn?"

cant job elements have been determined for quite a variety of occupations.

The Bennett, Seashore, and Wesman *Mechanical Reasoning Test* (1947) is a paper-and-pencil measure of mechanical aptitude. The items in this test are similar to the illustration in Figure 6–3. It is rapidly administered and scored, and likely to be of value for jobs like engineering where understanding machines is of prime importance.

Certain occupations, like drafting, require that the employee be able to visualize objects in space. Spatial visualization is measured by tests like the *Minnesota Paper Formboard* (revised, 1941) in which the individual responds to items similar to the ones illustrated in Figure 6–4. He must select the drawing that represents what the object will look like when the components are assembled.

Achievement or Proficiency. Intelligence and aptitude tests are useful measures of potential. They are most helpful for selecting personnel whenever the job to be filled requires unique skills or knowledges which the company expects to teach to new employees.

In addition these tests may be used for selecting personnel when the labor market is such that the company is compelled to hire employees who have certain capabilities even though these have not yet been augmented by training and experience, or when the company is specifically seeking persons who have the potential for growth and promotion within the organization.

Most often, however the employment office will seek employees who now know how to do certain kinds of work. In such cases, the selection tests will measure achievement, knowledge, or proficiency. The specific skills or proficiencies necessary for success in particular occupations are measured by *trade tests.*

Many of the trade tests currently being used are not available for com-

FIGURE 6–4

Item from the Revised Minnesota Paper Formboard Test

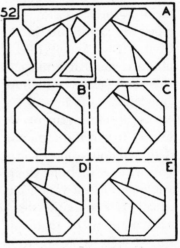

The subject must pick the figure (from A to E) which shows how the parts will look when assembled.

mercial distribution because they have been developed for and are the property of a specific company. Nevertheless, trade tests have been published in such areas as stenographic proficiency, machineshop tools, equipment and procedures, blueprint reading, and industrial electricity.

A special form of achievement testing worthy of note even though not available from test publishers is the "job sample." Here, the applicant is given an opportunity either actually to do the work in question or to simulate the actual tasks.

Although job sample testing has the obvious advantages of face validity and assessment based upon doing rather than merely writing about the work, it also has the disadvantages typically associated with performance testing. Furthermore, a job can never be completely replicated in a test setting. Much of the ultimate job performance may depend heavily upon situational factors associated with the work: for example, differing styles of supervision, unwritten work rules and practices, and so on (Albright, Glennon, & Smith, 1963).

Interests.   Intelligence, aptitude, and achievement testing are fundamental to most personnel testing programs. However, cognitive predictors alone rarely yield validity coefficients higher than 0.40–0.50. Thus, a number of job applicants selected for employment on the basis of scores on such tests will fail as employees; and especially significant in the light of our earlier discussion of the Civil Rights Act of 1964 (Chapter 5), a number of rejected applicants would if hired have been successful employees.

Several factors contribute to what might best be described as only "moderate" validity of cognitive predictors. One such factor is errors of measurement; every kind of measuring instrument is subject to a certain amount of error. A second contributing factor is the complex one of criterion relevancy (Bray & Moses, 1972). You will recall from Chapter 3 that many criteria are potentially available for test validation. However, not all available criteria are equally relevant either to the personal characteristics measured by a particular test or to the practical needs of an employer. For example, there is an important distinction between job *potential* and attained or demonstrated job *proficiency*. Absenteeism and turnover are two important criteria related to the latter, as are the obvious ones of quality and quantity of work. Clearly, a predictor measure of potential is not often as valid as we would like it to be for criteria of actual performance. Assuming performance reflects the effective utilization of one's potential, the validity of the cognitive measures alone should be subject to improvement by supplementing them with assessments of employee interests and personality. Unfortunately, as we will discuss in the following paragraphs, this logical expectation is rarely realized because of difficulties inherent in making assessments of interest and personality in pre-employment settings.

Interests are a product of the interaction of hereditary and environmental factors. It seems probable that human beings have capabilities which are never fully realized or exploited. The failure to reach the limits of our capacity in certain directions results primarily from lack of interest. The converse is also true to some extent. Heredity circumscribes the range of individual interests by limiting the range of possible achievement. Thus, we would hardly expect a color-blind person to display a strong interest in painting or other activity involving color perception or color matching. But the main limiting factor in the evolution of our interests is environmental rather than hereditary in nature.

Given two job applicants of about equal potential and prior experience, the one with the more significant vocational interests will probably be the better employee. Unfortunately, however, the measurement of interests is a much more satisfactory aid to vocational counseling with students than it is to selecting personnel. A fundamental objection to the use of interest inventories in the selection process is that the items in such inventories tend to be transparent. The applicant can often determine by reading the item which response will portray his interests most favorably for the job in question. He is thus able to make the best or most appropriate response even though it may not be indicative of his true interests.

Transparency is not regarded as a serious problem when students take an interest inventory for counseling purposes because it is likely that they are motivated to respond as carefully and accurately as possible. Job applicants, however, want to be accepted for employment. Thus, the validity of their replies to interest inventories may be open to question.

It follows, then, that interest inventories are probably of greater usefulness in a personnel testing program when the results are used for placement, classification, or counseling rather than selection. Once accepted for employment, the job applicant can probably be induced to respond as honestly as possible to an interest inventory on the grounds that it will facilitate his assignment to the kind of job in which he will most likely be successful.

The one noteworthy exception to this generalization is that the validity of interest inventories administered for the purpose of personnel selection has been demonstrated for certain groups of salesmen. The salesmanship scoring keys provided for standardized interest inventories contribute positively to selection in certain instances; in others, it has proven necessary to custom-tailor scoring keys for specific jobs.

The two most widely used interest inventories are the *Strong Vocational Interest Blank* (1951) and the *Kuder Preference Record* (1953).

The items in the Strong Vocational Interest Blank list occupations, school subjects, amusements, activities, and so on, which the respondent must rank in order of preference or respond to in terms of like, dislike, or indifferent. Every item in the inventory carries a positive or a negative weight based upon comprehensive statistical analyses. These weights are combined to produce occupational scoring keys. When the overall positive or negative weight is determined for each occupation, it is transformed to an indication of level of interest expressed as a letter grade (A, B+, B, B−, C+, or C). An A rating means that the individual's interests are similar to the pattern characteristic of persons successfully engaged in that type of work. A B rating means that his interests bear some resemblance to those of successful workers, while a C rating means that his interests bear little if any resemblance to those of successful workers.

This inventory has an exceedingly thorough and comprehensive research program behind it. One of the most impressive indications of the relationship between scores on the Strong Vocational Interest Blank and an occupational criterion has been reported for life insurance salesmen. The obtained relationship between score on the Life Insurance Salesman Key of the Strong, percent of salesmen retained after one and two years, and median amount of insurance sales during the first and second year is shown in Table 6–5. Salesmen who scored at the A level on the Strong were roughly twice as productive and much more likely to be retained than were the salesmen who scored at the B level or lower.

TABLE 6–5

The Relationship between Vocational Interest Blank Score, Rate of Retention, and Annual Sales by Life Insurance Salesmen

Score on Strong	Number of Salesmen Contracted	After One Year		After Two Years	
		Percent Remaining	Median Sales	Percent Remaining	Median Sales
A.	228	66.5%	$155,414	42.5%	$206,680
B+.	72	59.1	112,839	32.4	144,446
B, B−, C.	76	34.2	73,814	15.8	133,039

Personality. Many personnel officers regard personality as the crux of job success or failure. The feeling is rather widespread that for certain types of positions, particularly those requiring the exercise of supervision, personal characteristics may be even more important than skill or job knowledge. It is likely that an employment interviewer fancies as one of his primary functions, the determination of "what the applicant is really like." There is indeed little doubt that *personality traits* (characteristic modes of reaction) are vocationally significant. It is apparent also that adjustment, goal-directedness, and general mental health will all influence an employee's efficiency.

Of the several procedures for assessing personality, the two most often used are: paper-and-pencil inventories and projective techniques. *Paper-and-pencil inventories* contain a series of questions or statements like:

I worry a good deal about my health.
I frequently have headaches.
I concentrate easily.

The respondent is directed to reply to each statement by answering yes or no or always, sometimes, or never. Standardized paper-and-pencil personality inventories are as simple to administer and score as any other kind of objective group test. The results obtained from administration of such inventories for personnel selection have been, however, largely negative. The reason for this is that like interest inventories, paper-and-pencil personality inventories are highly transparent.

Projective techniques confront the examinee with a relatively unstructured or ambiguous set of stimuli which in the case of the Rorschach test look like ink blots and in the Murray Thematic Apperception Test are pictures. He is encouraged to respond freely, telling what he sees in the blot or making up a story about the picture. Responses to such stimuli are presumed to be projections of the subject's thoughts, wishes, desires, and needs.

Projective devices are not transparent. The subject does not know what responses are desired and hence cannot fake his replies in meaningful fashion. Administering projective techniques and interpreting responses to them does, however, require a high level of training and skill. Such instruments are typically administered individually and are both time consuming and expensive. In addition, projective tests have consistently been shown to be less reliable than objective tests.

The transparency of paper-and-pencil inventories and the expense as well as relative unreliability of projective techniques has kept personality appraisal in industry to a minimum. More research is needed to develop such measures particularly for predicting success in different types of high-level jobs within a given professional area. For such jobs, more of the variance of job success is attributable to personal noncognitive qualities; the cognitive attributes (ability, aptitude, knowledge) are pretty much assured by the education and training requirements imposed as qualification standards.

Note that we are speaking above only about high-level executive and managerial positions. For most industrial positions, personality assessment is of dubious validity and therefore may constitute an unwarranted invasion of privacy. Furthermore, even when personality assessments may be regarded as appropriate, their present state of development does not usually justify their inclusion in selection batteries (Biesheuval, 1965).

SUMMARY

This chapter considered the application blank, interview, and psychological test as three widely used preemployment evaluation techniques. Since the application form and interview are especially susceptible to subjectivity and potential invalidity, the efforts of the industrial psychologist have, for the most part, been directed toward these matters.

One approach to improving the validity of application blanks is to weight the responses to individual items and to score the blank by summing these weights. Such weights are derived from an investigation of the relationship between specific responses and some criterion of employee success. The stronger this relationship, the higher is the weight assigned to a particular response.

The biographical information blank is a refinement of the weighted application blank. It is a type of psychological inventory uniquely suited both to prediction and to research on the relationship between factors in the employee's past history and his level of job performance.

The employment interview serves two purposes in addition to the primary one of providing a basis for accepting or rejecting the applicant. The interviewer gives certain information to the applicant about the job and the company, and he strives to establish a friendly relationship with the applicant. The latter function is important because even rejected applicants are potential consumers of the product or services offered.

Interviews may be conducted in either unstructured or structured fashion.

In the unstructured interview, the pattern of questions, the circumstances under which these questions are asked, and the bases for evaluating the replies are not standardized. These factors vary from one interviewer to another and from one interviewee to another. Thus, the unstructured interview is subjective in the extreme. Such procedures tend to be markedly unreliable and invalid.

The structured interview is one in which the procedure is so controlled as to reduce the extent to which interviewer biases operate. The pattern of questions to be asked of all applicants by all interviewers is specified. In addition, the factors upon which the interviewer is to base his evaluation of the applicant are clarified.

Several suggestions for improving interviewing technique are discussed in this chapter. These suggestions relate to the influence of rapport, personal bias, halo effect, and contagious bias.

Finally, this chapter explored the range of standardized and commercially published psychological tests available for industrial application. The outstanding advantages of standardized tests include economy, immediate availability, and accessibility to norms. In spite of these advantages, the validity of such tests cannot be assumed; it must be established under the particular circumstance in which the test is to be used.

Psychological tests differ from one another in the way in which they are structured, administered, and scored. In addition to the frequently mentioned differentiation between subjective and objective tests, some tests have a time limit (speed tests) while others do not (power tests); some are suitable for administration to groups while others are designed for administration to one person at a time; and some require the respondent to perform on some kind of apparatus or equipment while others require him to reply by marking an answer to a written question.

In addition to differences in format, psychological tests are differentiated from one another on the basis of the functions they measure. These functions are identified as intelligence, aptitude, achievement, interest, and personality.

All tests of ability, including intelligence, aptitude, and achievement, measure the present level of cognitive performance. However, intelligence and aptitude tests are regarded as tests of capacity or potential because of their demonstrated success in predicting future cognitive accomplishments. Thus, these two types of test are most appropriate in situations wherein the job to be filled requires unique skills or knowledges which the company expects to teach its new employees. Most often, however, the employment office will seek employees who now know how to do certain kinds of work. In such cases the selection tests will measure achievement, knowledge, or proficiency.

7. Employee Training

Learning is a key factor in the development and modification of behavior, including those activities related to job performance. Behavior is learned as a consequence of certain kinds of experiences. *Training* refers to industrial efforts to provide those experiences calculated to facilitate the development of attitudes, skills, and knowledges most germane to satisfactory job performance.

The value both to management and employees of training for job-related behavior is self-evident. An effective training program may increase productivity, generate increased job satisfaction, decrease turnover and accidents, and so on. In one way or another, all of these desirable ends improve the quality of the product or service and reduce operating costs.

In addition, employee training has become a concern of great social importance. Educationally and socially deprived persons must through training be provided opportunities for productive citizenship. Likewise, automation makes imperative the provision of opportunities for retraining persons whose present skills are inappropriate to contemporary industrial technology.

Although automation and the social milieu have called attention to industry's need and responsibility for training in a dramatic way, this need has always existed, and industry has for a long time accepted the responsibility. An early form of on-the-job training, for example, is represented in the following agreement (United States Department of Labor, 1952) :

> Know all men that I, Thomas Millard, with the Consent of Henry Wolcott of Windsor unto whose custody & care at whose charge I was brought over out of England into New England, doe bynd myself as an apprentise for eight yeeres to serve William Pynchon

173

of Springfield, his heires & assigns in all manner of lawful employ-ment unto the full ext of eight yeeres beginnings the 29 day of Sept 1640 & the said William doth condition to find the said Thomas meat, drinke & clothing fitting such an apprentise & at the end of the tyme one new sute of apparell & forty shillings in mony: subscribed this 28 October 1640.

The kind of on-the-job training promised Thomas Millard was typical of New England apprenticeship in colonial days. The em-ployer's commitments were minimal. In return for receiving de-voted service for "eight yeeres," he was to provide merely "meat, drinke and clothing" and, at the end of the period, "one new sute of apparell & forty shillings in mony." Little enough perhaps, but even the full extent of the generosity provided by this indenture was not realized. Apparently, Millard became itchy to strike out on his own before completing the full term of his apprenticeship. The follow-ing statement appears at the foot of the indenture:

Tho Millard by his owne consent is released & discharged of Mr. Pynchon service this 22. of May 1648 being 4 months before his tyme comes out, in Consideration whereoff he looses the 40 s in mony wch should have bin pd him, but Mr. Pynchon giveth him one New sute of Apparell he hath at present.

It is apparent from the foregoing indenture agreement that in-dustrial training is far from a new concept. However, both the scope and methods of present-day industrial training differ considerably from colonial apprenticeship. Although development of job-related knowledges and skills has always been a fundamental objective of training, this objective has been considerably broadened, particu-larly since World War II.

One assumption underlying apprenticeship training which is par-ticularly called into question is that experienced employees with job skills are automatically thereby qualified to teach these skills to novices. Whereas training can be conducted in this way, it is often inefficient; that is, it takes longer than necessary and generally does not allow the trainee to make maximum use of his potential for development and job performance. Thus, the position taken in this chapter is that industrial training is most effectively conducted by capitalizing upon sound principles of human learning developed both in industry and in psychological laboratories.

Although training programs of various kinds permeate virtually all levels of the company, the present discussion is restricted to employee training. Special consideration is given to management and supervisory training in Chapter 13. The present chapter treats five main topics: (1) the scientific foundations of training programs in terms of principles of learning, (2) preliminary considerations in developing training programs, (3) implementing training programs, (4) evaluating training outcomes and procedures, and (5) training the trainer.

LEARNING PRINCIPLES UNDERLYING INDUSTRIAL TRAINING

Industrial training is a learning situation fundamentally similar to formal kinds of schoolroom learning. To be conducted successfully, a training program must take into account certain basic psychological principles of learning and forgetting. We cannot here review the very substantial body of evidence on learning theory. Rather, we will merely summarize some of the highlights.

What happens when a person learns? Attempts to describe and guide this experience must take into account something like the following sequence of events (McGehee, 1958):

1. The learner is motivated; he wants to attain some goal or goals.
2. The learner responds in ways calculated to attain these goals. However, his initial responses are limited by the "givens" which he brings with him into the learning situation. These initial givens include:
    a. The sum total of his past learning and abilities;
    b. The way in which he interprets the goal.
3. The learner practices behavior for goal attainment.
4. As he does so, the consequences of his responses are continuously fed back to him. He assesses these responses with respect to their adequacy for goal attainment.
5. Learning has occurred when the learner can attain his goal(s) using responses not formerly in his behavior repertoire.

Motivation

Repetitive practice or exposure is not by itself a sufficient condition for learning. A person learns only when he is motivated to do so. The importance of motivation as a precondition for learning has two major implications. First, any training program should be preceded by an orientation session (or sessions) to discuss and clarify the need for the program. Second, the program itself must provide continuing motivation during the course of training.

Clarifying the Need for the Program. Both new and experienced employees sometimes resent training. Such resentment may be based upon the feeling that the program really betrays a lack of confidence in their ability to do the work. Experienced supervisors likewise may object to the introduction of newfangled working procedures which are at variance with their familiar and accustomed ways of doing the job. Thus, one objective of the orientation to training is to attempt to forestall such resentments.

Another objective is to clarify the goals and the reasons for seeking to attain these goals. It is naïve to believe that work goals are self-evident for everyone alike. Whereas management, for example, may seek maximally efficient high-quality production, the employees may be influenced by work group goals established to maintain only whatever level of productivity will pacify the supervisor. Likewise, whereas a training program may be designed to teach a specific method of task performance, this method will not be perceived as desirable by those trainees who fail to understand its superiority to alternative procedures.

As a case in point, a company specializing in the manufacture of miniature motors for guidance systems in aircraft was disturbed by an unduly high rate of rejection during final inspection. The defects were attributable to poorly soldered connections. Further checking indicated that conditions caused by rapid expansion in the labor force had led management to utilize a kind of on-the-job training in which experienced solderers were teaching new employees how to do the work. None of these teachers was able, however, to explain the reason for using flux prior to applying the solder. As a result, new operators often regarded this as an unnecessary step in the soldering process. The simple expedient of explaining some elementary principles of soldering to the employees and to the new trainees led to an appreciable decrease in the rate of rejections.

Short-Term Goals. It has been found desirable to establish a number of readily attainable short-term subgoals throughout the learning sequence in addition to the fundamental long-term goal of "completion of training" or a "certificate" or achievement of "regular salary status." It would be difficult for most university students, for example, to attend school with a high level of motivation for the full four years if the only goal was eventual employment within a selected occupation. This goal is, to be sure, extremely important. Fortunately, from a motivational standpoint, it is supplemented by such subgoals as obtaining the diploma, earning satisfactory course grades, performing well on a specific final examination, and doing well on hourly examinations and even on 10-minute quizzes in any one course. In addition, the learner may derive considerable satisfaction from having grasped a difficult concept or gaining insight into a hitherto unknown process.

Individual Differences

We have said that once training begins, the trainee's initial responses are limited by the givens he brings with him. These "initial states" (Glaser, 1967) reflect the trainee's past history of demonstrated *utilization* of his aptitudes, interests, and so on. Hence the trainee's progress is influenced by such things as his idiosyncratic expectations or goals and the sum total of his past learning and of his abilities.

Idiosyncratic Goals. In spite of pretraining orientation some trainees may fail to understand the type of behavior finally desired. This failure may occur because the desired behavior is not in the response repertoire of the trainee. He therefore interprets what he is supposed to do in terms of whatever behavior *is* available in his repertoire.

For example, management may institute training for job rotation, anticipating that this will enable employees to cover for each other during vacation periods. However, unless this is clear to the trainees, they may simply view the training as an opportunity to appreciate something of the diversity of tasks performed by company employees. Such appreciation alone is not enough to insure satisfactory performance when jobs are actually rotated.

Past Learning and Abilities. Recognition of the existence of differences in capabilities, interests, attitudes, and so on between persons is fundamental to psychological testing programs. All men are *not* equal. Some are more capable than others of learning particular types of tasks. Contrary to popular belief, the effect of training is often to accentuate such differences rather than to cancel or reduce them. Thus, the spread between the best and poorest trainees in initial level of performance usually becomes progressively greater as the training program progresses. This is particularly noted when the task being learned is relatively complex or difficult, although it has even been reported when training was deliberately structured into a series of small, simple steps, one building upon the other (Welsh, Antoinetti, & Thayer, 1965).

The effect of individual differences upon subsequent performance in a training program is evident from the following study (Boring, 1945). Four groups of soldiers, classified on the basis of their scores on the Army Radiotelegraph Operator Aptitude Tests, received radiotelegraphic code instruction. The aptitude classifications ranged from I (highest) to IV (lowest). The rate of learning plotted for these four groups at two-week intervals during the training program is shown in Figure 7–1. Note that the early differences between these groups, which were pronounced even at two weeks, became even more accentuated as training progressed.

Individual Difference Variables in Interaction.   Having noted

FIGURE 7–1

Radiotelegraphic Code Learning as a Function of Trainee Aptitude

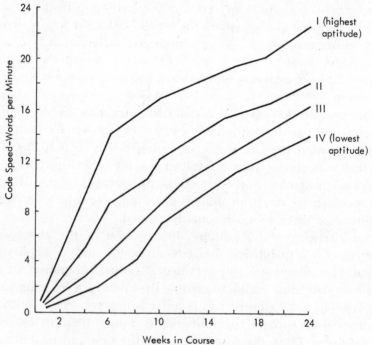

that idiosyncratic goals, past learning, and abilities influence the course of progress during training, we must emphasize that these factors interact with each other in mutually enhancing fashion. A trainee's expectations of how well he will be able to handle the training content will probably influence his motivation during training (Campbell, Dunnette, Lawler, & Weick, 1970). It seems likely that high-aptitude trainees have a past history of positive reinforcement through successful experiences in learning content similar to that to which they are now exposed during training, and therefore approach the training with the belief or expectation that they will be able to master the content or skill. Conversely, because of a past history of negative reinforcement, low-aptitude trainees probably approach training with an expectation that they will fail in it.

Practice

It is fairly obvious that trainees must actually practice a skill if they are to learn it. Even a highly motivated student attending lectures and seeing demonstrations of automobile driving, for example, is poorly trained to drive until after he has received supervised driving practice. Similarly, the foreman who merely attends lectures on how to train or how to lead is trained incompletely either as a trainer or as a leader. The essential element of supervised practice is lacking.

Thus, a training program must make provision for the trainees actually to practice their job in the way in which they ultimately will be expected to perform it. If a motor skill, like operation of a piece of equipment, is being taught, the trainees must have an opportunity to practice the operation of the equipment. The supervisor who is learning to train, in like fashion, must receive supervised practice in actually training employees.

In spite of the widely quoted maxim, practice may make imperfect. Improper or inappropriate behaviors which are practiced will be learned as effectively as correct behaviors. Thus, a key feature of the practice phase is that the trainees must be very carefully supervised. Mistakes must be corrected as soon as they occur. Anyone who has attempted to teach himself to play golf, for example, and then consults a professional is well aware of the fact that he must unlearn a number of bad habits that have become established as a result of unsupervised practice.

Whole versus Part Learning. One of the implications of the desirability of short-term goals for industrial training is that complex tasks should wherever possible be divided into their significant component parts for teaching purposes. The trainee is enabled thereby to attain a measure of satisfaction from successfully learning portions of the task even though he is not yet able to perform the entire task.

The nature of the parts to be learned and the sequence in which they are taught varies from one task to another. The disassembly of a weapon, for example, requires trainees first to learn to handle various subassemblies. Similarly, a typist must learn various subskills, including proper fingering and spacing, which she then integrates into a total behavior pattern.

The entire matter of the feasibility of teaching segments of the total task and, if this is done, of the optimal decomposition of the task and sequence for presenting its constituent parts requires examination in each specific training situation. In a general way, it has been shown that these matters depend upon two aspects of the task's components: complexity and organization. *Complexity* refers to the difficulty of each of the separate components of the overall task; *organization* refers to the interrelationships among task components (Naylor & Briggs, 1963).

When a task is highly organized, it has an essential cohesiveness the integrity of which would be destroyed by decomposing it into parts or subtasks. Thus, the whole method of training is particulary appropriate. Furthermore, its superiority to part training for such tasks increases as the difficulty of the constituent components of the overall task increases.

Part training, on the other hand, is particularly efficient when the constituent responses are not closely interrelated (that is, low task organization). The superiority of part over whole training for such tasks is increased when certain portions of the total task are much more difficult than others.

Massed versus Spaced Learning. Another aspect of the arrangement of training sessions is the matter of the optimal length of each session. Practice periods may be *massed,* in which case training consists of relatively few but long sessions, or they may be *spaced* so that there are more sessions, each of shorter duration. Five hours of training may be massed, for example, in a single session starting at 8:00 A.M. and continuing until 1:00 P.M. The same five hours may be spaced by setting up a 2½-hour session in the morning and another in the afternoon, or by establishing five one-hour sessions, or 10 half-hour sessions, and so on.

The primary advantage of spaced training is that it is generally easier to maintain a high level of trainee interest and to avoid fatigue during several sessions of shorter duration than during a few very long sessions. Spaced training has in general been demonstrated to produce more rapid learning and more permanent retention. Exceptions to this generalization occur in instances in which the skills or concepts to be learned are so simple that even massed practice periods will be of relatively brief duration.

The optimal spacing of training sessions must be determined for each task to be taught. If the time intervals between spaced practice periods are too long, the advantages of spaced practice may be more than offset by the amount of forgetting transpiring during the time interval. Similarly, if the individual practice periods are too brief in duration, they may be filled almost entirely by having the trainees check out tools and materials and receive instructions. Such periods will end just as the trainees are about to move into the task itself!

Transfer of Training.   Most training takes place in settings which are artificial in some degree. This is most obvious for training physically removed from the actual work site. However, it is true to some extent also even of training at the site because of subtle variations between training and working conditions. In the former, for example, the supervisor may tend to be more helpful than usual, and the wage may be independent of output.

Irrespective of *where* training takes place, the objective is to have the trainee learn to perform satisfactorily on the job. Thus, there must be some carryover, or transfer, from what is learned during training to actual job performance. This transfer may be either *positive,* in which case learning during traininig facilitates job performance, or *negative,* where training is actually an initial hinderance to job performance.

Positive transfer between two situations is encouraged when the stimulus-response requirements in those situations are similar. Furthermore, the more nearly similar these requirements, the greater will be the amount of positive transfer. Thus, it is clear that the more nearly the required behavior during training approximates the behavior required on the job, the greater will be the amount of positive transfer. If, for example, both speed and accuracy are required for satisfactory job performance, both of these response characteristics ought to be encouraged also during training.

Concern for transfer must also guide the way in which the training program itself is internally constituted and sequenced. Virtually any human task may be analyzed into subtasks, each critical to final performance. Consider, for example, a complex task like troubleshooting a radio. The mechanic is required, first, to know the rules of signal flow through each component. Second, he must know the proper use of electronic test instruments. Each of these subtasks can be further analyzed into subordinate subtasks. For example, proper instrument usage requires the mechanic to know which instrument to use for which kind of check, how to set up the test instrument, how to interpret the instrument reading, and so on.

Proceeding from a detailed analysis of the subtasks constituting final performance *(task analysis)*, the training program must be designed to insure that each subtask is fully learned. To accomplish this, the program must present the component subtasks in a sequence which maximizes the likelihood of positive transfer from learning one component to another.

Knowledge of Results

Trainees must be given a stream of information (or "feedback") about their performance if they are to maintain a high level of interest in the training program. The importance of feedback is evident from an investigation in which two groups of subjects were trained to aim a rifle at an unseen moving target (Stockbridge & Chambers, 1958). One group was given information indicating whether or not they were aiming in the vicinity of the target. The other group received no information of this kind. At the end of the 400th practice trial, the dissemination of information to the "knowledge" group was terminated, and both groups operated under conditions of "no knowledge" for 400 additional trials.

The results for these two groups of subjects expressed in terms of the mean number of seconds the rifle was actually aimed on the target are shown graphically in Figure 7–2. Knowledge of results produced a more rapid increment in performance than did the control condition during the original 400 trials. Furthermore, additional learning in the knowledge group ceased after the 400th trial paralleling the cessation of information about performance.

FIGURE 7–2

Effect of Knowledge of Results upon Accuracy of Rifle
Aiming

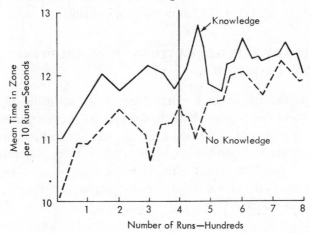

The no knowledge group eventually performed essentially as well as the knowledge group, but it required about twice as long for them to do so.

The incentive effect of knowledge of results is generally more important in the later stages of practice than during the initial stages. In the earlier stages, most trainees have a degree of enthusiasm tending to carry them forward. Later on this intrinsic enthusiasm diminishes, it must be rekindled by such externally imposed factors as proof of progress.

The provision of feedback information ought to follow the trainee's performance with as little time lapse as possible. You are aware in your own case of the instructional value of rapid feedback by the teacher of the correct answers to an examination. Similarly, the industrial trainee benefits most from a training environment permitting for frequent and rapid performance evaluations.

In spite of the clear necessity for feedback during training, it is possible for such feedback to be either too general or too specific to be helpful. Feedback that is too general fails to provide the learner with sufficient information by which he can improve his performance. However, overly specific feedback providing more detailed information than the trainee can use at his present level of sophistication may actually retard his learning. The latter situation is analogous to "overloading" the system. Generally speaking, in order to be useful the feedback must be of a type that will reinforce the training goals of successful trainees and lead to goal modification by the relatively unsuccessful trainees (Locke, 1967).

PRELIMINARY CONSIDERATIONS IN DEVELOPING TRAINING PROGRAMS

Granting the importance of the foregoing conditions of effective learning, these conditions alone do not specify the optimal nature of the training program. Training can take many forms, each incorporating appropriate learning principles. What, then, determines how the training program ought actually to be structured? And is there any evidence that certain kinds of instructional formats are more efficient than others?

Determining Training Needs and Objectives

A properly structured training program has certain well-defined objectives. These objectives follow logically from a systematic determination of training needs within the company and in turn suggest the ways in which training will be conducted, the persons who will be trained, and a scheme for evaluating the effectiveness of the program.

Often the need for some kind of training becomes evident because of the existence of a problem. Automation, for example, may be accompanied by layoffs and a consequent need to train displaced workers for other jobs. Rapid expansion of production or changes in the labor market may necessitate training designed to teach requisite job knowledges or skills to relatively inexperienced workers. Sometimes a company suddenly discovers a rather marked increase in accidents accompanying the introduction of new equipment and needs to institute a safety training program. Or, in anticipation of the retirement of a number of supervisory persons, the company may need to train replacements as effective leaders.

The foregoing problems merely suggest the kinds of situations that may create a need for training. The program begins with certain questions related to need: In what areas (safety, skills, supervision, and so on) is training needed? Which workers need to be trained? What are the specific training needs of these workers? Only after questions like these are answered can the company begin to think in terms of the kind of program that will be appropriate to its needs.

Discovering Training Needs. Analyses of training needs typically begin with an overview of the entire company in an attempt to identify areas of relatively inefficient operation. Interviews, studies of company records concerning turnover, accidents and customer complaints, and observations by the training analyst may all be suggestive.

Although this overview can suggest *general* areas of training need, it must be supplemented by studies to determine specific groups of workers in need of training. For example, safety training may be indicated for a company, but it is unlikely that all groups of workers will need such training. The analyst's focus narrows during this phase of training need determination as he studies the workers in particular departments. He may consult existing job analyses or make new ones of his own; he makes systematic observations; and he interviews.

Finally, the analysis of training needs gets down to the level of individual workers. Training may be necessary only for certain workers within a department; or differential amounts and types of training may be indicated for the various department members. Various tests of ability, skill, or job knowledge may be administered if these are appropriate to the identified areas of training need. Supervisory ratings may help identify particular workers most in need of training and indicate the kinds of training they ought to receive. Company records of individual productivity, accident frequency, and so on may provide further clues.

Training Objectives. A training program properly conceived permeates all levels and activities of an industrial organization. Its impact is felt by workers with varying amounts of experience and at various levels or classifications.

The diversity of training needs makes it impossible to present a really comprehensive list of the objectives that can be realized as a result of training. We will consider only some that are most generally applicable.

1. Orientation and Indoctrination. This kind of training is designed for newly hired personnel regardless of whether these workers have had prior experience. It serves primarily to explain the company's policies and practices. Secondarily, it may seek to develop

attitudes of pride in the company and personal identification of the employee with it.

2. Job-Related Skills and Knowledges. Such training is mandatory when a company is compelled to hire relatively inexperienced employees either because of conditions of the labor market or because the job to be filled is novel or unique to the particular company. A continuous program of skills-and-knowledges training for in-service personnel may be necessary also to upgrade present levels of employee performance.

3. Personal Improvement and Enrichment. This objective extends the impact of training considerably beyond the confines of the worker's job. It is based on the assumption that more broadly educated employees handle their work more efficiently. In addition, programs with more general educational objectives lay the groundwork for teaching new skills and knowledges demanded of workers by an ever-expanding technocracy. Thus, an organization like the National Secretaries Association has considered it desirable to sponsor courses for its members in such areas as art appreciation and human relations. Individual companies, likewise, provide opportunities for employees at various levels to take such courses as speed reading, blueprint reading, speech, and written communication.

4. Management Development. The executive, administrative, and human-relations skills required for effective leadership are not acquired by virtue of seniority or demonstrated job performance. As men progress to increasingly higher management positions, their responsibilities shift from the specific to the general; they must make decisions having broad impact and affecting many other persons.

5. Technological and Scientific Information. Rapid technological and scientific advances have necessitated special programs designed to keep employees abreast of the most recent developments. Many accounting procedures utilizing punched-card equipment "brand new" only 20 years ago, for example, have been superseded by the development of relatively inexpensive data-processing machines capable of storing and providing ready access to vast amounts of information. In a competitive society it is imperative that industrial organizations avail themselves of all pertinent technological advances. To do so requires that scientific and professional employees be provided the opportunity and incentive to learn about such advances.

Training and Personnel Selection.   It should be evident from the foregoing discussion that selection procedures and training goals for new employees are interdependent. The more qualified the selected employee, the less likely he is to require elaborate and lengthy job training. Conversely, the more comprehensive and effective the company's training program, the less elaborate need be its selection program.

This interaction between selection and training procedures must finally be interpreted in terms of cost. Both procedures require expenditures. Therefore, in the interest of economy, management must optimize the relationship between these two elements of its personnel program. Clearly, when selection test scores correlate positively with training success, acceptance of those applicants with the highest test scores is justified. They are the ones most likely to complete satisfactorily the training program. And by reducing the number of unsuccessful trainees, the overall cost of the training program is also thereby reduced. However, selection programs cost money too. If many applicants must be tested to identify a relatively small number with sufficiently high scores for training purposes, it may prove more efficient to modify the training program at some additional cost in order to effect more substantial economies in the selection program itself.

A cost analysis suggesting the optimum balance between selection and training expenditures is therefore dependent upon the (*a*) number of job applicants available, (*b*) validity of selection procedures for predicting success in training (*c*) cost per man of selection, and (*d*) cost per man of training.

Retraining. Retraining programs are developed in two kinds of situations. First, the retraining program may provide refresher instruction for present employees. Such refresher training may be required because of the introduction of new work methods and/or equipment, employee reassignment, or because a periodic performance review has indicated that the employee needs additional instruction in order more effectively to handle his present assignment.

Second, retraining may be necessitated by displacement. Retraining for displaced workers has become an increasingly important social concern because of automation and the changing nature of jobs away from repetitive short-cycle work. The area is a new one for psychological investigation; the meager results thus far available point to the importance of attitudinal factors to the success of this type of retraining.

188 *Psychology in Industrial Organizations*

A study of the feasibility of retraining factory employees for work as technicians concluded that only 15 percent were completely ineligible for such retraining. The primary limiting psychological factor was deficient educational background rather than a low level of learning ability. However, this is compounded by the increased cost of retraining men with minimally sufficient aptitude (McNamara, 1963).

Even when companies are willing to defray the cost of retraining persons with requisite abilities, there is likely to be a certain amount of initial employee resistance to change in work role (Fleishman, 1965). Retrainees, for example, were found to be much less satisfied with the company immediately following a retraining program than formerly. However, three years later, the level of job satisfaction returned to about the pretraining level (Rosen, Williams, & Foltman, 1965).

One particularly disturbing factor is the reluctance of older adults to seek retraining because of their conviction, or industry's, that they are too old to learn something new. To be sure, age is accompanied by some decrement in certain kinds of cognitive functions and abilities. However, in the age range of most employees eligible for retraining, the actual decrement is much less serious than the attitude of resistance.

The challenge to psychologists engaged in retraining is thus that of designing programs that effectively overcome such resistance by facilitating successful experiences by middle-aged trainees. That this is possible was demonstrated with inspection trainees for whom the training method emphasized active responses and minimized the possibility of making errors (Belbin & Shimmin, 1964).

Training the Disadvantaged. Considerable attention has recently been given to training directed towards disadvantaged persons. For one such program conducted by Lockheed Aircraft Company (Hodgson & Brenner, 1968) the applicants had to meet four of the following five criteria: (*a*) school dropout, (*b*) unemployed head of household, (*c*) income less than $3,000 during the previous year, (*d*) poor work history, and (*e*) no primary work skills. Given these requirements, none of the trainees could have met traditional company hiring standards. Nevertheless by developing programs using appropriate instructional methods, offering frequent reinforcement and recognition, dealing with content that was directly linked to a specific job, and providing jobs that were not dead-end ones, trainee retention during the program and after job placement was exceptionally high.

The key factor in this particular program seems to be that it lead directly to a job opportunity. The availability of such an opportunity is undoubtedly responsible for encouraging maintenance of a satisfactory level of motivation during training. In contrast, a follow-up six months after completion of a literacy training program without any provision for subsequent employment (Patten & Clark, 1968) indicated that the effect of the program was to generate an extreme lack of confidence associated with a feeling of being hopelessly undereducated.

In brief, successful training for the disadvantaged must have a tangible payoff for the trainee. Although it is technically feasible to enhance basic skills, unless the program provides for subsequent placement in a desirable job it becomes an additional exercise in futility for the trainee.

Considerations in Training Design

In many ways industrial training is essentially like other kinds of formal education. Neither training nor education should be permitted to evolve by happenstance. Both must be carefully designed most efficiently to implement the learner's attainment of the desired goals.

Terminal Behavior Desired.   The initial consideration in formulating any educational program is to specify the behavior ultimately desired. Broadly speaking, the goals of industrial training may be to convey knowledge (for example, orientation training), develop skills, or modify attitudes (for example, concerning accident hazards). Within each of these broad areas the training director must specify the training goals as precisely as possible. Clearly specified objectives serve two purposes. First, they guide the formulation of a training program that is calculated to implement goal attainment. Second, they suggest criterion measures which when applied to training program graduates permit evaluation of the effectiveness of the program for generating the desired terminal behavior.

Trainee Characteristics.   It is doubtful, even for a specified objective, that a single training format is appropriate for all learners. Instead, it is likely that the appropriateness of any training procedure depends both upon the objectives sought and the characteristics of the learner (Siegel & Siegel, 1967). The kinds of trainee characteristics that will most obviously concern the training director as he designs his program are ability or aptitude and previous job-related experience. If the trainees constitute a heterogeneous group with respect to these qualifications, he may well find it necessary to develop parallel programs for subsets of trainees. Each program, although designed to generate the same terminal behavior, may differ with respect to content, sequence in which the content is presented, instructional materials and methods used, and so on.

An Overview of the System.   The activities of training program graduates must mesh well with those of workers on related jobs. Otherwise, there is a danger that newly trained employees will either take over work responsibilities of other employees with a consequent duplication of effort and cost or that certain task elements will not be performed either by the newly trained or experienced employees. To prevent either occurrence, the training director must have a clear notion of the interdependence of related jobs within the overall company system.

IMPLEMENTING TRAINING PROGRAMS

Given an analysis of the terminal behavior desired, trainee characteristics, and the interdependence of work roles within the system, the training director may structure his program to be conducted at various sites and in various ways. The primary considerations in selecting a training site are (*a*) appropriateness of the site for the attainment of desired objectives and (*b*) economy, including the speed with which training is completed.

Two self-evident training sites are the classroom and some other unspecified location away from the company (for example, studying at home). Both of these settings are commonly used for training which involves acquisition of knowledge and/or attitude change.

Skills Training

Almost all reasonably large companies have formal in-house training programs. These programs rely most heavily upon the use of such well-established techniques as lectures, job rotation, and on-the-job training although techniques such as simulation, role playing, and programmed instruction are growing in popularity (Utgaard & Davis, 1970). Skills training may be contrasted with other kinds of training in that it requires some provision for actually performing the task under supervision. Such training may be conducted on the job, in a vestibule school or by otherwise simulating the work environment in an apprenticeship program or in a vocational school.

On-the-Job Training. The oldest and simplest approach to training a new employee is to orient him directly on the job under the close supervision of a foreman, a trained instructor, or an experienced operator. Ideally, on-the-job training should involve a systematic program of instruction, supervision, and evaluation of trainee progress. Too often, however, this type of training is conducted unsystematically.

The defects in unsystematic on-the-job training are all too obvious. Although the trainer is a skilled and experienced operator, he may be unable to teach this skill to others. Many husbands, for example, are excellent automobile drivers but are utterly incapable of teaching this skill to their wives.

Furthermore, the skilled employee who is supposed to act as the trainer may perceive the training situation as an opportunity to enjoy a vacation with pay. He may relax, read the paper, socialize with other on-the-job trainers while the trainee gains experience. Thus, the learner does not get the close supervision he needs and may require an unduly long period of time to become proficient at the job. He may, in addition, practice improper work habits leading to undue spoilage, and perhaps to unnecessary injury as well as to poor productivity.

Another difficulty sometimes encountered with on-the-job training results from the fact that the employee-trainer may actually resent the presence of the trainee. Such resentment, when it occurs, often reflects insecurity. Skilled employees may, for example, fear displacement by younger men and object to teaching skills and shortcuts developed through years of experience.

The aforementioned criticisms of on-the-job training apply, of course, only to such training at its worst. At its best, when the trainer has been taught how to teach, when he is made to feel secure and needed so that he does not fear displacement, and when he is made to realize the importance of maintaining vigilant supervision, this approach to training can be exceedingly valuable.

Vestibule Training. A vestibule school is a separate room or building within a company that is equipped with production equipment and staffed by full-time instructors. It is an industrial plant in miniature in which trainees learn their jobs under conditions like those found in the working environment except that close supervision by skilled trainers is assured and production pressures are not present.

In spite of the relatively high expense of vestibule training, it offers certain rather distinct advantages. Since the focus in vestibule training is learning rather than production, a greater amount of individualized attention can be given to the trainee's problems than is possible when he is trained on the job. Furthermore, whenever there are several openings, the vestibule school can allow the trainee to try out for various jobs rather than assuming a specific job assignment right from the beginning.

The advantages of vestibule training predicated upon provision of optimal learning conditions are, of course, immediately diminished whenever the vestibule school becomes a repository for obsolete equipment. Whatever economies management may seek to effect in this fashion are countermanded by the consequence that employees are trained to do a job with equipment they will not find in the plant.

Simulation. As is true for vestibule training, simulation provides opportunities to gain experience under close supervision but without the pressure of maintaining an output schedule or performing under circumstances where the stakes are real. Obvious applications of simulation training include flight training for pilots in transition to a new aircraft and the extensive simulations by astronauts prior to each mission. In these and similar situations the simulations provide tests both of equipment and men without actual risk to either.

Business games, role playing, and case problem discussions are often used for simulating managerial decisions for the purpose of management training as described in Chapter 13.

Apprenticeship. Apprenticeship training is utilized to prepare journeymen in skilled trade areas requiring relatively prolonged preparation. The period of apprenticeship varies from one to seven years, four years being quite typical.

Modern apprenticeship practices are quite different from the early practice described at the beginning of this chapter. Today's apprentice proceeds through a formal program of training, spending specified periods of time working at various kinds of jobs and taking certain courses. His hours of work are generally the same as those of employees within the department in which he is being trained, and he is paid a salary with provision for a systematic wage increase.

Satisfactory completion of apprenticeship makes the trainee eligible for admission to his trade union. Thus, apprenticeship training programs represent joint efforts of trade unions and industrial organizations to maintain a high level of preparation for certain skilled trades like carpentry and tool and die making.

Outside Training.   A good deal of vocational training is given outside of industry in trade and vocational high schools and in colleges and universities. Many schools offer shop training, specific vocational preparation in fields like automotive repair, and courses in clerical skills including typing and shorthand. The danger in such training is that it may tend to emphasize outmoded practices and obsolete equipment. It is an unusual publicly supported school, indeed, which can furnish its vocational shops with the most modern equipment and staff them with personnel familiar with current vocational practices.

Programmed Self-Instruction

The armamentarium of training techniques available to an industrial trainer is essentially like that available to any vocational teacher. These include such familiar techniques as lecture, discussion, demonstration, films and television, simulators, and so on. In addition, the training director has available to him such less familiar techniques as programmed instruction, sensitivity training, role playing, and case conferences. Since the three latter techniques are especially appropriate to supervisory and management training, their discussion is deferred until Chapter 13. We will consider programmed instruction in the remainder of this section.

All *good* instruction, regardless of the manner of presentation, is "programmed" in the sense that the material to be taught is organized, sequenced, and presented in steps calculated to maximize learning efficiency. Thus, although widely used as a designation for a particular instructional technique, the term *programmed instruction* does not fully convey the other essential components of the technique. These include: (*a*) self-pacing whereby the rate at which the learner masters the material determines the rate at which new material is presented; (*b*) active participation by the learner; and (*c*) immediate feedback to the learner about the correctness or incorrectness of his response. The designation *auto-instructional procedure* is sometimes used interchangeably with programmed instruction. Another frequently used synonym, *teaching machines,* implies that programmed instruction entails the use of some sort of hardware. Although in fact it often does, programmed material can be presented in other ways including books, films, computers, and sheets of questions. The essence of programmed instruction, regardless of how the materials are presented, is the program itself; that is, the sequence and organization of the informational bits contributing to the development of the desired terminal behavior.

Programmed self-instruction is not a new concept. The original teaching machine was invented in the mid-twenties as an elaboration of a device permitting students to score their own objective tests (Pressey, 1926). The rationale was that this machine would facilitate learning in two ways. First, by scoring his own test and *immediately* learning the right answer, the student learns from the test itself. Second, by including diagnostic self-testing along with other traditional forms of instruction, the student is encouraged to identify for himself those areas requiring further study. Thus, programmed self-instruction was originally conceived as a supplement to more traditional teaching procedures. The technique gained few adherents until the mid-fifties when the procedure was elaborated for complete rather than supplemental instruction and given support grounded in reinforcement learning theory (Skinner, 1954).

Programming. The teaching materials for programmed self-instruction are presented in small units or "frames." Each frame presents or reviews a bit of information building upon previously presented frames and requires the learner to respond. Immediately following his response, the learner is given feedback about its correctness or incorrectness.

These qualities are illustrated by the programmed segment shown in Figure 7–3. This segment is taken from a programmed booklet (Milton & West, 1961) describing the nature of programmed instruction. The frames preceding the ones selected for this illustration introduce the learner to the fundamental notions of stimulus, response, and association. Those following this segment apprise the learner of other elements of programming: frames structured with small, logical steps, presented at a rate appropriate to the learner; and provision of immediate knowledge of results following an active response by the learner.

FIGURE 7–3

A Segment of a Program concerning Programmed Instruction

Instructions: Read each frame carefully and fill in the blank(s). Verify the accuracy of your response against the answers provided in parentheses.

13. One important condition for effective learning is suggested by the phrase "learning by doing." The learner should not be passive. Instead, he should make an active _____ to each stimulus.   (Response)

14. The piano student does not learn a new "piece" just by silently reading the music; he plays it. He makes active responses to the printed notes which serve as _____.   (Stimuli)

15. Few of us are aware, however, that in *all* learning—not just in physical skills—it is preferable that the learner not be passive. On the contrary, he should make _____ responses to _____.   (Active; Stimuli)

16. Much of instruction consists of a teacher talking and students (sometimes!) listening. Stimuli are presented, but active _____ are not made to them.   (Responses)

17. Textbooks resemble lectures in that, although they present _____, readers rarely make _____ responses to them.   (Stimuli; Active)

18. Contrast the steps or statements you are reading here with those in an ordinary textbook. Here you not only read; you also fill in blanks. This is to insure that your responses are _____ ones.   (Active)

The program illustrated in Figure 7–3 is *linear,* that is, each learner proceeds in sequence through every frame. The steps presented in each frame are very small ones calculated to generate a high proportion of correct response and, hence, of positive reinforcement.

In contrast, a *branched* (or "intrinsic") program provides remedial material when the learner responds to a frame incorrectly. These remedial frames may differ depending upon the type of error made by the respondent.

Research on Programmed Instruction. The evidence concerning the relative effectiveness of programmed instruction in comparison with other training methods is equivocal. Savings in training time (and hence in cost) have, for example, been reported when programmed instruction was substituted for the original training program for mail-order employees and telephone relay adjusters (Hickey, 1961) and for teaching insurance fundamentals (Hedberg, Steffan, & Baxter, 1965). The most reasonable conclusion from these and similar studies is that, for appropriate material, programmed instruction is faster but probably does not lead to greater proficiency on an immediate posttest of acquisition (Campbell, 1971). Whether or not programmed instruction encourages superior long-term retention of the material learned is still an open question.

Although, as discussed in the ensuing section on "evaluating training outcomes and procedures," the assessment of any training method poses difficult problems, programmed self-instruction does seem to have unique strengths for certain purposes. Since it is individually paced, it may be more efficient than instruction geared to the average learner. And since programming by its very nature compels close attention to training objectives and the sequencing of information, well-designed programmed materials are likely to be well organized and free from extraneous details.

However, programmed self-instruction is not a panacea either for training or education. The development and pretesting of effective programs is costly. Whether or not the gain in training economy (when there is one) warrants the cost must be assessed in each instance. Furthermore, since the program is self-contained, it must provide a complete learning experience.

The sensible alternative to an all-inclusive, self-contained program is to combine programmed instruction with other procedures permitting the learner to obtain whatever clarification he needs. Otherwise, the necessity for comprehensiveness in structuring the program tends to lead to undue repetitiveness and miniscule increments of information from frame to frame. A consequent decline in motivation when the program is a lengthy one is almost inevitable.

EVALUATING TRAINING OUTCOMES AND PROCEDURES

The evaluation of a training program rests in large measure both upon the adequacy of the criteria of training effectiveness and of the research design for investigating the attainment of these criteria. There is a pronounced tendency for companies to evaluate their training efforts by assessing trainee reactions to the program (that is, how well they liked it) rather than measuring the consequences of the program for actual job behavior (Catalanello & Kirkpatrick, 1968). Trainee attitudes are, to be sure, one useful criterion for evaluating training outcomes and procedures. However, favorable attitudes in the absence of demonstrated corresponding improvements in job behavior are of only marginal utility.

The following list (Lawshe, 1944) is only a sampler of the kinds of behavioral measures that can be applied when evaluating training programs:

1. The number of man-hours per unit of product.
2. The amount of time required to bring a new employee up to a specified quantity or quality performance level.
3. The average production per unit of time after a specified number of hours or days on the job.
4. The average production performance of employees with varying amounts of training when length of the training period is not standardized.
5. The number of employees required to do a job or to produce a specified number of units.
6. The average straight time hourly earnings when piecework or a bonus plan is in use.
7. The average amount of merit increase received after a specific period of time on the job.
8. The average merit rating score.
9. The average quantity or value of scrap produced.
10. The average number of "reworks."
11. The accident frequency rate.
12. The number of man-hours of lost time from accidents.
13. The number of hospital visitations.

Procedural Comparisons

The time-honored research design for investigating the relative effectiveness of alternative training programs (for example, classroom versus programmed instruction) is to compare posttraining criterion scores for groups trained by each of the procedures under consideration. The overwhelming finding following this design, both for assessing formal educational procedures and industrial training procedures, is that of "no significant difference"; that is, groups of learners do about as well regardless of how they are taught.

However, it has been suggested (Siegel & Siegel, 1967) that this finding is frequently an artifact of an inappropriate research design which fails to take into account the interactions between the instructional procedure and other pertinent elements of the teaching-learning configuration.

Clearly, one such element is the learner. The finding that mean criterion scores are not significantly different for two groups trained in two different ways may mask the fact that procedure A is actually superior for learner type X and inferior for learner type Y, whereas the converse may hold for procedure B.

When this rationale was applied to learners differentiated by level of academic ability, for example, it was discovered that the conditions facilitating learning were quite different for low-ability and high-ability undergraduate students. The facilitating learning environment for *low-ability* students was one that reduced their perception of the likelihood of failure and directed their attention to the material to be learned. Their performance was adversely affected by circumstances increasing their perception of the likelihood of failure and/or directing their attention away from the content to be learned. The facilitating learning environment for *high-ability* students was one providing an intellectual challenge appropriate to the level of their ability. Again, the converse of this condition (that is, a perception that the material was too easy) adversely affected performance by high-ability students.

The implications of generalizations like the foregoing for training are relatively clear. Linear programming with small steps and considerable repetition is likely to be more appropriate for low- than for high-ability trainees. Likewise, classroom instruction to large groups wherein the students are relatively anonymous and therefore free from the likelihood of educational threat (for example, televised instruction) is more likely to satisfy the needs of low- than high-ability learners.

The implication of this emphasis upon studying interactions between features of the training procedure and other aspects of the teaching-learning complex rather than making control-group comparisons is also clear. It is relatively inappropriate to inquire whether one training procedure is as good as or better than another. The more significant question requires much more specificity; that is, for what kinds of learners, under what kinds of conditions, and for the attainment of what objectives does a given training procedure optimize learning?

Such a question recognizes the idosyncratic nature of learning. When properly answered, it will lead to one of two alternatives. First, it can specify a very carefully designed program for selecting trainees who are sufficiently homogeneous with respect to the critical learner characteristics required by the training procedure in use. Alternatively, if such selection is infeasible, it must lead to the development of multiple parallel training programs each calculated

to optimize training outcomes for homogeneous subgroups of trainees.

TRAINING THE TRAINER

The success or failure of a training program depends in large
measure upon the quality of instruction given to the trainees. A
criticism, mentioned earlier, of many training programs is that they
are founded upon the erroneous premise that men who know how to
do a job are automatically qualified to teach others how to do it.

The value of training the trainer is illustrated by a study conducted by Bavelas (1946). Learning curves were plotted for three
groups of trainees, all taught by the same instructor. At the time he
trained the first group, the instructor had received no training in
teaching methods; he had received partial instructor training in the
second group; and in the third, he had completed the training
program. The extent of instructor training is reflected in the performance of the trainees being taught by him as shown in Figure
7–4.

FIGURE 7–4

Learning Curves of Trainees of an Instructor at Various
Stages of the Instructor's Own Training

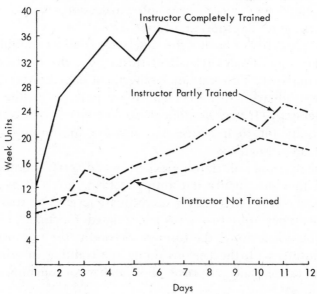

Granting the necessity for training the trainer, there remains the fundamental question of who should conduct the training of line personnel.

Who Should Train?

Industrial training may be regarded either as a line function or as a staff function. In the former instance, the employees are trained by their immediate supervisor. In the latter, training is administered either by a separate training department or by an outside consultant.

Although there may be certain circumstances in which training must be administered by the training department or by an outside consultant, this type of administrative arrangement is less satisfactory than is training by immediate supervisors and foremen. The danger inherent in classifying training as a staff function is that this arrangement may lead to behavioral change in the classroom but not in the working environment. The trainee learns to give the correct responses in the presence of the expert but does not transfer these responses to the job itself.

The immediate supervisor is in the final analysis the person who determines how employees will behave. He enforces certain standards of satisfactory performance and is most immediately responsible for the employee's success and job satisfaction. He is, in consequence, the most appropriate trainer.

The desirability of having the supervisor conduct training for his immediate subordinates is evident throughout the entire organizational framework. This kind of arrangement does, however, become increasingly difficult to implement as we progress up the management hierarchy. It may be difficult to convince busy executives of the necessity for their active participation in training their immediate subordinates.

Where does the staff training expert or industrial training department fit into the picture if training is to be given at each supervisory level to the immediately subordinate level? The staff training department performs two vital and related functions. First, it is responsible for training the trainers. Secondly, the training department consults with the persons doing the training in order to develop, evaluate, and improve the quality of ongoing training programs.

SUMMARY

Training objectives follow logically from a systematic determination of training needs. These objectives, in turn, suggest the ways in which training will be conducted, the persons who will be trained, and a scheme for evaluating the effectiveness of the program.

A properly conceived training program permeates all levels of an industrial organization. The need for management and supervisory development programs has been increasingly recognized in recent years.

Successful training programs are predicated upon certain basic psychological principles of learning. The most important of these principles is that a person learns only when he *wants* to learn. Motivation for learning requires that the trainee understand the reasons for training requirements, be provided with knowledge about his progress during the program, and be permitted to achieve short-term intermediate subgoals.

Motivation is enhanced also by the proper decomposition of a task into its meaningful parts for training purposes, the presentation of these parts in an appropriate sequence, and by training sessions that are of optimal length. These matters require that research be conducted in each instance to define the parts to be taught, the sequence in which these parts are to be presented, and the most appropriate spacing of training sessions.

In addition to providing for trainee motivation, the program must include provisions for selecting trainees. Marked differences exist in the ability of individuals to profit from industrial training.

Finally, skills training is sterile unless it contains the element of closely supervised practice. The reason for requiring very careful supervision during this phase of the program is that improper or inappropriate behaviors which are practiced may be learned quite as efficiently as correct behaviors. Mistakes must therefore be corrected as soon as they occur.

The training program must be internally constituted and sequenced to encourage positive transfer both within the program itself and from the program to actual job performance.

In many ways, industrial training is similar to other kinds of formal education. Neither should be permitted to evolve by happenstance. Both must be carefully designed most efficiently to implement the learner's attainment of the desired goals. This means that training programs must take into account the terminal behavior desired, the characteristics of trainees admissable to the program, and the interdependence of work roles within the entire system.

Training may be conducted in any number of sites including, in addition to the classroom and home study, training on the job and in a vestibule school. Likewise, the instructional procedures for training are diverse including lectures, discussions, demonstrations, simulation, and so on.

One technique that has gained recent attention is programmed instruction characterized by self-pacing, active learner participation, and immediate reinforcement. Programmed instruction is not a panacea either for education or training. The evidence concerning its effectiveness is conflictual. Furthermore, the cost of program development may mitigate against its use except when relatively large numbers of persons are to be trained.

The evaluation of alternative training procedures has generally not been fruitful. The typical research finding is that learners profit about equally irrespective of the instructional procedure. This chapter suggests that such findings may be artifactual, resulting from the application of an inappropriate research design to an inappropriate question. It suggests further that such evaluations are most meaningful when they delineate those interactions between learners, instructional conditions, and training objectives that optimize learning.

Retraining has become an increasingly important social problem. The evidence thus far available points to the greater importance of attitude over ability as a determinant of acceptance of new work roles and retraining programs.

A key feature of any training program, regardless of its nature, is the trainer himself. He must be capable of teaching his knowledges and skills to the trainee and be willing to do so. Many training programs are open to criticism because they are founded on the erroneous premise that men who know how to do a job are automatically qualified by virtue of this knowledge to teach others how to do it. Nothing could be farther from the truth. It requires the possession of skill as a trainer to be an effective teacher.

However, this does not imply that industrial training should be conducted only by training specialists, that is, consultants or the staff training department. The immediate supervisor is in the final analysis the person who determines how employees will behave. He enforces performance standards and is most immediately responsible for the employee's success and job satisfaction. He is, in consequence, the most appropriate trainer. The role of the staff training department is to teach the supervisor how to train and to consult with supervisors in order to develop, evaluate, and improve the quality of ongoing training programs.

III.

Human Factors Psychology

We turn now from concern with preemployment and training practices to consideration of some job-related factors influencing the employee's performance after he is hired. Appropriate selection, placement, and training procedures themselves contribute to facilitating job performance by increasing the likelihood of matching job requirements with abilities and interests. A further contribution is made by arranging working conditions, including equipment, to capitalize upon the strengths and to minimize the influence of the limitations of the human organism.

Chapter 8 considers the effect upon performance and attitudes of certain aspects of the physical work environment. In particular, attention is given to the relationship between work behavior and industrial illumination (including color), noise, music, and ventilation. In addition to summarizing information about the influence of these environmental conditions, this chapter discusses two methodological problems associated with investigations in this and other areas. One of these is the "Hawthorne effect"; that is, performance improvements attributable to improved motivation ancillary to changed environmental conditions rather than to the actual nature of the change. The other methodological problem is the discrepancy sometimes evident between findings from laboratory and field studies.

Even a well-trained employee working under optimal environmental conditions may experience fatigue as a consequence of prolonged work, or boredom as a result of monotonous work. Since both of these conditions interfere with effective performance, their assessment, nature, and procedures for their alleviation are also discussed in Chapter 8.

Another condition of efficient industrial performance is safety (Chapter 9). Accidents are here regarded as a kind of undesirable behavior due in part to correctable deficiencies in the working situation and in part to improper but correctable employee attitudes. The fact that proportionately few accidents can be attributed to equipment malfunctions seems to indicate that engineering principles related to safety have been relatively well developed and widely accepted. Thus, in this chapter, we are concerned primarily with the human factors responsible for accidents and with procedures for preventing their occurrence.

This part is terminated with a discussion of engineering psychology (Chapter 10). Machine and plant design were regarded as the sole province of the engineer until fairly recently. However, technological advances and man's activities in new environments, including space and ocean depths, made imperative an increased concern for planning and designing equipment in the light of the capabilities and limitations of prospective human operators. The engineering psychologist seeks to develop an optimally functioning unit of man and machine, that is, a man-machine system.

8. Work Environment

This chapter concerns two sets of factors potentially affecting job performance. One of these is the provision of appropriate working conditions, like rest periods and job rotation, to minimize the deleterious effects of fatigue and boredom. The other is the arrangement of the physical working environment in those ways calculated to make it easier for employees to do their work.

The physical working environment has probably been manipulated and studied by more legitimate professionals and self-styled experts than any other aspect of business and industry. Management is bombarded by literature describing the beneficial effects of certain color schemes and of piped music and is led sometimes to expect a tremendous increase in productivity if the water cooler is relocated or if bowling alleys are installed for employee recreation.

There is no doubt that an uncomfortable or unpleasant working environment may be partially responsible for lowered productivity, increased spoilage, and unnecessary accidents. Furthermore, work may be made less fatiguing and employee morale improved by creating a more pleasant and efficient work environment. The thing that must be remembered, however, is that often a change in the physical working environment is paralleled by a temporary increase in industrial productivity because of improved morale rather than a real improvement in conditions of work. It is imperative that environmental manipulations producing only transitory effects be distinguished from environmental changes having lasting beneficial effects. The phenomenon whereby environmental alterations lead to temporary improvements in productivity attributable to morale improvement is sometimes referred to as the "Hawthorne effect" after the initial studies which called particular attention to it. These studies are discussed in some detail in Chapter 11.

FATIGUE AND BOREDOM DIFFERENTIATED

Fatigue and boredom are factors of considerable consequence in industry. The most apparent indicators of either of these conditions is diminished output and increased spoilage. Secondary effects include increased turnover and accident rate. Although the correlates of fatigue and boredom are on the whole somewhat similar, the nature of these conditions and the factors responsible for them are quite different.

The Nature of Fatigue

Fatigue is a complex phenomenon from both a physiological and a psychological standpoint. Prolonged muscular activity eventually produces physiological changes, including the accumulation of waste products resulting from the activity of the muscles and depletion of the reserve of carbohydrates which serve as fuel for such activity. In addition, the continuation of activity ultimately leads to unpleasant subjective feelings of strain or tension. These two types of change, the physiological and the subjective, do not, however, parallel each other very closely. Furthermore, the time at which either of these changes occurs and the intensity of their occurrence correlates only imperfectly with a measurable decrement in productivity.

The absence of a close relationship between the physiological changes, the subjective experiences, and productivity are evident in situations in which persons fatigued from a physiological standpoint may continue to maintain a high level of productivity and may not report feelings of tiredness. It is apparent that strong motivation, like that encountered during athletic contests or in defense plants engaged in wartime production, may reduce or almost obliterate any noticeable deterioration in performance. Conversely, poorly motivated persons may experience subjective feelings of fatigue, and their output may decline, some time in advance of the physiological changes associated with fatigue.

It is difficult to formulate a definition of fatigue because of the imperfect relationship between its physiological and subjective components. The formulation of a definition is further complicated by the fact that the relationship between the physiological and subjective changes accompanying fatigue may be either reduced or accentuated by motivational factors. It will be satisfactory for our purposes to define fatigue in terms of its practical implications in the industrial setting. It is a temporary condition resulting from prolonged muscular activity and is manifest in a declining capacity for continued work.

The Nature of Boredom

Boredom is sometimes thought of as a kind of "mental fatigue," implying that it results from a psychological rather than a physiological cause. This distinction considerably oversimplifies the situation since, as we have already said, fatigue also entails a psychological or subjective component.

It is, perhaps, most meaningful to distinguish between fatigue and boredom on the basis of the kind of activity that generates these experiences. Fatigue results only when the person is engaged in prolonged muscular activity. Boredom results when the activity is regarded as monotonous or uninteresting. Prolonged muscular activity is not a necessary precursor to boredom. We may be bored, for example, when we read an uninteresting book, listen to a dull lecture, or watch a trite television program.

A further distinction between fatigue and boredom is predicated upon the fact that the former tends to generalize, while the latter is highly specific. When we are fatigued, we seek rest from all activity. When we are bored, we seek relief only from the monotonous activity. This fact should not be taken as an indication that boredom is somehow less significant or less important than fatigue. The production decrement for tasks regarded as monotonous is quite as real and as serious as that which accompanies the performance of fatigue-producing tasks.

FATIGUE

The fact that fatigue reduces the capacity for further work is amply illustrated by studies of industrial productivity or output during the course of a typical working day. A schematic plot of average hourly output for an industrial task involving motor activity is shown in Figure 8–1. The irregularities which are always apparent when such a curve is plotted have been smoothed in order to make the fundamental trends more apparent. Note that prolonged motor activity is characterized by an initial period of

FIGURE 8–1

A Schematic Plot of Average Hourly Output for Complex Motor Work

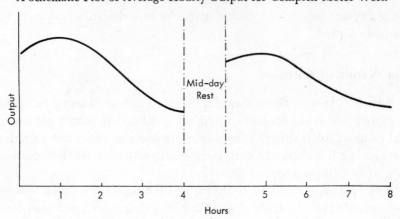

Hours

Source: R. A. Katzell. Fatigue and its alleviation. In D. H. Fryer & E. R. Henry, *Handbook of applied psychology*. New York: Holt, Rinehart & Winston, 1950. P. 75.

"warm-up" followed by a decline in output during the latter hours of the morning, and again toward the end of the work period.

Such a graph suggests that the examination of production records throughout the course of the workday may serve to identify the existence of fatigue. Furthermore, the comparative analysis of such records obtained under varying circumstances probably indicates something about the relative amount of fatigue experienced under these circumstances. Although output curves can be used in this way, they are not entirely satisfactory as indices of the existence of fatigue or as measures of the amount of fatigue generated by particular tasks. Any record of employee performance reflects the factor of motivation in addition to the effects of fatigue. Thus, a decline in output may be erroneously attributed to fatigue when in fact it may result from a progressive decline in interest. Conversely, of course, the output rate may remain high in spite of fatigue because of a high motivational level.

It is obvious, also, that many kinds of jobs do not lend themselves to work-curve analyses. It is possible to graph output only when the work is repetitive and when some kind of production unit can be counted. Work which varies in nature, like that of an office secretary, does not provide equivalent units which can be summated and graphed. Under such circumstances, the existence of fatigue must be verified by some other method.

Measurement of Fatigue

One of the first things to suffer as a person becomes fatigued is his "timing." This calls for precise receptor-effector coordination in order to produce the smooth patterns required for such skilled activities as hitting a baseball or flying an airplane.

Clearly related to the matter of timing is *vigilance*, that is, alertness in monitoring and responding to critical stimuli. The automobile driver, for example, must be continuously aware of and responsive to road conditions, other traffic, pedestrians, highway signs and signals, the feel of the car, and information provided by his instruments. A typical laboratory task for assessing vigilance requires the subject to respond in some way (say, by pressing a button) when a slowly moving light intersects the crosshairs marked on an oscilloscope. The variance of an individual's responses about his mean response has been found to increase as a function of fatigue. Thus, whereas pilots completing this task prior to a flight mission exhibited a relatively narrow range of response times, the variability of their vigilance responses increased markedly after a prolonged flight (Fraser, 1958).

Fatigue is obviously a complex phenomenon. There are individual differences in susceptibility to fatigue under similar circumstances and intraindividual differences in susceptibility on different occasions. We have previously alluded to one of the reasons for the complex nature of fatigue; it is both a physiological and a psychological phenomenon. The intimate relationship of these two components of fatigue has been clearly demonstrated in an investigation wherein the actual work load was increased without the subjects' knowledge (Hueting & Sarphati, 1966). In spite of the fact that they believed the physical demands of the experimental task to be constant, the subjects reported increased feelings of fatigue paralleling actual increases in the work load.

Some attempts separately to measure the physiological and subjective components of fatigue are described below.

Physiological Components. Some of the very early studies of fatigue were directed toward the measurement of the limitations upon prolonged work imposed by the musculature. The device used for such studies, known as an *ergograph,* permits for the conduct of fatigue experiments involving specific muscles or muscle groups. A weight is attached by a cord to an extremity of the body (for example, the fingertip or the hand) and the rest of the limb is strapped in order to inhibit movements of the muscles that are not under investigation. The subject is required to raise the weight periodically at a signal, and the height of each lift is automatically recorded. This recording, called an *ergogram,* is really a plot of the work decrement accompanying prolonged activity of the muscle or muscle group being studied. An ergogram produced by a subject required to lift a weight using one finger is illustrated in Figure 8–2. Note the progressive deterioration in his performance.

FIGURE 8–2

An Ergogram

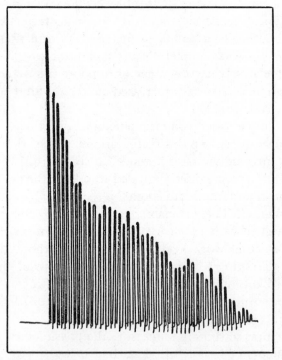

Each stroke represents a complete cycle of lifting and dropping the weight. The temporal sequence is from left to right.

Source: T. A. Ryan. *Work and Effort.* New York: Ronald Press, 1947. P. 50.

Ergographic studies clearly demonstrate that there is a considerable range of individual differences in the amount of prolonged muscular work that can be performed. The tracings obtained from different subjects vary tremendously with respect to the maximum level of performance, the length of the period during which near-maximum performance is maintained, and the rate at which performance deteriorates. This suggests, of course, that there are individual variations in susceptibility to the physiological components of fatigue. Again, however, it is important to realize that some portion of the differences obtained from ergographic studies must properly be attributed to variations in the motivational levels of the subjects rather than to variations in susceptibility to physiological fatigue.

A more direct approach to the measurement of the physiological aspects of fatigue requires a study of the involuntary physiological processes themselves while work is being performed. Such factors as oxygen consumption, muscular tension, and circulatory activity have been found to be related to fatigue and are relatively, although not completely, independent of motivational factors. This approach to the measurement of fatigue is, however, generally too unwieldy for use in industry.

Subjective Components.   The subjective component of fatigue (that is, feelings of strain or tiredness) have also been explored. It has long been known, for example, that feelings of weariness generally occur prior to a noticeable decrement in actual performance (Poffenberger, 1928). Such subjective fatigue does, however, tend to parallel production curves even though it anticipates them. Workers report the greatest feelings of tiredness when they begin work in the morning, immediately prior to lunch, and again immediately prior to the time that their shift ends (see Figure 8–3). You will recall that the typical curve of industrial productivity exhibits declining output also at these three periods.

Perhaps the most surprising aspect of industrial fatigue, defined either in terms of subjective feeling or in terms of output, is that it does not appear to accumulate continuously throughout the workday. Workers neither produce less nor do they feel more weary in the midafternoon than in the midmorning. Furthermore, both productivity and feelings of tiredness at the end of the shift are about the same as they are immediately prior to lunch. It is certain that a 45-minute or one-hour lunch period is not, itself, sufficiently long to dissipate completely the physiological component of fatigue. These

FIGURE 8–3

Percent of Employees Reporting Maximal Feelings of Tiredness at
Each Hour of an Eight-Hour Work Shift

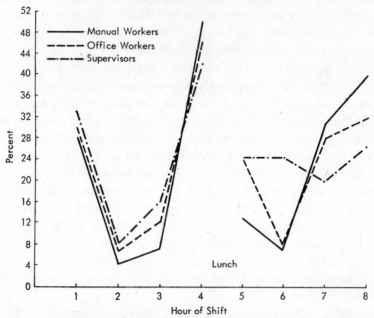

Source: J. W. Griffith, W. A. Kerr, T. B. Mayo, Jr., & J. R. Topal. Changes in
subjective fatigue and readiness for work during the eight-hour shift. *Journal of
Applied Psychology*, 1950, *34*, 163–66.

findings again reinforce the importance of motivational factors in
offsetting at least partially both feelings of fatigue and the concomi-
tant work decrement associated with it.

Alleviation of Fatigue

It is apparent that certain difficulties are encountered when the
psychologist studies fatigue. These difficulties are inherent in the
formulation of a definition of fatigue, in measuring it, in reconciling
discrepancies between its physiological and subjective components,
and in separating out the effects of fatigue from those attributable to
declining interest and motivation. In spite of these problems, however, the reduction of industrial fatigue is of extreme practical
importance.

The findings of ergographic studies and of other types of observations relative to the widespread individual differences in susceptibility to fatigue suggest that appropriate selection and placement procedures can serve as a partial solution to the problem. The assignment of employees to jobs should not be predicated solely on the fulfillment by them of the necessary experiential and educational requirements. The state of their physical health and the likelihood that they will experience real satisfaction from their work are factors that must be considered also in order to minimize susceptibility to fatigue.

The attempts of the psychologist to reduce the fatigue experienced by employees presently on the job are, in general, directed toward the maintenance of productivity or output while simultaneously reducing the effort or input required of the employee. Thus, the alleviation of fatigue involves for the most part the manipulation of certain features of the physical working environment. It is imperative that the beneficial effects accruing from the actual reduction of effort be sorted out from those effects attributable to the improved employee motivation which often accompanies the conduct of this type of investigation. You will undoubtedly recall the implications of the Hawthorne studies in this regard.

Length of the Work Period. Since fatigue is generated by prolonged activity, one avenue to its alleviation is the reduction of the length of the working period. The length of the typical working day and workweek has been progressively shortened during the past several years and in all likelihood will be further shortened within the next few years.

Unfortunately, the matter of the optimal length of the work period is too often approached with a background of misconceptions that appear on the surface to be reasonable. Representatives of management are sometimes heard to express concern about reduction in the length of the work period on the grounds that this will force an undue decline in productivity and create certain social problems related to the increase in available leisure time. Union representatives, on the other hand, may perceive reductions in the length of the workweek as an indirect device for increasing employee salaries and as a means by which the number of available jobs may be increased.

Both of these points of view stem from the erroneous assumption that productivity is directly related to the amount of time spent at work. The fact of the matter, however, is that changes in the length of the work period do not yield proportional changes in productivity. It is helpful, in this regard, to differentiate between *nominal* and *actual* hours worked. The nominal hours of work are defined by the clock, that is, the employee checks in and out at specified times and is nominally on the job for the number of hours elapsing between his check-in and check-out times. It is apparent, however, that he does not actually produce during this entire period. Virtually every job entails a certain amount of unproductive time, some of which is scheduled (for example, formally recognized rest periods) and some of which is not scheduled. We are dealing, after all, with a human being rather than with a machine. He alters his work pace, he has good days and bad days, he becomes tired and must rest, he experiences boredom and takes a break, and so on. Thus, the critical factor affecting productivity is actual rather than nominal hours worked. It has been found in general that increases in nominal hours decrease actual hours worked and conversely that decreases in nominal hours tend to be accompanied by increases in actual hours worked. Employees for whom the length of the workday and workweek both are lengthened spend on the average proportionately less time each hour in productive work.

The impact of lengthening the workday *without* a corresponding increase in the length of the workweek (for example, the 4-day, 40-hour week) is still in doubt pending further systematic research on this fairly recent innovation. One cross-sectional survey of employees who had been working on a four-day schedule for unspecified periods of time concluded that they overwhelmingly regarded the change as beneficial both to their work and to their home lives (Steele & Poor, 1970). Although a similar conclusion followed from analysis of questionnaire responses of pharmaceutical employees shortly after a four-day week was instituted, this conclusion was tempered by results obtained with the same employees about a year later (Nord & Costigan, 1973). One year after the change, the effects of the four-day week on home life were perceived as significantly less positive than at first, particularly for male employees. With respect to job performance a year after institution of the modified workweek, absenteeism continued to be low, but employees on slower paced jobs were less favorably inclined toward the change than those on faster paced jobs.

It seems clear that when additional data are available, the success of such programs will be seen to depend upon factors idiosyncratic to both the employee and the nature of his work. From the employee's viewpoint, the desirability of a three-day weekend every week depends upon his options for using his leisure time. Whether or not he can and will maintain a satisfactorily high level of performance during a 10-hour workday will also be influenced by the fatigue engendered by the task itself. The interaction of these two factors—the incentive value to the particular employee of longer weekends, and task-engendered fatigue—varies both with employees and jobs.

Rest Periods. The effect of authorized rest pauses during the day has been investigated rather extensively. It has been demonstrated that employees will rest regardless of whether or not rest periods are scheduled. A careful study of unauthorized breaks taken when formal rest periods were introduced into the work schedule of comptometer operators (McGehee & Owen, 1940) indicated that the effect of the authorized rest periods was to produce a sharp decline in unauthorized breaks and an increase in productivity.

The beneficial effects of scheduled rest pauses accrue from the fact that such pauses provide opportunities for a partial recovery from fatigue and for a change of pace which undoubtedly helps to relieve boredom. The mere fact of a scheduled rest period is, however, an insufficient guarantee of its effectiveness. The time of the day at which such breaks are scheduled, their frequency and duration, and the employee activity during the rest period may all be of considerable importance.

There is considerable variation between companies in the number and length of scheduled rest periods, even for jobs essentially similar. The typical procedure is to schedule one rest around midmorning and another around midafternoon, each period being 10 to 15 minutes in length. The ideal schedule for rest pauses is something that must be determined for each kind of work. It is likely that each rest period ought to be somewhat longer for very strenuous tasks than for light work. It is probable, also, that rest periods should be scheduled with greater frequency when the task is monotonous or physically taxing than when it is interesting or relatively sedentary.

An examination of the production curve during the course of the day can furnish very helpful clues about the specific times at which rest periods should be introduced if they are to be most beneficial. You will recall that the typical output curve for fatiguing work (Figure 8–1) indicates that productivity declines sometime after midmorning and again sometime after midafternoon. The usual practice is to schedule rest periods immediately prior to these declines in productivity in order to forestall their occurrence (see Figure 8–4).

FIGURE 8–4

Effects of Authorized Rest on Production during the
Morning Hours

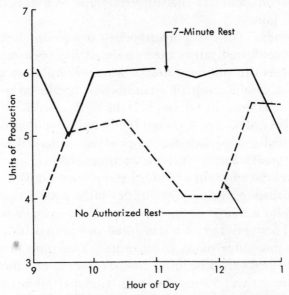

Source: J. Tiffin & E. J. McCormick. *Industrial psychology.* P. 489. Drawn from data by E. Farmer & S. M. Bevington, an experiment in the introduction of rest pauses, *Journal of National Institutional and Industrial Psychology*, 1922, *1*, 89–92.

The time scheduled for rest must be used wisely if the break is to be most beneficial. Employees engaged in heavy labor should relax; employees engaged in sedentary activity should move about and experience a change of scene. The rest period should provide a variation in pace and an opportunity for fatigue to be dissipated.

Miscellaneous Environmental Factors. Many of the environmental conditions that serve to accelerate or retard the development of fatigue are discussed later in this chapter. Reduction in the prevailing noise or vibration level and improvements in illumination and ventilation may lead to both improved output and diminution in subjective feelings of tiredness. Changes in work methods or in equipment design may materially decrease industrial fatigue by making it easier for the employee to do his work.

BOREDOM

We have already mentioned that the effects of boredom and of fatigue have much in common. Both may lead to increased turnover, spoilage and accidents, lowered morale, and subjective feelings of strain or discontent. Both factors also affect productivity. The output curve for monotonous work, however, is sometimes differentiated from that resulting from fatiguing work by the appearance of an "end-spurt" in anticipation of release from the task (see Figure 8–5).

FIGURE 8–5

Schematic Plot of Average Hourly Output for Monotonous Work

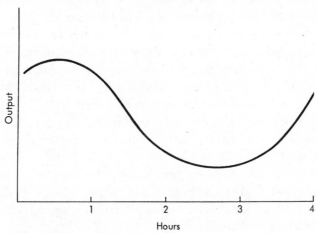

Source: R. A. Katzell. Fatigue and its alleviation. In D. H. Fryer & E. R. Henry, *Handbook of applied psychology.* New York: Holt, Rinehart & Winston, 1950. P. 75.

Whereas it was once believed that such an end-spurt output curve was invariably associated with monotonous work, there is evidence to the contrary. For example, Smith (1953) plotted the output of piece-rate operators in a knitwear mill against time of day and correlated these factors with self-reports of boredom. It was noted here that the shape of the output curves for any operator varied markedly from day to day. Also, there was no noticeable trend toward end-spurt curves for those operators reporting the most boredom.

In interpreting her findings, this investigator makes the important point that production curves are sensitive to factors other than the simple one of subjectively experienced boredom. An important such factor is self-pacing. Employees engaged in repetitive work often develop an output standard for themselves. If near the end of the day, they are behind schedule in terms of this standard, they tend to rush in order to catch up. Likewise, if they are ahead of this self-imposed schedule, they tend to slow down. The former would be reflected in an end-spurt, whereas the latter would, of course, have the opposite effect.

Personal Characteristics Related to Boredom

Monotonous tasks are thought of typically as being rather routine and highly repetitive. The relationship between the nature of the task and the experience of boredom is not nearly as direct, however, as the relationship between the kind of work performed and the experience of fatigue. Tasks that are monotonous for some workers may be rather interesting and challenging for others. Thus, boredom results from a lack of interest in the work. The experience of boredom is dependent upon the character of the work *as it is perceived by the worker* rather than upon the character of the work as it may be described objectively.

Remedies for boredom are predicated upon an understanding of the factors that lead workers to regard their jobs as monotonous. The factors which have been explored in this regard include intelligence, interest, and personality.

Intelligence of the Employee. It is reasonable to anticipate that jobs requiring either more or less intellectual capability than the worker possesses will prove to be monotonous. It is difficult for workers who are too intelligent for their tasks to maintain a continuing interest in it. The job does not challenge them sufficiently and therefore does not provide them with a feeling of satisfaction and accomplishment. Conversely, workers placed on jobs requiring more intellectual capability than they possess may also be expected to lose interest in their work because of the frustration of continual failure. It is not gratifying to be confronted continually by one's shortcomings.

It has been found, for example (Bills, 1923), that highly intelligent employees performing simple clerical tasks had a much higher turnover rate than did less intelligent employees on the same job. Turnover may be regarded as a partial indication of boredom since some employees undoubtedly terminate their employment in order to accept a more interesting job. It is likely, however, that many workers leave their present employment in order to accept a higher paying but not necessarily more interesting position. This factor confounds the utilization of turnover as a criterion of boredom.

The relationship between intelligence and boredom has been studied more directly by comparing the average intelligence test scores of workers who completed a questionnaire appraising the degree of boredom they experienced on the job (Wyatt, Langdon, & Stock, 1937). The average intelligence of the groups of workers reporting the most boredom tended to be higher than that of workers reporting the least boredom. The differences between the mean test scores of these groups did not, however, always meet the requirements for statistical significance, and the groups utilized for the study were very small in size (4 to 10 persons each).

Although there is some evidence in support of a relationship between employee intelligence and boredom, this relationship is by no means as strong as one might suppose. It is apparent that other factors, including interest and personal adjustment, may operate to counteract or minimize this relationship.

Employee Interests. The kinds of activities that interest us are determined in part by our intellectual capacity and to a large extent by our past experiences. We develop our own unique pattern of interests on the basis of the successes which we have experienced in the past and the environment to which we have been exposed. Thus, we each have proclivities toward certain kinds of industrial activities and away from other kinds of activities.

Individual differences with respect to interest were demonstrated by having workers in a candy packing department alternate on five different jobs for one month each. The employees were questioned about the amount of boredom they experienced on each of the five jobs, and highly individual patterns of boredom were discovered. A job that was the least interesting for one worker often proved to be the most interesting for another.

Personality. Attempts to establish a "personality pattern" characteristic of workers who are easily bored as differentiated from

those who withstand boredom have not been outstandingly successful. One investigation of the problem (Wyatt et al., 1937) led to
the conclusion that extroverted persons tend to experience boredom
more readily than introverted persons. Presumably, this relationship
exists because introverted workers are less dependent upon social
stimulation for personal gratification and are therefore better able to
function under conditions involving repetitive activity and relative
isolation. It has been found, also, that older employees and those
who prefer a degree of regularity in their daily activities are least
susceptible to boredom during repetitious work (Smith, 1955).

These bits of evidence provide meager clues to the relationship
between personality patterns and susceptibility to boredom. The
relationships are neither sufficiently strong nor sufficiently consistent
to permit the utilization of such measures for predictive purposes.

A more promising approach to this problem focuses upon employee needs and personal adjustment as the critical factors rather
than upon identification of a personality pattern associated with
boredom. A job which is satisfying to the employee and provides
him with a feeling of accomplishment and a sense of personal worth
is rarely regarded as monotonous. Work, on the other hand, that
does not provide the employee with a degree of job satisfaction is
often boring regardless of the nature of the activity performed. In
many ways, the factors responsible for job satisfaction are quite
similar to those responsible for deriving satisfaction from life in
general. Employees who seek variation in activities after working
hours tend also to derive the greatest amount of job satisfaction
when their work is varied in nature. Similarly, employees who are
dissatisfied with life in general and who are poorly adjusted in their
familial and home relationships tend to be dissatisfied with their
work and to be most susceptible to boredom.

Alleviation of Boredom

Industrial automation has made it possible within certain limits
to eliminate many routine and highly repetitive jobs. Automated
equipment cannot, however, relieve workers from all such tasks.
The equipment itself generates some new jobs of a repetitive nature
and many rather routine industrial activities are not amenable to
automation. In addition, the fact that boredom is a function of the
worker's perception of the job rather than of the characteristics of

the job as objectively defined implies that a certain amount of monotonous activity will always be present in industry.

Personnel Selection and Placement. One solution to the problem of boredom entails the utilization of appropriate personnel selection and placement procedures. A gross mismatching of the job and the worker relative to such factors as his intelligence, interests, and other personal characteristics should be avoided. Even the most careful selection and placement program will not, however, be a full solution to the problem. Selection and placement procedures must be supplemented by measures designed to reduce the boredom that is an inevitable consequence of certain kinds of work for some employees.

Motivation. The fundamental consideration in alleviating boredom is, of course, that of increasing the employee's interest and involvement in his work. This can be accomplished in a number of ways. Almost any job assumes additional significance for the employee when he is informed about the relationship between what he is doing and the end product being produced. It is imperative that the training program for new employees include some kind of an overview of the entire industrial operation and an indication of the role played in this operation by the individual worker.

Typically, employees are presumed to be motivated by instructions to do their best. However, laboratory findings confirm the superiority of a specific assigned work goal over this kind of abstract instruction. This superiority is evident both in terms of actual output and subjective reports of freedom from boredom. Subjects for this study (Locke & Bryan, 1967b) had to perform a complex psychomotor task requiring them to match patterns of lights shown on a display panel by manipulating controls consisting of foot pedals and a joy stick. Half the subjects were instructed to do their best; the other half were assigned a goal specifying the number of correct matches they were to attempt to make. For these latter subjects, the goal for each trial was always set above the number of matches successfully made during the previous trial. Figure 8–6 shows the superiority of establishing specific and relatively difficult performance goals for maintaining a reasonably high level of interest in an essentially monotonous task.

These findings suggest that it may be possible to reduce boredom on many repetitive tasks by having the worker periodically (each day or hour) set determinate goals. Further research is needed both

FIGURE 8–6

Effect of Performance Instructions upon Boredom Ratings
(higher scores indicate greater interest and less boredom)

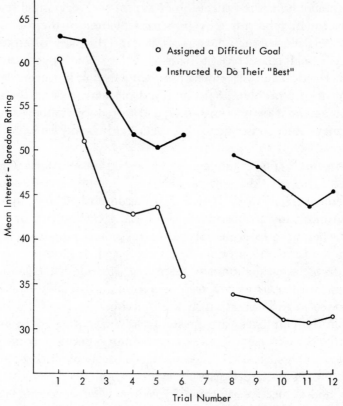

Source: E. A. Locke & J. F. Bryan. Performance goals. P. 127.

to test the applicability of this laboratory finding in the field and to determine the optimal level of difficulty at which goals should be set.

Job Enrichment. It is often possible to permit employees engaged in fragmented work a greater amount of responsibility for planning and organizing their activities. Such enlargement of the scope of the work, or job enrichment, provides the worker with a degree of variety which can be very helpful in counteracting boredom. Although we will note in Chapter 12 that some writers (Herzberg, 1968) regard job enlargement as a key factor in enhancing employee motivation, studies of its effectiveness have generated conflictual findings. Not all employees experience increased satisfaction following enlargement of the scope and, hence, the complexity of their work tasks.

It has been suggested (Hulin & Blood, 1968) that workers' attitudes toward tasks and job enlargement are affected by broadly based cultural factors. Those workers who feel alienated from middle-class values (for example, blue-collar workers in urban locations) experience *less* rather than more satisfaction when their work assignment is made more complex. Conversely, nonalienated workers (white-collar workers and blue-collar workers from rural locations) seem to derive enhanced job satisfaction from increased task complexity.

It is clearly premature to prescribe job enrichment as a motivational panacea for all employees engaged in monotonous work. As is true of such other efforts to enhance job satisfaction as the 4-day, 40-hour week, the effectiveness of job enrichment is moderated both by the nature of the task and by personal factors unique to the employee's history.

Other Approaches. When job enlargement is infeasible or judged undesirable, a lesser degree of variety may be introduced into work by job rotation. Several employees, each performing a different monotonous task, may be permitted to change jobs with each other periodically. The actual change in activity combined with a change in the physical and social environment relieves the routine and thereby often enhances the maintenance of task interest. This may well justify the added costs incurred by job rotation.

Certain other approaches to alleviating boredom are based upon factors other than that of increasing the employee's interest in his work. Strategically placed rest pauses, for example, are very helpful in forestalling the experience of boredom. Similarly, music may serve as a mild diversion acting to make time seem to pass more quickly and the job itself to seem more pleasant. Finally, bonus payments for productivity in excess of some established minimum may reduce the deleterious effects of boredom upon output.

THE WORK ENVIRONMENT

In addition to the job task itself, the physical environment in which work is performed may contribute to undue fatigue and have other deleterious industrial consequences. The sections that follow discuss selected aspects of the visual, auditory, and atmospheric surroundings in which work is done.

Illumination

The prevalence of visual defects among industrial employees is somewhat surprising. A company program to detect and correct such defects is likely to improve efficiency markedly. Motorola, Inc., for example, found that about 30 percent of the workers in one of its inspection departments had faulty vision (Piper, 1951). Correction of these defects led to decreased absenteeism, diminution in complaints about the product from the field, and a lower turnover and accident rate. Thus, the relatively small expenditure by a company to check upon and correct visual defects would seem to be extremely worthwhile.

Intensity. Industrial requirements in terms of the amount of light on a work surface vary considerably with the nature of the task to be performed. In general, work involving precise manipulation of small objects requires more intense illumination than does work involving the manipulation of large objects for which precision is not a critical requirement.

Although illumination intensity requirements increase as the task makes increased visual demands, attempts to formulate generally useful sets of intensity recommendations have generated considerable controversy. While Tinker (1947) concluded that 40–50 foot candles is sufficient illumination for even the most severe industrial tasks, others (General Electric Co., 1960) have recommended minimum intensities as high as 200 footcandles for automotive final assembly and inspection, and 2,000 footcandles for cloth inspection.

Such divergent recommendations result in part from differing definitions of criteria of "effective seeing." The criterion problem aside, however, it is evident that any set of intensity recommendations must properly be considered rough guides rather than definitive statements of illumination requirements for specific tasks in particular work settings. It is impossible accurately to generalize about intensity requirements alone, without regard for the factors that may interact with intensity. These potentially interactive variables include: (a) such other characteristics of illumination as glare, spectral composition, and amount of reflected light; (b) characteristics of the visual task, including the nature of the work, and the contrast between the work object and the background against which it is seen; and (c) the entire range of physical, social, and personal factors influencing job performance. Once these factors are specified for a particular job, it is a relatively simple matter to determine optimal illumination requirements for that job by empirical test.

Distribution and Reflection of Light. Virtually everyone is acquainted with the visual discomfort experienced when reading directly under a lamp that is the sole source of illumination in the room. Whenever the visual field is shifted from the well-illuminated page to the poorly illuminated surroundings, the pupil of the eye dilates. Similarly, the pupil contracts when shifting from low to high illumination. Excesses of pupillary activity are fatiguing; they cause eyestrain. Consequently, it is advisable to have the light well distributed throughout the visual field. It is for precisely this reason that television viewing in a moderately lit room is preferable to viewing in a totally darkened room.

Solutions to the problem of glare are relatively simple. They include the proper shading of lamps, the elimination of highly reflective surfaces from the visual field, and the diffusion of light at its source.

Color

Many extravagant claims have been made about the beneficial effects of using certain colors or color combinations in industry and in the home. Not all of these claims, however, are supported by valid evidence. It is quite true that the appropriate use of color can do much to provide a safer, more pleasant, and more efficient working atmosphere. Such benefits result from painting the equipment and background in such a way as to: (1) indicate danger zones, traffic patterns, fire and safety equipment, and so on; (2) focus attention upon the critical elements in the visual field; (3) provide ample reflection without glare; and (4) provide a restful visual relief when the employee turns momentarily from his work. About the only thing that can be said about the overall color scheme or *decor,* however, is that it should be one that is not regarded by employees as unpleasant.

The color of the walls and ceilings surrounding the immediate work area can do much to produce either visual comfort or discomfort. These surfaces must reflect an adequate amount of light without either producing glare or an undue contrast in brightness with the working area. Surfaces painted white, cream, or ivory reflect a considerable amount of light; pastel shades have intermediate reflectance values; and shades of brown, dark red, dark green, or dark blue have low reflective values. The appropriate wall and ceiling color will depend, quite obviously, upon the adequacy of the lighting and the specific type of work being performed.

Another factor that may affect decisions about the wall color to be used is the color of the material upon which work is being performed. All of us rest our eyes momentarily by looking away from the work surface. You look away from the textbook occasionally, for example, when you are reading; and your eyes wander away from the instructor or demonstration during a class period. Similarly, the industrial employee looks up from his work periodically.

An interesting illustration of the relationship between these brief visual rest periods and the optimal color for painting the surrounding surfaces occurred in the inspection room of a textile mill (Stauffer, 1947). The inspectors were scanning bluish denim, searching for defects. The walls were painted white to provide high reflectance on the assumption that the high illumination level would facilitate the inspection process. This assumption was entirely correct, but it neglected one important feature of the job. Since the employees were staring at the denim for relatively long periods of time, they reported a disturbing visual "afterimage" (peach color, in this instance) when they looked up from their work to rest their eyes momentarily. This negative afterimage, which is always the complement of the color to which the eye has been exposed for a prolonged period, interfered with normal vision for a while after the inspectors returned to their task. The simple solution in this case was to paint the walls in the color demanded by the eyes—that is, peach.

The aesthetic value of particular hues and their influence upon behavior has been the subject of some investigation and considerable discussion. Darker hues create the illusion of pulling walls in or ceilings down; lighter hues create the visual impression of added spaciousness and airiness.

Colors on the red side of the spectrum are regarded as *warm*, exciting colors; those on the green and blue end of the spectrum are regarded as *cool*, tranquilizing colors. The distinction between warm and cool colors is regarded as extremely important by most interior decorators and color consultants and is exploited in a variety of ways. Persons are presumed to move more rapidly, to talk with greater animation, and generally to maintain a higher level of excitation in a predominantly red-orange environment than in a blue-green environment. Thus, an environment that is meant to be relaxing and calming ought to be painted in cool colors. The suggestion is sometimes made that work involving the generation of considerable heat should be performed in a room painted in cool colors, while large, vaulty work areas should be painted in warm colors.

Such generalizations about the effect of color upon mood or subjective experiences of warmth and coolness are not well documented. We learn to make associations relative to particular colors and attach our own personal significances to particular hues. The range of such associations is tremendous, and generalizations about them are quite tenuous.

Noise

In assessing the industrial effect of noise, we must be concerned both with employee output (productivity) and with the input (or energy) necessary to achieve or maintain a given level of productivity. The finding, for example, that employees can adjust to noisy conditions without a production decrement would in itself be rather unimportant if this adjustment required them to expend considerable additional effort in order to maintain their productivity. Such additional effort would be reflected in undue fatigue, leading, perhaps, to job dissatisfaction and consequent personnel turnover and to an increased accident rate.

The interpretation of the effects of any environmental condition is complicated by differences in investigatory procedure. It is convenient in this regard to distinguish between "laboratory" and "field" studies. The former kind of investigation requires that groups of persons (either employees or persons assumed to be like employees) be removed from their actual working environment and required to perform in an artificially created environment. The task they perform for experimental purposes may be identical to the one they do on the job, or it may be a special task designed to incorporate the major elements of their job task.

Field studies, on the other hand, are performed in the working environment. It is possible within certain limits to manipulate the environmental conditions in an office or a factory. It is also possible on occasion to study groups of employees performing essentially the same job but working in different environments.

The fundamental difference between these experimental procedures is an important one. The Hawthorne effect, noted earlier, may be confounded in laboratory investigations by the fact that the entire setting is artificial. Thus, the discrepancy in experimental procedure (that is, laboratory versus field investigations) may account in part for discrepancies in the outcomes of studies concerned with noise and music. The amount of agreement based upon solid evidence concerning these variables is not outstanding.

Psychological Studies of Noise.   Sounds differ with respect to loudness, pitch, and quality. Furthermore, a given sound may be continuous or, as most often the case in industry, intermittent. Considered together, these variables serve to distinguish between "pleasant" or "desired" and "unpleasant" or "unwanted" sounds. For practical purposes, the latter is what is meant by noise. Virtually all studies of industrial noise have been concerned with sounds that are reasonably loud, unpleasant in pitch and quality, and varying in continuity. There is, however, another aspect of sound having some bearing upon work efficiency, that is, its meaningfulness. It is considerably easier to disregard meaningless extraneous sounds (like the clatter of a typewriter) than it is to disregard meaningful sounds (like the conversation of other students in the study hall).

Several of the early laboratory investigations indicated that following the onset of noise, there is a minor decrease in productivity after which productivity increases above the level attained when the environment was relatively quiet. The maintenance of productivity is accomplished, however, at the worker's expense. He must exert additional effort to maintain his output. It has long been known, for example, that noise leads to increases in muscle tension and metabolic rate (Harmon, 1933). These physiological changes are noted most immediately after the onset of noise. They decline, indicating diminished exertion, after a period of time during which the employee adapts to the noise.

The generalization that workers can adapt to noise and equal or surpass their former production level is, however, an artificial one. This generalization is founded upon laboratory investigations in which the participants were highly motivated and performed tasks requiring the exertion of short spurt-like efforts. These conditions are unlike those found in many industrial settings.

In contrast, Jerison (1959) examined the effects of noise upon sustained performance, leading to boredom and fatigue. Groups of subjects were required to monitor a panel of dials under conditions of "relative quiet" and "noise." The former condition consisted of a background sound of approximately 80 decibel intensity (about as loud as the noise present in a typical office). The noisy condition consisted of sound intensity in excess of 110 decibels (about as loud as the sound of thunder).

The subjects were required to work for periods of two hours. Under the control condition, the laboratory was relatively quiet for the full time; under the experimental condition, the laboratory was relatively quiet for one-half hour and noisy for the remaining 1½ hours. The results, showing the average performance at the end of each half hour under these conditions, are shown in Figure 8–7. It

FIGURE 8–7

Average Performance under Conditions of Relative Quiet and Noise

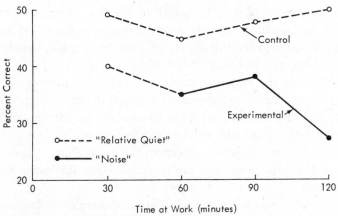

Note that the initial discrepancy between the experimental and control groups was maintained at a constant level for the first hour and a half. The deleterious effects of noise were apparent only after two hours.

is evident that the deleterious effects of noise upon the performance of this task (which required the maintenance of vigilance) became evident only after a relatively long period of time.

We will consider the results of one additional investigation (Broadbent & Little, 1960) of particular interest for three reasons: (1) it was a field rather than a laboratory study, (2) the performance investigated was manual rather than mental work, and (3) a deliberate attempt was made to control for the Hawthorne effect. The latter was accomplished by having the same subjects work under noisy and quiet conditions.

The investigators studied the output and other measures of efficiency for groups of employees working for periods under pre- and postnoise reduction conditions. These workers operated equipment perforating the side of movie film. Since they normally shifted from one room to another in a systematic cycle of six weeks, this was chosen as the length for experimental and control periods. Noise reduction in one of the workrooms was accomplished by baffling between rows of machines and acoustic treatment of the walls and ceilings.

The outstanding finding was that although noise reduction did not improve the rate of work, it significantly reduced shutdowns due to operator error and calls for maintenance. The magnitude of reduction in human errors following noise reduction led the investigators to hypothesize an interaction between noise and other features of this particular job, including the low illumination levels required for handling film. If such an interaction existed it might have acted to magnify the effects of noise reduction beyond what would be observed in other work conditions.

Nevertheless, the conclusions from this field study are consistent with those derived from laboratory investigations of high-intensity, meaningless, and continuous noise upon tasks requiring continuous attention. Noise does not markedly affect productivity defined by work rate. It does, however, increase the frequency of momentary lapses in attention and is thereby responsible for some kinds of human error.

As with other factors in the work environment, it is impossible to formulate a generalization about the psychological effects of noise applicable in all circumstances. Whether or not the potential of noise for increasing human errors is of practical importance depends upon such things as the kind of work being done, the characteristics of the noise, and other aspects of the physical and social working environment.

Physiological Damage.   Noise can have serious consequences apart from those regarded as fundamentally psychological in nature. Workmen's compensation is provided persons with hearing loss attributable to industrial noise. Legal proof of auditory damage is typically based upon the factors of intensity and length of time the worker is exposed to the noise. The New York State Workmen's Compensation Board, for example, uses the following standards in evaluating claims: (1) most persons will suffer permanent damage in a matter of months if exposed to over 120 decibels of noise for several hours daily; (2) a considerable portion of workers can suffer permanent hearing damage from exposure to 100–120 decibels for

TABLE 8–1

Typical Sound Levels for Selected Noise Sources and Environments
(distances are indicated in feet where appropriate)

Noise Source	Decibel Level	Environment
Hydraulic press (3')	Above 130	
Large pneumatic riveter (4')	121–130	Boiler shop (maximum level)
Trumpet auto horn (3')	111–120	Jet engine test control room
Cutoff saw (2')	101–110	Inside DC-6 airliner
Heavy trucks (20')	91–100	Inside Chicago subway car
10-hp outboard	81–90	Inside sedan in city traffic
Autos (20')	71–80	Office with tabulating machines
Conversational speech (3')	61–70	Average traffic (100')
	51–60	
	41–50	Average residence
	31–40	
	21–30	Broadcasting studio (music)

Distance in feet from noise source.
Adapted from A. P. G. Peterson & E. E. Gross, Jr. *Handbook of noise measurement*. New Concord, Mass.: General Radio Co., 1963. P. 4.

several hours daily; (3) a few persons may be permanently damaged by exposure for many years to noise between 90 and 100 decibels.

The meaning of these decibel levels is clarified in Table 8–1.

Other factors interact with noise intensity and duration of exposure to cause permanent hearing loss. These include the continuity and pitch of the noise, and the health, age, and susceptibility of the listener.

Music

You undoubtedly have certain personal feelings about the desirability or undesirability of having a radio or a record player operating while you are studying. It is likely, also, that you know someone (perhaps your roommate) who feels quite differently from you about this matter. The interesting thing about this kind of discrepancy in attitude toward music as a facilitator or inhibitor of work is that there is a direct relationship between attitudes toward music and productivity during music periods.

This relationship has been investigated in the following way (Baker, 1937). Two groups of subjects were each required to do arithmetic calculations during a sequence of music periods and non-music periods. The groups were each given a different *set* or expectation regarding the effects of music. One of the groups was informed at the beginning of the experiment that the music would probably interfere with its ability to do mental arithmetic. This expectation was reinforced by the presentation of data allegedly showing that this finding had resulted from a previously conducted experiment. The other group was told that previous research had indicated that music facilitates mental arithmetic, and appropriate documentation was presented to this group also. The actual arithmetic performance of the subjects in these groups indicated that their productivity was directly related to their expectations concerning the effects of the music (see Figure 8–8).

From these and other findings, it is evident that unqualified claims for increased production resulting from the introduction of music at work are not proven. Some of the factors influencing the effect of music upon productivity, aside from the individual's expectations, are the kind of work being done and his preferences concerning music. Not all workers, in fact, like music. It is estimated (Uhrbrock, 1961a) that from 1 to 10 percent are annoyed by it.

Nature of the Work. Music is most likely to be beneficial for work that is of a short-cycle and highly repetitive nature. Such work often does not utilize enough of the employee's abilities. His attention is not absorbed by the task, and he regards the work as monotonous. The hours of the day tend to move slowly, and the employee may experience very little personal satisfaction. In such circumstances, music may increase productivity and worker satisfaction. It is pleasantly diverting and may make time appear to move more rapidly.

FIGURE 8–8

The Effect of Expectation about the Effects of Music
upon Actual Performance

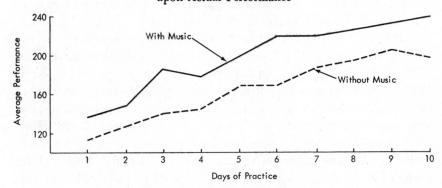

A. Music Suggested as Facilitating

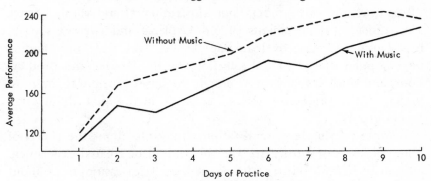

B. Music Suggested as Inhibiting

The performance of subjects during music and nonmusic sessions was compared for two groups.
A. Music was suggested as facilitating performance.
B. Music was suggested as inhibiting performance.

The beneficial effects of music under such circumstances were demonstrated quite clearly by a very careful investigation involving a large number of employees engaged in radio assembly (Smith, 1947). It was found that a production increase attributable to music was considerably more marked during the night shift than during the day shift, although music was beneficial also during the day. Employee reaction to the music was extremely favorable; only 2 percent of the workers indicated that they did not care at all for it.

The effect of music is, of course, to distract the worker. Music is beneficial both to productivity and morale only when such distraction is desirable. Thus, it must be emphasized that results favorable to music are generally obtained only for employees performing routine, repetitive jobs. More complex jobs requiring a greater amount of employee attentiveness generally are performed better in the absence of any distracting influence.

Kinds of Music. It is not clear whether output is affected by the type of music played, in spite of employee preferences for certain types of music. Factory operators participating in one study (Kerr, 1945), for example, were found to prefer popular and march-polka music over waltz-Hawaiian music. Furthermore, output and quality were lowest on days when the latter kind of music was played. However, comparable results were not obtained in a more recent study with assembly-line workers (Newman, Hunt, & Rhodes, 1966). Here, performance was compared for four kinds of music conditions and a control (no music) condition. The types of music were: show (Broadway musical numbers, both instrumental and vocal); dance (instrumental arrangements of old favorites and current songs); folk (vocal selections by Joan Baez, Peter, Paul, and Mary, and so on); popular (largely vocal selections by the Beatles, the Brothers Four, and similar groups). Although the latter music was the most preferred, this preference was not reflected in the quantity or quality of output.

Because no simple generalization is possible about the effects of different kinds of music, this variable should be treated experimentally in each work setting without making prior assumptions about the likely impact of different types of music.

The typical practice when making use of music in an industrial setting is to restrict each music session to a 20- to 40-minute period. These periods are generally inserted into the midmorning and midafternoon schedule at about the time when monotony and fatigue reach a maximum. Some companies make a practice also of scheduling music periods at the beginning and at the end of the shift. This procedure is presumed to create a pleasant working environment when the employees begin and terminate the day's work.

Temperature and Ventilation

Industrial ventilation is of considerable interest because of the demonstrated relationship between this environmental factor and such criteria as productivity, spoilage, and accident rate. A substantial body of research has been conducted relative to the three essential components of ventilation: temperature, humidity, and air movement. It has been found that control of any one of these factors is by itself relatively valueless unless the others are controlled also. A temperature of 90° F, for example, is much less comfortable when the humidity is high and the air relatively stationary than it is when the humidity is low and the air is in motion.

Thus, it is much more meaningful to consider *effective temperature* than it is to consider absolute temperature (as measured by a dry-bulb thermometer). The effective temperature scale combines the subjective effects of temperature, humidity, and air movement. When air movement is at a minimum, a dry-bulb temperature of 90° F at 10 percent humidity constitutes the same effective temperature (that is, is as comfortable as) a temperature reading of 75° F at 100 percent humidity or a reading of 80° F at 60 percent humidity.

The relative comfort or discomfort experienced in a particular effective temperature is, of course, partially a function of the kind of work being performed. One reviewer (Connell, 1948) concluded, as a cautious generalization, that the maximum effective temperature for the performance of simple sedentary tasks without serious impairment is 85° F. Tolerance limits for heavy physical labor are, of course, much lower.

SUMMARY

The effects of changes in the physical working environment must be interpreted cautiously for a number of reasons. First, employees respond not only to an objectively definable change in illumination or noise level but also to their attitudes concerning such changes. If they interpret a change as evidence for the fact that management is interested in their welfare, they will respond positively and their productivity may increase. If, however, the employees interpret the change solely as an economy measure designed by management to get more for its money, actual productivity may decline.

Related to the matter of employee attitudes are the facts that short-term effects of environmental changes are insufficient as a basis for determining the true worth of such changes, and that the results of laboratory investigations are not always verified when similar changes are instituted in the field.

Finally, environmental changes which lead to a production increase are not always desirable. It would be unwise to institute any such change, even if it increased productivity and reduced expenses, if these outcomes were accomplished by forcing a considerable increase in employee input or effort. Such additional effort may lead to job dissatisfaction, increased spoilage, and accidents, all of which may well offset the advantages relative to improved productivity and economy.

Fatigue and boredom are both undesirable consequences of industrial activity. These conditions lead to diminished output and subjective feelings of strain and tension. Although the effects of fatigue and boredom are somewhat similar, the factors responsible for these conditions are quite different.

Fatigue is a temporary experience resulting from prolonged muscular activity, and it is characterized by a declining capacity for continued work. Boredom is differentiated from fatigue by the kind of activity that generates it and its rather high degree of specificity. Monotonous work is uninteresting to the employee. Furthermore, the bored worker seeks relief only from the activity he regards as monotonous, while the fatigued worker seeks rest from all activity.

The alleviation of fatigue may be approached in several ways including: (a) the use of appropriate personnel selection and placement procedures; (b) modifications in the length of the work period and the insertion of authorized rest pauses into the schedule; (c) improvements in certain environmental conditions including illumination and ventilation, and the reduction of undue noise and vibration; and (d) changes in work methods and equipment.

Because of the different nature and consequences of monotonous activity, remediational measures for boredom differ from those for fatigue. Boredom may be somewhat reduced by assigning employees to jobs that are congruent with their interests and capabilities. In addition, provision should be made in the training program for informing employees about the relationship between their particular job and the total industrial operation. Other approaches to alleviating boredom include job enlargement, job rotation, authorized rest pauses, music, and bonus payments for high productivity.

Studies of industrial illumination have indicated that the critical requirements for light intensity vary with the nature of the task being performed. Work involving the manipulation of small objects with great precision requires more intense illumination than does work involving the manipulation of large objects for which precision is not a critical feature. Light distribution and reflection are also important aspects of the visual environment. The entire visual field must be relatively evenly illuminated and glare must be eliminated if visual comfort is to be maximized.

The use of color in the working environment has been the subject of many extravagant claims, not all of which can be documented. The appropriate use of color can contribute to the safety and efficiency of the work environment. About the only thing that can be said about the overall color scheme or decor, however, is that it should not be regarded by the employees as unpleasant.

Noise may, but need not, impede industrial efficiency. Whether or not the potential of noise for increasing human error is of practical importance depends upon such factors as the characteristics of the noise, the kind of work being done, and other aspects of the physical and social working environment. Aside from the possibility of undesirable psychological consequences, certain kinds of noises are clearly responsible for auditory damage.

Music is a distracting factor and is thus most likely to be beneficial for work that is of a short-cycle and highly repetitive nature. More complex tasks requiring a greater amount of employee attentiveness generally are performed better in the absence of any distracting influence.

Psychologists and engineers have been concerned with three essential and interdependent components of ventilation: temperature, humidity, and air movement. These components, considered together, constitute the subjective factor of effective temperature. The worker's tolerance for a relatively high effective temperature is greatest if he is engaged in simple sedentary tasks and lowest if he is engaged in heavy physical labor.

9. Safety and Accident Control

Everyone regards war as a cause of extensive devastation, death, and injury. The weapons recently developed by man for destroying the enemy are horribly effective. Even during World War II, fought with much more rudimentary weapons, our own casualties between the start of the war and the surrender of Japan numbered in excess of 900,000 persons, almost one third of whom were killed. Thus, war injuries and death affected a group of persons comparable to the entire population of a fair-size city.

The destructiveness of a war, however, is exceeded by the sheer waste of human resources attributable to civilian accidents. The number of deaths and injuries from civilian accidents during the period of World War II exceeded those classified as war casualties. Accidental civilian deaths during this period numbered approximately 350,000, and injuries numbered 36 million (National Safety Council, 1946). Accidents in the home were responsible for the greatest proportion of these injuries and deaths, but occupational and automotive accidents also contributed substantially to this enormous waste of manpower.

We cannot, as a society, afford to neglect the matter of accident prevention. Research and the application of knowledge in this area is as critical as it is in combating such medical scourges as cancer and heart disease. The fatalistic notion that accidents cannot happen to us or that they will occur because of bad luck regardless of our efforts to prevent them is contrary to the facts. The role of luck (including such things as unavoidable equipment malfunction) as a cause of accidents has been the subject of considerable study. Esti-

240

mates of the percentage of accidents due to such causes, and therefore unpreventable, vary between 10 and 20 percent. The large majority of accidents are clearly due to human factors rather than to fate. The most efficient eyeshield in the world is valueless, for example, if an employee refuses to use it. And even a smoothly functioning aircraft is subject to pilot error involving misinterpretation of its instrumentation or poor judgment relative to landing conditions.

Accident prevention requires the joint efforts of engineers and psychologists. The fact that proportionately few accidents are attributable to equipment malfunction would seem to indicate that engineering principles related to safety have been well developed and widely accepted. The psychological factors responsible for accidents have been studied also, but there is some reticence about applying the knowledge now available in this area.

This chapter is concerned primarily with the human factors responsible for accidents and with certain procedures for preventing their occurrence. The fact that relatively little attention is given to many of the engineering problems related to safety should not be taken as an indication that these factors are unimportant. Rather, this emphasis reflects the fact that the majority of accidents are due to human factors rather than to equipment malfunction.

CAUSES OF ACCIDENTS

It is not difficult to understand management's concern for employee safety. Accidents are expensive. They are responsible for a direct cost in terms of diminished productivity, as well as for the related costs of providing medical attention and compensation. Accidents, furthermore, may have a deleterious effect upon plant morale. It is understandably disturbing to employees, for example, to know that they are working at a job that has led in the past to a substantial number of injuries.

Work in certain industries is more hazardous than in others. The lumber, mining, and construction industries characteristically rank higher with respect to accident frequency than do communications and electrical equipment. This discrepancy in safety record as a function of the industry suggests at least three general factors which are potential causes of accidents. The first, and most obvious, of these is the *physical working environment*. The greater the exposure of an employee to dangerous equipment and to unfavorable working circumstances, the greater is his liability to accidents. A second causal factor suggested by interindustry differences in accident frequency is *personal* in nature. Certain industries are more selective than others in hiring and retaining employees on the basis of such personal variables as age, prior experience, and physical health. Finally, industries (and individual companies within an industry) may differ markedly in the extent of their concern about employee *attitudes* relative to safety. Workers who are unimpressed by the potential of their surroundings and job activities for causing accidents are more likely to be injured than those who have developed attitudes of appropriate caution.

The Physical Work Environment

A good deal has already been said about the working environment in Chapter 8. Unfavorable or unpleasant environments are responsible for diminishing productivity and lowering job satisfaction. It should be readily apparent also that certain environmental conditions may be either direct or indirect causes of accidents. Improperly anchored equipment, for example, would be regarded as a direct causal agent. Such factors as improper illumination or ventilation may either act directly as causes of accidents by making it virtually impossible for the worker to perform with safety, or may act indirectly by making the job unpleasant and the worker incautious.

Ventilation. The component of ventilation usually explored with reference to accidents is temperature. The relationship between accident frequency and temperature is shown clearly in Figure 9–1. The employees upon whom these data were based were all engaged in factory work. Fewest accidents occurred when the temperature was about 68° to 70°; a noticeable increase in accident frequency was observed when temperatures declined. The discrepancy between the accident rates noted for men and women as the temperature increased above 70° is of some interest. It suggests the possibility that the adverse effects of high temperatures may be sex-linked. This conclusion is confounded, however, by the fact that men are generally assigned to jobs requiring a greater amount of physical exertion and hence may be more vulnerable to accidents as temperature increases.

FIGURE 9–1

Accident Frequency in Relation to Temperature

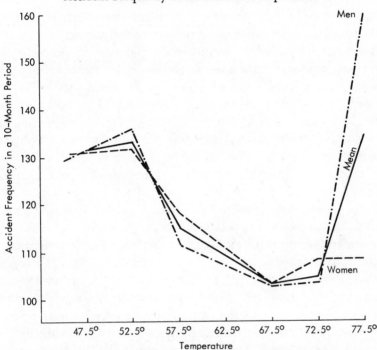

Source: E. E. Osborne & H. M. Vernon. *The influence of temperature and other conditions on the frequency of industrial accidents.* Industrial Fatigue Research Board, No. 19. London: H. M. Stationery Office, 1922.

The results discussed above were based upon records of relatively minor accidents. When coal mine accidents were classified according to severity (i.e., length of time absent from work), it was found that rising temperature increased the rate of minor accidents to a much greater extent than that of major accidents (Vernon, 1936). The discomfort associated with higher temperature probably leads to the kind of carelessness or indisposition toward work that is particularly responsible for minor accidents. The suggestion has been made, also, that workers may be more likely to use a minor injury as an excuse to take time off when the working environment becomes unpleasant.

Illumination. Twilight is a dangerous time of the day for driving simply because it is difficult to see under conditions of inadequate illumination. Defective illumination in industry is a rather obvious and easily correctible source of accidents.

Studies made some years ago of accident frequency under conditions of daylight and artificial illumination indicated that the latter circumstance produced a considerable increase in accident rate. Enormous improvements have been made by lighting engineers, however, since these investigations were conducted. The unshielded, low-intensity incandescent lamp should by now be a relic of the past. Proper artificial lighting still provides illumination that is somewhat inferior to daylight, but the differences are not great.

Equipment Design. The newspapers occasionally report an automobile accident occurring at night because the driver erroneously depressed his headlight button instead of his cigarette lighter. This kind of accident reflects the folly of poor equipment design and the sacrifice of safety in the interest of the aesthetics of dashboard arrangement. Many accidents can be avoided in circumstances in which rapid judgments are necessary by utilizing knobs of appropriate shapes and dials that are amenable to accurate interpretation. It is apparent that some automobile manufacturers are less impressed than they should be with the importance of proper equipment.

The design of manufacturing equipment with built-in safety devices and power cutoffs, and of special clothing that does not itself interfere with productivity, is a matter of very direct concern to industry. This is a particularly critical problem in circumstances in which the operation of the equipment demands continual exposure of the employee to moving parts, cutting edges, and flying debris.

This entire matter of the relationship between equipment design, intended function, and the capabilities and limitations of human operators is discussed in detail in the next chapter. As it relates to safety, proper equipment design requires a rather precise understanding of the sources of particular kinds of accidents.

This line of reasoning provided the rationale for a study of taxicab drivers with an abnormal number of accidents in which they were struck from behind (Babarik, 1968). These drivers were found to have a reaction pattern made up of slow initiation time and compensatingly fast movement time. Thus, they probably stopped their vehicles abruptly in a way that cannot be duplicated by a following driver. The two solutions proposed by the investigator are retraining and/or human engineering. The latter would call for changes in the braking system, perhaps adjusting it to the driver as one adjusts the seat.

Personal Characteristics of the Employee

The Metropolitan Life Insurance Company (1930) classified the causes of accidents experienced by employees of a railway company with the results noted in Table 9–1. About 20 percent of the acci-

TABLE 9–1

Causes of Accidents in the Cleveland Street
Railway Company

Faulty attitude	14%
Failure to recognize potential hazards	12
Faulty judgment of speed or distance	12
Impulsiveness	10
Irresponsibility	8
Failing to keep attention constant	8
Nervousness and fear	6
Defective vision	4
Organic disease	4
Slow reaction	4
High blood pressure	2
Senility	2
Worry and depression	2
Fatigue	2
Improper distribution of attention	2
Inexperience	2
Miscellaneous	6

dents were attributed to physical and personal disability (including defective vision, organic disease, worry and depression, and so on) ; the remainder were caused primarily by attitude factors.

Health. It is unnecessary to belabor the importance of physical health to safe industrial operation. An employee who is ill cannot devote the required amount of attention to his job and is likely to be somewhat careless.

The relationship between physical disability and accident liability is, however, a somewhat different matter. If the disability interferes with satisfactory job performance, the employee may experience an accident because of his defect rather than carelessness. One of the sources of accidents that can be most readily identified and easily corrected is defective vision. A comparison between the prevalence of visual defects among good and poor drivers, for example, indicated that accident-free drivers were significantly less susceptible to glare sensitivity, relatively free from astigmatism, and more likely to have adequate visual acuity (Fletcher, 1949).

Many companies have drawn up rather elaborate sets of physical specifications for various jobs in recognition of the fact that it would be utter foolishness to assign persons with certain disabilities to certain kinds of jobs. It is important to bear in mind, however, that the mere fact of the existence of a physical disability should not be construed as a contraindication for employment unless it is clear that the disability will interfere with satisfactory job performance. Quite often the handicapped worker, once aware of his limitations, can learn to compensate for a disability effectively. Thus, when handicapped workers are properly placed, employers report lower absenteeism and termination as well as accident rates than for able-bodied persons employed on similar jobs.

Age and Experience. The relationship between age and accident frequency reflects the operation of at least three variables which underlie the age factor: health, experience, and attitude. Younger employees as a group may be in better physical health than older workers, but they are more likely to be relatively inexperienced and somewhat more irresponsible. Studies of age as a cause of accidents are further complicated by the selective factors sometimes applied to older employees. Advancing age may be used by management as a reason for discharging an employee, particularly if he has a history of high accident frequency, or for reassigning him to less hazardous work.

The effect of this constellation of factors associated with aging is to produce consistent findings indicative of a lower accident rate for older than for younger employees. The data for workers in an ordinance depot, shown in Table 9–2, are typical of such studies. The incidental evidence apparent in this table, that men are more likely to have accidents than are women, is also a persistently recurring finding.

A similar pattern of accident frequency is discovered when accidents are plotted as a function of length of service or experience rather than of age. The more experienced employees (generally the older employees) have considerably fewer accidents than do the relatively inexperienced employees. That this is due to experience

TABLE 9–2

Tabulation of Accident Frequency
at an Ordinance Depot

Age Group	Male Rate per Hundred	Female Rate per Hundred
17–21	172	41
21–28	75	36
28–35	65	17
35–45	50	26
45–60	42	37
60+	35	0

Source: J. Mann. Analysis of 1,009 consecutive accidents at one
ordinance depot. *Industrial Medicine*, 1944, *13*, 368–374.

and is not merely an artifact of increased maturity is confirmed by
two studies: one with youthful employees (see Figure 9–2) and one
with older employees (see Figure 9–3).

In spite of the favorable safety record accumulated by older

FIGURE 9–2

Accidents Incurred by Young Employees as a Function of Years of
Experience

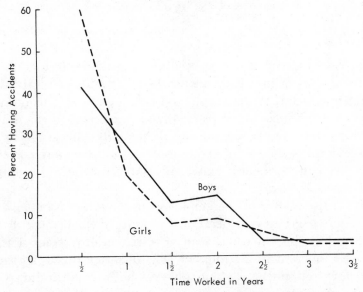

Source: H. M. Vernon. Prevention of accidents. *British Journal of Industrial
Medicine*, 1945, *2*, 3.

FIGURE 9–3

Accidents by Older Employees as a Function of Experience on the Job

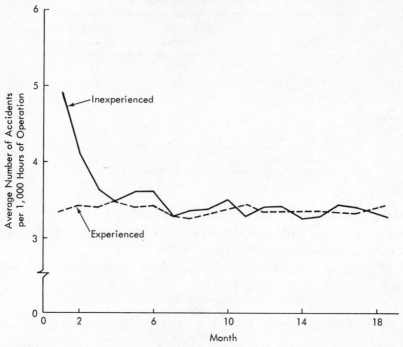

Source: R. H. Van Zelst. The effect of age and experience on accident rate. *Journal of Applied Psychology,* 1954, *38,* 313–317.

employees by virtue of experiential and attitudinal factors, there is a particular set of circumstances in which age must be regarded as a detrimental factor. Whenever the job makes physical demands upon the employee which are more readily satisfied by younger workers, the older employee is likely to be particularly susceptible to accidents. Thus, as shown in Figure 9–4, age is positively correlated with accident frequency under adverse temperature conditions when the work is strenuous.

The entire matter of the employment of older personnel is one that requires serious consideration by management because medical advances have increased our span of active, healthy years. There is no magic inherent in the number "65" dictating this as an age for mandatory retirement. Certain physical abilities, including vision and speed of reaction, are known to decrease with advancing age. There are, however, widespread individual differences in the rate

FIGURE 9–4

Accident Frequency of Coal Face Workers in Relation to Age
and Temperature

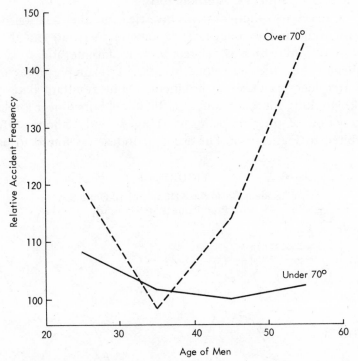

Source: H. M. Vernon & T. Bedford. *The absenteeism of miners in relation
to short time and other conditions.* Industrial Health Research Board, No. 62.
London: H. M. Stationery Office, 1931.

and severity of such impairments. Furthermore, the depth of job
knowledge accumulated by virtue of experience may act in many
instances to offset the physical accompaniments of aging. It is probably sensible to reassign many older employees to jobs that require
relatively little physical exertion and are not dependent upon rapidity of response, but it is both unwise and uneconomical to put all
older employees out to pasture.

Fatigue. You will recall from the discussion in Chapter 8 that
one of the effects of fatigue is to decrease productivity. This decline
in the output curve typically is observed during the periods immediately preceding lunch and the termination of the workday. The
same general kind of curve has been found to result when accidents

(rather than output) are plotted as a function of time of the day. Thus, there appears to be a relationship between production rate and accident frequency (Vernon, 1936).

It is necessary, therefore, in investigating the relationship between fatigue and accident rate, to somehow separate out the influence of output which is related both to fatigue and to accident frequency. This has been done by utilizing a simple index of accident frequency per unit of production. The resultant data (Goldmark, Hopkins, Florence, and Lee, 1920), obtained over a relatively long period of time in plants working 8- and 10-hour shifts, are exhibited in Figure 9–5. The accident index was found to parallel

FIGURE 9–5

Accident Ratio for 8-Hour and 10-Hour Day
with Production Rate Constant

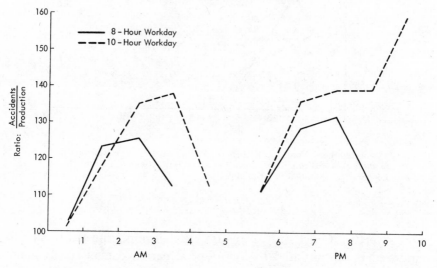

the output curve very closely during the 8-hour shift, indicating that production increases tend to be accompanied by an increment in accident frequency. The 10-hour shift, however, provided for the development of considerable fatigue leading to a rise in the accident index during the last two hours of the shift in spite of declining productivity.

Evidence of this sort leads to the conclusion that although fatigue can be rather directly responsible for accidents, it is not a causal factor of significant concern in most industrial settings. The 8-hour workday, which tends to prevent the occurrence of the kind of extreme fatigue associated with accidental injury, is fairly well standardized.

Attitudes, Adjustment, and Emotional Factors

An employee who is free from debilitating physical characteristics, who works under optimal environmental conditions, and who is aware of the limitations of his equipment is still quite likely to have an accident if his attitudinal pattern is one of recklessness, irresponsibility, or uncooperativeness. Such attitudes are, of course, symptomatic of more fundamental kinds of personal maladjustment. A mature, well-adjusted employee does not regard it as sissified to observe safety precautions and to avoid unnecessary risks. Thus, the entire matter of the relationship between attitudes and liability to accidents has generally been investigated within the broader context of adjustmental and emotional factors.

Some concrete evidence relative to the relationship between personal maladjustment and susceptibility to accidents was provided by a study of over 100 workers who had experienced more than 400 minor accidents (Hersey, 1936). More than half of these accidents occurred when the worker was emotionally disturbed, that is, worried, apprehensive, and so on. Such emotional states resulted either from concerns about the job or represented a transference of difficulties being experienced in the home. Some of the workers who experienced accidents were found also to be susceptible to rather regular periodic fluctuations in mood or emotional tone.

Alcohol and Drugs. Alcohol has been implicated as a causal factor in about half of the automobile accidents resulting in fatalities (Goldstein, 1962). This is so in part because of the direct performance decrements and deleterious subjective effects of alcohol consumption. However, it also reflects an intimate relationship between acute alcoholism or heavy consumption and such adjustmental problems as paranoia, suicidal thoughts, depression, and inclinations towards violence (Selzer, 1969).

Although the problem extends to drugs other than alcohol, comparable hard data for these other drugs are not yet available. We know that a substantial proportion of the population ingests perfectly legal prescription and over-the-counter drugs for various ailments and can guess that many ignore admonitions against driving because the drug sometimes causes drowsiness. In the case of illegal drugs like marihuana and the barbiturates, the investigator is limited to studies of driving performance under simulated conditions which are not valid indicants of actual driving behavior (Kalant, 1969).

Transitory Conditions. The picture that emerges of the person who is a high accident risk is that of one given to transitory and situational rather than more pervasive and basic emotional upset. Note, for example, in Table 9–3 that the distribution of automobile

TABLE 9–3

Distribution of Accident Frequencies for Patient Sample
and Random Sample of California Drivers

Accidents	California Drivers' Percentages	Patient Frequencies	Expected Patient Frequencies
None.....................	78.66%	133	129.79
1.........................	17.49	31	28.85
2.........................	3.20	1	5.28
3.........................	0.53	0	0.87
4.........................	0.10	0	0.17
5.........................	0.01	0	0.02
6 or more..............	0.01	0	0.02
Total..............	100.00	165	165.00

Source: M. W. Buttiglieri & M. Guenette. Driving records of neuropsychiatric patients. *Journal of Applied Psychology*, 1967, *51*, 97.

accident frequencies for neuropsychiatric patients admitted to a California Veterans Administration hospital closely approximates the distribution for a random sample of all California drivers.

Efforts to identify a personality type or a constellation of personality traits associated with high accident liability have not been particularly successful. Although the data from such studies have proven only minimally useful for predictive purposes, they have provided some important clues about the personalities of individuals who have repetitive accidents. Accident repeaters were found in one study to be differentiated from other workers by being overly fearful, fatalistic (feeling that they were unlucky), overly ambitious, revengeful, and desirous of pampering (Adler, 1941). A similarly unhealthy emotional pattern involving feelings of hostility and lack of concern for the social consequences of actions was discovered as a correlate of automotive accidents (Brown & Berdie, 1960). Emotional immaturity as evidenced by a tendency to become easily disturbed by minor irritations, to blow off steam in excess of that required by the situation, and by a kind of general irresponsibility and lack of considerateness was found to be related to accident frequency for route salesmen (Malo, 1954). A similar pattern has been identified using the Strong Vocational Interest Blank as a predictor. The difference between the standard scores on two of the subscales—"adventuresome" (the aviator scale) and "cautiousness" (the banker scale)—was found to correlate 0.28 with accident rate for an industrial population (Kunce, 1967).

It must be reiterated that the above noted relationships between personality and accident frequency are not strong. Were they more potent, we should have some basis for a statement to the effect that certain kinds of persons are accident-prone, that is, that their personality is such that we would expect them to have accidents with considerably greater frequency than dictated solely on the basis of chance. The issue of accident-proneness has received considerable attention in the professional literature, and it is appropriate that we direct our attention next to this matter.

ACCIDENT-PRONENESS

The reasons for interest in, and even excitement about, the possibility of demonstrating the existence of an accident-prone personality are relatively apparent. If it could be demonstrated that certain kinds of persons are much more susceptible than others to accidents, we would be provided with a powerful tool for the prevention of accidents. Accident-prone employees could presumably be identified and assigned to nonhazardous jobs.

The tenability of the principle of accident-proneness hinges upon the demonstration that some persons have many more accidents than one would forecast for them on the basis of chance, while others have many fewer accidents than one would expect if chance factors alone were operative. The typical evidence in support of the principle is based upon the demonstration that a relatively small percentage of employees have a disproportionately large percentage of accidents. One study of accidents in which taxicab drivers were involved, for example, found that 40 percent of the drivers had 70 percent of the accidents (Metropolitan Insurance, 1931). Thus, the argument was made that since some drivers never had an accident while others had several accidents, the latter must be accident-prone.

The critical feature overlooked in such demonstrations of accident-proneness is the proper definition of chance. The question of the number of accidents to be expected solely on the basis of chance is a little like asking how many heads in a row would result from flipping a coin. Assuming no bias in the coin or in the flipping procedure, we would expect to observe 50 percent heads and 50 percent tails *in the long run.* You are well aware, however, that it would be possible to observe five heads in a row on five consecutive flips just by chance. The odds against this occurring are high, but it can happen! The fact that it does happen occasionally is what tempts the inveterate gambler to try the long shots.

Mintz and Blum (1949) have been most articulate in pointing out the defect inherent in the interpretation of accident data like those cited for taxicab drivers as supportive of the principle of proneness. They write:

> The method of percentages of people and accidents implies an incorrect assumption, *viz.,* that chance expectation requires that all people in a population should have the same number of accidents. This is not the case. An obvious limitation that has often been overlooked is the fact that very often the reported total number of accidents in a population is smaller than the number of people in the population. For example, if a group of 100 factory workers had 50 accidents in one year, then a maximum of 50 people could have contributed to the accident record and accordingly a maximum of 50% of the population would have contributed to 100% of the accidents. Obviously, a small percentage of the population in this case does not establish the principle of accident proneness.

They follow this argument with another: there is no reason to assume that one accident immunizes the victim against the possibility of having other accidents. It is perfectly plausible to expect that some persons will just by chance have several accidents while others may not have any. The application of these arguments was used to develop an appropriate chance distribution of accident frequency for the taxicab accidents cited earlier, with the result shown in

FIGURE 9–6

Obtained and Expected Distributions of Accidents by
Taxicab Drivers

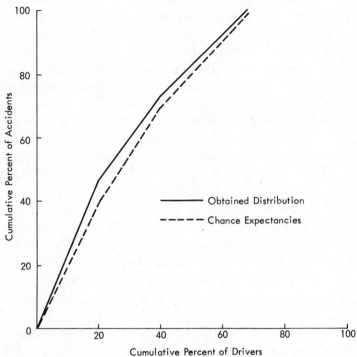

Figure 9–6. You will note that the obtained accident frequency and
the chance expectancies are very similar in shape. There is some
evidence for the fact that something other than chance was operating to produce the observed distribution of accidents because the
discrepancy between the obtained and chance distributions is statistically significant. It is quite clear, however, that the principle of
accident-proneness is not nearly as formidable as it was once thought
to be. Mintz and Blum concluded, from the examination of these
and similar sets of data, that the variance attributable to differences
in accident liability is about 20 to 40 percent. The effect of this
factor is small when compared with the estimated 60 to 80 percent
attributable to other factors.

A somewhat lower estimate of the accident variance attributable
to a constitutional or permanent predisposition is arrived at in

another way. If a person were accident-prone, he ought to experience an abnormally high accident rate over two different periods of time. It has been estimated from collating such correlations of accident frequency over time that constitutional predisposition accounts for a *maximum* of 15 percent of accidents (Kerr, 1957). Actually, since certain factors, like exposure to hazard, are uncontrolled in such studies and therefore may be systematic sources of error spuriously raising the correlations, the actual importance of accident-proneness may be even less.

Thus, the accident-proneness hypothesis has been placed in perspective. It was thought at one time that the primary route to the prevention of accidents was the utilization of appropriate personnel selection procedures designed to identify and eliminate those applicants who would tend to be accident-prone under virtually all circumstances. The most recent evidence, however, supports the contention that an individual's liability to accidents is highly specific. The fact that he is accident-prone under a given set of circumstances does not mean that he will be accident-prone under other circumstances. And the role of constitutional tendencies toward unsafe behavior is regarded as much less important than originally believed.

Two other concepts have been proposed as more powerful explanatory hypotheses than accident-proneness: (*a*) goals-freedom-alertness and (*b*) adjustment-stress (Kerr, 1957).

In terms of the "goals-freedom-alertness" hypothesis, the greater the worker's freedom to establish goals with a reasonable probability of attainment (that is, the greater his involvement in the task), the greater will be his alertness and work quality. Since an accident may be regarded as a variety of low-quality work, a participative and involving psychological climate may reduce accident frequency.

The "adjustment-stress" hypothesis holds that any adverse stress increases the organism's liability to accidents. Such stresses are temporary and may be internal to the organism (for example, disease) or external (for example, excessive temperature or noise).

All three hypotheses (accident-proneness, goals-freedom-alertness, and adjustment-stress) are complementary. Therefore, the focus of activity in the area of industrial safety has changed from that of a fundamental emphasis upon the identification of potential accident victims to a multidimensional approach emphasizing accident prevention.

ACCIDENT CONTROL

An industrial safety program must contain at least three elements in order to be of maximum effectiveness. Such a program must include provisions for (1) the identification and correction of unsafe working practices and conditions; (2) the specification of employee characteristics required for safe performance on certain jobs, and the consequent implementation of these specifications by means of appropriate selection procedures; and (3) a continuing program of preservice and in-service training.

Eliminating Unsafe Practices and Environmental Conditions

Certain environmental conditions which are potential sources of accidents are controlled by state regulations of various kinds. The placement of fire extinguishers and mandatory inspections of elevators and other moving equipment are illustrative of this kind of control. Ultimately, however, the responsibility for identifying and eliminating unsafe work practices rests with management and with every employee. It is management's responsibility to arrange the physical working environment in such a way that it provides adequate ventilation and illumination and the safest possible equipment. Management must arrange also to staff and equip a maintenance department adequate to the task of keeping the plant and its equipment in excellent working order. The fact that maintenance was too overworked to repair a defective rung on a ladder is small consolation to the painter who falls when the rung gives way.

The entire burden of accident prevention cannot, however, be placed upon management alone. Each employee must assume responsibility for reporting defective equipment or unsafe practices. In addition, every worker must appreciate and implement his own personal stake in a safe environment by observing certain rudimentary principles of industrial housekeeping, including mopping floors to prevent the accumulation of water or grease, piling materials properly, and removing loose objects from floors, stairs, and platforms.

There is some evidence for the fact that the psychological environment in which work is performed may be as important a consideration in accident prevention as is the physical environment. A comparison between employees in factory departments who had variable safety records indicated that accidents tended to occur with the greatest frequency in those departments with the lowest intra-company transfer mobility rates and the least promotion possibility for the typical employee. These factors are interpreted as symp-tomatic of an unwholesome psychological work environment. The lack of intracompany mobility and of promotional opportunities may lead to the development of attitudes of indifference toward the work. A more favorable psychological climate can provide incen-tives which act to raise the general level of alertness to potential hazards and to promote a desire to cooperate with safety personnel (Kerr, 1950).

Appropriate Personnel Selection Procedures

A comprehensive job analysis leading to an adequate set of worker specifications can quite often suggest certain of the physical or personal employee characteristics which are associated with acci-dents. Some of these kinds of characteristics, like defective vision or health, are self-evident. Others are a little more obscure but may nevertheless be of considerable importance. It has been suggested (Drake, 1940), for example, that accidents in certain kinds of activities are especially likely when the employee's perceptual speed is slow in relation to his motor speed. Since both of these factors appear to represent inherited capacities or limitations and are not amenable to training, they can be controlled only by the utilization of appropriate selection procedures.

Training

The discussion earlier in this chapter of the causes of accidents indicated that the majority of accidents are attributable to "faulty attitude." Although this is a rather vague classification, it implies that the utilization of selection procedures and the modification of the working environment can, at best, prevent only a relatively small proportion of industrial accidents. The most fundamental cause of accidents appears to be attitudinal in nature. Consequently, workers and supervisors must be taught to be safety-minded.

Such safety-mindedness does not always accompany the acquisi-tion of skill or knowledge about equipment operation. Most persons learn how to drive an automobile, for example, with relatively little difficulty. An attitude of maturity in its operation, however, is quite a different matter as shown by the comparison in Table 9–4 between the violations recorded for samples of accident-free and accident-repeater drivers.

Virtually all of the accumulated evidence about automobile accidents indicates that the safe driver is one who is skillful, knows the limitations of his equipment, and has a high degree of social aware-

TABLE 9–4

Motor Vehicle Violations Recorded for Driver Samples

	Number of Drivers	
	Accident Free (N = 59)	*Accident Repeater* (N = 88)
Minor Offenses		
Leaving vehicle running and unattended.............	1	1
Driving within 8 feet of streetcar stopped for passengers..	7	20
Not reasonably right for vehicle coming from opposite direction....................................	4	15
Not keeping to right half of road when view is obstructed.......................................	2	5
Crossing throughway without stopping...............	7	15
Failure to obey traffic signal......................	1	11
Speeding...	24	50
Left of streetcar..................................	0	2
Violation of traffic rules..........................	6	8
Mechanical defect.................................	0	1
Without proper lights.............................	1	5
Without proper brakes............................	0	2
Without proper muffler...........................	0	1
No vehicle inspection sticker......................	4	19
Improper operation...............................	5	7
Negligent collision................................	3	5
Serious Offenses		
Operating under influence of liquor..................	8	13
Operating so as to endanger lives and safety...........	8	15
Going away after injury to property..................	1	7
Going away after injury to persons...................	0	1
Operating after license suspension...................	0	7
Operating without proper registration................	0	10
Operating without being properly licensed............	4	9
Violation of compulsory insurance law...............	0	6
Operating without authority........................	0	4

Source: R. A. McFarland & A. L. Moseley. *Human factors in highway transport safety.* Cambridge, Mass.: Harvard University Press, 1954.

ness, including consideration for others. Safe drivers are neither resentful of authority nor do they regard the automobile as a tool for the extension of their own power. The National Safety Council's admonition that we reveal a good deal about our level of maturity by the way in which we drive is based upon solid evidence. It is likely that the relatively low proportion of accidents among drivers who are trained in a high school driver-training program can be attributed to the fact that such training emphasizes the acquisition of appropriate attitudes as well as of driving skills.

Since accident prevention is largely dependent upon the development of appropriate attitudes, industrial safety requires a continuing program designed to alert all personnel to the potential sources of accidents and to reinforce safe practices. The safety program must make provision for the systematic study of accident reports and regular inspection to detect unsafe procedures. The findings from such reports and inspections provide a firm base for the development of safety training programs.

Training of foremen relative to accident prevention has been shown to be highly effective (see Figure 9–7). The foreman, after all, is the person who is in the best possible position to see to it that safety precautions are observed.

FIGURE 9–7

Monthly Accident Frequency When Foremen Are Trained

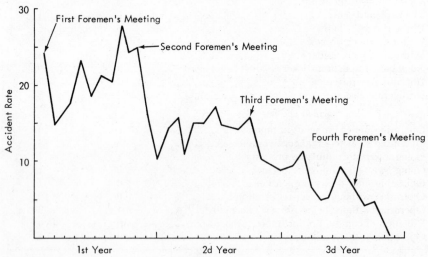

Source: Metropolitan Life Insurance Company.

FIGURE 9–8

"What Happened?" A Near-Accident Report

WHAT HAPPENED?
NEAR-ACCIDENT REPORT – INDIANA HARBOR WORKS

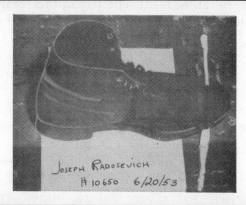

Joe Radosevich, #10650, missed losing his big toe by 55/1000th of an inch. He and another man were using a dolly bar to loosen a work roll. Joe lost his balance and the dolly bar went through his shoe, as shown in the picture.

HOW INJURY WAS PREVENTED

The dolly bar came within 55/1000th of an inch of Joe's big toe. This is the thickness of the safety cap in his shoe. The steel bar went between the leather and the safety cap. Wearing of safety shoes saved a toe or more for Joe.

76" Hot Strip Mechanical
Bulletin #35
July 1953

    Issued by . . . SAFETY DEPARTMENT

The training of foremen alone, however, is not sufficient. It is important also that a continuing program of in-service training be directed toward the workers. Such a program typically consists of several elements, all of which are designed to impress constantly the matter of industrial safety upon the individual employee. Publicity, including safety bulletins, payroll envelope inserts, charts, displays, and articles in the house organ can be highly effective in this regard. It is difficult to remain callous to the kind of evidence contained in the bulletin shown in Figure 9–8, for example. Other devices for encouraging safe work practices include the conduct of contests and the provision of awards to personnel or departments with outstanding safety records.

These apparently simple devices should not be dismissed lightly. The data on the effectiveness of organized safety programs are extremely impressive. Proctor and Gamble, for example, was able to reduce the frequency of disabling injuries from 36 per million man-hours in 1930 to 1 per million man-hours in 1955 by means of a program in which everyone was encouraged to "think" and "work" safety (Ewell, 1956). This kind of record is quite typical. The essence of successful safety training is the philosophy underlying the program rather than the specific methods whereby the program is implemented. Some companies with successful programs favor contests, others favor bulletin bombardments, and still others lean toward the use of the house organ for this purpose. All programs that work, however, are directed toward the fundamental objective of creating an attitude of pride in individual and company safety records, and of consideration and respect for one's fellow employees.

SUMMARY

The majority of accidents are attributable to three factors: (1) defective working environment and equipment design; (2) human limitations in the operation of equipment; and (3) improper worker attitudes relative to safety, including carelessness.

The role of the physical environment, including such factors as illumination, ventilation, and equipment malfunction, has been the subject of considerable study by engineers and psychologists. Although there is still room for further improvements in this area, it cannot be regarded any longer as a primary cause of accidents. The more fundamental problem in accident prevention is a human one and requires the application of appropriate selection and training procedures.

Efforts to identify a personality type associated with high accident liability have not been outstandingly successful. There is some evidence that the accident-repeater tends to be emotionally immature, somewhat hostile, and socially irresponsible. This pattern is not sufficiently consistent, however, to support the principle of accident proneness as the basic factor underlying accidents.

The importance of accident-proneness has quite often been overstated because of misinterpretations of studies, indicating that a relatively small percentage of employees have a relatively large proportion of the accidents. The proper application of chance expectancies to observed distributions of accident frequency leads to the conclusion that accident-proneness accounts for about 20 percent or less of the total accident variance. Thus, although of some consequence, this factor must be placed in proper perspective.

The most satisfactory approach to industrial safety involves the development of a comprehensive program of preservice training and in-service education relative to accident prevention. Such a program must place a continuing emphasis upon the study of the causes of accidents and near-accidents, the identification and correction of unsafe working procedures, and the development of an employee attitude best described as safety-mindedness.

10. Engineering Psychology

Until fairly recently, machine and plant design were regarded pretty much as the province of the engineer. The comfort of the person operating the machine and indeed his capability for operating various kinds of "mechanical monsters" was considered (if at all) almost as an afterthought.

With the equipment as a given, early attempts to improve worker efficiency had to rest upon an analysis of the job with a view toward task simplification. In this approach, tasks were reduced to their essential components and these components were arranged or sequenced so each could be performed in minimum time with the least wasted or fatiguing motion.

This rather one-sided regard for the machine could not continue indefinitely. Technological advancements made possible the design of even more powerful machines capable of performing previously unimagined tasks with staggering speed and precision *provided they could be operated effectively.* Such a provision removes the human operator from the realm of afterthought and makes his limitations and strengths essential considerations in machine and equipment design.

The urgent military rquirements of World War II focused particular attention upon the necessity for merging the talents of engineers, psychologists, physiologists, physicians and others in designing equipment (aircraft instrument panels, submarine diving controls) and structuring working conditions. This represented the beginning of the field designated "human engineering" or engineering psychology."

The point of departure for engineering psychology is information about man's capabilities and limitations. Utilizing such information, the engineering psychologist seeks to develop an optimally functioning unit of man and machine—a *man-machine system*. Virtually every major type of military equipment has, at least since World War II, received some attention from engineering psychologists. Nonmilitary applications have included such diverse products as aircraft and space vehicle instruments and cabins, artificial limbs, semiautomatic post-office sorting equipment, control panels for atomic reactors, telephone sets, and industrial machines of various kinds (Taylor, 1957).

Whereas this chapter is concerned primarily with engineering psychology, it is appropriate to begin by briefly considering its historical precursor: task simplification.

TASK SIMPLIFICATION

Task simplification entails a critical study of work activities with a view to revealing inefficient operations and working techniques. It may be discovered, for example, that employees are making unnecessarily fatiguing movements or that the sequence of operations is not conducive to expeditious job performance.

Time Study "Speedup"

Certainly there can be no quarrel with attempts to improve plant efficiency by eliminating unnecessary motions and reducing employee fatigue. However, the time-and-motion studies of some of the early efficiency experts were sometimes misapplied. They rested upon the erroneously simplistic view that employees want only high wages, employers want only low labor costs, and that both objectives can be attained by having employees accomplish more in less time (Taylor, 1911). The fallaciousness of this view is evident from an analysis of absenteeism in a paper products factory (Fried, Weitman, & Davis, 1972). Of the 40 job stations in this factory, those embodying conditions where employees (*a*) set their own pace and/or (*b*) could adjust or correct the machine had significantly lower absenteeism. Presumably, these employees were less alienated by their task demands than were others in the same company but without the same level of task control.

Attempts simply to speed up employee activity without regard for the consequent toll in human resources have always been repugnant to workers, psychologists, and many managers. The employees' primary defense against such speedup programs is to maintain social pressures which prevent exceeding what they consider to be a fair level of production. "Rate busters" who violate tacit agreements about production level are likely to find themselves ostracized by their fellow employees.

The usual procedure for such studies is to observe and time a relative brief sample of cycles of a repetitive task. Time standards for performing the constituents of the cycles are then established from averages based upon these limited observations.

Psychologists reject the utilization of time study data to set absolute performance standards because of the fallibility of certain assumptions underlying this application.

If the average times are to be used for setting standards, we must assume that the observed performances are sufficiently consistent and have been adequately sampled to produce reliable means. This assumption fails on two counts. First, only rarely is an adequate sample of observations recorded across employees, segments of the workday, days of the week, and so on. Second, times recorded for performance of various components of a total work cycle by individual employees tend to be characterized by a high degree of inconsistency. In view of the failure of these assumptions, we must conclude that average performance time calculated from observations is not a sufficiently reliable criterion for establishing normative performance rates.

A second psychologically fallible assumption is that there is one best way for doing a task regardless of who is doing it. This assumption disregards the body of evidence concerning individual differences. Although a sequence of motions or activities proving satisfactory for many persons may be discovered, it is likely that some persons will remain who could better perform the task using a different sequence or different motions. This realization has even permeated some of the aircrew training in the Strategic Air Command in which "Standard Operating Procedures" for particular elements of a mission have given way to "Crew Operating Procedures" which, although unstandardized, work best for the particular crews in question (Hood, Halpin, Hanitchak, Siegel, & Hemphill, 1957).

Thirdly, it is psychologically unsound to conceive of *rate* of production as the sole important criterion of industrial effectiveness. Increased productivity is undoubtedly extremely *inefficient* when it is accompanied by such things as heightened fatigue, worker dissatisfaction, and increased accident frequency.

Motion Simplification

Task simplification based upon the elimination of unnecessary motions and otherwise facilitating job performance is markedly different from the kind of speedup described above. Its emphasis is upon the individual and the effective utilization of his capacities rather than upon the job without regard for the characteristics of the worker. In jointly considering the nature of the work to be done and the person who is to do it, task simplification was a forerunner —and to some extent is still a component—of present-day engineering psychology.

Therblig Analysis. The primary principle of task simplification, as advocated and practiced by Frank and Lillian Gilbreth (1917), is that tasks can be modified to suit individuals rather than forcing individuals to comply with the requirements of the task. Thus, in an early study of bricklaying, Gilbreth (1911) was able to reduce the motions from 18 to 5, thereby increasing production from 120 to 350 bricks per man-hour without speeding up the work pace.

As practiced by the Gilbreths, task simplification entailed first a detailed analysis of each task into its constituent motions and activities. These constituents, termed "therbligs"—you can figure out why—included such activities as searching, finding, positioning, assembling, and so on. After identifying the therbligs, the task was simplified by eliminating those activities that were unnecessary, combining steps in task performance, and altering the sequence of activities.

Some Principles of Efficient Movement. A body of lore, based primarily upon experience rather than empirical evidence, supports the relative superiority of certain kinds of motions over others.

1. Symmetrical movements are more efficient than asymmetrical movements. It is preferable, for example, to have an assembler simultaneously reach for a bolt with his left hand and a nut with his right hand than to have him use the same hand to collect both components.

2. Parts, tools, and so on should be within easy reach. The region of most comfortable reach by a seated employee is defined by an arc circumscribed on the work surface by his hands extended to the

length of his forearms. Next in comfort is a region defined by arcs similarly drawn when his arms are fully extended. These areas of most comfortable reach without disturbing the worker's posture are sometimes referred to as "semicircular workpits" (see Figure 10–1).

FIGURE 10–1

Semicircular Work Pits

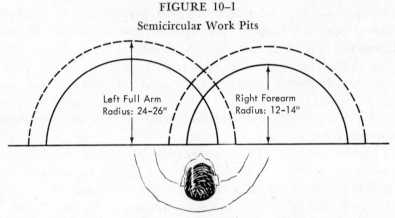

The semicircles delimit the areas of comfortable reach for each arm. The overlapping area is accessible to both hands.

3. Circular movements are more efficient than straight line movements.

4. Tasks that can be arranged in terms of rhythmic patterns are easier to perform than tasks requiring jerky or irregular movements.

5. Holding and carrying operations are more efficiently handled by equipment than by human operators. Unnecessary fatigue is generated by requiring an employee, for example, to hold a part while he works on it instead of clamping the part in a vise. Likewise, many part transport operations can be simply replaced by a "drop delivery" whereby the finished work is dropped down a hole leading to a chute and carrying it away from the work area.

6. Demands made upon the limbs and fingers should be proportional to their strength and dexterity. An outstanding and long recognized illustration of poor design in this regard is the typewriter keyboard. However, with the advent of electric typewriters the work load for the fingers has been so minimized that differences in finger

strength and dexterity have become relatively unimportant in spite of poor keyboard design.

MAN-MACHINE SYSTEMS

We have said that more recent psychological activity in the area of equipment design is founded on the *system* concept. To clarify the meaning of a man-machine system, which is an optimally functioning unit consisting both of the machine and its operator, we will first consider the components of mechanical systems. These components will then be related to those of human systems and man-machine systems.

Whereas a man-machine system entails the continuous interaction between an operator and his equipment, the systems concept is extended as well to complex configurations composed of many men and units of equipment. Thus, at a simple level of conceptualization a man-machine system like aircraft piloting entails the optimal interaction of two subsystems, one mechanical (the aircraft) and the other human (the pilot). However, this same man-machine system functions as a component subsystem in the still more complex coordination of several aircraft, each with its pilot and ground facilities, including their operators, comprising an air traffic control system.

Mechanical Systems

The simplest kind of system is designed to perform a specific function or group of functions indefinitely (or until it wears out) once it is triggered. This is an *open-loop* system. *Closed-loop* systems are ones in which the performance of a function by the equipment is sensed or fed back into the machine, making it self-regulating.

Open-Loop Systems. Many commercial buildings are equipped with sprinkler systems for fire control. The overhead sprinklers automatically spray water when there is a fire. The system is *controlled* by metal plugs which melt at a critical temperature. When the heat (the *input*) causes these plugs to melt, a water spray is released (the *output*).

The system is not self-regulating. It will continue to spray water as long as it is functional until it is shut down by some force ex-

FIGURE 10–2

Mechanical Systems

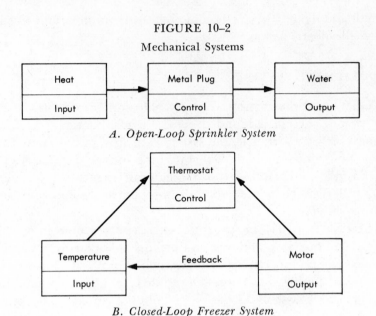

A. Open-Loop Sprinkler System

B. Closed-Loop Freezer System

ternal to the system itself. Figure 10–2 shows the system diagrammatically.

Closed-Loop Systems. A thermostatically controlled home freezer is a closed-loop system because it is self-regulating (see Figure 10–2). Once the thermostat is set for a particular temperature (say, 10° F), the refrigerating motor will operate whenever the temperature rises above that level. However, the output itself serves to change the input, in turn signaling to the control when the temperature again drops to 10° F and motor operation ceases.

Human Systems

We may consider man also as a closed-loop system. This analogy is not difficult if we substitute for the terms stimulus-interpretation-response, the mechanical concepts input-control-output. Viewed as a system, man receives information, somehow processes it, and reacts to it.

Inputs for the human system take the form of receptor organ activity. These sensations are processed by such interpretive control functions as thinking, reasoning, deciding, and so on. The output, of course, is some kind of behavior. This response in turn affects the input and the cycle continues.

Consider the operation of a human system performing a relatively simple task like maintaining a constant driving speed of 55 miles per hour (see Figure 10–3). The basic input is a set of visual

FIGURE 10–3

A Human System: Maintaining Driving Speed at 55 Miles per Hour

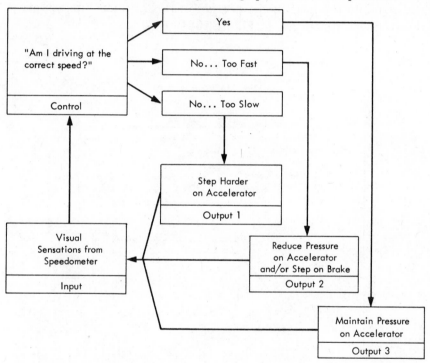

sensations from the speedometer. These are supplemented by other inputs not considered in Figure 10–3, including the sound of wind rushing past the car, the feel of the wheel, or the sound of certain squeaks or rattles we have learned to associate with certain speeds. The visual sensations from the speedometer are processed, and an appropriate response is made, depending upon the interpretation.

Note that the situation described and diagrammed in Figure 10–3 provides for *branching*. Instead of a system limited to a single control action and a single output, we have a variety of control decisions each eliciting a different output. Branching is not limited to human systems. Electronic computers, for example, are often controlled by branching programs permitting specified operations to occur under specified circumstances.

A Man-Machine System

It has undoubtedly occurred to you that the human system we have just described is only a part of the total system involving both the man and the machine. A portion of this man-machine system is shown diagrammatically in Figure 10–4.

FIGURE 10–4

A Man-Machine System

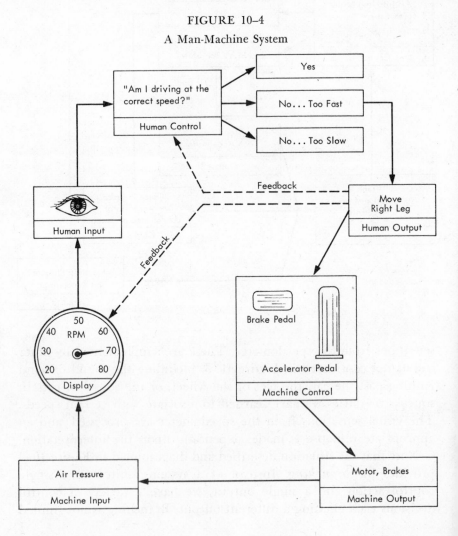

The essence of this system is that the human portion with its inputs, controls, and outputs constitutes an overall control system for the mechanical portion of the system. The entire man-machine system thus is mediated by the human operator. Should he fall asleep at the wheel, the mechanical controls become useless.

This suggests what is at once the strength and weakness of man-machine systems compared with systems that are entirely mechanical. The latter are foolproof except for mechanical breakdown. However, they lack the precision of control and flexibility of output that can be exerted only when the higher cognitive processes of a human being are incorporated within the system. In oder for man to function as part of the system, there must be an optimal rapprochement between the human being and the machine. The inputs, controls, and outputs required of him must be facilitated by the machine's design and within the range of human capability.

Allocation of Functions between Men and Machines

Any man-machine system can be designed in alternative ways. Variations are possible in the numbers and complexity of machine components, the number of people in the system, and the functions performed by these people. Since the proportional work load assigned to machines and people comprising the system can be varied, it is important to consider the kinds of things best done by men and those best handled by machine (Chapanis, 1965).

Several attempts have been made to list the relative advantages of people and machines for various kinds of functions. These lists include such things as the superior flexibility of man, superior computational speed of machines, and so on. However, such comparisons have not themselves proven helpful in designing man-machine systems. Such lists neglect two important principles of man-machine design.

First, social, economic, and political values partially determine the allocation of functions. The technology of automation cannot be applied irrespective of its broad social ramifications including employee displacement, job retraining, and unemployment.

Second, assignment of functions must be continuously reevaluated. As technology advances, machines are made capable of performing functions not contemplated when the system was instituted. Post-office mail sorting for destination using machines to read zip codes is a case in point. In this instance, the development of a machine to read has caused the entire system to be redesigned.

Although the initial allocations of functions to men and machines are often based upon the judgments of the systems designers, these judgments are usually amenable to empirical test. Such a test, for example, has confirmed the superior reliability of a space vehicle navigation system when a well-trained man provides redundancy in the system, over various orders of redundancy where all components are machines. This superiority, as shown in Figure 10–5, is attributed to the flexibility which man brings into the system.

The remainder of this chapter is devoted to a discussion of various human factors (or if you prefer, the human subsystem) in man-machine sytems. As shown in Figure 10–3, the linkage between man and machine requires sensory inputs (receipt of information),

FIGURE 10–5

The Reliability of a Double Redundant Navigation System in Which One of the Redundant Components Is Man (dashed line) as Compared with the Reliability of Systems with Various Orders of Redundancy in Which All Components Are Machines (Solid Lines)

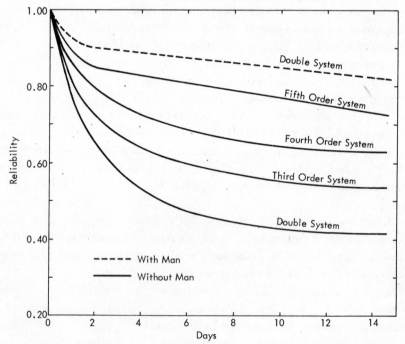

Source: M. A. Grodsky. Risk and reliability. *Aerospace Engineering*, 1962, *21*, No. 1 21–33.

central control processes (information processing and decision making) , and outputs (actions of various kinds) .

INPUT LINKAGE BETWEEN MAN AND MACHINE

The input to man is received by his sense organs. Any of the receptor organs could theoretically provide this input linkage, but for most practical purposes inputs are presented either visually or auditorially.

Choice of Input Modality

Four factors influence the choice of sense channel for presenting information to the human operator and qualify the nature of the input itself: appropriateness, precision, present load on the input channel, and efficiency.

With respect to appropriateness, it makes more sense to provide input by sound rather than light when the operator is sometimes absent from the input source. For example, we rely upon the telephone ring to signal us from any location in home or office. Visual inputs, on the other hand, are most appropriate when an auditory signal would interfere with other listening activities.

Other things being equal, inputs *not* providing precise information can be presented either by light or sound. Thus, low engine oil pressure can be signaled either by a warning light on the dashboard or by a warning buzzer. Such inputs have an "all-or-none" character; they provide information that a mechanical system either is or is not working properly, that some critical point has or has not been reached, and so on. Although such gross inputs frequently are satisfactory, there are many circumstances wherein the operator must be provided with more precise information about machine function. Here, the input must indicate quantitative variations in function on some kind of dial or scale. A pilot, for example, needs accurately to know his altitude and rate of climb. Generally, such information is provided visually; auditory discrimination along a graduated scale is difficult.

If there is a choice of sense modality for providing inputs, the systems designer will take into account the demands already being made upon the various receptor channels. When the operator is already much occupied with visual inputs, the designer will seek to provide any needed additional inputs by sound or touch.

Finally, the efficiency of the input modality must be considered. Whereas all receptor systems usually considered for input linkage have about equally fast response times, some are more efficient for certain purposes than others. Comparing the efficiency of the two most frequently used receptor systems, sight and hearing, the latter is generally superior for simple, brief messages calling for immediate action. The converse conditions favor visual input. Furthermore, visual input is obviously more efficient than auditory input when the receiving environment is noisy. And, auditory input would be required when dark adaptation integrity must be maintained (Morgan, Cook, Chapanis & Lund, 1963).

Visual Displays

Matters of display design have received considerable attention by engineering psychologists. The arrangement of display clusters like those on automobile dashboards, airplane cockpits, and spacecraft presents several problems for the human engineer. It has been shown, for example, that when the operator must keep abreast of information simultaneously conveyed by several different dials, his task can be simplified by patterning the dial display (Woodson, 1954). This is done by orienting each dial so the normal position of the pointer is the same for every one. Thus the operator can quickly spot and identify a dial pointer indicating an abnormal condition.

The typical design of an aircraft panel includes instruments having a profusion of different scales and a lack of uniformity from one instrument to another. Of particular concern is the speed and accuracy of readings of those instruments at the periphery of the field of vision. This matter was studied for alternative arrangements wherein the peripheral instruments were (a) all arranged vertically, (b) all arranged horizontally, (c) arranged in mixed fashion—some vertically and some horizontally (Bauer, Cassatt, Corona, & Warhurst, 1966). The latter arrangement was found to be superior both with respect to detection accuracy and detection time, both of which are aspects of vigilance.

Vigilance

Monitoring mechanical equipment requires a particular type of attentiveness termed *vigilance*. The characteristics of vigilance include prolonged attention to infrequently occurring stimuli which signal the necessity for some kind of action. This describes the fundamental activity of such diverse tasks as monitoring a radar scanning device for detecting approaching aircraft and monitoring electronic telescopes for extraterrestrial sounds. In both instances the normal condition, requiring no response, is the *absence* of a critical stimulus. The critical condition, requiring a response, is the occurrence of some kind of visual or auditory signal.

There appear to be two principal determinants of vigilance performance: expectancy and level of arousal (Poulton, 1966). Both factors are probably related to the monotonous nature of the monitoring tasks.

Expectancy. The most frequently occurring vigilance error is an error of omission, that is, failure to respond appropriately to an infrequently occurring signal. Laboratory studies have confirmed that this error can be reduced by familiarizing subjects with the approximate frequency with which they can expect to receive critical signals. Thus, the accuracy of infrequent signal detection during a test period was found to be affected by the rate at which these signals were presented during the pretest orientation period. Vigilance performance over a prolonged period was best when the pretest orientation presented signals with about the same frequency as presented during the vigilance test itself. The implication is, of course, that vigilance training must be realistic in the sense that trainees should develop an awareness of the likelihood of occurrence of critical signals during a finite time period (Colquhoun & Baddeley, 1964).

Arousal. Since the normal condition in vigilance tasks is absence of the critical stimulus and since the abnormal condition requiring a response occurs infrequently, it is essential to maintain a satisfactory level of operator alertness or arousal.

The importance of this factor was clearly demonstrated in an investigation (Deese, 1957) of the percentage of signals detected when varying numbers of signals were presented each hour. Whereas almost 90 percent of the signals presented at a rate of 40 per hour were detected, this percentage declined to about 65 percent when the rate was 20 per hour, and dropped below 50 percent when the rate was 10 per hour.

There are limits, of course, to this relationship between signal rate and arousal. Signals which come too frequently can also produce a performance decrement, perhaps because of a perceptual "overload." Given this U-shaped function between signal frequency and accuracy of identification, there is probably an optimum frequency for maximizing arousal and minimizing perceptual overload which varies with the nature of the signal.

To maintain a proper state of arousal when critical stimuli occur rarely, it has been helpful sporadically to present "artificial signals" (Wilkinson, 1964). These artificial signals should be identical to the real signals (but presented only for arousal purposes) and followed by feedback to the operator concerning the adequacy of his response. The rationale for artificial signals is clearly similar to the intended arousal function of an unanticipated question suddenly asked of you during class by the lecturer.

Other ways to maintain a satisfactory level of arousal have been suggested (Bergum & Lehr, 1962). These include making the signals as obvious as possible (for example, by signaling with very bright, large lights); allowing operators to work in pairs and when possible permitting conversation; providing ample rest and brief work periods (up to 10 minutes rest after every 30-minute work period); and observations by a supervisor on a random interval schedule.

CENTRAL CONTROL PROCESSES

Once an input linkage between man and machine is established, the operator must identify and process the information he has been provided and decide upon an appropriate course of action. This is shown as the controlling aspect of Figure 10–3. Information processing may involve any one or combination of such processes as evaluation, comparison, computation, judgment, reasoning, and so on. These processes eventuate in a decision about the type of action to be taken.

The one outstanding characteristic of human information processing functions is that they involve "recoding." The input data are manipulated and interpreted in some fashion. Such recoding is man's unique contribution to a man-machine system. When recoding is unnecessary, that is, when each input uniformly predetermines a specific output, the system can be automated.

Most kinds of decision making have three components: information collection, subjective assessments of this information, and some sort of appreciation of the overall pattern of evidence (Poulton, 1966). The two latter components are involved in recoding.

All of the components of decision making are enormously compounded and the resultant decision made more difficult as the inputs become more numerous and complex. Too much informational input may hinder rather than facilitate decision making. This was demonstrated in an investigation of the quality of decisions concerning the allocation of aircraft to search for a reported submarine (Hayes, 1962). The subjects (naval enlisted men) could choose up to eight aircraft and could use up to eight characteristics (distance and speed of the aircraft, fuel carried, and so on) in making their choices. Decision-making time was found to increase both with the number of aircraft available as alternatives and the number of characteristics to be considered. The increase in decision quality gained by additional information input did not always offset the resultant increase in decision-making time. In other words, although decisions were improved *to a point* by providing more information, the time required to reach a decision was thereby increased. Thus, it is possible to present too much information for efficient decision making.

Aside from such input overload, another condition adversely affecting decision-making time is an overload in the variety of decisions that may be potential alternatives. This was demonstrated in the above-mentioned investigation. It was also demonstrated in another study (Hick, 1952) wherein subjects had to respond by using a particular finger assigned to a particular signal. The fewer the number of signals used and hence the fewer the number of response alternatives, the more rapid was the decision or response time.

The interaction between number and quality of inputs with number and variety of decisions required as joint determinants of decision-making time and decision quality is compounded by still other conditions of the system. One of these is the amount and quality of other simultaneous inputs which are extraneous to the particular decision in question. This is a realistic consideration since decision processes rarely interrupt the flow of information related to potential decisions about other matters. For example, while deciding whether or not to pass the car ahead of you, you must still remain attentive to the possibility of a blowout or an overheating motor.

From the above, it follows that information processing and decision making is facilitated by three conditions:

1. Input should consist of the minimum number and variety of information required to make the decision. Where possible, inputs which otherwise might have been separately presented may effectively be combined as an integrated signal. Thus, an efficient way to present information about an aircraft's turn, bank, and airspeed is by a combination auditory signal to both ears with variations in

steadiness, frequency, and modulation of the tone (Forbes, 1946).

2. Decision alternatives should be limited to the smallest number possible to accomplish the objectives of the system.

3. When attention is divided, input stimuli must be more intense (louder, brighter) than when attention is undivided. This was demonstrated by presenting bursts of noise, some of which contained a barely audible tone, to one ear. Simultaneously, a six-digit number was sounded in the other ear. The subjects were instructed to rate the certainty with which they were able to discriminate the tone from the noise under two conditions: while listening to the six-digit number and while ignoring it. Discriminability was superior under the latter condition, that is, when attention was undivided (Broadbent & Gregory, 1963).

OUTPUT LINKAGE BETWEEN MAN AND MACHINE

Man's output affecting machine function can be mediated by a wide assortment of equipment controls including levers, knobs, buttons, pedals, and so on. At least three factors must be considered in designing any control: (1) its operation must not require undue force; (2) it must be easily distinguished from other controls for different functions; and (3) it must be as conceptually simple as possible.

The first of these requirements is self-evident and need not be discussed further.

Distinguishability is a particularly important consideration when the operator is confronted by an array of controls in close proximity and must select the appropriate one very quickly. This situation is typical in high-speed aircraft. One study of aircraft controls found that certain shapes are more readily identifiable by touch than others even when gloves are worn (see Figure 10–6) (Jenkins, 1947).

Conceptual simplicity is sometimes facilitated by the shape and direction of movement of the control. Controls shaped as reminders of their function and moving in the same direction as the resultant machine operation tend to facilitate man-machine linkage. The automobile steering wheel is a realistic control. You turn it to the right to move the vehicle to the right. It would be confusing indeed if the control and resultant operation were to act in opposite directions.

FIGURE 10–6

Knob Shapes That Are Readily Identified by Touch

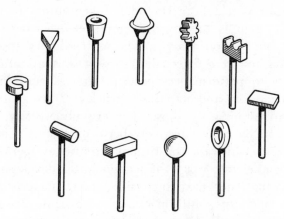

Another approach to conceptual simplicity is that of reducing the number of alternative controls and arranging them in meaningful patterns.

The usual typewriter keyboard illustrates conceptual *complexity.* It consists of approximately 45 different keys arranged in illogical fashion and operated by 10 fingers. An alternative arrangement is a chord keyboard whereby letters are signaled by pressing a pair of keys, one with each hand. With this arrangement the fingers remain poised above their own keys (except for numerals) and the correspondence between pairs of keys and the letters is logical. Postal workers learned to operate this chord keyboard two weeks sooner than did a matched group learning to type on a conventional keyboard. Furthermore, even after seven weeks of training, the group on the chord keyboard was about four days ahead of the group practicing on the typewriter keyboard (Conrad & Longman, 1965).

Although it is doubtful that the results of studies like this one will lead to significant changes in the typewriter keyboard for ordinary secretarial work, they suggest the importance of conceptual simplicity in arranging keyboard controls.

SUMMARY

Engineering psychologists seek to develop an optimally functioning unit of man and machine, that is, a man-machine system. Such systems capitalize upon man's unique capabilities and minimize the effects of his limitations.

Previous to World War II and the beginnings of engineering psychology, attempts to improve employee efficiency emphasized time study and motion analysis. The most salutary applications of these approaches were directed towards task simplification rather than merely to performance speedup. In task simplification, the constituent motions and activities of each task are analyzed with a view toward eliminating those that are unnecessary, combining those that can be more effectively performed jointly, and altering the sequence in which the constituent activities are performed.

With an accelerated pace of technological development, it became increasingly necessary to consider the characteristics of potential human operators while machines were being designed rather than as an afterthought. From the human engineering point of view, man operates as a subsystem within the total man-machine configuration. Viewed in this way, man receives information (inputs), somehow processes this information and makes appropriate decisions, and takes action (outputs).

The inputs from machine to man are transmitted through the sense modalities, particularly vision and audition. Hence, the engineering psychologist is much concerned with optimal arrangements of input displays. A particular input problem area of considerable concern is that of vigilance; that is, prolonged attentiveness to infrequently occurring stimuli which signal the necessity for some kind of action. Vigilance is required whenever the task is characterized by monitoring. The two principal determinants of vigilance performance are expectancy and the level of arousal.

Once an input linkage between man and machine is established, the operator must process the information he has been provided. Information processing (or recoding of the inputs) may involve any one or combination of such processes as evaluation, comparison, computation, judgment, reasoning, and so on. These processes eventuate in a decision about the type of action to be taken.

The action, itself, can be mediated by a wide assortment of equipment controls including levers, knobs, buttons, and pedals. At least three factors influence the design of controls: ease of operation, distinguishability from other controls, and conceptual simplicity.

IV.

Human Relations Psychology

During the first quarter of this century, industrial management was largely influenced by Taylor's scientific and relatively impersonal approach. However, the Hawthorne studies, described in Chapter 11, were responsible for profound changes in the field of industrial psychology generally, and management in particular, by clarifying the importance of such interpersonal factors as leadership style, informal work groups, and group norms. The results of the Hawthorne studies and other research, like the Tavistock Institute Coal Mining Studies (also described in Chapter 11), combined with the practical experiences of many industrial psychologists to generate the human relations movement. The philosophy of "scientific management" emphasized the rights and responsibilities of management in making decisions, determining direction, and providing controls affecting the entire industrial enterprise. Hence, it pretty much neglected the realm of social relationships at work and employee participation in decision making—issues central to the human relations movement.

The human relations movement began to flourish in midcentury. The theories of three psychologists especially important in this movement, McGregor, Herzberg, and Likert, are described in Chapter 12. McGregor's major contribution lay in clarifying certain largely implicit assumptions about human behavior which serve as a basis for management action. He designated two of these sets of assumptions "Theory X" (the traditional assumptions) and "Theory Y" (assumptions with a human relations flavor). Herzberg's major contribution is his two-factor theory of job satisfaction. He maintains that the factors generating job satisfaction are qualitatively different from those generating job dissatisfaction, and he attempts to specify the nature of this difference. Building upon the work of McGregor, Herzberg, and others who are much concerned with the individual employee, Likert's theoretical position primarily concerns organizational structure. He is a particular advocate of employee participation as fundamental to enhancing organizational effectiveness.

Part IV concludes in Chapter 13 with a description of leadership research and a review of the major management development techniques currently used in industry. The classic experimental research on leadership is reviewed in our attempt to indicate something of the complexities involved in specifying the conditions of effective leadership. In addition, several management development techniques, like laboratory training, are described and evaluated.

11.

The Human Relations Movement: Two Classic Experiments

This chapter describes the two studies responsible for stimulating the development of the human relations movement in industrial psychology: the Hawthorne studies (Roethlisberger & Dickson, 1939) and the Tavistock Institute coal mining study (Trist & Bamforth, 1951). Both studies emphasized the importance of interpersonal relationships at work, and especially the influence of the informal work group and its norms on employee behavior.

THE HAWTHORNE STUDIES

What was originally supposed to have been a one-year research project was initiated in 1927 at the Hawthorne (Chicago) plant of the Western Electric Company. The original purpose of this study was to determine the relationship between quality and quantity of illumination and industrial efficiency. This modestly conceived research project eventuated in a 12-year comprehensive study now regarded as a classic research effort. Its findings were influential far beyond the investigators' initial expectations. Indeed, the origin of the human relations movement in industrial psychology can be traced directly to these studies.

As we will shortly see, the Hawthorne studies introduced the concepts of group norms and leadership styles into the field of industrial psychology. Moreover, they demonstrated the existence of complex interactions of such variables as hours of work, employee attitudes, rest pauses, and informal interpersonal relationships.

It is interesting to note that although these studies were completed and reported about 35 years ago (Roethlisberger & Dickson, 1939) contemporary investigators often seem to rediscover some of the same findings. To be sure, the Hawthorne studies suffered some methodological deficiencies. However, they were vastly superior to much of the research previously conducted.

The Hawthorne studies were comprised of five major parts, each of which will be described separately:

1. Experiments on illumination;
2. Relay assembly test-room study;
3. Interviewing program;
4. Bank wiring observation-room study;
5. Personnel counseling project.

Experiments on Illumination

Five studies concerned the effects of varied illumination. More than one study was required because the relationship between illumination and productivity proved to be more complex than the researchers had anticipated. The three most important of these studies are summarized below.

Illumination: Study One. The objective of this study was simply to investigate the relationship between illumination (quantity and quality) and productivity. The experiment involved workers in three different departments of the Hawthorne plant: small parts inspection, relay assembly, and coil winding. The first step in the procedure involved establishment of a base or control rate of production within each department. Thus, the employees worked initially under the existing lighting installation.

After the base rate of productivity was established for each department, the intensity of the illumination was increased in graduated steps, and the corresponding changes in production efficiency were noted. No clear-cut relationship between productivity and intensity of illumination was evident. The report of this study (Snow, 1927) concludes that the results

> brought out very forcibly the necessity of controlling or eliminating the various additional factors which affected production output in

either the same or opposing directions to that which we can ascribe to illumination.

Illumination: Study Two. This experiment, conducted only with operators in the coil winding department, was designed to overcome some of the deficiencies apparent in the first study. The workers were divided into two groups which were equated for experience and average output. The groups were housed in different buildings in order to reduce the possible effects of competition upon productivity.

One of the groups, the "test group," worked under three different illumination intensities (24, 46, and 70 footcandles). The other group ("control") worked under a more or less constant illumination level of 16–28 footcandles. The variations in the intensity of illumination for the control group resulted from variations in the amount of daylight which supplemented the artificial light.

Although this seemed like an excellent research design for comparing the effect of varying illumination intensities, the results were somewhat surprising. The report of the findings (Snow, 1927) states:

> This test resulted in very appreciable production increases in both groups and of almost identical magnitude. The difference in efficiency of the two groups was so small as to be less than the probable error of the values. Consequently, we were again unable to determine what definite part of the improvement in performance should be ascribed to improved illumination.

Illumination: Study Three. The third study involved the same test and control groups but further refinements were made in the experimental design. The control group now worked under a constant illumination of 10 footcandles of purely artificial light. The test group was provided with intensity levels from 10 to 3 footcandles in steps decreasing 1 footcandle at a time. Again, quoting from the summary of findings (Snow, 1927):

> After the level of illumination in the test group enclosure changed to a lower value, the efficiences of both the test and control groups increased slowly but steadily. When the level of illumination for the test group finally reached 3 footcandles, the operatives protested, saying that they were hardly able to see what they were doing, and the production rate decreased. The operatives could and did maintain their efficiency to this point in spite of the discomfort and handicap of insufficient illumination.

The results of these experiments on illumination were considerably different from those anticipated; they raised more questions than they answered. Hence, the second major part of the Hawthorne series, the relay assembly test-room study, was initiated.

Relay Assembly Test-Room Study

This study (hereafter abbreviated RATR study) was designed to control several of the variables that were found earlier to influence productivity in the illumination studies in order to answer the following questions:

1. Is it desirable to introduce rest periods during the work shift?
2. Can the workday be shortened without appreciable decreases in output?
3. What are the employee attitudes toward the company?

The experimenters decided to use a small group of employees. These employees were placed in a separate room where they were away from the rest of the workers in the plant. The task these employees performed, the assembly of small relays, was quite simple and highly repetitive. Two women with considerable work experience were selected to participate in the study. These two women who were already friends then selected the three other relay assemblers and the layout operator who assigned the work and obtained the needed parts. These six women comprised the work crew. There was one additional person who was present in the RATR. His job was to keep records of what occurred in the room. These records included both production output levels and a daily diary of the social interactions in the room. The observer also recorded the significant bits of conversation occurring in the room.

The special experimental test room had work layouts, chairs, and light fixtures identical to those in the regular department. A recording device was added to the equipment so that the number of relays assembled and the time required to assemble each relay were recorded.

Thirteen test periods were employed in the relay assembly test-room study. These test periods are grouped for purposes of discussion into four phases, based on their similarity of purpose.

Phase 1. The first phase of the study included three test periods. In the first test period, the experimenters obtained an accurate measure of each woman's productivity under typical working conditions. In the second test period, they determined the effects of a change in the location of the work setting upon the level of production. In the third period, a new method of payment was instituted. The women were now being paid on the basis of the production level of their own six-person group, instead of on the production level of all of the approximately 100 other relay assembly operators.

Phase 1 was successful in accomplishing its purpose of transferring the women from the regular factory situation into the test room set up. The women in the test room became a *social* group in addition to a *work* group. The observer recorded a substantial amount of personal conversation as well as work-related conversation.

Phase 2. The second phase of the research was comprised of four test periods all primarily concerned with the introduction of rest periods. In period 4, two rest periods of five minutes each were introduced. These rest periods were increased to 10 minutes each in test period 5. In period 6, six rest periods of five minutes each were used. In period 7, two rest pauses were given, a morning one of 15 minutes and an afternoon one of 10 minutes, and a free morning lunch was given to the women. These test periods lasted on the average about six weeks.

The results of Phase 2 indicated that, despite the reduction in the number of hours worked due to the rest periods, average production increased substantially. This can be seen in Figure 11–1 summarizing the production level of the women in the 13 test periods.

The production records of each of the five operators were examined. Two of the women (operators 3 and 4, see Figure 11–1) had shown steady increases in productivity, and one woman (operator 5) had fairly constant output. However, the other two women (operators 1a and 2a) had periods of increased and decreased productivity. Moreover, these two women were considered to be uncooperative and antagonistic. Therefore, at the end of Phase 2, they were replaced by two other cooperative women (operators 1 and 2) for the remainder of the study.

Phase 3. The purpose of the third phase of the RATR study was to determine the effect of a shorter workweek on productivity. Period 8 had the same work conditions as period 7 except that the workday was reduced a half hour. In period 9, the workday was

FIGURE 11-1

Total Weekly Output, Experimental Periods 1-13,
Relay Assembly Test Room

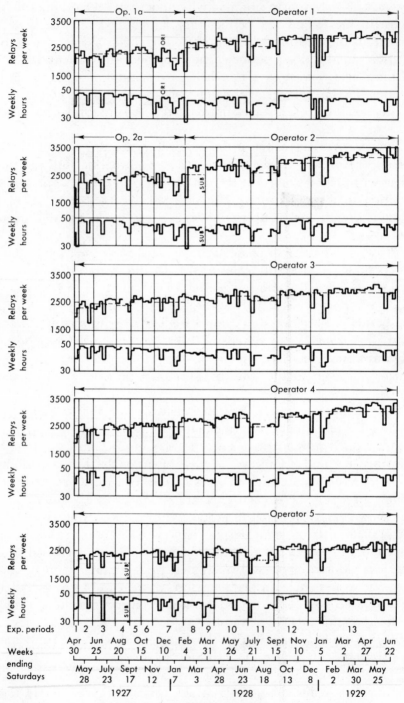

Source: F. J. Roethlisberger & W. J. Dickson. *Management and the worker.* P. 78.

shortened an additional half hour. In period 11, the five-day work-week was introduced. The women were paid the regular hourly rate for Saturday even though they did not work. These three test periods lasted about seven weeks on the average.

Although the workweek was reduced from 48 hours (test periods 1, 2, and 3) to approximately 42 hours (test periods 9 and 11), overall productivity increased substantially. Moreover productivity in Phase 3 was higher than that in Phase 2 (see Figure 11–1). As expected, the women reported they liked the shortened work schedule.

During test period 9, the women were questioned about their attitudes toward their work. The women were asked, "What do you think has made it possible for you to increase your earnings since you have been in the test?" The results of the responses to this item and the questioning that followed it indicated that the women attributed their increased productivity to the absence of rigid and excessive supervision in the test room. The women liked the "absence of bosses" and the "opportunity to set one's own pace." These results are very interesting in that freedom from excessive supervision was regarded as more important than the rest breaks, a shorter workweek, and free lunches.

Phase 4. Phase 4 was primarily a check on the validity of the previous findings. Period 10 was identical to period 7. Period 12 was identical to period 3—no rest breaks, no free lunch, a full six-day workweek. Period 13 was a replication of periods 7–10 except the company did not provide the midmorning lunch. Periods 10 and 12 lasted 12 weeks and period 13 lasted 31 weeks.

The results indicated that once again production rose. However, by this time, the girls were taking rest pauses whether or not they were scheduled and they overtly resisted attempts to eliminate these unscheduled breaks. By the end of the experiment, the women preferred the test-room situation with its friendly atmosphere and pleasant working conditions to the regular factory. The observer was regarded as a friendly representative of management and not as a repressive supervisor.

Again in the relay assembly test room as in the illumination experiments, the researchers were surprised by the results. Production had increased dramatically and the attitudes of the employees had become substantially more positive. What caused these changes?

Conclusions and Implications. Four tentative explanations of the improved performance were given: (*a*) fatigue was reduced by working shorter hours; (*b*) boredom was reduced by working shorter shifts; (*c*) motivation was improved by the wage incentive plan; and (*d*) motivation was improved because of changes in supervisory methods.

The first two explanations were dismissed after examining the daily output levels over the course of the study. The third possible explanation—improved motivation attributed to the wage incentive plan—was tested with two additional studies which concluded that part, but not more than half, of the increased productivity could be attributed to the incentive plan. In their words:

> [1.]   There was absolutely no evidence in favor of the hypothesis that the continuous increase in output in the Relay Assembly Test Room during the first two years could be attributed to the wage incentive factor alone.
>
> [2.]   The efficacy of a wage incentive was so dependent on its relation to other factors that it was impossible to consider it as a thing in itself having an independent effect on the individual. Only in connection with the interpersonal relations at work and the personal situation outside work, to mention two important variables, could its effect on output be determined. [Roethlisberger & Dickson, 1939, p. 160.]

Therefore, the researchers concluded that the most important determiner of increased productivity was the change in supervision to a more permissive and democratic style.

When the relay assembly test-room study was completed, the experimenters realized they had not been investigating the effects of rest breaks and a shortened workweek on productivity but rather they had been studying the effects of the social situation on employee attitudes. The RATR study clearly demonstrated the importance of interpersonal relations, supervision, and employee attitudes for industry. These results were at variance with some basic managerial assumptions of that time. Productivity was demonstrated not to be solely determined by such environmental factors as illumination. Instead, the work situation was shown to be extremely complex and composed of many factors previously not even considered relevant. As a result of this study, rest pauses were introduced in Western Electric plants throughout the country. In addition, the management of Western Electric was so satisfied with the results of the research that additional studies were undertaken.

Interviewing Program

At the conclusion of the RATR study, the researchers believed that employee morale was closely related to satisfaction with supervision. Moreover, this study also demonstrated that productivity and morale were positively correlated. Therefore it became clear that the area of supervision merited additional study.

It was at this point that the investigators changed their focus from studying the impact of enviromental manipulations to investigating employee attitudes, supervision, and morale. This change in focus can be considered to represent the birth of the field of human relations with its recognition of the importance of human needs relating to interpersonal relationships. The decision systematically to study employee attitudes and morale affected the subsequent development of the entire discipline of industrial psychology.

Procedure. A mass interviewing program was initiated in the inspection branch, employing about 1,600 workers. Three male and two female supervisors were trained to obtain accurate information about the attitudes of employees toward such things as working conditions and the quality of supervision.

Since the cooperation of the supervisors was extremely important, only a few employees from each section were interviewed each day. This minimized the interruption in a section and permitted the work therein to continue as normally as possible. The supervisors were also involved in providing lists of eligible interviewees and providing a place where the interview could be conducted.

The entire program would have failed without the willing cooperation also of the employees being interviewed. Toward this end, the interviewers were trained to exercise care in explaining the purpose of the interview and assuring respondents of the confidentiality of their replies. Furthermore, employees were paid their usual wage for time missed from the job because of participating in the interviewing program.

The interviewers recorded replies verbatim in order to minimize forgetting and misinterpretation. Initially, the investigators feared that this procedure might cause the interviewees to be reluctant to talk. However, this fear was groundless. The respondents freely expressed both favorable and unfavorable attitudes toward company policies and practices. These attitudes were categorized relative to (*a*) supervision, (*b*) working conditions, and (*c*) the job in order to facilitate their interpretation.

Results. Largely because of the care given to clarifying the purpose of the study, the use to be made of the data, and the confidential nature of the replies, the overall reactions to the interviewing program from both employees and supervisors were very favorable. More than 20,000 employees were interviewed before the program was suspended because of the economic depression.

The rather rigid initial form of the interviewing procedure was substantially loosened as the study progressed. With the less structured procedure employees were given considerable freedom to discuss those matters they felt were important. Although this procedural change tripled the length of the average interview (to 90 minutes) the additional amount of significant information obtained and the resultant cooperation of the interviewees justified the increase.

The results of the interviewing program were incorporated into subsequent supervisory training programs and were widely distributed throughout the company. The Hawthorne management undertook a comprehensive program to investigate employee complaints and possible solutions.

The most important finding from the interviewing project in terms of understanding industrial behavior was the discovery of the previously unsuspected importance of employee work groups. These informal clusters of workers were found to exert considerable control over the behavior, including job output, of the individual members.

Bank Wiring Observation Room

The bank wiring observation room (BWOR) study was designed further to investigate the impact of informal employee social structure.

Procedure. This study entailed a detailed investigation of a work group under nearly normal everyday working conditions. Although no experimental manipulations, such as illumination changes, were performed, one change from normal working conditions was required: the workers were moved from the plant into an experimental room. This was done because previous findings had demonstrated that it was infeasible to conduct research in the plant itself where rivalries tended to develop between the "special" research group and the rest of the employees. These rivalries and jealousies interfered both with the research efforts and with the normal work routine. In spite of this change in work setting, attempts were made to make the work situation in the experimental room as realistic as possible.

As in the RATR study, an observer was placed in the room. He was instructed to avoid any supervisory or leadership activities and against violating any employee confidences. The primary task for the observer was to determine how both the formal and informal social group functioned. Further, he was instructed to assess the interrelationships between these two types of groups.

As in the earlier Hawthorne studies, the researchers demonstrated their receptivity to information tangential to the fundamental issue under consideration. Thus, although the observer was instructed to focus on formal and informal work groupings, he was encouraged to note any other behavior he considered important.

Data recorded by the observer were supplemented by those obtained by an interviewer who remained outside the test room. The general plan was for the observer to record actual behavior and for the interviewer to uncover the reasons for that behavior.

During the first week the artificiality of the work setting, including the presence of the observer, appeared itself to influence the workers' behavior. The men worked constantly and were suspicious of the observer. Shortly, however, they appeared to return to their more usual work routine: they took frequent rest breaks and violated several company policies. After a month, the researchers were confident that the work group was operating in its usual manner. The observations in the BWOR continued for approximately seven months.

Division of Work.   Fourteen men worked in the BWOR. Nine were wiremen, three were soldermen, and two were inspectors. These men made parts of switches for telephone equipment. Wiring and soldering required different lengths of time. One solderer could solder the connections made by about three wiremen. As a result, the men were divided into soldering units. Two inspectors could handle the work of all the men. The arrangement of these work groups is shown in Figure 11–2.

The wiremen worked on two kinds of switches for the telephone equipment: connectors and selectors. The method of wiring was the same for both types of switches and the differences between them were very small. The men in the front of the room (W_1, W_2, W_3, W_4, W_5, W_6, S_1, S_2, and I_1) worked on connectors while the men in the back (W_7, W_8, W_9, S_4, and I_3) worked on selectors. The more skilled men were moved to the front to work on connectors. Men

FIGURE 11–2

Bank Wiring Room: Division of the Group into
Inspection and Soldering Units

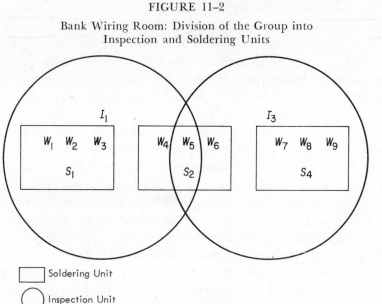

Soldering Unit

Inspection Unit

Source: G. C. Homans. *The human group.* P. 56.

began as solderers, progressed to selector wiremen and then to connector wiremen. Being transferred to connector wiremen was considered a promotion even if not accompanied by an increase in pay.

The Social Organization in the BWOR. Although the 14 men in the test room felt an identity as a group, two smaller cliques developed. The men in the front of the room, Clique A, consisted of W_1, W_3, W_4, S_1, and I_1. W_2 participated in the games that the clique played but he rarely participated in the conversation. The men in the back of the room, Clique B, consisted of W_7, W_8, W_9, and S_3. W_6 joked around quite a lot with the men in Clique B but at times he was excluded from their activities. W_5, S_2, and I_3 did not participate in the activities of either clique. These social relationships are summarized in Figure 11–3.

Men within a clique tended to help each other on the job when it became necessary and they occasionally traded jobs with each other. The men within a clique tended to become friends and they also played games together during breaks at work. Each clique had its own games and activities. The men in Clique A felt superior to those in Clique B. They felt they bought higher quality candy, indulged in less horseplay, and perceived that their conversations were on a higher plane. Moreover, their productivity was greater.

FIGURE 11–3

Bank Wiring Room: Division of the Group into Cliques

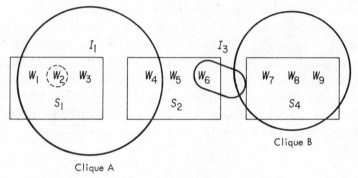

Source: F. J. Roethlisberger & W. J. Dickson. *Management and the worker.* P. 509.

Results. There were two major findings from this study: (1) Informal social groups were found to exert considerable influence on the behavior of the men; and (2) The men often violated company rules on important issues.

The results clearly indicated that the informal groups strictly enforced certain rules, or norms, of their own even when these conflicted with established company policy. These norms defined "proper" behavior in the work group. Thus, although the men were capable of higher productivity, they established and enforced a norm of 6,000 units per day as "fair" production. If any employee attempted to "bust the rate" by producing more than this number in order to receive more pay, strong informal pressures were brought to bear against him by the rest of the work group which perceived rate-busting as a serious threat. They feared that if production became too great, fewer employees would be needed and some employees would be fired. It is interesting to note that a "chiseler" (a person who produced less than the standard) was subjected to the same kind of peer group pressures as a rate-buster.

The group was found to have several norms relating to its supervisor. One forbade "squealing" or telling the supervisor anything that might hurt one of the men in the group. Another governed the supervisor's behavior by providing social sanctions if he acted officiously or attempted to take advantage of his position of authority. The men were able to put sufficient pressure on one supervisor to cause him to request a transfer.

The observer also noted that the men broke company policy on a number of significant issues. For example, they frequently traded jobs thereby reducing the boredom and increasing opportunities for socialization. Company rules prohibited job trading because each man was trained only for his own job and was presumed to be unqualified for another one.

The men also violated company policy by reporting uniform productivity each day whereas, in reality, their daily output rate showed considerable variation. Since such a violation required supervisory complicity, it is clear that the supervisors also violated company regulations.

Personnel Counseling Project

This project was the last one in the Hawthorne series. It was initiated four years after the others were completed. (Research had been suspended during the intervening years because of the economic depression.) The goal of the personnel counseling project was to improve the quality of supervision and communication.

"Personnel men" were assigned to the various departments to talk to and counsel with the employees. The effects of this counseling program were improved supervisor-employee relations in the plant, reduced management-labor tensions, and improved personal adjustment of certain of the employees.

Conclusion

The Hawthorne studies called attention for the first time to the importance of the interpersonal environment at work. In particular, they emphasized the partial dependence of both productivity and job satisfaction on two types of social interaction: those between fellow workers and those between workers and supervisors. The human relations movement was encouraged by these findings as well as those of the Tavistock Institute Coal Mining Study described in the following section.

THE TAVISTOCK INSTITUTE COAL MINING STUDY

The Tavistock Institute of London, England, engaged in the late 1940s in a study of the effects of changes in coal mining procedures (Trist & Bamforth, 1951). The procedure entailed individual and group interviews conducted over a two-year period. The approximately 20 miners interviewed performed different coal mining jobs and had all been employed in the industry for a considerable time. Representatives of various levels of management were also interviewed.

The Short Wall Method

Coal mining procedures had remained essentially unchanged for a very long time until mechanized equipment was introduced in the 1940s. The premechanized, short wall method relied upon small work groups working autonomously at the coal face. Each work group was comprised of a highly skilled leader, his mate, and several unskilled laborers who removed the coal in tubs. The size of the work groups varied from two to eight men. The leader negotiated a contract with the mine management for a piece of the mine. Management bought the coal mined by the group but exercised no supervisory function.

Each work group was responsible for the entire coal mining task. The leader and his mate performed the many complex and highly skilled operations that were required. Although the equipment was simple, the tasks were varied and the men considered themselves artisans.

The choice of work mates was obviously of crucial importance. This choice was made by the leader—a highly skilled and respected man in the community. Once a work group was formed, the relationships among its members tended to become stable and long lasting. When a man was injured or killed, the other group members typically cared for his family. The powerful interpersonal bonds between the work group members were often reinforced by composing the groups on kinship lines.

These autonomous closely knit work groups were remarkably adaptive to the mining environment. Mining was accurately perceived by the men as a dangerous occupation; they reported that the fear of death and the extreme darkness of the mine made the work environment a source of constant anxiety. The close relationships between the men helped them overcome their fears. The importance to the men of this group function was considerable.

The short wall method encouraged conflict between the various work groups centered about the availability of tubs for moving the coal. These tubs were always in short supply and many rather unethical practices were followed by each work group in its attempt to have access to as many tubs as it needed. This interteam conflict, which sometimes spilled over from the mine to the community, tended to increase intragroup loyalty and cohesiveness.

A type of graft developed in this mining environment. The leader often paid off a mine official in order to secure a prime section of the mine for his work group: i.e., one wherein the coal was reputed to be soft and easy to work. The mining community was rough and tough; the short wall system of mining was well suited to the general environment.

The Long Wall Method

The coal mining industry was nationalized in the 1940s, and the engineering consultants suggested the installation of mechanical coal cutting equipment and automatic conveyors. Consequently, coal mining became technologically more complex. Whereas the earlier procedures emphasized human effort, the newer ones emphasized mechanical effort. Mechanization made possible the working of a single large face of the mine.

The new procedure, referred to as the long wall method, resulted in the creation of a work relationship very different from that associated with the earlier procedures. The artisan relationship between a skilled leader and his mate assisted by one or more laborers was not compatible with the new job demands. The need arose for a work unit somewhat analogous in size and complexity to a small factory department. The basic unit became a work group of 40–50 men and their supervisors.

The long wall method divided the work into a standard series of constituent and sequential operations. The work groups were spread over approximately 200 yards in a mining tunnel approximately 2 yards wide and 1 yard high. Production engineers wrote the simple equation: 200 tons of coal mined daily equals 40 men over 200 yards over 24 hours. Things did not turn out to be that simple.

Trist and Bamforth (1951, p. 10) stated:

> Anyone who has listened to the talk of the older miners who have experienced in their own worklives the changeover to the long wall cannot fail to be impressed by the confused mourning for the past that still goes on in them together with a dismay over the present coloured by despair and indignation. To the clinical workers, the quality of these talks has at times a ring that is familiar.

A primary reason for the morale decrease following institution of the long wall mining system was that this system eliminated the close-knit work group. No comparable social structure emerged to help the men cope with their psychological and emotional problems.

Changes other than those of morale were also apparent. Productivity decreased considerably. The men replaced their former norm of high productivity with a lower standard. Whereas externally imposed supervision was unnecessary under the short wall method, it became critical with the new system. Unfortunately, effective supervision was essentially impossible with the long wall; the men were spread out too far to supervise effectively, and combined with the darkness in the mine, they were able to do much as they pleased. Absenteeism increased and contributed further to decreased productivity.

Conclusions

Trist and Bamforth interpreted their observations psychologically. They attributed the production decreases to an increasing sense of anomie. The workers lost their sense of meaning in life. Withdrawal in its many forms characterized the miners' behavior. It is clear that changes that are technologically advantageous may yet prove to be harmful to an organization whenever such changes ignore human needs. Moreover, the results of the Tavistock Institute study replicated an important finding of the Hawthorne studies: the importance both to morale and productivity of the social context of work.

THE HUMAN RELATIONS MOVEMENT

The results of the Hawthorne and Tavistock studies, along with the findings of others, led to the development of the field of human relations. Unlike Taylor, who neglected the social context of work, these social interactions are central to the approach of the human relations psychologists. The objective is to apply behavioral knowledge in organizations to build human cooperation toward attainment of organizational goals. Thus, it is an action-oriented, goal-directed discipline (Davis, 1967). In addition to studying organizational behavior for its own sake, human relations psychologists seek to do something constructive about it. That something is to develop more productive and humanly rewarding outcomes of work. The general approach is amplified and clarified in the next chapter wherein we consider the view of three major human relations psychologists.

SUMMARY

Although completed over 30 years ago, the Hawthorne studies remain as a classic and most significant research effort in the field of industrial psychology. The findings of the Hawthorne studies helped turn the discipline of industrial psychology toward a more human relations viewpoint. The initial experiments on illumination produced some unexpected and interesting results. Therefore, a second more comprehensive experiment, the relay assembly test-room study, was undertaken. The variables manipulated included the introduction and removal of rest pauses and the shortening and lengthening of the workday and workweek. Women assemblers were the subjects in this study.

The results indicated that all changes, whether beneficial or detrimental to the employees resulted in increased production. The researchers concluded that the most important determinant of the increased production was the change in supervisors from an authoritarian style to a more permissive democratic style. The importance of the social situation on productivity and employee attitudes was also demonstrated in this study.

The next study was the interviewing program. The results of this study clearly demonstrated the importance of the social context of work. The employee's informal work groups were found to exert considerable control over worker's behavior.

The fourth Hawthorne study was the bank wiring observation room study. The purpose of this study was to examine a work group under as real-life conditions as possible. There were two major results. First, as demonstrated in the interviewing program, the informal social groups were found to exert significant control over worker behavior by generating and enforcing group norms. These norms sometimes provided social pressure to disregard company rules. The personnel counseling project concluded the Hawthorne studies. The most significant conclusion from these studies is the importance of the social relationships at work on worker's behavior.

The Tavistock Institute coal mining study investigated the effects of a change in English coal mining procedures. Before the change, coal was mined for generations using the short wall method. Small autonomous work groups (2–8 men) mined the coal. Each group worked together as a unit for many years. These closely knit work groups helped the workers cope with the problem of fear that is a part of the mining profession. An engineering study indicated that mining would be more efficient if mechanical equipment was installed. This suggestion was followed and a new system of mining, the long wall method, was initiated. This method increased the work group size to approximately 40. The stable social relationships between workers that were present with the short wall method now disappeared. Production decreased and absenteeism increased as a result of the change in mining procedures. These results are attributed to the workers developing a sense of anomie. The important conclusion to be drawn from this research is that changes dictated by rational engineering considerations that ignore human social needs may prove to be harmful to the organization.

These two studies and other work led to the formation of the field of human relations psychology, a discipline that emphasizes the social factor in the work setting.

12. Behavioral Management Theorists

The Hawthorne and Tavistock studies described in the previous chapter marked the beginning of systematic consideration of interpersonal factors in industrial organizations. Three psychologists—McGregor, Herzberg, and Likert—have had an especially significant impact on contemporary industrial psychology and management theory. Moreover, elaborations of their views are likely to dominate these fields for many years to come. Hence this chapter summarizes and evaluates the theoretical positions of these three men.

McGREGOR: THEORY X AND THEORY Y

McGregor published his major work, *The Human Side of Enterprise*, in 1960. This book is an examination of the assumptions implicit to industrial management. It will be helpful briefly to summarize McGregor's views on human motivation before discussing these assumptions and their implications.

Motivation

McGregor's notions about motivation were heavily grounded in the work of Maslow, a personality theorist. According to Maslow (1954), man is a wanting animal. That is, when one of his needs is satisfied, that need is replaced by another one. This process of continual wanting motivates behavior from birth to death; the human organism continually attempts to satisfy his needs.

Maslow further postulated that man's needs are hierarchically ar-

304

ranged. This hierarchy is comprised of five levels arranged in order of their importance to biological survival; physiological, safety, social, egoistic, and self-fulfillment.

Physiological Needs. The physiological needs (for example, for food and water) stand lowest in the hierarchy. However, they are preeminent in importance when thwarted. A man deprived of food or water is obviously not going to be concerned with satisfying a higher level need such as that for status or personal recognition.

The placement of the physiological needs at the bottom of the hierarchy reflects Maslow's position that a satisfied need is not a motivator. Since physiological needs are pretty well satisfied for most members of our society, these have little practical significance as motivators, and attention can be given to those needs at the next higher level: the safety needs.

Safety Needs. These include the need for protection from physical danger and threat. Gratification of such needs clearly preoccupies the serviceman engaged in battle. Although the threat of *physical* danger is rarely present in everyday life, and hence is not typically a powerful motivator, the need for *psychological* safety (that is, security) does have significant motivational consequences for large numbers of persons in our culture. The need for security becomes especially important when man is in a dependent relationship wherein he fears arbitrary action. The fear of such action characteristically has supported efforts to organize labor and has motivated seniority provisions in virtually all union contracts.

Once the safety needs are relatively well satisfied, the social needs become increasingly important motivators of behavior.

Social Needs. These needs include those for giving and receiving friendship, belonging, and association. According to McGregor, management is aware of the social needs but often incorrectly assumes that these needs conflict with the attainment of organizational goals. Hence management may attempt to thwart satisfaction of the social needs. In consequence, the employee may become antagonistic and uncooperative.

Egoistic Needs. These needs stand at the next higher level and probably assume greatest significance both for management and employees. The egoistic needs are of two types:

1. Those related to self-esteem, including the needs for self-respect, self-confidence, and competence.

2. Those related to one's reputation, including the needs for recognition, appreciation, and status.

Unlike the lower level needs, the egoistic ones remain unsatisfied in typical industrial organizations, particularly for employees in the lower levels of the job hierarchy. There is obviously little satisfaction of egoistic needs for routine production workers. In McGregor's view, the rigid application of principles of so-called scientific management has had the unfortunate consequence of blocking the satisfaction of some of man's most important needs.

Self-Fulfillment Needs. The needs standing at the top of the hierarchy are those for self-fulfillment. These include the needs for fully realizing one's potential, being creative, and continued self-improvement throughout one's lifetime. Hence the self-fulfillment needs are sometimes referred to as needs for self-actualization.

Relatively few jobs provide opportunities for self-actualization. Furthermore, the deprivation experienced at lower levels of the needs hierarchy (particularly with reference to social and egoistic needs) prevents most employees from attending to their need for self-fulfillment.

An Integration. McGregor postulated two major categories of assumptions by management relative to the needs-hierarchy concept outlined above. He designated these assumptions *Theory X* and *Theory Y*. As you will shortly see, Theory X and Theory Y are caricatures of managerial styles; no manager literally adheres to either set of principles. Most management styles fall somewhere on a continuum between these two extreme sets of assumptions. At one extreme, the assumptions of Theory X are inconsistent with Maslow's need hierarchy theory: at the other, the assumptions of Theory Y are entirely consistent with Maslow's theory.

Theory X: The Traditional View of Direction and Control

Although it is doubtful that any manager would agree that he subscribes to the three assumptions underlying Theory X behavior, it is clear that some or all of these assumptions are implicit in many management actions. The three assumptions of Theory X managers are (McGregor, 1960, pp. 33–35):

1. "The average human being has an inherent dislike of work and will avoid it if he can." McGregor maintains that the stress placed by management on a "fair day's work" and the evils of output re-

striction reflect the underlying belief that the average worker is lazy and therefore tries to work as little as he can safely get away with. Theory X managers perceive that the evidence for this assumption is overwhelming.

2. "Because of this human characteristic of dislike of work, most people must be coerced, controlled, directed, threatened with punishment to get them to put forth adequate effort toward the achievement of organizational objectives." Theory X managers feel that the promise of reward is not sufficiently strong to overcome the fundamental dislike of work. Hence the threat of a punishment, such as that of employment termination, is necessary to achieve reasonable levels of productivity.

3. "The average human being prefers to be directed, wishes to avoid responsibility, has relatively little ambition, wants security above all." This viewpoint assumes the mediocrity of the masses; Theory X managers bemoan the low quality of their workers.

Although the extreme position of Theory X management is somewhat of a straw man, the implicit assumptions do influence much contemporary managerial strategy. Theory X managers focus upon the reinforcements provided through wages and job tenure—both of which relate only to the workers' physiological and safety needs. You will recall that in laying out the needs-hierarchy theory, Maslow states that once these lower level needs are satisfied, the social and egoistic needs assume added importance. Theory X managers provide little opportunity for these latter needs to be satisfied.

McGregor also addresses a classic counterargument sometimes made by management. This argument states essentially that it is virtually impossible to attempt to gratify higher level needs (for example, for status or personal recognition) for most employees because they are essentially unwilling to work efficiently. In McGregor's view, when employees are reluctant to cooperate with management in the attainment of organizational goals, this reluctance is attributable to management rather than employee deficiencies. He points out that the rewards offered by Theory X managers (pay, fringe benefits, and so on) are useful to workers only when they leave their jobs and go home. Wages or medical benefits are useless to an employee while he is on the job. Therefore, it is reasonable to expect that by thwarting ego needs, work is a source of punishment rather than reward. To the extent that work is thus perceived as an evil that must be endured to provide for subsequent pleasures *off* the job, it is not surprising that some workers attempt to do as little of it as they can.

McGregor acknowledges that this analysis of management may appear unduly harsh and that the lot of the industrial employee has been greatly improved during the 20th century. Management has become more humanitarian and equitable. However, he insists that this has been done without any fundamental change in management's understanding of employee needs. He stresses that a new set of assumptions of workers' needs (Theory Y) must replace those of Theory X if present conditions are to be further improved.

Theory Y: The Integration of Individual and Organizational Goals

The six assumptions of Theory Y (McGregor, 1960, pp. 47–48) are:

1. "The expenditure of physical and mental effort in work is as natural as play or rest." This assumption implies that man does not inherently dislike work. Rather, depending upon conditions over which management has control, work may be perceived as satisfying and voluntarily performed or dissatisfying and avoided whenever possible.

2. "External control and the threat of punishment are not the only means for bringing about effort toward organizational objectives. Man will exercise self-direction and self-control in the service of objectives to which he is committed."

3. "Committment to objectives is a function of the rewards associated with their achievement." If the rewards provided at work result in the satisfaction of the egoistic and self-fulfillment needs, then the workers will direct their efforts toward organizational objectives.

4. "The average human being learns, under proper conditions, not only to accept but to seek responsibility."

5. "The capacity to exercise a relatively high degree of imagination, ingenuity, and creativity in the solution of organizational problems is widely, not narrowly distributed in the population."

6. "Under the conditions of modern industrial life, the intellectual potentialities of the average human being are only partially utilized."

These assumptions have very different implications for management than do those of Theory X. Theory Y implies that collaboration between labor and management is possible, while Theory X assumptions offer management an easy rationalization for organizational failures.

The central principle of organization derived from Theory Y is *integration:* that is, the creation of conditions such that organizational members can best achieve their own goals by directing their efforts toward the success of the enterprise. This principle implies that maximally efficient organizations make significant adjustments to member needs. The Scanlon plan is one strategy for achieving integration.

Scanlon Plan

The plan devised by Scanlon, an associate of McGregor, implements a philosophy of management consistent with Theory Y and the principle of integration (Lesieur, 1958). The two important features of this plan are cost-reduction sharing and effective participation.

Cost-Reduction Sharing. Improvements in organizational effectiveness and consequent economic gain resulting from employee suggestions are shared with the employees. The method for sharing cost-reduction savings requires the development of a ratio between the organization's total manpower costs and a measure of output, like total sales. This ratio is derived after considerable study and is generally unique to that particular organization. Improvement of the ratio, representing an economic gain to the organization, is shared with the employees on a monthly basis.

Effective Participation. Taken alone, the cost-reduction sharing feature of the Scanlon plan is simply a form of incentive or profit sharing. The distinctive feature of the plan is that it provides, in addition, a mechanism whereby every organizational member can contribute to organizational efficiency. In so doing, it provides opportunities for every member to satisfy his higher level needs through efforts directed toward organizational (rather than external) objectives.

Effective participation is implemented through a committee structure with representation from all organizational groups and levels. The function of these committees is to discuss and critically evaluate all suggestions for improving the organizational effectiveness ratio.

Membership is rotated thereby giving everyone in the organization a chance to serve as a committee member. Departmental committees of workers and lower level supervisors have the authority to implement immediately ideas appropriate to their level. Suggestions which have broad organizational implications are referred to higher level "screening committees" consisting of representatives of both workers and management. Minutes of all meetings are kept to insure that ideas are never lost and that the screening committee is aware of the actions taken throughout the organization.

McGregor, despite the absence of research support, claims that in Scanlon plan companies participation is significantly greater than that obtained from conventional suggestion plans. He attributes this to the absence of impersonal suggestion boxes and remote committees evaluating worker ideas. In the Scanlon plan, the individual in his own work setting or at a screening committee meeting presents his idea. Then, in his presence, the idea is discussed and evaluated. If the idea is accepted, the individual is reinforced for his contribution to the company. If not, he is often encouraged to seek help from others in the company in order to improve the original idea. McGregor claims, again without research support, that in a Scanlon plan company a climate is created which encourages individuals to work together to develop ideas rather than one which encourages secrecy to prevent someone from stealing his idea and getting the reward for himself. Individuals are encouraged to cooperate rather than compete for monetary rewards. The economic gains from an employee's suggestions are shared with his fellow employees while providing him with considerable satisfaction of social and ego needs.

An Overview

McGregor's contributions to the field of human relations are those of a formulator of theory and not those of a validator of theory. McGregor did not perform controlled experiments to substantiate his theoretical positions.

As previously stated, McGregor's views on motivation were based on Maslow's need hierarchy theory. While Maslow's theory has found considerable acceptance in the industrial community, there is very little experimental evidence to indicate that it has the degree of validity that McGregor assumed it possesses. Similarly, Mc-

Gregor's confidence in the Scanlon plan was not based on research but rather on personal observation. The enthusiasm of those personally involved with the plan has never been questioned. (Lesieur & Puckett, 1969.) However, the presumed financial benefits of the plan have not yet been empirically demonstrated.

Despite the absence of research support for McGregor's theories, he has had a significant impact on management thought. His caricature of American industry as a Theory X institution has hit home with a substantial number of executives. The *Human Side of Enterprise* has been credited with helping turn management thinking around in the last decade toward the human relations viewpoint. Furthermore, McGregor is credited with being the first to identify the dichotomy between the human relations viewpoint (Theory Y) and Taylor's (1911) scientific management position (Theory X).

HERZBERG: MOTIVATION-HYGIENE THEORY

In 1959, Herzberg, Mausner, and Snyderman published *The Motivation to Work*. This book contained the results of their research and presented the motivation-hygiene theory of job satisfaction to explain these results. A second book *Work and the Nature of Man* (Herzberg, 1966) summarizes the theory and presents its industrial implications. Herzberg's theory is one of the most controversial in the field of industrial psychology. It will be summarized and critically evaluated following the presentation of the research which provided its underlying rationale.

The Preliminary Research on Job Satisfaction

Herzberg, Mausner, and Snyderman (1959) sought to identify events predisposing increased or decreased job satisfaction by interviewing 200 accountants and engineers. They began by asking the interviewees to recall a time when they felt particularly good about their job. The interviewers then determined the reasons for the good feelings. The workers were asked if their positive feelings at that time affected their job performance, their interpersonal relationships, and their overall well-being. After a positive sequence of events was completed, the interview was repeated, but this time the workers were asked to describe events at work that resulted in negative feelings about their jobs. The interview was continued until a worker could think of no further sequence of events associated with increased or decreased job satisfaction.

The interview responses generated five factors as primary determiners of job satisfaction: achievement, recognition, work itself, responsibility, and advancement. The last three were determined to be of greater importance for a lasting change of attitudes. These same five factors appeared very infrequently when the workers described events that resulted in job dissatisfaction. Therefore when one of these five factors was present, workers were satisfied. However, when they were absent, the workers were not dissatisfied. Instead, they held neutral feelings.

An entirely different set of factors was found to determine job dissatisfaction. The major dissatisfiers were factors extrinsic to the task itself: for example, company policy and administration, supervision, salary, interpersonal relations, and working conditions. Unlike the satisfiers, these dissatisfiers produced short-term changes in job attitudes. These five factors were mentioned only infrequently when the workers discussed satisfying circumstances.

The findings of the original studies led to the conclusion that the factors involved in producing job satisfaction are separate and distinct from those leading to job dissatisfaction. In other words, semantics aside, job satisfaction and dissatisfaction are not opposites of each other. The opposite of job satisfaction is *no* job satisfaction; the opposite of job dissatisfaction is *no* job dissatisfaction.

The motivation-hygiene theory seeks to integrate these findings by defining and differentiating the essential qualities of these two presumably distinct sets of factors.

Motivation-Hygiene Theory

The two dimensions designated above as satisfiers and dissatisfiers are presumed to reflect two different human needs systems.

One need system is derived from man's biological structure; it is comprised of his primary drives (hunger, for example) plus all of the learned drives which have become conditioned to these primary ones (for example, to earn money in order to buy food). The foundation of this need system is the biological drive to avoid pain and discomfort.

The other need system derives from man's unique ability to achieve and grow. He needs challenge, a sense of achievement, and a feeling of accomplishment in order to feel fulfilled.

Note the similarity between Herzberg's and Maslow's views of motivation. What Maslow classifies as the lower level needs (physiological, safety, and social) correspond to Herzberg's need to avoid unpleasantness. Similarly, Maslow's higher level needs (egoistic and self-fulfillment) correspond to Herzberg's need for growth.

Proceeding from the postulation of these two distinct systems, Herzberg regards the "need for growth" system as fundamental to the satisfiers and the "pain-avoidance" system as fundamental to the dissatisfiers. Any aspect of the job catering to the need for growth is a potential satisfier or *motivator;* likewise, any aspect of the job environment catering to the biologically based need system is a potential dissatisfaction-reducer, or *hygiene* factor. The predicted effects of the motivator and hygiene factors are shown schematically in Figure 12–1.

FIGURE 12–1

Schematic Representation of the Two-Factor Theory of Job Satisfaction*

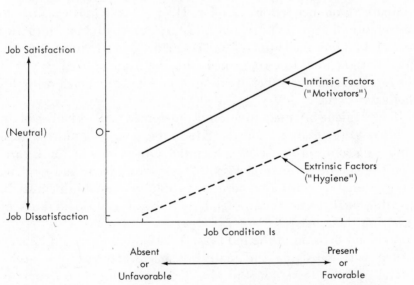

* Although shown as linear functions, no assumption of linearity is made by the theory.

Implications

If Herzberg's distinction between the effects of motivator and hygiene factors is correct, it calls into question a number of current practices in the area of industrial relations which tend to emphasize the hygiene factors.

Remember that Herzberg does not deny the importance of such factors. On the contrary, he recognizes that failure to satisfy hygiene needs may generate considerable organizational distress. However, he sees as a frequent error the assumption that preventing dissatisfaction will automatically generate positive feelings with a resultant increase in creativity, productivity, and profits and a corresponding decrease in absenteeism and turnover. According to Herzberg, satisfaction of hygiene needs leads only to a temporary absence of dissatisfaction. Hygiene demands, including those of increased salary and improved fringe benefits, tend to be recurrent.

Therefore, Herzberg feels that it is especially important for organizations to recognize and respond to employee needs for personal growth. Herzberg's position on this matter is similar to that taken by McGregor in arguing for Theory Y management.

What concrete steps can be taken by an organization to improve its response to needs for personal growth? Although Herzberg regards himself primarily as a theorist and critic, he has some preliminary recommendations to offer. He feels that it is essential to restructure the present-day industrial relations division into two formal divisions in an attempt to meet man's dual structure of needs. One division would be concerned with the hygiene need system of the worker and the other division would be concerned with his motivator needs.

The hygiene-oriented division is presently well established in industrial organizations. Herzberg feels this area of industrial relations will continue to be of substantial importance in the future. The hygiene needs of employees will inevitably recur and escalate. Thus, there is a continuing need for ingenuity to establish equity in distributing hygiene rewards and to discover additional ways of satisfying these needs.

A second division of the industrial relations effort would be concerned with satisfying the motivator needs. Herzberg identifies several specific tasks for this division, including one generally designated "job enrichment." Job enrichment is an attempt to make work tasks more meaningful, thereby enabling the employee to experience feelings of pride and accomplishment in his work.

Some of the principles involved in job enrichment are (Herzberg, 1968):

1. Removing some controls while retaining accountability.
2. Increasing the accountability of persons for their own work.

3. Granting additional authority to an employee.
4. Introducing new and more difficult tasks not previously handled.
5. Giving employees opportunities to become experts in specific or specialized tasks.

Note that these and related principles emphasize responsibility, achievement, recognition, and personal growth; in short, they emphasize what Herzberg designates as motivators.

Critical Evaluation

This theory has been responsible for giving direction to a tremendous amount of research in the general area of job satisfaction. The evidence has been contradictory, sometimes supporting but generally refuting the theoretical propositions.

The methodology of the original research providing the rationale for the theory, and hence the theory itself, has been the subject of much criticism. For example, it has been suggested (Vroom, 1964) that the conclusions from the interviews were artifacts of the open-ended nature of the interview procedure itself. Attempts to replicate the original findings do, indeed, seem to indicate that whereas use of the (Herzberg, Mausner, Peterson, & Capwell, 1957) original procedure confirms the original findings, variations in the interview procedure generate other findings (Dunnette, Campbell, & Hakel, 1967). In particular, needs for achievement, responsibility, and recognition have, in Herzberg's terminology, power both as motivator and hygiene factors. It has been suggested that Herzberg's procedure prevented discovery of this dual action because of the tendency of interviewees to attribute the causes of satisfaction to their own achievements on the job and to project dissatisfaction to conditions beyond their control (that is, to the job environment).

A second difficulty with Herzberg's theory is that it generates a prediction that is contrary to what is known about the relationship between job satisfaction and job performance. If the two-factor theory were correct, one would expect highly satisfied employees to be motivated to high productivity. However, this expectation is not confirmed; the extent of the relationship between job satisfaction and productivity is slight (Brayfield & Crockett, 1955).

Because of conflicting evidence and the failure to confirm certain predictions from Herzberg's motivation-hygiene theory, it must be regarded as an oversimplification of the complex relationship between motivation and job satisfaction or dissatisfaction (Dunnette et al., 1967).

LIKERT: PARTICIPATIVE ORGANIZATION

As director of the University of Michigan's Institute of Social Research, Likert and his colleagues have, for the past 25 years, engaged in studies of organizational management. Many of these studies have contrasted the best and poorest units within an organization with respect to such variables as leadership style, communication, and group process. Although the institute's program is still active, two major works summarize the research thus far completed and integrate these findings theoretically: *New Patterns of Management* (Likert, 1961) and *The Human Organization* (Likert, 1967).

The Empirical Bases

The theoretical formulations follow from two lines of empirical work which we will describe separately. The first is comprised of studies of specific variables (for example, communication, employee loyalty) in the organizational context. The second derives from analysis of the results of large-scale administration of an attitude survey designated the "Profile of Organizational Characteristics."

Specific Organizational Variables. Two representative studies will serve to indicate something of the scope and direction taken by this type of research: one on superior-subordinate communication, and the other on work-group loyalty.

The first was a study of perceived communication patterns in a public utility company (Mann, cited in Likert, 1961) and generated the results shown in Table 12–1. This table reveals marked discrepancies between supervisors' and subordinates' perceptions about the effectiveness of the communication process; the former perceived the communication process as more effective than the latter. Such findings are probably not unique to this particular company.

The second study here considered tested, and refuted, a proposition derived from Theory X assumptions which suggest a fundamental schism between loyalty to the work group and loyalty to the organization. As shown in Figure 12–2, closely knit industrial work groups (high peer group loyalty) tend to hold more favorable at-

TABLE 12–1

Extent to Which Superiors and Subordinates Agree as to Whether Superiors
Tell Subordinates in Advance about Changes

	Top Staff Says as to Own Behavior	*Foremen Say about Top Staff's Behavior*	*Foremen Say as to Own Behavior*	*Men Say about Foremen's Behavior*
Always tell subordinates in advance about changes which will affect them or their work..........	70%	27%	40%	22%
Nearly always tell subordinates.................	30 } 100%	36 } 63%	52 } 92%	25 } 47%
More often than not tell...	—	18	2	13
Occasionally tell.........	—	15	5	28
Seldom tell.............	—	4	1	12

Source: R. Likert. *New patterns of management.* P. 52.

FIGURE 12–2

Relationship between Peer-Group Loyalty and
Attitude toward Superior

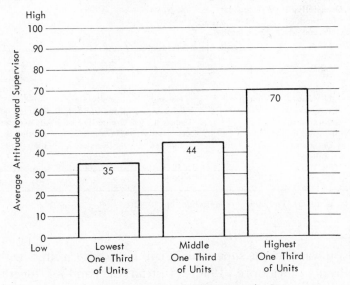

Units Grouped by Peer Group Loyalty Score

Source: R. Likert. *New patterns of management.* P. 33.

FIGURE 12-3

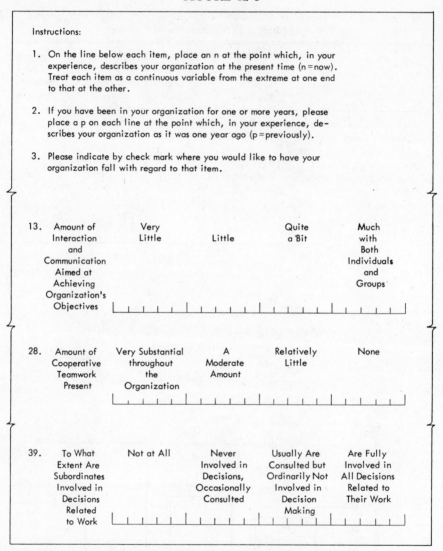

Instructions:

1. On the line below each item, place an n at the point which, in your
   experience, describes your organization at the present time (n=now).
   Treat each item as a continuous variable from the extreme at one end
   to that at the other.

2. If you have been in your organization for one or more years, please
   place a p on each line at the point which, in your experience, describes your organization as it was one year ago (p=previously).

3. Please indicate by check mark where you would like to have your
   organization fall with regard to that item.

13. Amount of   Very   Quite   Much
    Interaction   Little   Little   a Bit   with
    and   Both
    Communication   Individuals
    Aimed at   and
    Achieving   Groups
    Organization's
    Objectives

28. Amount of   Very Substantial   A   Relatively   None
    Cooperative   throughout   Moderate   Little
    Teamwork   the   Amount
    Present   Organization

39. To What   Not at All   Never   Usually Are   Are Fully
    Extent Are   Involved in   Consulted but   Involved in
    Subordinates   Decisions,   Ordinarily Not   All Decisions
    Involved in   Occasionally Involved in   Related to
    Decisions   Consulted   Decision   Their Work
    Related   Making
    to Work

Source: R. Likert. *The human organization.* Pp. 197-211.

titudes toward their supervisor than do work groups with low
peer loyalty (Seashore, 1954). Instead of banding together in
opposition to the supervisor, as suggested by the assumptions of
Theory X, closely knit work groups are likely to perceive him—and
presumably the organization he represents—*more* favorably.

Profile of Organizational Characteristics. This survey form has been administered during a period of several years to thousands of industrial employees. Three of the constituent items and a portion of the instructions are reproduced in Figure 12–3.

Organizational Typology

Based on the findings of the Institute for Social Research, Likert has classified organizations into four categories for theoretical purposes: exploitative authoritative, benevolent authoritative, consultative, and participative group. Table 12–2 summarizes some of the essential distinctions between these four systems of organization. In Table 12–2 note that an exploitative-authoritative organization (sometimes referred to as System 1) can be considered to have a Theory X orientation while a participative group (System 4) organization can be considered to have a Theory Y orientation. Similarly, Systems 2 and 3 organizations lie somewhere between on a Theory X-Theory Y continuum. Although Table 12–2 is based on empirical research, it should not be regarded as a summary of fact but instead as a statement of theory that awaits verification.

System 4 Organizations

It is clear from Table 12–2 that Likert regards System 4 as the most effective organizational system. He regards three principles as fundamental to the development and maintenance of such participative organizations: (1) supportive relationships, (2) group decision making, and (3) higher performance goals.

Principle of Supportive Relationships. System 4 organizations genuinely attempt to insure supportive interpersonal interactions among their members. Such supportive interactions enhance each organizational member's sense of personal worth and importance to the attainment of organizational goals (Likert, 1961). Although this principle can be used to guide all interpersonal relationships within an organization, its application is especially crucial in superior-subordinate relationships. The supervisor can encourage employee commitment to organizational objectives by enhancing the latter's sense of individual contribution to the successful attainment of organizational goals. As noted by Likert, this principle can only be implemented with regard for the employee's values, expectations,

TABLE 12–2

Organizational and Performance Characteristics of Different Management Systems Based on a Comparative Analysis

	System of Organization			
Operating Characteristics	Exploitative Authoritative (System 1)	Benevolent Authoritative (System 2)	Consultative (System 3)	Participative Group (System 4)
1. Character of motivational forces				
a. Underlying motives tapped	Physical security, economic security, and some use of the desire for status	Economic and occasionally ego motives	Economic, ego, and other major motives	Full use of economic, ego, and all other major motives
b. Kind of attitudes developed toward organization and its goals	Attitudes usually are hostile and counter to organization's goals	Attitudes are sometimes hostile and counter to organization's goals and are sometimes favorable to these goals	Attitudes may be hostile but more often are favorable and support behavior implementing organization's goals	Attitudes generally are strongly favorable and provide powerful stimulation to behavior implementing organization's goals
2. Character of communication process				
a. Amount of interaction and communication aimed at achieving organizational objectives	Very little	Little	Quite a bit	Much with both individuals and groups

3. Character of decision making				
a. At what levels in organization are decisions formally made?	Bulk of decisions at top of organization	Policy at top, many decisions within prescribed framework made at lower levels	Broad policy and general decisions at top, more specific decisions at lower levels	Decision making widely done throughout organization, although well integrated through linking processes provided by overlapping groups
4. Character of interaction-influence process				
a. Amount of cooperative teamwork	None	Virtually none	A moderate amount	Very substantial amount throughout the organization
5. Performance characteristics				
a. Productivity	Mediocre	Fair to good	Good	Excellent
b. Excessive absence and turnover	Tends to be high when people are free to move	Moderately high when people are free to move	Moderate	Low

Source: Adapted from R. Likert, *New patterns of management.* Pp. 223–233.

and background. The entire notion of *support* rests upon a perceptual phenomenon reflecting these values and expectations. What is viewed by one employee as supportive may well be viewed by another as punitive. Even more likely differences in background variables may generate a considerable discrepancy between what the supervisor perceives as supportive and what the employee himself perceives as supportive. This is perhaps most evident in, but certainly not limited to, instances where the supervisory-subordinate relationship involves persons of different races, sexes, vastly different educational backgrounds, and so on.

Group Decision Making. We have already noted (Table 12–2) differences in decision-making and interaction patterns within the

FIGURE 12–4

Man-to-Man and Group Patterns of Organization

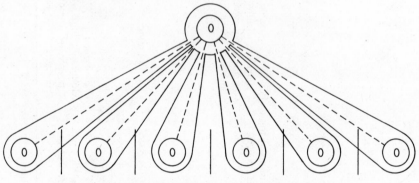

A. Man-to-Man Pattern of Organization

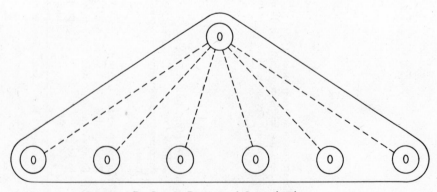

B. Group Pattern of Organization

Source: R. Likert. *New patterns of management.* P. 107.

four organizational systems posited by Likert. These differences are further clarified in Figure 12–4 which schematically summarizes interactions with two different organizational structures. The man-to-man model shown in that figure is the traditional one characteristic of System 1 and System 2 organizations. This is essentially a hierarchical, or chain-of-command structure with progressive delegation of authority to successively lower levels of the organizational hierarchy.

In contrast, a group pattern of organization (Figure 12–4*b*) involves subordinates at each level of the organizational hierarchy in making and implementing the decisions that affect their own work group. Obviously, some mechanism is required to insure coordination of the decisions and efforts of each of these work groups toward the attainment of *organizational* goals. This mechanism is provided by the "linking pin" structure (see Figure 12–5) suggested for System 4 organizations. Each linking pin is both a supervisor of one work group and a subordinate in another (next higher level) work group. He is thus the key person insuring adequate communication throughout the organization and, while representing his subordinates, is fully accountable to *his* supervisor for the effectiveness of decisions made and their execution within the group.

FIGURE 12–5

The Linking Pin

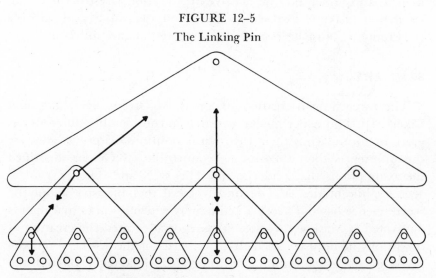

Arrows Indicate the Linking Pin Function

Source: R. Likert. *New patterns of management.* P. 113.

High Performance Expectations. The third fundamental principle of System 4 organization is that it expects high levels of performance from its members. This expectation must not be management's expectation alone; all employees at all levels must share and be committed to the goal of high performance. Likert (1967) postulates that this shared expectation of superior performance will follow from the development of supportive relationships and the involvement of the group members in decisions affecting them.

Critical Evaluation

Likert's theoretical position is more heavily grounded in empirical research than the theories of either McGregor or Herzberg. Many of Likert's concepts (for example, linking pin, supportive relationships) are now accepted parts of the human relations vocabulary and his profile of organizational characteristics has been widely used for research purposes.

However, Likert has probably not had as significant an impact on operational procedures in industry as has Herzberg; hence his propositions have not yet been as extensively tested. This difference in operational impact probably reflects the fact that it is easier to apply some of the principles derived from the motivation-hygiene theory than it is to undertake the massive organizational restructuring advocated by Likert. Further judgment on the validity of Likert's contributions must be reserved until more data are available.

SUMMARY

The three human relations theorists, McGregor, Herzberg, and Likert relied on experimental research to considerably different degrees in formulating their theoretical positions. However, despite this difference, their theories are compatible. McGregor identified the assumptions that underlie the Theory X and Theory Y managerial philosophies. McGregor advocated that industry adopt the social science based Theory Y philosophy which assumes that man is motivated as Maslow theorizes. McGregor advocated the creation of conditions in industry such that the needs of the workers and the needs of the organization are integrated. McGregor offered the Scanlon plan as an example of the practical application of the principle of integration.

Herzberg's motivation-hygiene or two-factor theory was based on the job satisfaction research of Herzberg, Mausner, and Snyderman. According to this theory, the factors that produce job satisfaction are separate and distinct from those that produce job dissatisfaction. The two-factor theory had been severely criticized and it is currently believed to be an oversimplified view of job satisfaction. However, Herzberg's views have had a significant impact on current operating procedures in industry.

Likert's theoretical positions are largely based on the research of the Institute of Social Research. He has devised a four-category organizational classification typology. Likert believes that the participative group organizational structure (System 4) is the most effective. System 4 organizations are characterized by supportive relationships, group decision making, and linking pins. There is some preliminary experimental evidence supportive of Likert's theories.

All three theorists believe that the higher level needs must be satisfied at work before man will be committed to organizational objectives. In addition, they feel that human engineering has simplified many industrial jobs to the point where it has become a liability instead of an asset. More fundamentally, however, the three theorists believe in the innate goodness and worth of the average man.

13. Leadership Research and Management Development

Such techniques of management development as sensitivity training and management gaming are applications of empirical findings in the general area of leadership. Hence, we will examine some of this leadership research first before discussing its various applications to improving managerial effectiveness.

LEADERSHIP RESEARCH

The present chapter concerns two levels of industrial leadership: line supervision and management. Although leadership is required at both levels, there are important differences between line supervisors and managers in the kinds of things they are expected to accomplish.

Supervisory Roles

The foreman or line supervisor is an intermediate in the relationship between nonsupervisory employees and higher levels of management. He typically has been promoted to his position from the line on the basis of seniority and/or merit, and often receives little or no training for his new leadership role. Although the line supervisor exerts a most direct influence upon the activities of individual employees and is the key figure in implementing decisions originating with management, he often is not accepted as a member either of the management or worker group.

326

Thus, whereas the supervisor lacks the status and authority associated with management, he must accept responsibilities far exceeding those of line employees. These responsibilities may include inducting the new employee into the work group and providing on-the-job training, encouraging safety, handling grievances, encouraging efficient job behavior, making performance ratings of the men he supervises, and scheduling the work activities in his section. In addition, he must represent the views of management to those he supervises and effectively communicate the needs of his subordinates to higher management.

Managerial Roles

Successively higher levels of industrial leadership (mid- and top management) tend less and less to interact with line employees. Managerial concerns are organizational in the sense that they are oriented more toward the company than toward a component work unit and are directed toward such broad issues as organizational goals, budgets, markets, and so on.

Hemphill (1960), using questionnaire responses of a sample of executives, identified the following ten dimensions of management activities:

1. Providing staff service in nonoperational areas—including gathering information, selecting employees, training supervisors.
2. Supervising work of others. (This dimension is characteristic of mid-management and lower positions. It is not a dimension of higher level management positions.)
3. Business control, including cost reduction and budget preparation.
4. Technical concern with products and markets.
5. Concern with human, community, and social affairs in consequence of company activity and policy.
6. Long-range planning.
7. Exercise of broad power and authority.
8. Concern with company reputation through public relations and maintenance of product quality.
9. Concern with personal status within the company and community.
10. Preservation of company assets.

All management positions emphasize some of these dimensions more than others. Indeed, certain of these dimensions are relatively incompatible. For example, managers concerned with preserving company assets through manipulating large operating expenses and taxes tend not to be involved in industrial relations or technical operations. Furthermore, these 10 dimensions of management activity are not all-inclusive. Differences in organizational settings, task requirements, and personal predispositions of managers may lead them to engage heavily in such other activities as personnel staffing (including selection, placement, and training), coordination, and communication.

The importance of the interaction between certain organizational characteristics and the primary roles of *mid-management personnel* has been clarified in a study of civilian managers working for the Department of the Army (Katzell, Barrett, Vann, & Hogan, 1968). Nine possible management roles, somewhat overlapping the 10 dimensions listed above, were identified for these employees: (*a*) long-range planning; (*b*) staffing; (*c*) technical consultation; (*d*) budgeting; (*e*) responsibility for sharing information versus personal responsibility for taking action; (*f*) concern for operations versus concern for advising others on technical matters; (*g*) involvement in technical activity versus administrative activity (coordination, communication, and so on); (*h*) controlling activities, including cost reduction; and (*i*) time spent with others.

These nine roles were related to certain organizational characteristics like the organization's mission, level relative to the Department of the Army, location, and size. It was found with respect to mission, for example, that organizations with an administrative mission tended to emphasize the staffing and controlling roles, and to deemphasize long-range planning. In contrast, organizations with a research and development mission tended to deemphasize staffing and controlling roles. With respect to organizational size as an interactive variable, larger organizations tended more than smaller organizations to emphasize the importance of time spent with others, and to deemphasize long-range planning activities by middle managers.

In spite of differences in managerial roles as a function of the organizational setting and of differences in roles between managers and line supervisors, all persons in these positions exercise some form of leadership. Therefore, it is necessary to make some general observations about the leadership process by way of background for the discussion of industrial supervision and management.

Nominal versus Effective Leadership

It is considerably easier to describe the ways in which leaders can function than it is to define the personal requirements for effective leadership, or to conceptualize the process of "leading." Investigations in the general area of leadership have pointed to the necessity for differentiating between leadership and status, and abandoning the prevalently held "great man" theory of leadership. Leaders are status figures; they occupy positions of esteem and wield power. However, the converse need not be true. Persons can have considerable status and power without being effective leaders.

Nominal leadership is imposed upon the group. The person occupying a position of nominal leadership has been appointed to this position by his superordinates. His status is generally reinforced by a title and salary sufficient to differentiate between himself and the members of the group he is assigned to head. A title on the door and a carpet on the floor may denote power as well as status. With enough of each, nominal leaders can command obedience. Whether or not they function as effective leaders, however, is an entirely different matter.

A person cannot be regarded as an *effective* leader unless he has willing followers. Workers who accept their supervisor or manager, and willingly implement his plans, behave and feel quite differently from those who are compelled to do so unwillingly. This is most apparent for elected leaders who are in a position to evoke a high level of subordinate effort and satisfaction by virtue of the fact that they have been chosen by the persons they lead. Elected leaders have behind them a feeling of group solidarity which gives them a powerful edge over a titular head.

Although many companies do take employee preferences into account when making supervisory appointments, the election of leaders is relatively uncommon in industry. Nevertheless, the distinction between nominal and effective leadership is useful because it alerts us to some of the potential difficulties entailed in the imposition of leadership. In order for an appointed leader to function with maximum effectiveness, he must be the sort of person who would have been elected by the group itself if it had been given the opportunity.

The distinction between nominal and effective leadership is perhaps most apparent in the military services. Virtually all enlisted men are obedient when an officer issues commands. Such obedience results from the threat of dire consequences for insubordination. However, the officer who can command on the basis of willing followership and whose men respect his superior knowledge and ability, feeling that they are part of a cohesive group pursuing common goals, is in an enviable position indeed. Unpleasant tasks are performed more willingly by the group members, and the general level of performance and personal feelings of satisfaction are considerably heightened under such circumstances.

From the foregoing discussion, it is evident that nominal leaders must be selected and trained with utmost care if they are to function effectively.

Specific techniques aside, what underlying attitudes, objectives, and concerns differentiate effective from ineffective leadership in contemporary society? If it were possible to select only one key phrase in reply to this question, it would have to be human relations. Effective industrial leadership is concerned with managing the interpersonal relationships at work in ways calculated to encourage both employee satisfaction and organizational goal attainment.

This dual emphasis upon effective human relations and organizational productivity as joint responsibilities of the industrial leader contrasts sharply with the notion of scientific management prevalent during the early part of this century. In this earlier view the leader's sole function was to expedite organizational productivity. This was to be accomplished impersonally through refinements in bureaucratic structure and increased efficiency of the methods of work.

The Successful Leader

Many studies of the characteristics of successful as opposed to unsuccessful managers implicitly assume that certain traits characterize successful leaders irrespective of the work setting. Adherents to the *trait theory* of leadership seek to identify certain characteristics or combinations of personal characteristics that underlie "natural" leadership. They assume that this general leadership quality attracts willing followers regardless of the particular circumstance wherein it is displayed.

This approach is illustrated by one study (Ghiselli, 1963) which identified five major traits displayed by effective managers. These traits are most apparent for managers at the higher organizational levels.

1. Initiative: a willingness to try new things.
2. Intelligence: high verbal and symbolic abilities.
3. Perceived occupational level: seeing oneself as deserving of high status and properly associating with others at the upper socioeconomic level.
4. Self-assurance: a favorable self-evaluation.
5. Supervisory ability: the ability to direct other's activities.

In a similar vein, executives and personnel managers were asked to describe the type of person most likely to succeed as a key member of top management (Jurgenson, 1966). The dozen adjectives selected from a list of 120 were:

decisive	energetic	creative
aggressive	self-starting	intelligent
productive	responsible	well-informed
enterprising	determined	clear-thinking

These adjectives clearly overlap the list of five traits of effective managers cited above.

We have mentioned that the trait view of leadership anticipates that persons who are effective leaders in one situation will tend also to be effective leaders in other situations. However, this expectation is open to serious question. One estimate of the correlation between leadership ability in *different* situations is a maximum value of 0.35 (Matthews, 1951). The correlations between several measures of leadership ability in a *given* situation, on the other hand, are considerably higher and support the view that effective leadership is *situational*. Whereas specific leader characteristics may predispose a person to assume leadership, his effectiveness in this capacity is heavily influenced by the circumstances under which he is required to function. We will return to this point again later in the chapter.

332   *Psychology in Industrial Organizations*

Leadership Styles

The behavior of leaders is often classified along a continuum ranging from *authoritarian* (or boss-centered) leadership at one pole to *democratic* (or subordinate-centered) leadership at the other (see Figure 13–1). Although the distinction between authoritarian and democratic leadership is a convenient one, it is apparent that these two styles rarely exist in pure form. It is generally recognized also that classification of leadership solely on this dimension does not do justice to the multidimensional nature of leadership climates.

FIGURE 13–1

Continuum of Leadership Behavior

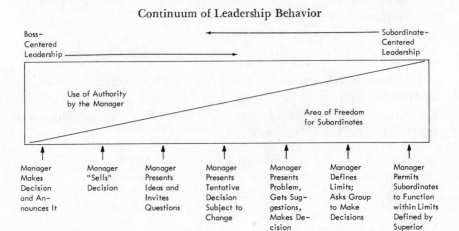

Source: P. Tannenbaum & W. H. Schmidt. How to choose a leadership pattern. P. 96.

Authoritarian Leadership. A group operating under authoritarian leadership is wholly dependent on the leader for a determination of policies and goals. The authoritarian leader wields absolute power and is the sole unifying factor within the group. He is the only person within the group who knows the overall plan of activity; and he alone has the responsibility for assigning tasks to individual members. The morale and productivity of the group deteriorates rapidly when such a leader is temporarily absent because the followers have become wholly dependent upon his direction.

Democratic Leadership. The democratic leader is an agent of the group. He facilitates and encourages the members' involvement and participation in achieving the group's goals and, whenever possible, in actually forming its objectives. Thus, the democratic leader encourages a maximum amount of group solidarity founded upon a network of strong interpersonal relationships between group members. Since each of the members is an active and informed participant in the group's activity, democratically led groups tend to perform quite effectively even during periods when the leader is temporarily absent.

Studies of Leadership Style.   There is a classic extensive study concerned with the relative effectiveness of authoritarian and democratic leadership (Lewin, Lippitt, & White, 1939; Lippitt, 1940). The groups in which these investigations were conducted each consisted of five boys who were 10 years old. These were extracurricular hobby groups and were led by adults primed to exercise three different kinds of leadership behavior: authoritarian, democratic, and laissez-faire. The behavior of the leaders in their attempt to establish each of these three group "atmospheres" is described in Table 13–1.

The experimental design required that the adult leader be changed periodically in order to expose each hobby group to all three types of leadership. The order of leadership was *rotated:* that is, the sequence for one group was democratic, authoritarian, and laissez-faire leadership; for another it was authoritarian, democratic, and laissez-faire, and so on.

In general, the results indicated that democratic leadership is superior for the purpose of evoking creative behavior and cooperativeness. Productivity and member satisfaction were poorest in the laissez-faire situation. It is important to note, however, that there were exceptions to the generalization that democratic leadership was responsible for the highest level of morale. Some of the youngsters, particularly those from autocratic homes, were perfectly satisfied to take orders from an authoritarian leader.

Many investigations of industrial leadership styles have been stimulated by this research with children. In general, such studies point to two conclusions:

First, a particular style may be relatively effective for one purpose and relatively ineffective for another. Thus, a style affecting productivity may not influence employee attitudes, and vice versa; and whereas a particular style may increase quantity of output, another may be required to increase quality (Anderson & Fiedler, 1964).

TABLE 13–1

Three Types of Leadership

Variable	Leader's Behavior		
	Democratic	Authoritarian	Laissez-faire
1. Control over policy formulation.	All policies a matter of group discussion and decision, encouraged and assisted by the leader.	All determination of policy by the leader.	Complete freedom for group or individual decision with a minimum of leader participation.
2. Control over member's activities.	Activity perspective gained during discussion period. General steps to group goal sketched, and when technical advice was needed, leader suggested two or more alternative procedures from which a choice could be made.	Techniques and activity steps dictated by the authority, one at a time, so that future steps were always uncertain to a large degree.	Various materials supplied by the leader who made it clear that he would supply information when asked to do so. He took no other part in the discussion.
3. Control over working associates.	The members were free to work with whomever they chose, and the division of tasks was left to the group.	The leader usually dictated the particular work task and work companion of each member.	Complete nonparticipation of the leader.
4. Dispensation of praise and criticism.	The leader was "objective" or "fact-minded" in his praise or criticism.	The leader tended to be "personal" in his praise or criticism of each member.	No attempt to appraise or regulate the course of events.
5. Participation by leader.	Leader tried to be a regular group member in spirit without doing too much of the work.	Leader remained aloof from active group participation except when demonstrating.	Infrequent spontaneous comments about members' activities.

Source: R. K. White & R. Lippitt. Leader behavior and member reaction. In D. Cartwright & A. Zander (Eds.), *Group dynamics*. P. 528.

Second, whereas our society tends to give an edge to democratic leadership styles, there are yet circumstances wherein authoritarian leadership may be superior. Persons who are unprepared for democratic group action because of lack of prior exposure to and training for such leadership may feel relatively insecure unless provided with the kind of direction afforded by an authoritarian leader.

Thus, the best leadership style is a function of such situational factors as the specific type of problem confronting the group and the group's constituency. With respect to the former, for example, it has been found that problems which depend for their solution upon coordinated action are more efficiently solved when the leadership is centralized and authoritarian than when it is democratic (Roby, Nicol, & Farrell, 1963). With respect to group constituency, there is evidence from several studies that individuals vary in their preference for constraining (authoritarian) versus freer (democratic) environments, and that this preference interacts with the leader's style jointly to determine both the employee's level of performance and satisfaction (Forehand & Gilmer, 1964).

Leadership Dimensions

Two dimensions of leader behavior, *consideration* and *initiation of structure,* have been the subject of considerable research. Typically, these dimensions are assessed by means of a questionnaire on which subordinates describe the way in which their supervisor leads (Fleishman, 1953).

Consideration entails awareness by the leader of his subordinates' feelings. It is the dimension of leadership emanating from the human relations view and is revealed by affirmative responses to such questionnaire items as:

"He expresses appreciation when one of us does a good job."

"He puts suggestions that are made by foremen under him into operation."

Initiating structure is supervisory behavior facilitating group interaction toward goal attainment. The supervisor may accomplish this by organizing, planning, and scheduling the work or by direct intervention in the group's goal-directed activities (Fleishman, 1955). Questionnaire items illustrating this dimension are:

"He offers new approaches to problems."

"He insists that foremen follow standard ways of doing things in every detail."

Dimensions versus Styles. Although there appears superficially to be a parallelism between the dimensions "consideration" and "initiation of structure" and the styles described earlier as "democratic" and "authoritarian," it would be erroneous to equate leadership dimensions and styles. A leader may have *either* a democratic or authoritarian style (to use the extremes of this scale) without his style necessarily implying anything about the dimensions of his leadership behavior. Either style can be exercised in a climate of high or low consideration.

Furthermore, contrary to what one might expect, the dimensions consideration and initiating structure are independent of each other. Considerate supervisors may or may not avoid initiating structure.

Consideration. The effective supervisor tends to regard his subordinates as individuals, each with his own motives, feelings, and goals. He recognizes that the motives, feelings, and goals of his subordinates are likely to be quite different from those held by himself (Meyer, 1951). Such an attitude of consideration in dealing with subordinates has been found to correlate positively both with ratings of supervisory effectiveness (Bass, 1958) and productivity of the work group (Likert, 1968).

This respect for the individuality of each subordinate probably underlies certain specific behaviors that have been found to differentiate between effective and ineffective supervisors. The former (1) evidence trust in the worker's ability to handle the task by not supervising too closely, (2) communicate effectively, and (3) delegate job tasks and provide the delegated persons with sufficient authority to carry out the tasks with which they are charged (Kahn & Katz, 1953).

Initiating Structure. A supervisor who initiates structure actively organizes and defines the group's activities. He assigns tasks, defines roles, plans ahead, and generally establishes ways of getting things done.

Thus, in initiating structure the supervisor behaves in a somewhat authoritarian manner. However, as we have previously said, this need not have any implication for the level of consideration displayed by him. It is quite possible for a supervisor to initiate structure and be regarded by his subordinates as high on consideration, low on consideration, or somewhere between these extremes on the consideration dimension.

There is evidence that with respect to at least one criterion of industrial behavior, grievance rate, initiation of structure is an especially important dimension for those supervisors who are "moderately considerate" (Fleishman & Harris, 1962). Those supervisors who were perceived by their subordinates as "highly considerate" generated a low grievance rate irrespective of their score for initiating structure. Also, those supervisors who were perceived as "inconsiderate" generated a high grievance rate irrespective of their

FIGURE 13–2

Interaction of Leadership Dimensions as Joint
Determinants of Grievance Rate

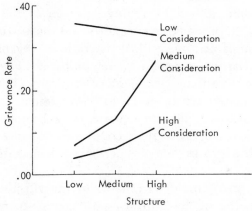

Source: E. A. Fleishman & E. F. Harris. Patterns of leadership behavior. P. 50.

score for initiating structure. But of supervisors perceived as being medium in consideration, those low on initiating structure generated a low grievance rate whereas those high on initiating structure generated a high grievance rate. These relationships are shown in Figure 13–2.

Thus, although initiation of structure *may* contribute to an elevated grievance rate, *it need not*. The determining factor is the interpersonal atmosphere in which the leader provides his direction and structure. If he can develop a climate of consideration, then his efforts to initiate structure can be well received.

Campbell, Dunnette, Lawler, and Weick (1970) conclude (based on the research of Fleishman, Harris, and Burtt, 1955, and Halpin, 1957) that the best dimensions of leadership like the best styles of leadership are a function of certain situational variables. The complexities of human behavior preclude generalizing about simple relationships between leader behavior or leadership style and effectiveness.

Employee Participation

The supervisor's role in initiating structure or, alternatively, in encouraging subordinate participation in setting goals, defining work roles, and so on must be appropriate to situational factors associated with the group's activities and structural properties of the group itself.

This was demonstrated in an investigation of the relationship between the flavor of management policy and the attitudes of supervisors. Two companies, one with democratic management and one with authoritarian management, were compared. The investigator concluded that the success of a democratic approach to leadership rests upon the employees' readiness to accept responsibility and the possession by them of sufficient experience and knowledge to deal with their work problems. If these conditions do not exist, authoritarian leadership proves to be superior to democratic leadership (Stanton, 1960).

One of the important determinants of the effectiveness of employee participation is the legitimacy of such participation as perceived by the workers themselves. Worker attitudes are positively influenced by participating in situations in which they regard it as right and proper for them to engage in the decision-making process (French, Israel, & As, 1960). However, there are a variety of situations in which the workers regard such participation as inappropriate and look toward the supervisor for concrete action of a structure-initiating nature.

The tolerance of workers for supervisors who exercise power depends also upon the perceived personal characteristics of the supervisor himself and the psychological needs of each of the subordinates. Workers may express satisfaction with a relatively powerful and directive supervisor who does not encourage much participation, provided such a supervisor is perceived by them as considerate of his men (Mann & Hoffman, 1960). Furthermore, there are individual differences among workers in their desire for, and hence satisfactions derived from, participation in decision making. Persons who have strong needs for independence react more favorably to participation than do persons with weak independence needs (Vroom, 1959).

Finally, even within a single industrial organization attitudes toward directive and participative supervision may vary because of differences in the structure of various work groups. Large groups characterized by little personal interaction among the workers and between workers and their supervisor were found to favor authoritarian leadership. Conversely, workers within small, highly interactive groups had more positive attitudes toward equalitarian leaders (Vroom & Mann, 1960).

It is evident from the foregoing that it is impossible to make blanket generalizations about the most effective supervisory styles. Effective leadership behavior in certain situations may prove relatively ineffective in others because of interactions between variables within the work group. Among others, these include the personal needs of the group members, the tasks in which they are engaged, their perceptions about the legitimacy of participating in decision making, and the structure of the group. These worker and work-group variables are further compounded by the personal characteristics, including the needs, attitudes, and perceptions, of the supervisor himself.

A Situational Model

In somewhat oversimplified form, the issues raised thus far in our discussion of effective leadership have contrasted the human relations and scientific management points of view. We have asked whether it is better for the manager to lead using a democratic or authoritarian style; to evidence a high level of consideration or structure initiation; to encourage or discourage employee participation. To these and similar questions, we have concluded uniformly that the effectiveness of any kind of leader behavior depends upon the configuration of the situation in which leadership is being exercised. The situational factors to be taken into account include characteristics of the task or problem, the participants (both leader and followers), and the organizational environment. Thus, instead of regarding one form of leadership as generally better than another, it is more accurate to speak of types of leadership as being best for particular combinations of circumstances.

Following this conclusion, it remains to identify those combinations of circumstances under which various kinds of leadership are most effective. This is precisely what has been attempted in the "contingency model" described below (Fiedler, 1964, 1967). This model regards effective leadership as a joint function of three interactive sets of situational variables:

1. *Leader-member relations.* The degree to which group members trust the leader and are willing to follow his guidance.
2. *The task structure.* The extent to which the task can be spelled out step by step and performed according to a standard procedure (as opposed to tasks which must be left nebulous and undefined).
3. *Position power.* The power inherent in the leader's position including his freedom to hire, fire, promote, or demote.

Any group can be classified with respect to these three situational variables in accordance with the model shown in Figure 13–3. Each

FIGURE 13–3

Situational Determinants of Effective Leadership: A
Contingency Model

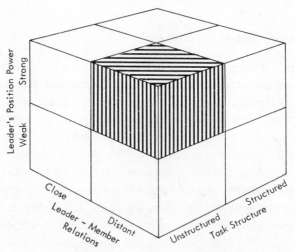

Source: F. E. Fiedler. Contingency model of leadership effectiveness. In L. Berkowitz (Ed.), *Advances in experimental social psychology.* P. 163.

cell of this model represents the integration of a particular combination of these variables. Thus, the shaded cell in the figure identifies a group characterized by distance rather than trusting closeness between the leader and members, working on an unstructured task, and supervised by a powerful leader.

Predictions. Eight different kinds of groups are portrayed in the model shown in Figure 13–3. These groups are ranked in Table 13–2 according to whether circumstances in the group are favorable to the leader. (This ranking assumes that "leader-member relations" is the most important and "position power" is the least important of the three situational variables.)

Referring to this table, the easiest group to lead is the one wherein the members like their supervisor, have a highly structured task, and where the supervisor is powerful. The most difficult group to lead is one wherein the members dislike their supervisor, work on an unstructured task, and where the supervisor has little power.

Using this classification of conditions favorable and unfavorable to exercising leadership, the contingency model makes the following two predictions:

1. Autocratic, highly structured leadership will be most effective in situations either very favorable or very unfavorable to exercising supervision. (These are the conditions ranked at the top and bottom of Table 13–2.)

2. Human-relations oriented, democratic, permissive leadership will be most effective in situations intermediate in favorableness to exercising supervision (that is, the middle ranks in Table 13–2).

Implications. When put to the test, these predictions seem generally to be supported by the data (Fiedler, 1971). However some recent work has questioned the validity of the contingency model (Ashour, 1973; Graen, Alvares, Orris, & Martella, 1970). Although more evidence is needed, the contingency model shows promise of specifying the circumstances wherein the two polar leadership styles, authoritarian and democratic leadership, will each prove most effective.

Using the model, it becomes possible to engineer the situation to fit the manager (Fiedler, 1965). The company can most effectively capitalize upon a manager's particular leadership style by arranging an optimal work setting for him; that is, a setting with the proper combination of leader-member relations, task structure, and leader position power. The kinds of modifications that are possible include:

1. *Leader-Member Relations*

To encourage greater closeness—increase homogeneity of the group by including men with attitudes, beliefs, and backgrounds similar to those of the manager.

To encourage greater distance—increase heterogeneity of the group by including men with attitudes, beliefs, and backgrounds dissimilar to those of the manager.

2. *Task Structure*

To increase task structure—give the manager precise operating procedures for the group to follow.

To reduce task structure—assign the manager to groups which perform tasks that cannot be reduced to clearly specified operating procedures.

3. *Position Power*

To increase position power—assign men to the group who are several ranks below the manager; allow communication only through established channels; give the manager greater autonomy.

To decrease position power—assign men to the group who are almost equal to the manager in rank; communicate directly with each group member without going through the manager; require the manager to consult with his subordinates in making work-related decisions.

Research on the Contingency Model. The model was developed from data gathered from over 800 groups functioning in many different organizations. Two of the major attempts to validate the model are reported below.

In one (Fiedler, 1966), 288 Belgian navy recruits and officers were constituted into three-man groups half of which were led by an officer and half led by a recruit. In addition, half the men spoke French whereas the other half spoke Dutch. Leader position power was a function of the rank of the leader: whether officer or recruit. Task structure was manipulated by requiring the groups to work on different kinds of problems. An additional structural element was introduced by virtue of language: some of the groups were favorably constituted by placing together men with homogeneous linguistic backgrounds; others were unfavorably constituted by assigning men from heterogeneous backgrounds to the same group. Finally, leader-member relations were measured by a post session questionnaire. The results of this study were somewhat disappointing in that they departed substantially from the predictions cited in Table 13–2.

TABLE 13–2

Situational Factors Facilitating and Inhibiting Leadership

Rank (*Reflecting Ease of Leadership*)	Situational Variables		
	Leader-Member Relations	Task Structure	Position Power
1 (Most favorable)................	Close	Structured	Strong
2	Close	Structured	Weak
3	Close	Unstructured	Strong
4	Close	Unstructured	Weak
5	Distant	Structured	Strong
6	Distant	Structured	Weak
7	Distant	Unstructured	Strong
8 (Most unfavorable).............	Distant	Unstructured	Weak

A second more successful partial test of the model (Shaw & Blum, 1966) held all but one of the situational variables constant. The one situational variable systematically manipulated was "task structure." The three tasks (ranked from least to most structured) were:

(*a*)   A discussion problem requiring the group to list the five most important traits required for success in our society.

(*b*)   A discussion problem requiring the group to describe which of five possible courses of action would be best for a young politician who had an alcoholic wife.

(*c*)   A task requiring the group to identify five objects by asking a maximum of 40 questions.

It is clear that although the contingency hypothesis is a provocative stimulus to further studies of leadership the model, in its present form, is far from validated. One of the important unresolved issues is that of the relative strength of the three posited situational determinants of leadership effectiveness.

MANAGERIAL SELECTION AND ASSESSMENT

The underlying objectives of programs for selecting managers are similar to those discussed earlier (Part II) for selecting other kinds of personnel. The intent of all selection programs is predictive; in the case of management selection and assessment, the aim is early identification of persons with management potential. However, unlike many other jobs, effective managerial behavior is highly situational. Success as a manager in one organization or in one division of an organization does not necessarily imply equal success in other organizations or divisions.

A further complexity in selecting upper level managers is introduced by virtue of the incumbent's potential influence upon the organization's destiny. Planned organizational change (discussed in Chapter 17) requires managers with vision about alternatives to present courses of action concerning markets, products, procedures, and so on, and with sufficient influence to implement that vision. To the extent that incumbents specify the requirements for a new member of the management cadre, they may merely perpetuate the course that they have set for the organization.

Generally speaking, predictions of subsequent behavior can be made from two very different kinds of predictors: signs and samples. The former typically are provided by the results obtained from paper-and-pencil tests measuring variables like intelligence; the latter predict subsequent behavior from systematic observations of samples of present behavior exhibited, for example, under simulated job task conditions. There is growing sentiment favoring the use of behavioral predictors of management talent (Lopez, 1970) and a consequent rapid growth of the "assessment center technique."

Predictive Signs

The two classes of psychometric predictors most often used in this essentially traditional approach to managerial selection entail measures of high level intelligence and selected personality characteristics.

A manager's effectiveness clearly depends, in part, upon his ability to keep abreast of technological changes and to plan accordingly, to analyze problems and solve them expeditiously. These aspects of management performance would seem, on their face, to require above average intellect. And the evidence (Ghiselli, 1963) is that this is clearly the case.

Aside from high level intellect, an effective manager obviously must possess superior skill in dealing with people. However, as a sign of such skill tests of *information* about desirable supervisory practices typically prove to be invalid (Rosen, 1961). Better predictive efficiency is generally obtained with personality inventories assessing such more general characteristics underlying interpersonal effectiveness as self-esteem and self-confidence.

The Sears executive test battery illustrates a management assessment program largely comprised of paper-and-pencil psychometric signs (Bentz, 1968). The components of the test battery measure in the areas of intelligence, personality, interests, and values. Evidence accumulated over a 25-year period supports the utility of this battery for predicting both executive promotability and the morale of subordinates under the executive's jurisdiction. More recently this battery has been expanded and elaborated to include behavior sample assessments with a consequent further increase in validity.

Behavior Samples: Assessment Centers

The central feature of the assessment center approach to managerial performance prediction is its focus on behavior samples (by using simulations) rather than relying solely upon predictive signs. The rationale is that the best predictor of subsequent performance is actual evidence reflecting present behavior. This rationale does not obviate the need for management development programs for further training persons thus identified as having managerial talent. On the contrary, it provides an added basis for interfacing selection and development programs since such techniques as gaming, case-study, and the in-basket (described in the following section) simulate management problems and are useful both for training (development) and assessment purposes.

Conservative estimates indicated that over 100,000 persons have participated in the assessment center process; 75,000 of these persons have been assessed by the Bell System alone since its introduction there about 25 years ago (Bray & Moses, 1972). The assessment center method typically provides simultaneous evaluations of small groups (6–12) of people who participate in the program for several days. In addition to completing the usual sign predictors (that is, cognitive ability tests and personality inventories) the assessment also includes a lengthy interview and simulations. The latter are the heart of the procedure. For example, one application (Bray & Campbell, 1968) used the three following simulations:

Leaderless Group Discussion. The group of assessees participates in a meeting ostensibly to discuss candidates for promotion from among their fictitious subordinates. Each is given a description of a "subordinate" to present as his candidate. Following the presentations and subsequent group discussion, the assessees must rank order the candidates.

Oral Fact Finding. The assessee plays the role of arbitrator in a labor-management dispute. He is provided an outline of the dispute and given an opportunity to determine additional facts and issues by questioning an assessment center staff member. The assessee then presents his decision orally to the staff member and is questioned intensively about it.

Consulting Case. The assessee is given written material concerning the operation and problems of a business concern. After studying the material he makes oral recommendations to two assessment center staff members who role play the two controlling partners. He also provides written recommendations.

At the end of the assessment period, the center staff—which is made up of company management personnel—evaluates each assessee using all of the evidence displayed during the performance samples in conjunction with the psychological test scores. The growing interest in this procedure for identifying managerial talent stems from the judgment that it generates information particularly about interpersonal behavior that is not obtainable from traditional personnel records including the more commonly used predictive signs (Hinrichs, 1969).

MANAGEMENT DEVELOPMENT

Management training or development has four characteristics (Campbell et al., 1970):

1. It is intended as a learning experience.
2. It is planned by the organization.
3. It occurs after the individual has joined the organization.
4. It is intended to further the organization's goals.

The objectives of management development programs are generally to increase the knowledge, problem-solving ability, and interpersonal competence of the participants.

The specific training procedures typically include some combination of (a) lectures, (b) assigned readings, (c) formal courses in public speaking, human relations, and so on, (d) job rotation providing an overview of company operations, (*e*) sensitivity training, (*f*) managerial grid, (*g*) management gaming, (*h*) case study, (*i*) role playing, and (*j*) in-basket technique.

The principles of learning discussed in Chapter 7 are applicable to all of these techniques, but most obviously to the first four listed. Therefore in this section we will consider only the procedures designated (*e*) through (*j*) above.

A preliminary note about training for line supervisors and foremen is in order. Such employees typically are promoted from the line on the basis of job experience and proficiency. Once in his new position, the supervisor is required to spend much of his time in activities broadly classified as human relations; he must deal with people rather than with machinery or equipment. Although the supervisor needs to have the technical know-how required for the kind of work he supervises, this alone is not enough; he needs also to develop leadership skills.

One of the major problems in leadership training is the distinction made within many companies between supervisory behavior as it is taught in theory or in the classroom and as it is actually practiced in the plant. An excellent training program may be utterly ineffective whenever higher management provides an example of leadership contradicting what the supervisors have been taught in their training classes. It is futile, for example, to attempt to train foremen in techniques of democratic leadership if when they return to the plant they are exposed to autocratic leadership from their superordinates. Thus, it is not surprising to find that some leadership training courses are relatively ineffective; that is, they produce no noticeable changes in foremen's attitudes or behaviors when they return to the plant (Fleishman, 1951). One of the implications of a negative evaluation of supervisory training programs is simply that such training cannot be effective if it is conducted solely at the level of the line supervisor. Middle and top management benefit also from participation in leadership training programs.

Sensitivity Training

Sensitivity training entailing the use of T-groups is one of the most controversial but widely used of the management development techniques. Often it is included as a part of the more general training endeavor designated "laboratory training." Our description of the technique and its goals is followed by a summary of some of the evaluative research.

Description. Sensitivity training is difficult to describe because of the many procedural variations employed by different trainers. The following summary is based upon Campbell and Dunnette's (1968) effort to extract common procedural elements.

The heart of sensitivity training is the T-group usually comprised of 10–15 persons confronted by an unstructured activity. Typically, no topics for discussion and no specific tasks are planned for the group. A trainer is usually present, but he tends to reject the leadership role. He may set limits on the length of the meeting and state the objective of the group as "enhancing the understanding of one's own and others' behavior."

T-groups emphasize the "here and now." That is, the behavior displayed in the group by its members is the object of study and discussion. Whereas T-groups explore the feelings and emotions of members at the instant they occur, they tend to reject consideration of past behavior and future problems along with the feelings and emotions associated with these past and future events.

The session is usually initiated with a brief statement by the trainer who then falls silent and, as a rule, refuses to guide the group. The vacuum of silence is often filled with feelings of frustration and hostility. Eventually one or more of the group members attempt to assume leadership and give direction to the group's activity. These attempts become the issue for group study with the objective of enhancing each member's understanding of how he affects and is affected by the others in the group.

Given the unstructured group as the primary vehicle and the behavior emitted as the principal topic of conversation, the group's success depends almost entirely on the *feedback* process. Each participant is encouraged to tell the others how their behavior is seen and interpreted and to describe the feelings generated.

Two elements are considered necessary for the feedback process to be successful. First, a certain amount of anxiety or tension must be generated. Anxiety is generally evoked in the T-group sessions when a participant discovers that his previous methods of interaction do not suffice in this new situation. The second prerequisite to effective feedback has been termed "psychological safety" (Schein & Bennis, 1965). A group member must feel that the others in the group will act in a supportive and nonevaluative way when he reveals himself.

The trainer's behavior is crucial to the group's ability to learn to give constructive feedback and to promote psychological support. He serves as a model for the participants to imitate. He absorbs feelings of hostility without acting aggressively or becoming defensive. He provides feedback to others and is open and honest in expressing his own feelings.

The following is a brief episode from a sensitivity training session.

> At the fifth meeting the group's feelings about its own progress became the initial focus of discussion. The "talkers" participated as usual, conversation shifting rapidly from one point to another. Dissatisfaction was mounting, expressed through loud, snide remarks by some and through apathy by others.
>
> George Franklin appeared particularly disturbed. Finally pounding the table, he exclaimed, "I don't know what is going on here! I should be paid for listening to this drivel? I'm getting just a bit sick of wasting my time here. If the profs don't put out—I quit!" George was pleased; he was angry, and he had said so. As he sat back in his chair, he felt he had the group behind him. He felt he had the guts to say what most of the others were thinking! Some members of the group applauded loudly, but others showed obvious disapproval. They wondered why George was excited over so insignificant an issue, why he hadn't done something constructive rather than just sounding off as usual. Why, they wondered, did he say their comments were "drivel"?
>
> George Franklin became the focus of discussion. "What do you mean, George, by saying this nonsense?" "What do you expect, a neat set of rules to meet all your problems?" George was getting uncomfortable. These were questions difficult for him to answer. Gradually he began to realize that a large part of the group disagreed with him; then he began to wonder why. He was learning something about people he hadn't known before. " . . . How does it feel, George, to have people disagree with you when you thought you had them behind you? . . ."
>
> Bob White was first annoyed with George and now with the discussion. He was getting tense, a bit shaky perhaps. Bob didn't like anybody to get a raw deal, and he felt that George was getting it. At first Bob tried to minimize George's outburst, and then he suggested that the group get on to the real issues; but the group con-

tinued to focus on George. Finally Bob said, "Why don't you leave George alone and stop picking on him. We're not getting anywhere this way."

With the help of the leaders, the group focused on Bob. "What do you mean, 'picking' on him?" "Why, Bob, have you tried to change the discussion?" "Why are you so protective of George?" Bob began to realize that the group wanted to focus on George; he also saw that George didn't think he was being picked on, but felt he was learning something about himself and how others reacted to him. "Why do I always get upset," Bob began to wonder, "when people start to look at each other? Why do I feel sort of sick when people get angry at each other?" . . . Now Bob was learning something about how people saw him, while gaining some insight into his own behavior [Tannenbaum, Wechsler, & Massarik, 1961, p. 123].

Goals. The following objectives of sensitivity training were extracted from an extensive review of the literature on the technique (Campbell & Dunnette, 1968) :

1. To increase self-insight and self-awareness concerning one's behavior and its impact in social situations. To learn how other people perceive and interpret one's behavior.

2. To increase one's sensitivity to the behavior of others. To increase one's empathy: i.e., the ability to infer accurately what other people are feeling.

3. To increase awareness and understanding of the processes that inhibit and facilitate group function.

Evaluative Research. We will restrict our discussion of attempts to evaluate the effectiveness of sensitivity training to just two of the many criteria that have been employed for this purpose: the impact of such training upon (*a*) self-perceptions, (*b*) changes perceived by others.

1. Self-Perceptions. Several studies (for example, Gassner, Gold, & Snadowsky, 1964) have investigated changes in participant's self-perceptions following sensitivity training. Generally these studies compare pretraining and posttraining measures of the participant's perceptions of his actual or real self and his ideal self. Occasionally, as in the Gassner et al. study cited above, the research design entails an experimental and control group. The pre measures and post measures are obtained for the latter group with the same intervening interval as for the experimental group but *without* exposure to sensitivity training. Instead, the control group merely engages in its normal activity during the period intervening between pretesting and posttesting.

The finding from implementing this particular control group design was that persons in *both* groups (experimental–with sensitivity training; control–without sensitivity training) reported less discrepancy between their "real" and "ideal" self on the posttest measure than on the pretest measure. If a control group had not been utilized, it would have been easy to interpret the partial data obtained from the experimental group only as supportive of sensitivity training since the direction of change was consistent with the goals of such training. Such results emphasize the critical importance of using a control group design in studies of change following the application of sensitivity training or, indeed, of any other procedure.

2. Changes Perceived by Others.   Advocates of sensitivity training usually cite studies using another criterion: perceptions by others of changes in the sensitivity training participants. In one such study (Bunker, 1965) superiors, subordinates, and peers of participants in training were asked the following question:

> Over a period of time people may change in the way they work with other people. Do you believe that the person you are describing has changed his (her) behavior in working with people over the last year as compared with the previous year in any specific ways? If *yes,* please describe.

The experimental group was comprised of 229 persons who had participated in sensitivity training. The control group was comprised of 112 persons who were selected by asking each experimental subject to nominate a person in his organization who held a similar position to his own and who had never participated in sensitivity training. Perceptions about changes in behavior were obtained from the experimental and control subjects and from their coworkers about a year after the experimental subjects had completed their training.

On 11 of the 15 categories of change investigated, the experimental subjects were reported to have changed significantly more than the controls. The largest differences favoring the experimental group were related to increases in openness, receptivity, and tolerance of difference. The results of this study appear to support strongly the assertion that sensitivity training has utility for organizational development.

However this and similar studies have been criticized on methodological grounds (Campbell & Dunnette, 1968). One criticism is that the raters knew whether or not the ratee had participated in sensitivity training; hence they may have been more likely to perceive change in those persons who they knew were *supposed* to change. Also, there was at least the possibility that the raters discussed their ratings with each other thereby contaminating each other's observations. Finally, since no measures were taken prior to training, the raters' estimations of change were based entirely on recollections of events occurring at least a year previously. Such delayed recollections are notoriously unreliable and subject to considerable distortion as any amateur lawyer knows.

One final point must be noted before leaving this matter of sensitivity training. Even were changes in interpersonal behavior following sensitivity training to be convincingly demonstrated—and they have not!—there is no established relationship between such changes and increased effectiveness on the job. That improved interpersonal sensitivity generates improved managerial effectiveness is, at present, merely an article of faith of sensitivity training advocates. This simple but crucial proposition still awaits empirical justification.

Managerial Grid

The managerial grid (Blake, Mouton, Barnes, & Greiner, 1964) is offered to industry as a packaged management development program with a clear-cut financial payoff. The rationale for the managerial grid rests on a bipolar conceptualization of leadership dimensions. The two key dimensions are designated: (1) concern for people and (2) concern for production. By keying each of these dimensions to a nine-point scale and assuming that the dimensions are uncorrelated, it is possible to classify a manager in terms of his position on the managerial grid. This grid, showing the placement of five hypothetical managers, is illustrated in Figure 13–4. The 1,1 manager behaves in least desirable fashion; the 9,9 manager, who is maximally concerned both with production and with the people with whom he interacts, is presumed to behave in optimal fashion. The managerial grid training program seeks to develop 9,9

FIGURE 13–4

Managerial Grid

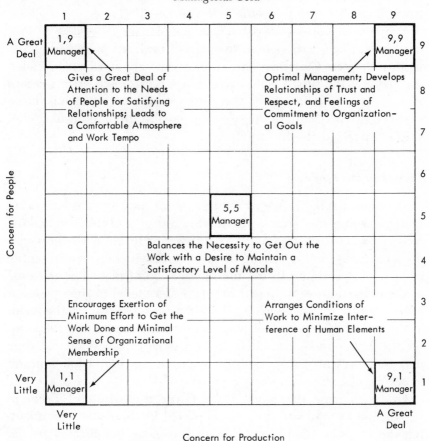

Source: R. R. Blake, J. S. Mouton, L. B. Barnes, & L. E. Greiner. Breakthrough in organization development. P. 136.

managers. This is to be accomplished by a program involving elements of sensitivity training leading both to management development and organizational change. The initial steps in training are designed to teach each individual how the other group members see his managerial style. A modified T-group approach is utilized. The group then works through a series of problems and various exercises which enable each individual to demonstrate his style of leadership and receive constructive feedback from the other group members. This process has as its goal the movement of the individuals toward the 9,9 region of the managerial grid. The individuals are then supposed to return to their organization and help move it towards the 9,9 approach (Blake & Mouton, 1964).

Whether or not the 9,9 pattern on the managerial grid is, in fact, optimal can be questioned on the basis of evidence presented earlier in this chapter. Certainly, this simple view about effective leadership ignores the situational factors that several other writers regard as highly important. Also, the assumption that task and interpersonal orientations are the two most critical dimensions of leadership is merely that—an assumption.

Management Gaming

Decision making is one of management's most critical functions. Management games attempt to develop a degree of decision-making facility by constituting groups of trainees as teams, each representing a company, and requiring them to make decisions governing the company's operations during the next period of play. The outcome of these decisions is evaluated in terms of a model of the operation of the industry or economy. This evaluation is fed back to the teams at the end of each period of play and they then make new decisions for the next period. Anywhere from a week to a year of real time may be represented in periods of play ranging from a few minutes to several hours.

One such game, developed at the Carnegie Institute of Technology for use by graduate students, is played by three teams constituting the industry. The complexity of this game is indicated by the fact that each set of decisions, covering a month of real time, requires two to three hours. An IBM computer is tied up for about 45 minutes each time the results of a move are computed (Dill, 1967).

The players in this particular game are provided with many kinds of information, including basic background data on the history of their company's operations and constraints on its policies and operations. They receive quarterly balance sheets and income statements for their competitors. The status of the team's own company is indicated monthly by a variety of reports, including balance sheets, income statements, summaries of financial commitments, cost of raw materials, cost of goods sold, warehouse stocks and shipments, finished product inventories, and work force as well as equipment down time data. Other information including market survey data, availability of financing, results of product preference tests, and so on are available to each team as requested or required.

The teams are required to make a full range of production, marketing, and finance decisions, including such things as price levels, sales, forecasts, amount of production, applications for financing, allocation of products to regions, and others.

Management gaming has opened tremendous possibilities both for training managerial personnel and for investigating the effectiveness of various industrial policies and practices. The latter application of gaming is, of course, dependent upon the adequacy of the model upon which the game is constructed. To the extent that it realistically simulates industrial conditions, the game itself becomes a research tool whereby answers may be provided to fundamental questions about management theory and practices.

Case Study

A fundamental objective in training managers and supervisors is to develop an understanding and appreciation of human relations problems and the acquisition of skill in dealing with personnel problems. The case conference method is one way in which these objectives may be realized.

This method involves group discussions of actual business problems or cases. The case is a realistic situation requiring some kind of supervisory action. It lends itself to various solutions, none of which can be judged in absolute terms as being right or wrong. Some solutions are, however, better or more appropriate than others. The following cases designed for line supervisors typify this kind of situation.

Case 1

The other day Miss Black went to the personnel office and asked to be transferred out of your section. Joe, the personnel manager, informed you that she gave as her reason that you are favoring Miss White. According to Miss Black's story, Miss White, who is of the same grade level as she but with six months' seniority, has entrenched herself in your favor by being an informer. As a result, Miss White is allowed to while away the day doing just enough work to make it look good, while she (Miss Black) carries a heavy work load and is closely supervised by you.

This is news to you. You are careful to distribute the work evenly. Miss White has a better aptitude for the work, completes it rapidly, and needs little supervision. On the other hand, Miss Black has difficulties, so you are giving her job training—not close supervision. In relation to the charge of informing, you think this might arise from the fact that Miss White often gives you good suggestions on methods of improvement. You think Miss White is supervisory material, while you doubt if Miss Black is.

How are you going to handle this situation (McLarney, 1959)?

Case 2

The other day the personnel department informed you that one of your men had quit—Smith, an operator you had hired about a month ago. During the exit interview, he told the personnel interviewer he was quitting because in your section the regular workers were a clique, there were no opportunities for an outsider, and he had been told that he was not wanted.

You began to investigate by talking to Jack White, the old-timer whom you had selected to help Smith get acquainted with the job and with the other men. Jack informed you that he went to lunch with Smith the first day. During the meal Smith kept boasting of how he was going to be top man in the section before long because of his wonderful experience—that you had practically guaranteed him rapid advancement by stating that his past experience would be of great aid to him. Jack claimed that he tried to show Smith that this attitude wouldn't do him any good in getting along with the group. The next day Smith turned down Jack's suggestion that they go to lunch together and went instead with Bill Brown, who had recently been demoted and transferred to your section. Smith and Brown continued going to lunch together.

Then you began to check up on Smith's work. You found that he made less than normal progress during the month he was in your section. You spoke to several of the men who worked with Smith. They told you that none of the men liked him—that he criticized everything and everybody and was constantly saying that in the company where he had worked previously conditions were better and better work was turned out. One of the group said he told Smith that, if he didn't like the way things were done here, he ought to quit.

You review your actions in hiring Smith. You recall from the application blank and the interview that he came to work for a wage that was less than he had received on his previous job, also that he had received no raises on his last two jobs. During the interview he stated that he didn't mind getting less than his previous wage if he had the opportunity to advance—that the reason he quit his last two jobs was the lack of opportunity on them. You told him there were always opportunities in the company for a good man. During the month Smith was on the job, you spoke to him several times, and he told you that he was coming along fine.

1. What might be some of the things wrong with Smith, the man who quit?
2. Which of these might you have uncovered in the interview?
3. Which mistakes might you have made in the induction?
4. How should you have inducted Smith?
5. Suppose he is right about the clique—that your group does try to discourage new men who are good workers. How are you going to clean up that situation?
6. What are you looking for in an induction follow-up?
7. How do you get this information (McLarney, 1959, p. 358)?

The trainees are given a period of time in which to study the case and to think about alternative solutions. They are encouraged, during the conference, to discuss the problem, to suggest solutions, and to evaluate the ramifications of the various solutions.

Role Playing

Role playing is in a way an extension of the case approach. The case conference terminates with a discussion of alternative solutions. Role playing, however, requires that the trainee actually carry out his solution in a supervised practice situation.

A problem for consideration at a role-playing session, for example, might be the case of employee Jones who has an unusually high accident rate. One of the supervisor-trainees would be assigned to the role of the employee and several others would be assigned to the supervisory role. Each of the role players would then act out his solution to the problem with the remainder of the training class as an audience. The class sees several alternative solutions acted out before it and is in a position to compare and evaluate each of them. Furthermore, the role players have an opportunity to experience the feeling of reacting in a particular way. And the one who is assigned to the role of the employee gains some appreciation of how it feels to be on the receiving end of various kinds of supervisory reaction.

Aside from some embarrassment during the initial role-playing sessions, this technique appears to be quite valuable for helping supervisors gain an understanding of the human element in business and industry. Furthermore, it has been suggested that much of the embarrassment arising from being observed can be sharply reduced by the technique of *multiple role playing*. In this procedure the entire training class is split into small groups, each confronted by the same problem. Since every member of the group is assigned a role to play within his own group, the method tends to reduce feelings of self-consciousness. An additional advantage of multiple role playing is that subsequent discussion across groups often reveals a variety of solutions to the same problem as a function of the particular personalities interacting within each group (Maier & Zerfoss, 1952).

The In-Basket Technique

The in-basket technique (Frederickson, Saunders, & Ward, 1962) has been used as a training aid, as a selection device for prospective managers, and as an instrument for assessing the performance of prospective managers.

The trainee is confronted with an in-basket filled with realistically assorted items including important memoranda, daily reports, social items, and so on. His task is to go through the items, handling each as if he were on the job. He can refer, delegate, plan meetings, issue memoranda, and write letters. Each of his actions must be taken in writing, thereby providing a record of his test responses. When he finishes with the in-basket materials, he completes a form which allows him to describe his reasons for taking each of his actions.

In-basket responses are scored by trained judges who evaluate such things as decisiveness, imagination, courteousness to subordinates, and so on. The technique has been found to tap three major areas of behavior: (1) making decisions and taking action versus deferring decisions and actions; (2) high work output versus low work output; and (3) acting independently versus seeking advice and guidance from superiors (Frederickson, 1962).

Although these areas of behavior seem clearly related to managerial success, and as intriguing as the technique is, there are two issues needing further attention. First, performance across in-basket tests tends to fluctuate (Frederickson, 1961). Thus, extreme care must be taken in selecting items for inclusion in an in-basket test in order to insure that they closely approximate those that would actually be encountered on the job. Because of the tremendous variety of managerial jobs, this poses obvious difficulties for standardizing in-basket tests. Second, the validity of the technique requires further study, with particular reference to test-taking attitudes. Whether a person's real life responses are like those he makes on the in-basket test is still an open question.

SUMMARY

The essence of effective leadership is a willing group of followers. This fact is recognized in the distinction sometimes made between "nominal" and "effective" leadership. A nominal leader is invested with power by virtue of his appointment to a status position. However, unless his subordinates willingly follow him, such a person is merely a titular head. He may, to be sure, issue orders and command obedience; but high morale and the maximum expenditure of effort by individuals to achieve the group's goals are beyond the realm of command.

The fact that persons serving as nominal heads may be relatively ineffective as leaders poses a particularly significant problem for industry. The organizational structure of most companies requires that certain individuals be appointed to positions of authority. In order for these nominal heads to function as *effective* leaders, they must be carefully selected and trained.

Effective industrial leadership is concerned with managing the interpersonal relationships at work in ways calculated to encourage both employee satisfaction and organizational goal attainment. Three of the factors in interpersonal management discussed in this chapter are leadership style, ranging from authoritarian to democratic; leadership dimensions, including consideration and the initiation of structure; and employee participation. In each instance, conclusions about the effectiveness of particular kinds of leader behavior (for example, democratic versus authoritarian) depend upon the configuration of the situation in which leadership is being exercised. The situational factors to be taken into account include characteristics of the task or problem, the participants, and the organizational environment. Thus, instead of regarding one form of leadership as generally better or worse than another, it is more accurate to speak of types of leadership as being most appropriate for particular combinations of circumstances.

Two approaches to management selection and assessment are discussed in this chapter. The more traditional approach, based upon predictions from signs, tends to emphasize the results of high level intelligence tests and personality inventories. A more contemporary trend in managerial assessment emphasizes an evaluation of behavior samples displayed under simulated conditions. Some of the techniques of behavioral assessment overlap some of the techniques of management development, but with a different emphasis. The objective of assessment is early identification of managerial talent whereas the objective of development is to train persons identified as having such talent.

V.

Organizational Psychology

Organizational psychology is a relatively new special interest within the broad context of industrial psychology. Organizational psychologists study motivation, job satisfaction, group functioning, and planned organizational change and typically do so by experimental manipulation.

Chapter 14 discusses three organizational psychology experiments in considerable detail. These are presented as illustrative of the general approach.

Since group effort is characteristic of industry, Chapter 15 considers two major aspects of the research on effective group functioning. We are here concerned first with the evidence concerning the relative effectiveness of group and individual performance for problem solving and related tasks. Secondly, this chapter considers the impact on group effectiveness of variables like group size, group norms, and communications networks.

Chapter 16 is addressed to two questions often asked of industrial psychologists: How can em-

players be motivated? What conditions generate job satisfaction? The early attempts to motivate employees primarily through financial incentives were predicated upon an erroneously simplistic view of human motivation. As we will discuss in this chapter, human motivation is very complex; many factors other than pay contribute to job satisfaction or dissatisfaction. Furthermore, the correlation between job satisfaction and job performance is weaker than was originally anticipated.

The ultimate test of research and theory of organizational and human relations psychology is their utility in planned organizational change. Hence, Chapter 17 is divided into two sections. The first elucidates the principles of planned change; the second illustrates various change strategies by describing five field studies.

14. The Experimental Approach to Organizational Research

Organizational psychology is the study of the behavior of organizational members both as it influences and is influenced by that organization. This intentionally broad definition reflects the wide scope of activity in this field. Organizational psychologists study such matters as job satisfaction, motivation, conditions of effective group functioning, leadership, and organizational change.

Three organizational psychology experiments are described in considerable detail in this chapter. Our twofold purpose is (a) to clarify something of the nature of research in this field and (b) to enhance your appreciation of the variety of procedures encompassed by the term *experiment*. With respect to the latter objective, you may wish to review the section on psychological experiments in Chapter 2, since the essential properties of the experimental approach are constant irrespective of procedural variations.

The three illustrative experiments to be considered in this chapter differed in the amount of control over the research environment exercised by the investigators. The first (Morse & Reimer, 1956) was a field study conducted in an organizational setting and typifies careful research but with less control over the research environment than is possible in experimental settings. The second (Adams & Rosenbaum, 1962) was conducted in an experimentally manipulated real-life situation. And the third study to be described (Lane & Messé, 1972) was a straightforward laboratory study.

DECISION MAKING IN AN ORGANIZATION

This classic research by Morse and Reimer (1956) was one of a large series of studies of social behavior performed by the staff of the University of Michigan's Survey Research Center. The major purpose of this particular study was to investigate the relationship between the level at which decisions are made in a large hierarchical organization and two dependent variables: (*a*) satisfaction and (*b*) productivity. Based on the results of previous research the investigators hypothesized that both satisfaction and productivity would be enhanced by increasing employee participation in decision-making processes.

Procedure

The research was conducted in a department of a nonunion company with four very similar divisions each engaged in routine clerical work. All employees in these four divisions were women—mostly young, unmarried, with a high school education; their long-range plans typically involved marriage and a family rather than a career. Research preliminary to initiation of the experiment proper demonstrated that these four divisions were similar with respect to the independent variable (pattern of decision-making authority) and both dependent variables (satisfaction and productivity).

The experimental manipulation consisted of increasing the amount of decision making by clerks in two of the divisions (the *autonomy* condition) and decreasing the amount of decision making by clerks in the remaining two divisions (the *hierarchy* condition). The investigators devoted approximately six months to establishing these conditions through appropriate supervisory training. In order to establish the autonomy condition, two divisional supervisors were trained to decrease the proportion of decisions made by them in favor of increasing the proportion of decisions made by their subordinates. To establish the hierarchy condition, the two remaining supervisors were trained to exercise even more authority and to make a higher proportion of decisions than formerly.

After completion of the supervisory training phase, the experiment was continued for approximately a year with the clerks working under one of these two types of supervision. Measures of satisfaction and productivity were taken again at the end of this year to determine if there was any change attributable to the manipulated supervisory patterns.

Results

Success of the Manipulations.   Before interpreting their findings, the researchers first had to demonstrate that they had successfully manipulated the independent variable: that is, the decision-making patterns in the two sets of divisions. The success of the manipulations was partially corroborated by observation. Clerks in the autonomy divisions were seen to make decisions about such matters as work methods, personnel, and rest periods. Conversely, the researchers observed that following the initial supervisory training in the hierarchy divisions, there were decreased opportunities for clerks in these divisions to control and regulate their own activities.

Although such observations were reassuring concerning implementation of the desired conditions, additional and more convincing evidence of this issue was obtained from the clerks themselves. Their perceptions concerning each major area of company operation were recorded through administration of premanipulation and postmanipulation questionnaires inquiring into the degree that:

1. Company officers, or other higher ranking employees make decisions about policies, rules, procedures, or methods;
2. The girls in the section make decisions about these matters.

From the statistically different responses to these questions by clerks working under the two manipulated conditions, the experimenters concluded that they had accomplished their objective: they had decreased the locus of centralized decision-making control in the autonomy divisions and had increased it in the hierarchy divisions. Hence, any changes in the dependent variables (satisfaction and productivity) could logically be attributed to this experimental manipulation.

Satisfaction.   One aspect of the hypothesis under investigation stated that increases in the decision-making roles of employees should result in increased satisfaction and, conversely, that decreased opportunities for decision making should result in decreased satisfaction. Three areas of satisfaction were studied: (1) supervision; (2) the company; and (3) the research program.

1. Satisfaction with supervision. Evidence concerning possible changes in satisfaction with supervision was obtained by administering premanipulation and postmanipulation questionnaires. On both occasions the employees were asked to assess (*a*) the quality of their interpersonal relations with the supervisor and (*b*) the supervisor's effectiveness as a representative to upper management. Four representative questions are reproduced below; the first two ask about interpersonal relations whereas the last two deal with the supervisor as an employee representative.

(1)   Can you count on having good relations with your supervisor under all circumstances?

(2)   In general, how well do you like your supervisor as a person to work with?

(3)   How much does your supervisor go out of her way to help you get things for girls in your section?

(4)   How much does your supervisor try to help people in your section get ahead in the company?

On all questions concerning satisfaction with the supervisor, the patterns of replies shifted in the predicted direction. A shift toward increased satisfaction was noted in the autonomy divisions and a shift toward decreased satisfaction was noted in the hierarchy divisions.

2. Satisfaction with the company. The employees were asked, "Taking things as a whole, how do you like working for this company?" Compared with their premanipulation replies, the responses at the end of the study confirmed increased satisfaction with the company for employees in the autonomy divisions and decreased satisfaction for employees in the hierarchy divisions.

3. Satisfaction with the research program. The clerks were asked an open-ended question about their satisfaction with the changes made during the study. Those in the autonomy divisions typically replied that they wished the changes to continue indefinitely; those in the hierarchy divisions generally indicated that they would prefer for the experimental program to end immediately.

In view of the consistency of findings concerning satisfaction, the investigators concluded that increasing local decision making increased satisfaction whereas decreasing employee participation in decision making decreased satisfaction.

Productivity. Although a parallel relationship between locus of decision-making control and productivity was also hypothesized, this expectation was not confirmed. Production levels were found to increase in both the autonomy and hierarchy divisions; moreover, the increase was significantly greater in the latter!

This finding is difficult to interpret because of a contaminating factor. During the experimental period nine clerks terminated employment because of dissatisfaction with the job. As you would expect from the results reported above for satisfaction, virtually all of these (eight of the nine) worked in hierarchy divisions. The effect of their departure was to produce a spurious increase in the individual productivity records of the remaining employees because the same amount of work now had to be accomplished by fewer workers. However, taking this contaminating factor into consideration, the experimenters concluded that their findings still did not substantiate the expected relationship between locus of decision making and productivity.

Discussion and Overview

Morse and Reimer's study is included in this chapter because it is one of the few investigations conducted in an ongoing organization that fulfills the requirements of a controlled experiment. The noteworthy aspects of their design leading to its classification as an experiment were the following:

1. The independent variable was deliberately manipulated; the locus of decision making was experimentally lowered in the autonomy divisions and raised in the hierarchy divisions.

2. The groups compared were demonstrated to be similar with respect to critical variables before the independent variable was manipulated. Hence postexperimental differences in the dependent variables could be attributed with some confidence to manipulation of the independent variable.

WORKER PRODUCTIVITY AND COGNITIVE DISSONANCE ABOUT WAGE INEQUITIES

We will consider next an experiment embodying some of the properties of a field study and some of a laboratory investigation.

Like the Morse and Reimer experiment, the one we will now consider was conducted in a real-life situation. The primary procedural difference is in the degree of control over the situation exercised by the investigators.

Adams and Rosenbaum (1962) investigated the norm of equity or fairness. In a general way this currently fertile area of research is concerned with determining what individuals in our culture consider to be "fair." Adams and Rosenbaum assume that when an individual performs work in exchange for pay he thinks about what he contributes on the job (his inputs) and what he receives for performing the work (his outcomes). They also assume that an employee's perceptions about his inputs and outcomes are influenced by what he thinks are the inputs and outcomes of other persons. Using the investigators' terminology, *Person* designates the individual whose perceptions the study focuses on and *Other* designates the individual with whom Person compares himself.

Based on previous work (Festinger, 1957), Adams and Rosenbaum assert that a psychological state of *cognitive dissonance* (a feeling of unpleasant tension) should exist for an individual whenever he perceives that he is in an inequitable or unfair situation. Likewise, they assert that cognitive consonance (a feeling of harmony) should exist whenever the person perceives himself as functioning in an equitable situation.

But when is a situation fair or equitable? The investigators accept the following equation (Adams, 1965) as defining equity:

$$\frac{\text{Person's outcomes}}{\text{Person's inputs}} = \frac{\text{Other's outcomes}}{\text{Other's inputs}}$$

This equation states that equity exists whenever a person perceives the ratio of his own rewards (outcomes) to effort (inputs) as equal to this ratio for Other. For example, if Person and Other were equally qualified for a job (equal inputs) and they received the same pay (equal outcomes) the equation posits a state of equity for Person. The existence of equity should be accompanied by cognitive consonance, or job satisfaction. However, if Person were less qualified for the job than Other (lower inputs for Person) and they both received the same pay, Person should experience inequity and the resulting cognitive dissonance should be reflected in dissatisfaction.

Festinger's theory of cognitive dissonance mentioned above predicts that persons experiencing dissonance attempt in some way to reduce their unpleasant feelings and restore consonance. The experiment we are about to describe tested this prediction in the framework of equity theory. Adams and Rosenbaum reasoned that if Person experiences dissonance because of perceived inequity he will attempt to reduce this dissonance by establishing consonance between his inputs and outcomes in relation to the inputs and outcomes of Other. The procedure examined changes in an individual's productivity when he is made to feel that he is being overpaid relative to his coworkers.

The hypothesis was: If Person is paid an hourly wage, his productivity will be higher if he perceives that he is being paid too much (inequitable overpayment) than if he perceives that he is paid the correct amount (equitable payment).

The rationale for this hypothesis is that when Person perceives that he is overpaid he experiences unpleasant feelings of dissonance which he will attempt to reduce by restoring equity. His options are either to reduce his outcomes or to increase his inputs. However, the former option is denied Person in an hourly wage situation. Hence, he can only restore equity by raising his inputs: that is, by working harder thereby increasing his productivity.

Procedure

The method used to test this hypothesis was devised and first used for this study by Adams and Rosenbaum. Subsequently, this method has been used by many other investigators interested in studying the norm of equity.

Twenty-two male university students were hired for part-time temporary work as interviewers with an advertised pay rate of $3.50 per hour. When the subjects reported to the prospective employer they were randomly assigned to the experimental (overpayment) and control (equitable payment) condition. Although this assignment was random it was made to appear that it was based upon the candidate's replies to a background questionnaire concerning previous work history and educational background.

The actual implementation of the experimental (overpaid) and control (equitably paid) conditions is best clarified by quoting the experimenter's statements to subjects assigned to each condition.

Experimental (Overpaid) Condition. "You don't have any (nearly enough) experience in interviewing or survey work of the kind we're engaged in here. I specifically asked the Placement Service to refer only people with that kind of experience. This was the major qualification we set. I can't understand how such a slip-up could have occurred. It's really very important for research of this kind to have people experienced in interviewing and survey techniques. (Agonizing pause.)

We're dealing with a limited alternative open end kind of questionnaire. There's no "correct" answer to an item. Research in this area has shown that the nature of the response elicited by a skilled and experienced interviewer is more accurate and representative of the respondents sentiments and differs substantially from the responses elicited by inexperienced people.

Who interviewed you at Placement? (E scans the New York University phone directory, picks up telephone receiver and dials a number. Gets busy signal and slams receiver down. Pause, while E thumbs papers and meditates.)

I guess I'll have to hire you anyway, but please pay close attention to the instructions I will give you. If anything I say seems complicated, don't hesitate to ask for clarification. If it seems simple, pay closer attention. Some of this stuff, on the surface, may appear deceptively easy.

Since I'm going to hire you, I'll just have to pay you at the rate we advertised, that is $3.50 per hour." [Adams & Rosenbaum, 1962, p. 162.]

Control (Equitable Payment) Condition. "Well, this is very good. We can use you for this work. You meet all the qualifications required for the job, which is good because we often have to turn people down because they're poorly qualified. Poorly qualified people can really make a mess of a study of this kind. Why even the census, where they were dealing with simple demographic material, got fouled up. They hired inadequately qualified people, some of them housewives for example, and the result was the gross deficiencies in their data that were so widely criticized in the press, if you recall.

Well, anyway, I'm pleased you have the background we're looking for.

So far as pay is concerned, the people at the Placement Service have probably advised you that we pay $3.50 per hour. This rate is standard for work of this kind performed by people with your qualifications." [Adams & Rosenbaum, 1962, p. 162.]

Implementing the Design. Referring to the theoretical statements made earlier, the subject is Person whereas the other unnamed, but presumably qualified, interviewers are Other. The Person's qualifications are his inputs; his pay of $3.50 per hour is the outcome. In the experimental condition, Person is induced to feel that his inputs are out of line with his outcomes and the input/outcome ratio of Other. In the control condition the subject is induced to feel that his input/outcome ratio is in line with that of Other.

Once these conditions were established, the experimenter gave the subject instructions for the interviewing task: to interview adults for 2.5 hours. The interview was a relatively simple one so that many interviews could be completed during the work period. Also, it could be perceived as requiring more skills than the subject possessed or as requiring the amount of skill the subject possessed. Before the subject left to begin work he was briefly reminded of the relationship between his qualifications for the job and his pay of $3.50 per hour.

Following completion of the work assignment each subject was asked to reply to a questionnaire concerning his reactions to the job. The experiment and its purpose were explained, and the subject was paid the $3.50 per hour promised him.

Results

The validity of the experimental findings hinged on the credibility of the procedure. Judging from the questionnaire responses and replies during a postexperimental interview, the procedure was entirely effective. None of the subjects felt they were participating in a psychological experiment; all believed that they had been hired for and had worked on a real job for real wages.

The hypothesis was substantiated by the findings. Subjects in the experimental group averaged approximately 40 completed interviews during the 2.5 hours whereas control group interviewers averaged 28 completed interviews in the same length of time. This mean difference was statistically significant.

Discussion and Overview

The problem investigated in this study concerned the reaction of employees to a perceived wage inequity. This problem and the finding has obvious practical implications for industrial organizations as well as theoretical significance. Adams and Rosenbaum derived their hypothesis from a psychological theory (dissonance theory). Their findings stimulated many subsequent investigations to further clarify the norm of equity.

The method of this investigation is especially interesting. The researchers manipulated variables in a real-life situation while concealing this fact from the subjects. Thus they were able to exercise considerable experimental control without sacrificing realism.

A FURTHER CLARIFICATION OF EQUITY THEORY

The third study considered in this chapter is a laboratory experiment typical of most of the research in organizational psychology. For comparison, and to clarify the wide array of strategies that can be used to investigate the same research area, we have selected another study of equity: this one by Lane and Messé (1972).

Lane and Messé's research concerned the norm of equity and its influence on the way rewards are distributed. Specifically, they sought to determine which of two alternative conceptions of the norm of equity generated the more accurate predictions.

One conception was that posited by Adams (1965) and presented earlier in this chapter. You will recall following his definition of equity, Adams' equation predicts that an individual will distribute rewards (outcomes) so that each group member will receive a reward proportional to his contribution to the group (his input).

An alternative theoretical position was developed by Lane and Messé expanding a formulation by Weick (1966). In brief, they theorized that Adams' prediction has a second order of priority and that individuals are *first* concerned with establishing their own equity.

In testing predictions from the two formulations, subjects were required to distribute monetary rewards to themselves and to a coworker. The experimental design established equal inputs for both the subject and his coworker: they worked for the same length of time on the same task. A preliminary study established a fair amount of reward for the work performed. Following this determination of a fair reward, three experimental tests were conducted. In one the subject was asked to distribute an amount of money which, if divided equally, would have given both the subject and his coworker a fair reward for the work performed. In the other two tests the subject was required to distribute either double or one half of the amount required for fair payment both to himself and his coworker.

The prediction from the Adams' formulation is that all three conditions (insufficient, sufficient, oversufficient) should lead to an equal distribution of money by the subject to himself and his co-worker. Since the subject and his coworker made equal inputs under all three conditions, the subject can only create equity by allocating the rewards equally without regard to the total amount of money available.

The alternative formulation predicted that when the total amount available was insufficient to provide a fair reward both to the subject and his coworker, the subject would take most of the reward for himself: that is, the person is more interested in es-tablishing equity for himself than for a coworker. Following this logic, the condition under which the total amount available was just sufficient to generate a fair reward to both the subject and his coworker ought to lead to an even distribution of the available reward. Finally, Lane and Messé predicted that the oversufficient reward condition would lead the subject to take more than half of the total reward for himself.

Procedure

The subjects were 39 male university students randomly selected from approximately 500 respondents to an advertisement in the campus newspaper. This advertisement stated that the respondents would be paid for their participation in "motivation research" projects.

The experimental procedure was initiated by having subjects complete an industrial opinion questionnaire—the task for which they were to be paid—in groups of 8 or 10 persons. Of the 8–10 persons in each group, half were subjects and half were confederates. Although unknown to the subjects, the confederates were working for the experimenter and knew what the experiment was about. The real subjects sat at one table; the confederates were seated at another, adjacent table.

Following completion of the questionnaire (requiring 90 min-utes) the experimenter announced that each person at Table 1

374   *Psychology in Industrial Organizations*

(real subjects) was going to determine both his own pay and the pay of one person seated at Table 2 (confederates). Each subject was then given an amount of money, two envelopes one marked "My Pay" and the other marked "His Pay"), and a one-item questionnaire that asked how he divided the money. The total amount of money that each subject was given to divide was announced to the group; this amount was $3 for groups working under the insufficient reward condition, $6 for the sufficient reward condition, and $12 for the oversufficient reward condition.) While the confederates remained seated at Table 2, each subject went to a separate cubicle, divided the money given him, sealed the envelopes, and answered the one-item questionnaire, returned the sealed His Pay envelope to the experimenter, pocketed the My Pay envelope, and left the room.

Results

The percentage of the total reward assigned by each subject to himself and to Other was, of course, easily determined from the amount in each His Pay envelope. The results confirmed Lane and Messé's predictions: subjects in the sufficient reward condition allocated approximately half of the total reward to themselves whereas subjects in both the insufficient and oversufficient conditions allocated significantly more than 50 percent of the reward to themselves.

Discussion and Overview

The research just described is typical of many experiments in organizational psychology. Its purpose was to determine which of two alternative theoretical formulations best predicts behavior under specified circumstances. In this instance the predictions from theory were tested in the laboratory. However, as we have previously noted, predictions may be tested also in an artificially created real-life situation or in the natural environment.

POSTSCRIPT

The three studies described in this chapter illustrated three different approaches to research in organizational psychology. In common with most research they generate other issues and questions even while helping resolve the particular ones they were designed to address. For convenience we have organized many of these issues for more detailed discussion under the next two chapter headings: "Effective Group Functioning" and "Motivation and Job Satisfaction."

15. Effective Group Functioning

Group decision making and problem solving are held in low esteem by American folklore proclaiming: "A camel is a horse designed by a committee." "A committee is comprised of the incompetent led by the uninformed."

Such whimsy aside, it is clear that group endeavor is a necessary and significant aspect of American industry. The highly skilled craftsman working alone and completing a product from raw material to finished result has been replaced by work groups and assembly line technology. This is particularly true, of course, when an end product (like an automobile) requires such diverse and highly specialized skills that the manufacturing process exceeds the reasonable capabilities of a single worker. Even with mounting evidence favoring job enlargement—a topic previously considered— to counter what in some industries has become unbearable task fragmentation, the work group rather than the employee working alone is typically the structure of choice.

Group effort is important also at managerial levels. Almost all organizations have a standing committee system with most important decisions made in committee meeting. Each participant contributes his particular expertise to the management group's solution of complex problems.

We have already alluded to the significant impact of work groups in the two studies described in Chapter 11: the Hawthorne studies and the Tavistock Institute studies. Assemblers in the relay assembly test room part of the Hawthorne studies constituted a closely knit work group that strove to achieve organizational objectives. In contrast, employees in the bank wiring observation room formed into two cliques which at times worked against organizational objectives by restricting output and breaking company policy on various issues. In the Tavistock Institute studies, the work groups were of great importance to miners using the short wall method. However when the long wall method was introduced the informal work groups disappeared and, in consequence, productivity decreased markedly.

The present chapter examines the research on group functioning. It is divided into two major sections. The first concerns the efficiency of group versus individual performance with particular reference to problem solving, decision making, and risk taking. The second section summarizes research on variables, like group size and group norms, which affect the quality of group performance.

GROUPS VERSUS INDIVIDUALS

It is convenient to differentiate three areas of research on the effectiveness of group versus individual effort. These areas, designating the criterion behavior investigated, are: problem solving, decision making, and risk taking.

Problem Solving

Do individuals or groups solve problems more efficiently? In the absence of evidence this question could be debated both ways. It can be argued, for example, that the stimulation of some group members by the activities of others is a facilitative process. Two persons may, through mutual stimulation of ideas, be able to solve a problem that neither could solve alone. On the other side, it can be argued that a group may get bogged down in trivia and its members may distract each other from constructive activities. Fortunately, we do not need to rely on speculation to settle the issue of group versus individual effectiveness for problem solving. The pertinent empirical data are available.

The early research comparing the effectiveness of group with individual problem solving presented the same problems to groups (comprised of from two to five persons) and to individuals working alone. One study of this type (Shaw, 1932) compared the performance of four-person groups with that of individuals on complex intellectual puzzles. Two types of problems were used: one, a straightforward intellectual exercise like rearranging the words to complete the last lines of a sonnet; the other, a puzzle requiring an insightful solution. The latter problem is exemplified as follows:

> Three missionaries and three cannibals are on one side of a river. Get them across to the other side by means of a boat which can hold only two persons at one time. All the missionaries and one cannibal can row. Never under any circumstances or at any time may the cannibals outnumber the missionaries since this may lead to a disaster.

For both types of problems groups offered a higher proportion of correct solutions than did individuals. This finding has been confirmed in many similar studies. Simply stated, this general line of research supports the conclusion that problems are solved more efficiently by groups than by individuals working alone (Lorge, Fox, Davitz, & Brenner, 1958) .

However, this line of research fails to answer a more basic and practical question: Does a group of people working together solve problems more effectively than the *same number* of people working alone? If you had four potential problem solvers, are you better off constituting them as a working group or having them work independently? The research on *brainstorming* has been concerned with answering this particular question.

Brainstorming (Osborn, 1957) is a widely used problem-solving technique in industry. When a group brainstorms a problem, they typically adhere to four rules:

1. Criticism is prohibited.
2. Group members are encouraged to think of wild or "outlandish" solutions.
3. Quantity of ideas is emphasized. The greater the number of possible solutions suggested, the greater is claimed to be the probability of good ones.
4. Group members are encouraged to improve upon the suggestions of other group members and thus to combine or chain ideas.

In one study comparing group brainstorming with individual problem solving (Taylor, Berry, & Block, 1958) , the subjects were randomly assigned either to a five-man group or to the individual condition. Following this assignment they were presented with problems like: "What steps can you suggest to get more European tourists to visit the United States?" The subjects were asked to offer as many creative solutions to each problem as they could.

The number of solutions generated by the five-man groups working together for a total of five hours was compared with the number of solutions produced by the nominal groups (five individuals working alone for one hour each). The actual group generated fewer solutions (37.5) than the nominal groups (38.1) and fewer unique ideas (10.8 compared with 19.8).

These findings have generally been confirmed by other studies of brainstorming, leading to the conclusion that individuals working alone are more effective problem solvers than individuals working in groups. This finding is often taken to signify that the facilitative effects of mutual stimulation in groups are outweighed by the negative effects of distraction.

We must note two limitations in generalizing from research on brainstorming. These limitations have opposite effects: one leading to an underestimate and the other to an overestimate of the effectiveness of group problem solving.

The limitation leading to an underestimate derives from the typical experimental procedure wherein newly constituted groups usually work together for a brief period of time. It is possible that once groups have learned to work together effectively they may become significantly more effective than they seem to be in their early stages.

A second limitation of brainstorming research derives from the type of problem ordinarily used in such studies: that is, a problem with no correct solution. It has been suggested that utilization of problems with a single correct solution (mathematics, for example) would cause the stimulating effect of group interaction to diminish in importance while simultaneously heightening the distraction operative in groups (Freedman, Carlsmith, & Sears, 1970). Hence, for this type of problem groups are probably even less efficient than the research on brainstorming would suggest.

In summary, the research that has thus far been performed clearly indicates that individuals working alone are more efficient problem solvers than the same number of individuals working as a group. However, as with most broad generalizations, there are probably exceptions to such a uniformly negative assessment of group problem solving. It is conceivable, although thus far difficult to demonstrate empirically, that special circumstances of problem complexity and group constituency might mitigate against the superiority of individual over group problem solving.

Decision Making

Research on group and individual decision making can be conveniently classified under two headings. The first concerns the relative *accuracy* of group versus individually made decisions. The second concerns the *process* by which individuals and groups make decisions.

Accuracy.   Accuracy of decisions made by individuals and groups was originally investigated over 50 years ago (Knight, 1921). Students were each privately asked to estimate the temperature in a classroom wherein the actual temperature was 72 degrees. Although the individual judgments varied widely, the mean estimate (that is, the group average) was 72.4 degrees. This average estimate was more accurate than the judgment made by most of the individuals.

However, we cannot conclude from this or other similar studies using a similar procedure that groups make more accurate judgments than individuals. We can conclude only that the average of individual judgments likely is more accurate than one person's judgment. Unfortunately, the relative accuracy of persons meeting face-to-face in groups as compared with individual judgments still remains an open issue.

Process.   How do group meetings eventuate in some kind of decision?

To arrive at an answer to this question it is helpful at the outset to differentiate two polar decision-making processes in groups. At one extreme the decision may be made unilaterally. Here one individual—typically the committee or group chairman—authorizes himself to decide. At the other extreme, decisions may evolve through consensus. We will have more to say about these processes in the following paragraphs. However it should be clear that groups may reach decisions by means of yet other processes (for example, taking vote without reaching consensus) and that even unilateral decision making may entail a wide range of potential inputs by the group to the single ultimate decision maker.

We will look first at unilateral decision making.

A characteristic form of unilateral decision making entails what we have termed *self-authorization*. Hence one participant in the meeting—usually the ranking executive—authorizes himself to decide for the group. A *committee meeting* may be called less for the sake of making a decision than to gain acceptance for a decision already made by the convener. The decision maker may himself leave such a meeting feeling that agreement has been reached when, in fact, there has been no agreement by the participants and therefore no commitment to a course of action. The appearance of participatory assent may reflect simply apathy, resignation, or a desire to end the meeting. In spite of a superficial appearance of acceptance it is evident that unilaterally made decisions fail effectively to marshall and utilize the potential resources of the group.

In a variant of self-authorized decision making by the convener alone, two or three especially vocal group members may make decisions for the entire group. Here, by remaining silent, the majority abdicates decision-making authority to a vocal minority.

Decision by *consensus* contrasts markedly with both of the processes described above. True consensus is obtained when everyone in the group agrees with and accepts the final decision. Before consensus can be reached, everyone in the group must feel free to state his opinion and all must be willing to work together towards a decision reflecting the wishes of the group as a whole. Thus, consensus makes it possible for each member to utilize his unique resources. It can be attained only when all facts are presented and considered in terms of the different perspectives and values of the various group members. (Bass, 1965) .

Unfortunately, consensual agreement is rarely possible in complex group problem-solving situations (Guetzkow & Kriesberg, 1950) . However it is a goal worth striving towards. When consensus cannot be reached it is important that everyone be aware of the fact and that no one be deluded into feeling that agreement has been reached.

Clearly, chairing a group with the goal of attaining consensus requires a high level of interpersonal skill and patience. The leader must avoid making the decision himself; he must also guard against attempts by a vocal minority to terminate discussion before the group has made its decision. In a consensually oriented group disagreements occur, tempers may be short, and the final decision may not satisfy every participant. The time required to make decisions

is longer, reflecting the involvement of a greater number of participants with divergent views. However, the probability of commitment to the decision is greater when that decision reflects consensus
based upon participation and involvement than when a decision is
imposed upon the group by a single participant or a subgroup of
participants.

Risk Taking

Although risk taking is sometimes considered a special type of
decision making, we have separated the two on methodological
grounds. The experimental approaches to studying these two kinds
of behavior tend to be quite different.

Much of the research on risk taking has concerned the *risky shift*.
As we will shortly see, the risky shift refers to the tendency of individual group members to adopt decisions entailing a greater
amount of risk following group discussion than each was willing to
endure prior to such discussion.

In a risky shift research the subject is presented with several problems wherein he must choose between two alternative courses of
action: one with a moderately desirable outcome that is fairly likely
to occur; the other with a very desirable outcome but a low probability of occurrence. An illustrative item from the risky shift dilemma questionnaire follows (Kogan & Wallach, 1967) :

> Mr. D is the captain of College X's football team. College X is play-
> ing its traditional rival, College Y, in the final game of the season.
> The game is in its final seconds and Mr. D's team, College X, is
> behind in the score. College X has time to run one more play.
> Mr. D, captain, must decide whether it is best to settle for a tie
> score with a play which would be almost certain to work or, on
> the other hand, should he try a more complicated and risky play
> which would bring victory if it succeeded but defeat if not.

> Imagine that you are advising Mr. D. Listed below are several
> probabilities or odds that the risky play will work.

> Please check the LOWEST probability that you would consider
> acceptable to make it worthwhile for Mr. D to try the riskier play.

> _____   Place a check here if you think Mr. D should *not* attempt
> the risky play no matter what the probabilities.
> _____   The chances are 9 in 10 that the risky play will work.

_____ The chances are 7 in 10 that the risky play will work.
_____ The chances are 5 in 10 that the risky play will work.
_____ The chances are 3 in 10 that the risky play will work.
_____ The chances are 1 in 10 that the risky play will work.

The individuals in this type of risk-taking research (Kogan & Wallach, 1967; Marquis, 1962) responded individually to each problem. They did not discuss the problems or their choices, and they did not know that they were to discuss them subsequently. After they had made their choices, they were placed in a group and asked to reach a unanimous decision.

The initial results from this line of research indicated that the group almost invariably preferred a more risky alternative than did the individuals working alone. Moreover, when the individuals completed the same questionnaire in private following the group discussion, they tended to favor the more risky alternative. Therefore, this initial research indicated that the group's decisions were not only riskier than individual decisions, but also that the individuals were committed to the group's decision. This shift toward riskier decisions in a group setting is designated *risky shift*.

As the matter of risky shift was investigated further, it was discovered that in spite of the general finding noted above, 1 of the 12 items on the original risky shift questionnaire consistently generated a shift toward a more cautious alternative. Subsequently, other items have been devised for demonstrating a *cautious shift* and the original conclusion that groups are willing to take greater risks than individuals no longer seems justified (Pruitt, 1971; Cartwright, 1971). More research is needed to clarify the conditions under which groups will exhibit either a cautious or risky shift.

VARIABLES AFFECTING GROUP PERFORMANCE

Many investigations have been concerned specifically with variables (like group size, cohesiveness and group norms, personality of group members, and so on) affecting group performance.

Group Size

Group size is an excellent illustration of a variable which superficially seems to be a simple one but which, from a psychological standpoint, exerts complex and competitive influences.

An increase in the number of persons comprising the group should add to the total talent possessed by the group. Each individual brings different skills and viewpoints which, if used effectively, should add to the group's effectiveness. Another potentially positive effect of increased group size is that it increases the probability that each group member will find someone with whom he wishes to interact. A two-person group provides only one possible interaction between members; obviously, as the number of group members is increased, the number of possible two-person interactions increases geometrically. The significance of increased potential for interaction is the corresponding increase in the probability that each group participant will be involved in rewarding interpersonal interactions.

However, there are also several negative consequences of increasing group size. Individuals are less likely to express their ideas in larger than in small groups (Gibb, 1951). This conclusion follows from studying group behavior in solving a public relations problem presented to groups of various size. The first 30 minutes of the session were devoted to listing possible solutions; the next 30-minute period was used to evaluate the suggestions. The results indicated that the percentage of members who never talked and the percent who said they had ideas that they did not express increased dramatically as group size increased. In part, this limitation on participation is a mechanical accompaniment of increased group size. Since most groups have individuals who dominate the discussion, the likelihood that a member will be denied an opportunity to participate increases as a function of group size. The inability to participate may generate dissatisfaction, resentment, and withdrawal, all of which are detrimental to effective group functioning.

Aside from the mechanical constraints, individuals in larger groups are more likely to experience feelings of inhibition about participation; they become more conscious of sounding silly or being misunderstood (Gibb, 1951). Apparently, large groups are perceived as more threatening than smaller ones. Increased group size tends to encourage the formation of subgroups (Collins & Guetzkow, 1964). When these subgroups have goals in opposition to those of the larger group, their influence is likely to be decisive.

Taken together, the experimental evidence indicates that the negative effects of increased group size generally outweigh the positive effects. For example, Worthy (1950) reports decreased morale and productivity across a wide variety of jobs as work-group size was increased. Whereas work-group size has traditionally been determined by technological considerations (for example, the number of employees required efficiently to conduct an assembly function), there is growing evidence that worker satisfaction and commitment both improve when a relatively small number of employees share responsibility for a relatively large or meaningful segment of the work.

Cohesiveness and Group Norms

Cohesiveness refers to the degree to which the forces acting on the members to hold the group together are stronger than the forces atcing to break up the group. The more cohesive the group, the less likely it is to dissolve. Cohesive groups are collections of individuals who are attracted to each other and enjoy interacting. Typically a cohesive group perceives its task as compatible with the goals of a large proportion of its members.

With reference to group behavior, a *norm* is a standard of appropriate or acceptable behavior. Some norms are widely held in our culture: for example, honesty and fairness. Work groups develop their own norms over time. You will recall that men in the bank wiring observation room study developed production norms and made attempts to bring rate-busters into line.

These two factors—cohesiveness and norms—interact to affect group performance. If a group is cohesive and employees share a norm of high productivity, these factors reinforce each other positively as demonstrated in the relay assembly test room part of the Hawthorne studies. In contrast, when cohesiveness is high and the group norm favors low productivity, production will be low. It should be evident that whereas group norms can only operate to affect performance when the group itself is cohesive, cohesiveness itself is neither an asset nor a liability to an organization.

Development of Norms. An early study of norm setting entailed use of a perceptual phenomenon known as the autokinetic effect (Sherif, 1936). This effect is the apparent movement of a stationary point of light in a darkened room. Although the light is stationary, the illusion of movement is almost universally experienced. Subjects who were unaware that the movement was an illusion were asked to estimate how much the light was moved. These estimates were made by individuals working alone, by individuals in groups, and by individuals in groups after initially working alone.

The results indicated that each inexperienced subject was fairly consistent in his judgments all of which fell within a fairly narrow range. However there were substantial individual differences: some tended to perceive much movement whereas others reported little movement. Following the establishment of this *personal norm* the subjects were placed in groups and again asked to judge the amount of movement. Here the judgments of the individuals began to converge. Even without the benefit of conversation and without reaching any group decision, the individuals began changing their judgments to approximate the mean judgment of the group. When subjects were removed from the group and placed again in the individual setting they carried the group norm with them. That is, without any form of group pressure, they continued to hold the norm established in the group setting. Apparently, they had developed a genuine acceptance of and commitment to the group norm.

It is clear that group norms are developed and persist even when the subject matter of the norm is not particularly crucial to the individual. The pressures toward norm formation and commitment are even stronger for issues, like production level, which are of great importance to employees than for judgments of autokinetic movement.

Social Reinforcement of Norms. How does the group respond to a member who deviates from the group's norm? To study this question, one investigator (Schacter, 1951) recruited subjects as members for editorial, movie, radio, and case study clubs. Some recruits were assigned to those clubs for which they indicated a preference ("high cohesive clubs"); others were assigned to clubs for which they did not express an interest ("low cohesive"). All groups were presented a case summary of a juvenile delinquent for discussion eventuating in agreement about the kind of treatment he should receive. This assignment was presumably relevant to the group's interest in the case study and editorial clubs and irrelevant to the interests of the members of the other two clubs. Hence, the experimenter created four conditions: high cohesive with a relevant assignment; high cohesive with an irrelevant assignment; low cohesive with a relevant assignment; and low cohesive with an irrelevant assignment.

Of the nine members in a typical group, three were confederates of the experimenter. Two of the confederates initially advocated severe punishment for the delinquent. One remained adamant in this view; the other shifted toward the popular group view. The third confederate advocated the position that was found to be the most popular before the experiment began.

After the task was completed, the subjects were asked to select persons for inclusion in further group meetings of smaller size and also to assign persons to various committees. The subjects consistently voted to exclude the deviant member from further group meetings and to assign him to the least important committees. This rejection of the deviant member was greatest in the cohesive groups. Given the social rejection of a deviant group member in an artificial situation without real stakes, one can imagine the magnitude of social pressure toward conformity with group norms in real situations with real stakes.

Communication Networks

The various forms of communication—downward, upward, and horizontal; one way and two way—have been extensively studied in the laboratory as well as in natural settings. The laboratory studies establish and analyze the effectiveness of communication networks; that is, artificially established pathways for transmitting information among members of the group (Bavelas, 1950). Four such networks are shown in Figure 15–1. To facilitate comparison, each of these illustrative networks includes the same number of participants, and each is shown with a two-way communication flow.

The star group: All information is sent to a central figure (C) who in turn relays it to the persons on the periphery of the group (P). This is a miniature representation of a simple autocratic communication structure.

FIGURE 15–1

Four Communication Networks

Star   Chain   Circle   All-Channel

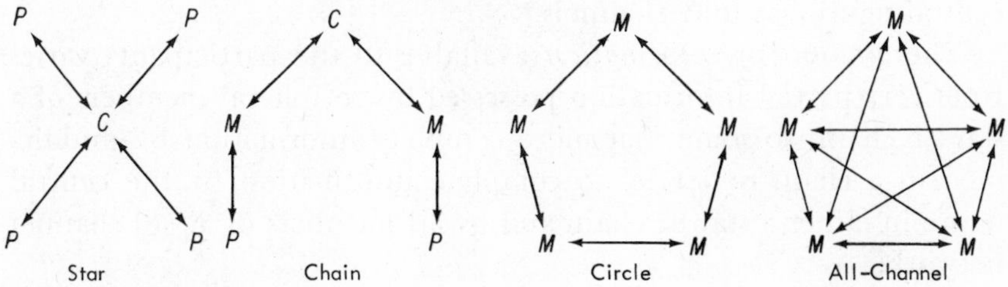

The chain: The communication pattern is complicated by placing middlemen (M) between the star and the men on the periphery. This is a miniature bureaucratic structure.

The circle: This pattern permits communication between adjacent group members but lacks centralized organization. It is an artificial pattern useful for research, but not often found in industry.

The all-channel group: In this pattern all members are free to communicate with all other members. This is typical of the communication network among members of a governing board or other group composed of members with equal status and influence.

The relative efficiency of these and other communication networks is typically investigated in a particular kind of laboratory setting. The subjects in each group are seated around a table but are separated from one another by partitions. They can communicate only by passing notes through slots in the partitions and the experimenter establishes the network by opening and closing the slots. The group must solve problems utilizing only the channels of communication open to it.

Dimensions of Networks.   The four networks shown in Figure 15-1 differ from each other in three important respects: the number of communication channels provided each member, the amount of information available to each member, and the total number of channels (*links*) available for the communication.

With respect to the *number of channels open to each member,* you will note that the circle provides every member two channels of communication; that is, he can communicate directly with only two other members of his group. The all-channel network provides every member with four channels of communication. In the chain, members at the periphery (P) have only one channel, whereas each middleman (M) has two channels (one to C and one to P). And in the star, the peripheral members each have one channel while the central figure has four channels.

The *amount of information* available to the participants varies from very partial information possessed by peripheral members of a star or chain, to somewhat more complete information by middlemen in a chain or circle, to complete information by the central figure in either a star or chain and by all members of an all-channel network.

The greater the number of links available for transmitting information, the greater is the possibility of overburdening a network with messages. The various five-man networks shown in Figure 15–1 entail 4 links for the star and chain, 5 links for the circle, and 10 links for the all-channel network.

Relative Effectivenes of Networks. By combining two of the dimensions discussed above—number of channels open to each participant and amount of information available to participants—it is possible to distinguish between networks that are highly centralized and those that are decentralized. Highly centralized networks are those, like the star and chain, wherein one participant (C) has more channels of communication and more information than the other participants. Networks low in centralization are those, like the circle and all-channel, wherein all members have an equal number of channels and have access to the same amount of information.

In summarizing the results of several studies of communication networks, the following generalizations emerge (Costello & Zalkind, 1963) :

Highly centralized communication networks facilitate:

1. Efficient performance of routine problem solving of the type involving assembly of information;
2. Development of a strong leadership position for the central figure;
3. Development of a quickly stabilized set of interactions among group members.

Decentralized communication networks facilitate:

1. Development of higher levels of member satisfaction;
2. Handling ambiguous and unpredictable situations;
3. Innovative and creative solutions to problems.

Thus, research does not identify one type of network as uniformly superior to another. Highly centralized and decentralized networks each have unique advantages, depending upon the nature of the task. However, whereas the latter tend to be characterized by high member satisfaction, the former tend to suffer low morale (Leavitt, 1951) .

The reason for the relative efficiency of highly centralized networks for collating information and using it to solve problems is that the structure of these nets facilitates assemblage of all relevant information with a minimum of communication overload (that is, too much and sometimes irrelevant communication). In contrast, decentralized nets (circle, all-channel) are less efficient in this regard because their arrangement prevents them from developing a hierarchy wherein a central figure collates information (Guetzkow & Simon, 1955), and because they are characterized by more linkages encouraging communication overload (Dubin, 1959).

Evidence for this view comes from a study wherein decentralized groups were deliberately given an opportunity to restructure themselves in order most efficiently to solve assigned problems. They typically elected either a star or chain network (Guetzkow & Dill, 1957). Both of these networks elected by originally decentralized groups are characterized by imposition of a communication hierarchy and a reduction in the number of communication linkages.

In summary, generalizations about the superiority of particular kinds of communication networks, judged either by the criterion of task performance or member satisfaction, must be tempered by considering the constituency of the group and the purpose for which it is formed. A highly centralized network is most efficient when the task is routine and collation of individual activities is necessary from the very beginning. However, there are circumstances wherein a freer network permitting more active participation by the group members is highly desirable. It would probably be unwise to impose a rigidly patterend communication network when flexibility is required of the group by virtue of the complexity of the problem confronting it and/or the diversity of knowledges and backgrounds possessed by its members.

Highly centralized and decentralized communication networks can coexist within the same organization. Thus, whereas a decentralized net is highly appropriate to communication between professional and technical personnel in a research, academic, or scientific organization, there is also a need in the same organization for more centralized communication networks for effective support services.

Homogeneous versus Heterogeneous Groups

A homogeneous group is one in which the members are relatively similar with respect to personality, ability, and interests. Bass (1965) has noted advantages and disadvantages of homogeneous grouping as a function of the interaction between this and other variables in the work context. Homogeneous group members can influence each other more readily; there is less resistance to an attempt to persuade when the persuader is someone similar to rather than different from us. Another advantage of homogeneous groupings is that they tend to promote friendship. Because of these and other factors, satisfaction with group membership is generally higher in homogeneous groups. In addition, such groups tend to function smoothly and to evidence a high level of coordinated effort.

The desirability of homogeneous grouping for task performance depends upon the nature of the task. Productivity is higher in a homogeneous group than in a heterogeneous group when the task is simple or when it requires coordinated effort. However, if the task is complex, a heterogeneous group comprised of persons with varied skills often proves to be superior because of the breadth of experience and training they bring to bear upon the problem at hand.

Personality and Intelligence

Empirical findings support the conclusion that the general intellectual level of the group members is positively correlated with the group's performance. However, this generalization must be accepted cautiously; often the correlations, while statistically significant, are relatively low. One explanation sometimes given for the finding that this correlation is not higher is that aspects of the interpersonal activities in a group may impede the more intelligent group members from making full use of their special abilities (Mann, 1959; Heslin, 1964).

Several studies have concerned the relationship between member personality and group performance. Personality traits like dominance, authoritarianism, interpersonal sensitivity, and extroversion-introversion have been investigated. Invariably the results of such studies demonstrate at best only a very slight correlation between personality and group performance (McGrath & Altman, 1966). This generally negative finding probably reflects, to some unknown degree, difficulties in assessing personality. However, even with better personality measures it seems doubtful that a very strong relationship between these variables can be demonstrated.

SUMMARY

This chapter considered first the research on the relative effectiveness of group versus individual effort with particular reference to problem solving, decision making, and risk taking. The studies concerning problem solving have focused on the technique of brain-storming. This research indicates that, with few exceptions, individuals working alone tend to be more productive and creative than the same number of persons working as a group. A parallel generalization cannot be made for decision making; the evidence is equivocal. Finally, recent studies of risk-taking behavior by individuals and groups indicate that this behavior is more complex than was originally believed. Whereas the initial research on risk taking seemed to demonstrate that groups are more inclined toward risk taking than are individuals, this generalization has been modified by demonstrations that, on occasion, groups behave more cautiously than individuals. Specification of the circumstances generating both risky and cautious shifts awaits further study.

Many of the variables affecting group performance other than risky shift have been explored in considerable detail. For example, small work groups typically are more effective than larger ones. Presumably this is so because of the interaction between group size and two other factors—cohesiveness and group norms—exerting direct effects upon performance. The impact of the group's performance norm is most evident in cohesive groups which exert pressure toward conformity with these norms.

The impact of many aspects of group structure is conditioned by the task at hand. For example, homogeneous groups function best for simple tasks and those requiring cooperation; heterogeneous groups function best when the task is complex and/or when speed of response is a liability.

16. Motivation and Job Satisfaction

One of the questions most frequently asked by management is: "How can employees be motivated to do their best work?" Ability, aptitude, and knowledge are clearly important prerequisites for satisfactory job performance. Likewise, proper placement, training, and job and equipment design facilitate satisfactory performance, but these are of little avail unless the employee is motivated.

Among the various sources of motivation, one is related to work itself. Employees are engaged in company activities for more than a third of their waking hours. As an important aspect of life in our culture, satisfying work contributes to man's sense of general well-being and feeling of personal worth. Work that is not personally satisfying tends to have the opposite effects. The conditions and effects of job satisfaction or dissatisfaction have been extensively examined; by one estimate (Lawler, 1971) between 2,000 and 4,000 studies of this matter have been published in the last 30 years!

The fundamental question central to this research seems simple enough: Just what is it that employees seek from their work, and how can the realization of personal satisfactions be facilitated? As we will see, despite its apparent simplicity, this is really a rather complex question. To answer it requires that we first discuss some general principles of human motivation and then apply these principles to the matter of job satisfaction.

MOTIVATION

The most obvious answer to the question, "Why does man work?" is that he does so to earn money. The simplicity of this explanation of motivation for work is so appealing that virtually all early efforts to motivate employees entailed some manipulation of wage or salary through incentive plans. As we will shortly see, wage or salary is but one of a constellation of gratifications provided by work.

Incentive Plans

As described in Chapter 10, Taylor's early studies (1911) were predicated on the premise that money was the primary incentive for work. Largely because of the respect that industry had for Taylor, incentive plans proliferated in this country, peaking in popularity at about the beginning of World War II. The most favored plan was the piece-rate system wherein employees were payed for each unit of work produced.

The war itself interrupted the growth in popularity of incentive plans. High productivity during that period was motivated by patriotism and associated social pressures. Following that war, incentive pay plans never regained their former popularity in spite of empirical demonstrations of increased performance following institution of an incentive system (Burnett, 1925; Locke & Bryan, 1967a).

The postwar decline in implementation of incentive plans has been explained by one writer (Lawler, 1971) on the basis of what he regards as a relatively prevalent condition of distrust in industry. Employees paid a bonus for productivity in excess of an established work norm or quota suspect that this baseline quota will be raised whenever the level of bonus earnings becomes substantial. And these suspicions are frequently confirmed. A secondary explanation for the diminished impact of incentive plans is that these plans require that relatively large pay increases be given to the most meritorious workers; companies often are unwilling to satisfy this requirement.

The Complexity of Human Motivation

Human beings are driven to satisfy a wide variety of needs. Some of these are physiologically based (for example, the need for food, water, and rest) ; others, like the needs for peer approval, self-esteem, and achievement, are socially derived. Clearly, many drives simultaneously influence an individual's behavior at any one time.

The observed behavior is not itself an absolute index of the underlying motivation. Two employees engaging in the same behavior —say, excessive absenteeism—may be doing so to satisfy quite different needs. Likewise, the same actions by any individual on different occasions may result from different motivation on these occasions.

One additional fact further complicates the study of motivation: persons are not always aware of the reasons for their actions. Many of our feelings about a predisposition towards circumstances and persons encountered in adult life are rooted in early, and often repressed, childhood experiences.

In view of this complexity, it is not surprising that psychologists cannot respond affirmatively to management's request to find an employee's "hot button" which can be pressed to improve his level of productivity. Such a request reflects an essential Theory X viewpoint: that is, that motivation is supplied by management in the form either of rewards or threats of punishment. The contrasting Theory Y view emphasizes that employees wish to do their jobs well but are often impeded in this endeavor by obstacles imposed by management. According to the latter view, management cannot motivate employees; what it *can* do is to remove obstacles to employee motivation by, for example, job enrichment and increasing opportunities for employees to display initiative.

Two Theories of Motivation

An overall view of motivation is that it directs behavior in two ways: (1) by causing the individual to seek one of several available goals and (2) by causing him to seek certain goals not present at the moment.

The former is illustrated by an employee who must choose between remaining in his present position or accepting advancement within the company entailing greater income but less security than he presently enjoys. Other things being equal, the choice he makes will reflect a discrepancy in the value he places upon income and security. Similarly, an employee dissatisfied with his present position because it provides little opportunity for advancement may be motivated to seek a job with another company providing greater opportunities.

The "needs-hierarchy" theory and the "valence-expectancy" theory are two attempts to explain the goal choice and goal search aspects of motivation. Each of these theories is considered separately below. The needs-hierarchy theory was described in some detail in Chapter 12 and is summarized here again because of its importance to the present discussion.

Needs-Hierarchy Theory. It is evident that needs, and hence the goals we seek, are arranged in a hierarchy of importance. At any given time certain needs are stronger than others (Maslow, 1943). However, this hierarchy is flexible rather than static because of the interdependence of needs. Relatively less important goals may assume real importance after previously more basic ones have been satisfied (Haire & Gottsdanker, 1951).

We will have occasion to invoke the notion of interdependence of needs throughout the ensuing discussion of job satisfaction.

The needs-hierarchy operative at a given time for any employee reflects the interaction of two sets of factors: his personal history and the immediate situation. The situational determinants of the needs hierarchy are provided by the organizational environment which rewards certain kinds of behavior and discourages others. Thus, attempts to generalize about the perceived importance of specific job factors must take into account the overall job picture (Herzberg, Mausner, Peterson, & Capwell, 1957). As an illustration, in certain job situations pay and security may be reasonably satisfactory while working conditions are poor; in others working conditions may be good but pay and security are unsatisfactory. Workers in the former situation would probably perceive working conditions as more important than pay and security while the converse would be characteristic of workers in the latter.

The importance of the interaction between personal and situational factors as joint determinants of needs hierarchies has been clearly demonstrated for technical personnel engaged in governmental research and development work (Friedlander, 1966). The relative importance assigned by these employees to three areas of need was investigated: (*a*) social environment (for example, working relationship with supervisor, relationship with co-workers); (*b*) intrinsic self-actualizing work (challenging assignments, a feeling of achievement); and (*c*) recognition through advancement (increased salary, promotion). When these employees were separated into high and low performers based upon salary controlling for age and tenure, the results were as shown in Figure 16–1.

FIGURE 16-1

Differences in Expressed Needs as a Function of Age and Performance

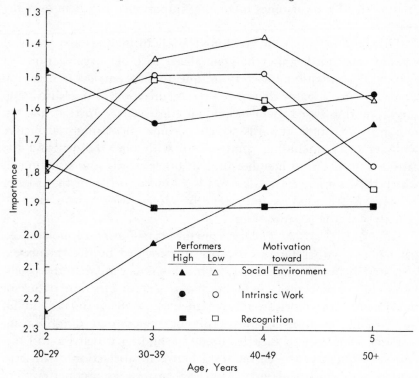

Source: F. Friedlander. Motivation to work and organizational performance. P. 148.

For high performing employees, irrespective of age, the needs hierarchy was: intrinsic work, most important; recognition, second; and social environment valued least. For low performers, irrespective of age, the hierarchy was: social environment, valued most, intrinsic work, second; and recognition was least important.

The interesting thing about the findings shown in Figure 16–1 is that the hierarchies in the two performance subgroups are affected in important ways by age, which is a personal factor.

For all younger employees—both high and low performers—the greatest importance is assigned to intrinsic, self-actualizing work. But whereas this emphasis is maintained by high performers, it soon shifts for low performers in favor of the social environment. Conversely, whereas the discrepancy in the importance of the social environment is very evident when employees are young (with high performing employees ranking it at the bottom of their needs hierarchy), this factor assumes increasing importance for them over the years.

This finding cannot be attributed *solely* to the personal factor of age and therefore cannot be generalized to other organizations. It reflects also situational factors unique to this particular organization. The investigator describes this organization as one discouraging promotion based upon individual effectiveness. Instead, the system provides some rewards which become increasingly attractive with seniority, including comradeship with one's fellows and the satisfaction of group membership. In other words, the situation in which these employees work rewards a kind of behavior that sooner or later is regarded as important by all employees who elect to remain with the organization.

Valence-Expectancy Theory.   Further clarification of motivation, particularly with reference to work, is provided by the valence-expectancy theory (Vroom, 1964). This theory is similar to the needs-hierarchy concept in that both emphasize the idiosyncratic nature of motivation. Since motivation is regarded as specific to the individual, motivational patterns cannot easily be generalized to *groups* of workers. Hence, both theories predict a finding which we will discuss subsequently: the correlations between satisfaction or dissatisfaction with work and such behavioral criteria as productivity are weak.

A second similarity follows from the above. Both concepts seek to explain the origins of idiosyncratic motivational patterns evident at any point in time. In other words, instead of asking whether job dissatisfaction is related to a criterion like turnover, both emphasize the question: "Why does this dissatisfied employee leave his job whereas that equally dissatisfied employee elects to remain?"

The two approaches provide complementary answers to this question. The needs-hierarchy theory says, in essence, that behavior is dictated by those needs with greatest primacy. The valence-expectancy theory attempts to explain how such primacy develops among several competing needs.

The term *valence* refers to the attractiveness of any goal or outcome. Before following a course of action, we assign valences (consciously or unconsciously) reflecting our expectations about the

TABLE 16–1

A Hypothetical Decision Using Value-Expectancy Theory

Alternatives	Expected Consequences (and Valences)				Total Valence
	Immediate Income	Opportunity for Advancement	Nature of Work	Hours of Work	
Remain on present job.............	Present level (0.00)	Fair (0.25)	(0.00)	Convenient (0.50)	0.75
Change to job A.............	Slightly above present level (0.25)	Good (0.50)	More interesting than present work (0.75)	Very inconvenient (−0.50)	1.00
Change to job B.............	Slightly above present level (0.25)	Excellent (0.75)	More interesting than present work (0.75)	Moderately inconvenient (−0.25)	1.50

consequences of each alternative open to us. We behave in the direction of the strongest or most positive valence.[1]

To illustrate, let us consider a hypothetical employee's drive for changing jobs. As shown in the top row of Table 16–1, he assigns a valence of 0.75 to his present job. This valence is compounded of the importance to him of present salary, opportunity for advancement, the nature of the work he does, and the hours of work. (Although other factors will also enter into this decision, we have limited the number for the purpose of illustration.)

His expectations concerning these same factors are also shown in Table 16–1. The valence-expectancy theory predicts that this employee is predisposed to move from his present job to job B. If the valence for job B were higher than 1.50, the likelihood of his actually making the move would be even greater.

JOB SATISFACTION

It usually, and often incorrectly, is assumed that an employee who is satisfied with his job will be motivated to greater productivity, diminished absenteeism, and other evidences of superior job performance. Even when this anticipated relationship between job satisfaction and performance is not obtained, there are nonetheless substantial benefits accruing to organizations from obtaining job satisfaction information from employees. Most managers, if given a choice, would prefer to have satisfied rather than dissatisfied employees. The remainder of this chapter is devoted to exploring such topics as the relationship between job satisfaction and productivity, the characteristics of satisfied workers, and the components of job satisfaction.

Hoppock's Research

An early study of job satisfaction was conducted by Hoppock in 1935 using the questionnaire method. Three of his items are shown along with the replies in Table 16–2. Note that in reply to item 1, 77 percent of the respondents indicated that they either liked, were enthusiastic about, or loved their jobs. This result may seem somewhat surprising since it is often assumed that workers typically are

---

[1] The psychologically sophisticated reader will note the origins of this concept in "field theory."

TABLE 16–2

Responses on Hoppock's Questionnaire

1. Choose ONE of the following statements which best tells how you like your job. Please place a check mark in front of that statement:

Response	*Percentage*
I hate it..	2
I dislike it..	2
I don't like it..	11
I am indifferent to it..................................	9
I like it..	63
I am enthusiastic about it.............................	9
I love it..	5
	101

2. If you could have your choice of all the jobs in the world, which one would you choose? (Check one)

Response	*Percentage*
Your present job.......................................	48
Another job in the same occupation....................	16
A job in another occupation	36
	100

3. Which gives you more satisfaction? (Check one)

Response	*Percentage*
Your job...	66
The things you do in your spare time..................	34
	100

Source: R. Hoppock. *Job satisfaction.* Pp. 250–252.

dissatisfied with their jobs. It is interesting to note that the finding that most workers are reasonably well satisfied with their jobs has more recently been replicated with automotive workers (Kornhauser, 1965).

Hoppock also determined the relationship between the worker's job level and his job satisfaction. These results are summarized in Table 16–3: an index of 100 represents extreme dissatisfaction; 700 represents extreme satisfaction. It is clear that there is a positive correlation between job level and job satisfaction.

This relationship between job level and job satisfaction is consistent with predictions from Maslow's theory of motivation. Jobs at the higher classifications undoubtedly facilitate satisfaction of those needs standing at or near the top of Maslow's needs hierarchy, thereby increasing the likelihood of the employee experiencing job satisfaction.

TABLE 16–3

Job Satisfaction as a Function of Occupational Classification

Classification	Number of Cases	Range of Indices	Mean Index
Unskilled manual..........................	55	100–650	401
Semiskilled..............................	74	125–650	483
Skilled manual and white collar..............	84	125–675	510
Subprofessional, business, and minor supervisory..................................	32	250–700	548
Professional, management, and executive.......	23	300–700	560

Source: R. Hoppock. *Job satisfaction.* P. 255.

Components of Job Satisfaction

A procedure often used to answer questions like these requires employees to consider a list of job characteristics and to rank or rate them in order of their perceived importance. The 10 factors ranked as most important by employees in six companies is shown in Table 16–4. This table also shows the expectations of executives in these companies and labor leaders about the ranks that the employees would assign to these factors.

One very important conclusion from such studies is that the needs of employees often are not well understood either by executives or by labor leaders. A factor, for example, like "information on success or failure at the job," was ranked as quite important by workers but excluded from the top 10 ranks expected by executives and labor leaders. The latter group, in particular, tended to overestimate the extent of employee concern about union matters.

The rank assigned by employee groups to any job factor is, of course, a function of the specific factors that employees are asked to consider. It is a function also of the employee's position and job context. Thus, a rank ordering of the importance to industrial supervisors of various job characteristics (Gruenfield, 1962) differed in important ways from the ranks shown for line employees in the first column of Table 16–4. The supervisors included as important several characteristics that did not enter into the ranking by line employees; for example, increased personal responsibility and greater opportunity for independent action. The supervisors also

TABLE 16–4

The 10 Most Important Factors Contributing to Job Satisfaction as Ranked
by Employees, Executives, and Labor Leaders

Rank	By Employees	Expected by Executives	Expected by Labor Leaders
1.....	Security	Pay	Pay
2.....	Advancement	Security	Security
3.....	Pay	Vacations	Hours
4.....	Benefits	Advancement	Working conditions
5.....	Information on success or failure at job	Working conditions	Unions
6.....	Type of work	Company attitude	Company attitude
7.....	Vacation and holiday practices	Type of work	Handling of grievances
8.....	Supervisor	Benefits	Vacations
9.....	Profit sharing	Supervisor	Union-management relations
10.....	Working conditions	Hours	Job Evaluation programs

Source: National Industrial Conference Board, *Factors affecting employee morale.* P. 21.

assigned lower ranks to some characteristics, like fringe benefits, than did line employees. However, for both groups of workers, working conditions were ranked as least important and security and opportunity for advancement were ranked as most important.

The next several sections focus upon employee perceptions of the relationship between job satisfaction and the following aspects of the job and work setting: pay, security, opportunity for participation and personal recognition, hours and working conditions, and supervision. This is followed by a discussion of the importance to job satisfaction of employee expectations about the conditions of work.

Pay. It is evident in Table 16–4 that management tends to overemphasize the importance of pay as a determinant of job satisfaction. As we noted earlier, quite elaborate incentive pay systems have been developed to recompense employees on the basis of productivity (either as individuals or in groups) or some related criterion. However in this particular study pay rate was noted as the most important job factor by only 7 percent of the workers. A recent extensive review of the literature on job satisfaction (Lawler, 1971) concludes that employees rank pay as the most important determinant of job satisfaction only in about 30 percent of the studies of the issue.

The relative importance attached to this factor by workers is undoubtedly a function of the wage currently being received in relation to that being paid to other employees in similar jobs or in jobs requiring similar training and experience. Its perceived importance is also a function of the employee's needs relative to what he can purchase with the wage he is receiving.

The fact that employees quite often rate factors related to ego-satisfaction and personal recognition as more important than salary is apparent from the results obtained from a large group of workers and shown in Table 16–5.

TABLE 16–5

Importance of Various Job Factors as Rated by Workers

	Percentage of 7,000 Workers Including This Item in the First Five	Percent Assigning It First Choice
A steady job	61.9%	36.1%
Pay rate	52.6	7.2
A chance to get ahead	41.9	6.9
A square boss	39.6	4.8
Working on the job you prefer	35.3	15.2
Credit for the job you do	29.6	2.2
Vacations and holidays	21.5	0.4
Friendly working companions	21.3	0.7
Medical and health facilities	20.8	0.6
Pension	9.7	7.1

Source: R. Stagner. Psychological aspects of industrial conflict: Motivation. P. 6.

It would be incorrect, of course, to maintain that rate of pay is unrelated to job satisfaction. The point, however, is that once the employee surpasses some minimum income, his feelings about the job tend to reflect the extent to which it satisfies certain of his socially derived needs. Thus, financial rewards cannot be regarded as a panacea or even as the most important incentive governing employee motivation.

Job Security. The importance attached by workers to the factor of security is clearly evident in Table 16–5 and substantiated by other investigations of a similar nature (Hersey, 1936; Wyatt, & Langdon, and Stock, 1937.)

The relative importance of security in comparison with other aspects of the job, such as pay or personal recognition, varies as a function of the job classification and the extent to which the workers actually do feel secure in their job. It is likely that workers who are not confronted by the possibility of precipitous dismissal will regard factors other than security as being of primary importance. Many employees, however, remember the widespread unemployment and the real economic pinch of the depression and, in consequence, place a very high value upon job security.

Participation and Personal Recognition. Improvements in industrial efficiency are often accompanied by fragmentation of the task performed by each employee. The craftsman's feeling of satisfaction and personal pride derived from his ability to transform raw materials into a finished product is rarely experienced within our present factory structure. The employee today has the same needs for a feeling of accomplishment, pride, and personal worth as did his artisan predecessor. The importance of these factors is evident from the high ratings consistently assigned by workers to such questionnaire items as "opportunity to use own ideas" and "credit for the job you do."

Although it is often impossible to enable each employee to experience the pride of a craftsman, it is both possible and necessary to provide the kind of training that will enable each worker to see how his sometimes miniscule task fits into the manufacture of the total product. This kind of training has been found, by way of illustration, to improve materially the net good yield produced by a manufacturer of miniature motors utilized in guidance systems and on space satellites. Prior to training, the assemblers tended to be somewhat careless in handling components. This lack of caution often produced microscopic chips which were ultimately responsible for motor malfunctions. The solution developed by the company was to organize a training program in which all employees became aware of the importance of their motor to the successful performance of the satellite and of the importance of their own job to the proper functioning of the motor.

Hours and Working Conditions. It is of some interest to note that the hours worked and the physical conditions under which work is performed are generally not regarded by employees as very important determinants of job satisfaction. The consistently low ratings assigned to these factors probably indicates that most jobs are performed on a tolerable work schedule and under at least minimally adequate working conditions.

Supervision. One of the significant findings of the Hawthorne study was that it was possible to change the attitudes of the employees by developing a cooperative spirit between workers and supervisors (Roethlisberger & Dickson, 1939). A friendly supervisory-subordinate relationship appeared to generalize to a favorable work climate. The importance attached by workers to the quality of supervision probably results from the fact that the supervisor is in a way a representative of the company. When perceived in this light, he is a primary force facilitating or inhibiting the satisfaction by the employee of his needs for personal recognition.

A strong relationship has been found, for example, between dissatisfaction with certain aspects of supervision and the subsequent termination of employment during the year subsequent to completion of a job satisfaction questionnaire. The comparison between the responses made by these groups relative to certain supervisory matters is shown in Table 16–6 (Weitz & Nuckols, 1955).

TABLE 16–6

Responses of Groups of Insurance Salesmen to Selected Items concerning Supervision

	Percent of Survivors	Percent of Terminators
Like freedom from supervision	56	34
Like helpfulness of supervision	62	41
Like personal friendship with the manager	70	53
Dislike manager misrepresenting or failing to explain all provisions of the contract	6	16
Manager doesn't devote enough time to the agent's problems	4	12
My job was misrepresented by the manager during the hiring interview	9	19
Feel free to talk over personal problems with the manager	94	74
Feel free to discuss selling problems with the manager	99	90
Manager makes you feel you are doing a worthwhile job	90	78
Enjoy manager socially	92	83
Manager spends part of his time handling agents' personal problems and grievances	83	64
Manager gives each agent a detailed explanation of changes in company policy or procedure	88	73

Employee Expectation. Both the newly hired employee and his employer have certain expectations concerning the behavior of the other party. The term *psychological contract* has been applied to these expectations. In addition to this contract's obvious features, like amount of work to be performed and pay rate, it implies a pattern of rights, privileges, and obligations both for the worker and his employing organization. For example, the employee may expect that his supervisor will not be punitive; or the employer may expect that the worker will purchase products manufactured by the company. Such expectations are neither written into any formal contract nor verbalized at the time of hiring. However, they have a significant effect upon the contractual parties (Argyris, 1960).

The importance of employee expectations was demonstrated in a field study for a life insurance company experiencing a high turnover rate: 27 percent of the new salesmen were terminating within the first six months (Weitz, 1956). In order to determine if this high turnover rate was attributable to inaccurate employee expectations, half of the new employees were given a booklet describing the job in considerable detail whereas the other half (following usual control procedures) were not given the booklet. Turnover in the former group was reduced to 19 percent, presumably because the information provided in the booklet provided the men with more realistic expectations about the job.

Personal Characteristics of Satisfied Workers

The emphasis in the remainder of this chapter is upon the factors or conditions associated with employee attitudes of satisfaction or dissatisfaction with the job. It is convenient for this discussion to separate the personal from the situational components of job satisfaction.

That certain personal characteristics like sex, age, intelligence, and mental health or adjustment should be related to job satisfaction is not surprising. Work is an aspect of the total life experience. To some extent, our attitudes toward work reflect our personal history.

Sex. A higher overall level of job satisfaction has been reported for women than for men (Morse, 1953).

Differences in the relative importance attached by men and

women to specific aspects of the job have also been investigated. A sample of workers completed a questionnaire in which the following five factors were presented in various combinations as pairs: advancement, hours of work, salary, security, and supervisor. The respondent was required to check the item in each pair of statements that he (or she) regarded as most important in a job (Blum & Russ, 1942). The choices, expressed as percentages of the total number of choices attainable, are summarized by sex and by martial status in Table 16–7.

Men attached considerably more importance than women to advancement possibilities and somewhat greater importance to salary. The women, on the other hand, regarded the supervisor as a more potent determinant of job satisfaction than did the men. However, this research was performed about 30 years ago. In the intervening

TABLE 16–7

Attitude toward Various Incentives by Sex and Marital Status

	Men			Women		
	Married	*Single*	*Total*	*Married*	*Single*	*Total*
Salary.................	46%	46%	46%	34%	36%	39%
Security...............	76	65	69	65	73	72
Supervisor.............	32	34	33	51	45	45
Hours of work..........	13	16	15	29	18	21
Advancement...........	83	89	87	71	78	76

years the role of women in the work force has changed dramatically and surely will continue to do so. Therefore, the validity of Morse's findings for understanding the relationship between sex and job satisfaction at present is questionable.

The replies of unmarried female workers corresponded in some ways more closely to those of men than to those of married women. This is particularly apparent for the ratings assigned to the supervisor, hours of work, and advancement. Thus, these data are suggestive of some fundamental differences in the gratifications which employees seek from their job and of the role of work in overall life adjustment as a function of sex and marital status.

Age. There is some evidence indicative of increased job satisfaction with increased employee age (Morse, 1953; Hoppock, 1936).

This relationship has been attributed to a combination of factors, including the termination of employment by dissatisfied older personnel and a kind of conservatism or resignation with advancing age to the realities of life and the job. In addition, some of the factors responsible for job dissatisfaction, like lack of opportunity for advancement and low salary, are of somewhat lesser importance to older workers than to younger employees who are in the midst of raising a family.

Intelligence. The level of intelligence does not itself appear to be a determinant of job satisfaction or dissatisfaction. The employee's intelligence in relation to the nature of the job he performs is, however, a factor of considerable consequence. Employees who are either insufficiently challenged by their work or who are engaged in activities that are too demanding relative to their intellectual capabilities are often dissatisfied with their job. The implication of this relationship for the implementation of adequate personnel selection procedures is self-evident.

Experience. Job experience is related to satisfaction in a rather interesting fashion. As one might expect, new employees tend to be relatively well satisfied with their jobs. This "honeymoon" terminates after a period of time, however, unless the worker feels that he is making rather steady progress toward the satisfaction of his occupational and social needs.

Almost every company employs a number of persons who after several years with the company feel that advancement or salary increases have not been forthcoming with sufficient regularity and that they are working at a dead-end job. The effect of this is to cause a perceptible decline in the prevailing level of job satisfaction during the several years following the start of employment. The level of job satisfaction appears to increase again after six or seven years and reaches a maximum for workers who have remained with a company for about 20 years (Hull & Kolstad, 1942). This is undoubtedly due to the fact that the most dissatisfied employees have sought other employment either voluntarily or involuntarily. In addition, employees who have been encouraged to remain with the company for as long a period as 20 years have probably been provided with the kind of incentives that lead to feelings of job satisfaction.

Personal Adjustment. The existence of a relationship between job satisfaction and adjustment to, or satisfaction with, life in general has been implied throughout the preceding sections of this chapter. One study concerning this relationship interviewed more than 400 automotive workers to assess both personal adjustment and job satisfaction; the correlation between ratings of these factors was positive (Kornhauser, 1965). In addition to this positive relationship between personal adjustment and job satisfaction, adjustment was found to be positively related also both to the employee's occupational level and his perception that his skills were being effectively used.

The interpretation of a relationship between job satisfaction and life adjustment is somewhat risky as regards cause and effect. It might be assumed that a worker who is personally maladjusted and unhappy about cricumstances outside of the plant will generalize this attitude to include dissatisfaction with his company and job. There is some evidence, however, that the relationship may also work the other way; that is, job satisfaction is partly responsible for a general feeling of well-being and satisfaction with life (Brayfield, Wells, & Strate, 1957). In any event, either as cause or effect or as some combination of the two, management has reason to be concerned with the worker's adjustment to the job itself and, in a larger sense, to life.

Job Satisfaction and Job Performance

We have already mentioned that the correlation between job satisfaction and such performance criteria as productivity, accident rate, absenteeism, and turnover tends to be weak. This finding is contrary to what common sense leads us to anticipate.

Productivity. Quite a number of investigators have correlated a measure of job satisfaction with supervisory ratings of employee performance and been forced to the conclusion that these two factors are not particularly related. The correlations actually obtained for groups of office clerical workers, for example, ranged between -0.06 and $+0.13$ (Brayfield & Crockett, 1955). Similarly low values have been reported for plumber apprentices, farmers, IBM operators (Gadel & Kriedt, 1952), retail salesclerks (Mossin, 1949), and other employee groups. The median correlation reported in a recent summary of various studies across many occupational groups was only 0.14 (Vroom, 1964).

Such studies are open to a certain amount of criticism because of the subjective nature of the criterion of employee performance.

Supervisory ratings of performance leave much to be desired in the way of reliability and validity. An objective criterion, sales volume, was correlated with an index of job satisfaction for insurance agents with positive results. The two measures yielded a correlation coefficient of 0.26 (Baxter, Taaffe & Hughes, 1953). Although this correlation is not high, it provides some support for the contention that there is a slight tendency for satisfied employees to be more productive than dissatisfied employees. However, even such a slight positive relationship is not uniformly obtained where an objective performance criterion is used. For example, a correlation of only 0.22 has been reported between job satisfaction and performance of positioners (Mann, Indik, & Vroom, 1963).

Turnover.   Another plausible, but often unsubstantiated, hypothesis is that job satisfaction ought to be related to such criteria as absenteeism and turnover. It seems reasonable to anticipate that employees who are for some reason unhappy with their job will seek other employment when possible. Although this expectation has been supported in several studies (Ross & Zander, 1966), the evidence for it is not very strong. Furthermore, contrary findings showing no relationship between job dissatisfaction and turnover have also been reported in the literature (Giese & Ruter, 1949).

Job satisfaction is clearly only one part of the answer to turnover. Again, we must invoke the notion of individual needs hierarchies and the susceptibility of these hierarchies to personal factors (like sex, age, and education) and situational factors (including the availability of other jobs and economic obligations). Taken together, these conditions influence the worker's propensity to leave if dissatisfied with his job.

It has been hypothesized that those workers with a high propensity to leave if dissatisfied tend to be young, highly skilled employees with few economic obligations who live in an area where there is a demand for their skills. The opposite conditions generate a low propensity to leave if dissatisfied (Hulen, 1966). This interpretation fits nicely into the valence-expectancy theory of motivation discussed earlier.

Factors Influencing the Relationship.   It would be erroneous to conclude from the foregoing discussion that job satisfaction is an unimportant consideration in industry or that it cannot be improved regardless of management's efforts to do so. The point is simply that job satisfaction is complex (Schwab & Cummings, 1970; Wanous &

Lawler, 1972) . This complexity makes it difficult to generalize about the factors contributing to job satisfaction and dissatisfaction and about the influence of these attitudes upon job performance.

There are widespread individual differences between employees in the goals which they seek (individual needs hierarchies) and hence in the effectiveness of specific factors as determinants of job satisfaction and behavior. Furthermore, as we have already pointed out, needs hierarchies are exceedingly flexible since they reflect the valences currently attached to potential outcomes.

This situation is quite analogous to your own experience in school. It is unlikely that the amount of effort you expend in a particular course is affected solely by your feelings about that course. Regardless of whether you are happy or unhappy in it, and whether you have elected to take it or have been compelled to take it in order to fulfill a university requirement, you are under a certain amount of pressure to produce (that is, to earn a passing grade) in order to be graduated.

Employees also function under conditions of constraint. Productivity or job stability may be no more of an ultimate goal for them than earning a satisfactory grade is for you. High productivity or job stability may for some employees be a means toward the realization of certain other goals like status or ownership of a new car. When the pressure for productivity is high, the employee may perform efficiently either in the absence of any real job satisfaction or even when he is quite dissatisfied. (Triandis, 1959) .

Furthermore, it is naïve to assume that management's goals and the employee's goals always coincide. Whereas management may value efficient productivity, at least some employees are more intensely driven toward other ends also satisfied in work settings. For example, the worker who is highly motivated by a desire for social acceptance by his fellow employees may actually derive increased satisfactions from limiting his productivity and thereby gaining group acceptance.

The reported correlations between measures of job satisfaction and job performance are undoubtedly underestimates resulting from certain procedural and definitional difficulties adversely affecting the reliability and validity of both measures (Schwab & Cummings, 1970) . To some extent this is a function of the subjectivity inherent in certain of the satisfaction and performance criteria. In addition, it results from such things as inadequate record keeping and certain evaluative problems inherent in assessing attitudes.

SUMMARY

Early attempts to motivate industrial employees tended to focus on money as a primary incentive; hence financial incentive plans proliferated in number and variety during the decades preceding and immediately following World War II. The relative demise of such plans at present reflects an appreciation of the complexity of human motivation. Salary, wages, and financial incentives generally have idiosyncratic effects depending both upon the employee and situational factors in and outside of work.

Two complementary views about motivation are presented in this chapter: needs hierarchies and valence expectancy.

The needs-hierarchy concept refers to the arrangement of our needs, and hence the goals we seek, in a hierarchy of importance. Certain needs are stronger than others at a given time. The relative strength of any need at a particular time depends upon the interaction of both personal and situational factors.

The valence-expectancy concept further clarifies the organization of idiosyncratic needs hierarchies. It regards the predilection for a course of action as dependent upon our expectations about the consequences of that action. In these terms, behavior is directed toward the outcome from which we anticipate the strongest and most positive consequence.

Although there are some conflicting findings, the bulk of evidence indicates that the majority of employees are reasonably well satisfied with their jobs. The level of job satisfaction is positively correlated with job rank or status, age, and personal adjustment. In addition, women tend more often than men to report job satisfaction.

The relationship between job satisfaction and job performance (including productivity and turnover) has been extensively studied with indications that this relationship is, at best, rather weak. The fact that these relationships are not stronger reflects the complexity of motivation and its highly individualized nature.

17. Planned Organizational Change

The theories and research findings of organizational psychologists ultimately must stand the test of successful application to planned organizational change. This application entails the transformation of a financially troubled and otherwise distressed organization into a prosperous and healthy one. Although there are still large gaps in knowledge about both organizational and human relations psychology, the preceding chapters indicated that these gaps are being rapidly closed. This chapter considers several attempts to apply this knowledge.

It will be helpful to begin by elucidating certain principles of planned change introduced in previous chapters. Following this introduction, we present summaries of five field studies wherein planned organizational change occurred.

PRINCIPLES OF PLANNED ORGANIZATIONAL CHANGE

We have organized the principles of planned change under three headings. First, we describe the chronology of change. Next we consider the objectives of organizational change by reviewing the theories of the human relations psychologists previously presented in Chapter 12. The final section discusses the principles of change.

Chronology of Planned Change

Although planned organizational change does not necessarily progress in an orderly and logical sequence, the following phases

414

have been differentiated as characteristic of most change (Lippitt, Watson, & Westley, 1958) :

1. Recognition of the Need for Change. The client organization needs to be aware that a problem exists and must believe that a more desirable state of affairs is possible before any sort of planned change can be initiated. This phase is sometimes termed "unfreezing."

2. Establishment of a Change Relationship. The client organization must communicate its problem to the change agent, must respond favorably to his views, and agree to expend the effort required for successful change to occur.

3. Clarification or Diagnosis of the Problem. The client organization must provide the change agent with enough information for a comprehensive diagnosis. This often proves to be an especially trying time for management because previously unsuspected ramifications of the original problem are frequently uncovered.

4. Establishing Goals. Organizational management and the change agent must ultimately agree on a course of action after duly examining alternative goals and procedures for their attainment. Typically some apprehension is experienced at this stage as management realizes that it will have to relinquish and/or modify certain of its characteristic and long-established modes of behavior.

5. Transformation of Intentions into Change Efforts. Because of the departure from previously accustomed patterns of behavior, the client organization requires considerable support and encouragement from the change agent as it attempts to implement the attainment of its new goals. Such support and encouragement is possible only in a climate of acceptance of the desirability of change at all organizational levels.

6. Generalization and Stabilization of the Change. The diffusion of change throughout the organization and the incorporation of the change into the fabric of the organization can be encouraged by management in two ways. First, it must be alert to evidences of appropriate new behavior and reinforce these occurrences. Secondly, it must institute organizational procedures consistent with the desired change.

7. Achieving a Terminal Relationship. The termination of the relationship between the change agent and the organization sometimes proves difficult because of the dependency of the latter upon the skills of the former. It is one of the change agent's responsibilities to wean the organization away from such dependence.

Objectives of Organizational Change

Psychological change agents generally have a preconception about the "ideal" organization—one they wish the client organization to become after the change program is completed. This ideal typically combines the essential properties of Theory Y, System 4, motivator-oriented organizations as described respectively by McGregor (1960), Likert (1967), and Herzberg (1966) and summarized in Chapter 12. Four properties of such organizations are reviewed below.

1. Participative Decision Making.   Participative decision making involves the worker facilitating his participation in decisions appropriate to his organizational level. It carries with it the implication that workers may occasionally reach decisions with which management disagrees. Nevertheless, their participation in the decision-making process enables employees to satisfy their higher level needs on the job and helps to remove the feelings of powerlessness and helplessness so prevalent in contemporary industrial organizations.

2. Integration of Organizational and Employee Goals.   If an organization is to function effectively, the workers and management must be working toward attaining the same goals. When the goals of these two parties are not integrated, each side dissipates a large share of its creative talent and energy in a power struggle to the detriment of the organization.

3. Meaningful Jobs.   Organizational psychologists generally believe that many present-day jobs do not enable workers to satisfy their higher level needs. Hence, whenever possible, jobs must be enriched to enable employees to assume greater responsibility and derive a greater sense of achievement. It is assumed that job enrichment encourages employee motivation.

4. Effective Communication.   This fourth property of an effective organization is an essential precondition of the three properties stated above. Effective organizational communication is open in the sense that communication flows freely in all directions: upwards, downwards, and laterally.

Psychological Aspects of the Change Process

Both psychological research and the experience of change agents have resulted in recognition that effective change is impossible without (*a*) the commitment of top management and (*b*) open confrontation with those organizational forces resistant to the change.

The importance of top management's commitment was demonstrated in a supervisory training program study for the International Harvester Company (Fleishman, 1953). Lower level managers attended training sessions designed to teach them to be more sensitive to the feelings of their subordinates ("consideration") and less involved in planning and setting task schedules for task performance ("initiating structure"). Posttraining measures of the two variables —consideration and initiating structure—appeared to substantiate the validity of the training. However, this initial finding did not hold up over time. On later readministrations of these measures, the trainees were found to score even lower on the former and higher on the latter than they did prior to the training. These rather surprising results were attributed to the fact that top management did not participate in and were not sympathetic to the objectives of the training program. Hence, the trainees were discouraged from putting into practice in the plant those behaviors for which they had been reinforced during the training.

It is likely that any contemplated organizational change will encounter a certain amount of resistance. Many organizational members prefer to stay with accustomed patterns of behavior; for them the prospect of change engenders insecurity and anxiety. Rather than neglecting this resistance, the successful change agent typically encourages its expression as a first step toward overcoming it. Hence, sensitivity training, including its many variants, is probably the single most widely used technique for effecting organizational change. As described in Chapter 13, the goals of such training are to increase self-insight and sensitivity to the behavior of others.

FIVE FIELD STUDIES OF ORGANIZATIONAL CHANGE

Glacier Metal Company

As a result of intermittent contacts with the company, the Tavistock Institute of Human Relations (Great Britain) approached the organization with a proposal to collaborate on a project to investigate and improve Glacier's methods for developing satisfactory group relations. The project spanned approximately two and a half years with an initial period of several months devoted to insuring that the research team was not perceived either by management or labor as a protagonist for either side. The project is reported by Jacques (1951).

Solution of the immediate pressing problems confronting the company was *not* the researchers' primary goal. Instead, they were concerned with implementing methods of assisting the organization in developing the capabilities to solve its own problems more effectively. They defined a healthy organization as one that is capable of successfully handling its own technical, economic, and social problems in a realistic way. Note that in this view a healthy organization is not characterized by freedom from problems; instead, it is one that is capable of successfully adapting to problem situations. The goal of the Tavistock team was to help Glacier become this kind of organization.

The research team began by making a historical study of the organization. During this period they gained an understanding of how the organization functioned and of the factors leading to its current status. Furthermore, during the two-month period required to complete this phase, they had the opportunity to become acquainted with many organizational members at all levels of the hierarchy. Glacier was found to employ 1,800 persons, 1,300 of whom worked in the London factory where the main study was conducted. The company was founded in 1899 and initially manufactured antifriction metals; approximately 20 years later it expanded by manufacturing bearings for automobiles and other machinery. In 1941, by initiative of the managing director, the employees elected 24 representatives to form a Works Committee from which 11 representatives were elected to the Works Council. These groups were created to enable employees at all levels of the company to share in developing and modifying company policy.

Although the company had never reached a contractual agreement with any union, a majority of the hourly rate workers were members of trade unions by 1942. By 1949, shortly after the Tavistock group began work with the company, the demand for Glacier's products decreased leading to a layoff of about 250 employees in a four-month period. The criteria for layoff were formulated by a committee comprised of representatives of all levels of management, staff, and workers. At the end of that same year market conditions improved to the point that the company began once again to hire additional personnel.

One of the change agent's fundamental strategies was to uncover the previously concealed forces that were reducing the efficiency of the company. This approach is very reminiscent of conventional clinical psychotherapeutic procedures and relies upon self-examination accompanied by consultative interpretation. The object is to clarify the psychological, cultural, and technological forces impeding organizational effectiveness. The expectation is that the organization will acquire a capacity to function more effectively when phenomena like rivalry, suspicion, and hostility are uncovered and dealt with by the entire group.

This general approach was applied by the change agent to help the company's service department develop an equitable pay plan. Management had proposed a change from piece-rate to hourly rate payment because of perceived worker dissatisfaction with the former. A committee was formed to evaluate management's proposal; this committee, in turn, requested assistance from the Tavistock researchers.

The hourly rate suggested by the service department manager was based on the average level of piece-rate earning for the shop with a built-in deduction to allow for a possible slight decrease in productivity. This proposal was rejected by the workers and the ensuing discussion revealed considerable distrust of management's motives and intentions. In particular, there was considerable worker suspicion that management knew that the new pay plan would not work and would use its failure as an excuse to rescind the plan in favor of a lower piece rate than presently prevailed. It became evident to all concerned parties that the prolonged and heated discussions of pay plans were masking the more fundamental problem, that is, lack of trust. After management agreed to drop the originally proposed deduction for the anticipated decrease in productivity, the workers became more confident of the integrity of management's motives and a new wage plan was agreed upon. Furthermore, in recognition of the more fundamental underlying problem, a shop council was formed as a mechanism through which the department could become aware of and solve its problems.

The change agent also consulted for the Works Council which had inadvertently surfaced an unanticipated problem while instituting a system of standing committees. The problem that was raised by the formation of these committees concerned the council's power and authority. Although the council had been constituted almost 10 years earlier upon management initiative, its role had never previously been clearly defined. A weekend conference was convened for this purpose and revealed that the council itself was at least partly responsible for its ambiguous status. By insulating itself from inputs from the organizational members it was supposed to be representing it had, over the years, progressively diminished its own power. After working through the problem of open communication permitting free expressions of feelings, a more representative Works Council was created.

Food World

Unlike the changes described above, the management of Food World, a regional supermarket chain, rather than an outside consultant, served as the agent of the changes next to be described (Lawrence, 1958).

The entire grocery industry underwent fairly radical changes during the second quarter of this century. The most important modification was the development of the supermarket concept: that is, larger store size, increased variety of stock, self-service, and reduced gross profit margin.

Back in 1935 Food World was a chain of about 600 small neighborhood grocery stores emphasizing the sale of a limited number of products and personalized attention to customers. It was a highly centralized operation with close authoritarian, paternalistic supervision of store personnel. The growth of the company was attributed to the drive and leadership of the president who was personally known to and respected by most of the employees. Responding to the industry trend, this picture changed considerably over the next 20 years. By 1954 Food World had 100 large self-service stores each employing about 50 persons. Although the president was less active than formerly, he was still the dominant figure in the company.

Organizationally, the district managers and assistant district managers were intermediaries between top management and departmental supervisors. Each market employed three department managers: one each for produce, grocery, and meat. These department managers spent all of their time in one store working directly with the merchandise and supervising the clerks. At this stage of develop-ment Food World seemed to be an effective organization which, over the years, had evolved a smoothly functioning managerial pat-tern. However, in reviewing industry trends the five top managers anticipated that their greatest competition in the future would come from strong independent stores. They felt that the competitive edge in the future would go to the company that could effectively com-bine the advantages of large size with flexibility at the local level. These five managers proceeded to act as the change agent for this developmental direction at Food World.

In reviewing their own organization they concluded that they had to overcome certain current problems if Food World were to develop in the desired direction. Among these problems were: (*a*) overly centralized leadership at the top with a consequent dirth of initiative by mid-management, (*b*) a virtual absence of communica-tion from lower to higher levels of management, and (*c*) a tendency at all management levels to fight fires rather than to make orderly progress toward the attainment of planned objectives. Hence, two major changes were instigated:

1. The creation of the store manager as a new position. This position was considered the key to retaining the advantages of chain operation while simultaneously adding the advantages of strong independent operations. The store manager was supposed to per-ceive himself as a relatively self-sufficient businessman responsible for the overall operation of his market.

2. The responsibilities of the assistant district managers were considerably enlarged. Whereas they formerly supervised the perish-able departments (produce and meat), they were now to advise the store manager in all facets of his operation. Since this relieved the district managers of some of their former responsibilities, their functions were simultaneously upgraded to encompass long-range planning.

The district manager-store manager interaction was regarded as one of the key factors in implementing the change program; three patterns of interaction have been described by Lawrence (1958).

The first district manager (DM–1) treated his store manager (SM–1) as dictated by the reorganization plan. He coached SM–1 in leadership methods and encouraged store personnel to accept SM–1's leadership; he delegated responsibility for immediate super-vision of employees to SM–1. SM–1, in turn, appeared willing to accept this responsibility and exercised supervision by working mainly through his department managers.

A different situation prevailed in a second store. Here DM–2 bypassed SM–2 in dealing with department heads and clerks, often giving them detailed and rather obvious instructions. In spite of this SM–2 assumed leadership as prescribed by the reorganization plan with the result that the DM–2–SM–2 pair achieved the desired results in spite of the fact that the district manager persisted in his traditional, prereorganization role.

Yet another pattern of interaction occurred between DM–3 and SM–3. DM–3 made virtually all decisions, both major and minor, and treated SM–3 as a person who was to carry out his detailed instructions and relay them to subordinates. As you would expect, DM–3 often bypassed SM–3 and dealt directly with store personnel himself. This interaction was essentially a continuation of the pattern existing prior to the change effort.

These three types of interaction patterns, reflecting differences in receptivity to the change program, were found to be correlated with two variables. One of these was the amount of time DM spoke (as opposed to listened) when he was with his SM. DM–1 talked about 58 percent of the time whereas DM–2 and DM–3 talked about 74 percent of the time. This difference in DM behavior probably reflects something about the personality both of the DM and the SM. Indeed, Lawrence found that the SM's own self-concept tended to be consistent with and helped explain his attitude—either favorable or unfavorable—to the reorganization.

A follow-up two years later demonstrated that DM–2 and DM–3 had modified their behavior to bring it into closer accord with the desired organizational model. Presumably, this change would have occurred sooner if, in addition to being supported by top management, more intensive advance planning had been directed toward securing support from all persons affected by the change.

Automotive Assembly: Plant Y

Following the end of the Korean War early in 1953 the demand for automobiles rapidly increased. Plant Y along with five sister plants in the same company stepped up assembly-line speeds and instituted a two-shift operation. Nevertheless, the production at Plant Y lagged behind that of its sister plants, and its absenteeism and turnover rates were by far the highest in the division. This dismal record persisted in spite of the manager's efforts to pressure improved efficiency through threat.

The manager was retired in the fall of that year and was replaced by Cooley—formerly a production manager at one of the sister plants. This personnel change was not suggested by an external change agent; it was made by executives of the company itself. The consequences of this naturally occurring change have been reported by Guest (1962).

Cooley's initial efforts at the plant were devoted to familiarization. He got acquainted with each of his staff; he sent letters to each foreman asking to be invited to visit his section. Within his first few days on the job he met with the union shop committees and requested their suggestions for possible plant improvements. One observation from these activities was that the plant had historically operated on a day-to-day crisis basis with little evidence of long-range planning.

When Cooley assumed the plant managership, the division manager (his supervisor) suggested that he make a number of personnel changes including terminating many of the plant supervisors. Cooley rejected this advice and requested resignation from only three of over 300 salaried employees. In his attempt to turn the organization around with its present personnel he convened regularly scheduled meetings involving all levels of supervision. These meetings reviewed the past month's performance and planned the next month's activities, often successfully anticipating emergencies before they occurred.

Two avenues were open for new expenditures of money at Plant Y: one for improving working conditions, the other for acquiring new machinery to increase assembly-line efficiency. Cooley and his staff decided upon the former course. Over $15,000 worth of renovations were made in the cafeteria; new fixtures, clothes lockers, heaters, and fans were installed in the washrooms; and so on. All of these changes were made gradually, and many followed suggestions originating from hourly employees and union representatives.

By 1956 fear of demotion or job termination was no longer the primary motivating force behind the actions and responses of the supervisors. Guest made three general observations comparing superior-subordinate relations in 1956 and 1953. First, he noticed that the expressed opinions of superiors toward subordinates and toward each other were considerably more positive in 1956. Second, there was a greater amount of information flow upwards in 1956, and subordinates reported that they had easier access to their supervisors. Finally, a higher proportion of the communications were concerned with future planning than with present crises.

These changes in the direction and nature of communication and in the attitudes of employees were paralleled by performance changes. By 1956 Plant Y's direct labor costs had decreased 14 percent—a savings of more than $2 million a year. Furthermore, this plant which had the second highest number of monthly labor grievances in 1953 recorded fewer grievances than any other plant in the division in 1956. Its absenteeism dropped from 4.1 percent in 1953 to 2.5 percent in 1956, and in the same period, turnover of hourly employees decreased from 6.1 percent to 4.9 percent.

Obviously, this is a success story attributable largely to the influence of a single change agent who, by improving the work and psychological environment in the plant, generated improved worker attitudes and increased productivity. Guest concludes that a key factor in this success, aside from the change agent's talents as an administrator, was the fact that he did not have a history of prior association with Plant Y. He speculates that there is some critical point after which an organization may be incapable of changing itself through internal manipulation and requires intervention by someone new brought into the organization from the outside.

Sigma Plant, Piedmont Company

As one of the plants in a large petrochemical corporation, the Sigma Plant had a reputation of being technically competent and had consistently been able to meet its production goals. However, this plant began experiencing some difficulty early in 1960 precipitated by the parent company's (Piedmont) merger. Following this merger, Sigma was instructed to become more autonomous by making more of the decisions relevant to its own operation. Sigma could not comply with this change in its operation, and its departments became increasingly competitive with each other.

Because of earlier success with the program in the parent company, the managerial grid training program (see Chapter 13) was installed in the Sigma Plant at the end of 1962. Its implementation consisted of six phases:

1. Laboratory Seminar Series. A one-week conference in which each participant explores his own managerial style and devotes about 50 hours to practice in problem solution. This series also included some structured sensitivity training focusing upon managerial style.

2. Team Development. The results of phase 1 are transferred to the actual job situation.

3. Intergroup Development. The objective of this phase is to change the perception of intergroup effort from that of a competitive win-lose pattern to one encouraging joint problem solving (a win-win situation).

4. Organization Goal Setting. Members from different organizational levels confront the important task of establishing realistic organizational goals.

5. Goal Attainment. This phase involves planning, the steps needed to accomplish the goals set in phase 4.

6. Stabilization. The final phase is designed to support the changes brought about in phases 1–5 and to reinforce these changes.

The change agents (Blake, Mouton, Barnes, & Greiner, 1964) were aware that evaluation of the effectiveness of their program would be confounded by many uncontrolled variables. Nevertheless a pre-posttraining evaluation was attempted using both production and attitudinal data as criteria. Average productivity per employee following the grid program was found to increase from 103.9 to 131.3 even though there was no noteworthy addition of new plant equipment. A similar positive shift in employee attitudes toward supervisors was noted following training. Although the authors of the study attribute the favorable shifts to installation of the managerial grid technique, it is possible that the technique itself has a less significant impact than does the climate for change generated by any systematic attempt to facilitate cooperation and planning by organizational members.

Weldon Pajama Company

Marrow, Bowers, and Seashore (1967) report a widely quoted study of organizational change. Marrow was president of Harwood—a middle-sized corporation in the pajama manufacturing industry. Harwood bought Weldon, one of its leading competitors, in 1962; the basis for the acquisition was Weldon's demonstrated success in the higher price market that had largely eluded Harwood.

Weldon had become one of the fastest growing producers of

quality pajamas early in the 1940s. By 1950 Weldon was employing about 3,500 people in its five plants. Its growth and success were not accompanied by any change in management practices; it was still run largely by its two owners whose personal role in every decision had contributed to the company's growth for about a decade but by the late 1950s appeared to be contributing to its decline. By 1960 increased labor and manufacturing costs caused Weldon to consolidate its operation into one main plant employing a maximum of 1,000 persons during peak season.

At the time of its purchase by Harwood, Weldon's facilities were inadequate. The building was large, but not well maintained; modern equipment was lacking. Weldon's work force included a small nucleus of highly skilled employees and a larger group of relatively unskilled workers. The supervisors and managers were competent but, for the most part, made few decisions and assumed little responsibility. The one exception to this generalization was the production manager, who spent most of his working day directing activities in the sewing rooms.

The situation at Weldon contrasted markedly with that at Harwood which had, since 1939, been applying principles of group dynamics to the problems of management. Harwood's top management had become convinced that a job is done best when the employees feel that their needs are considered in ways that sustain their self-respect and generate a sense of responsibility. The employees and management worked at creating an environment of trust and openness wherein problems were approached in a spirit of joint inquiry with a view toward full participation in their solution.

With the acquisition of Weldon, Harwood became the largest company in the field producing about 20 percent of the world supply of pajamas. While many factors enter into the successful operation of an organization, Marrow was convinced that Harwood's long history of employee efficiency and loyalty reflected its application of a behavioral science approach to management. In consequence, the Harwood organization became the model for the Weldon change program.

A study undertaken soon after the acquisition revealed that the employee populations at Harwood and Weldon were basically similar. For example, about 80 percent of the employees in both plants were women, and about two thirds were married. However, based upon replies to an anonymous questionnaire, the Weldon organization demonstrated an authoritarian profile while Harwood's demonstrated a more participative profile. In terms of organizational performance, Harwood was superior to Weldon; Harwood's return on its investment was 17 percent while Weldon's was −15 percent. Harwood's average monthly absenteeism was 3 percent while Weldon's was 6 percent; and whereas Harwood's average monthly turnover was 0.75 percent, Weldon averaged 10 percent turnover monthly.

The change program instituted after acquisition had three major features: (1) virtually all Weldon personnel were retained; (2) the physical plant and work methods were modernized; and (3) the existing organizational pattern was changed by emphasizing participative problem solving. We will examine this last feature in more detail.

Midway in its two-year change program the organization began to build relationships of trust and cooperation between its members, using methods derived from sensitivity training procedures. The first group attending these sessions was comprised of the five department heads in the main office who were mainly concerned with marketing and administration. The next group to attend was comprised of the top six staff members from the plant, which included the plant manager. Eventually all management personnel down to the level of assistant supervisor attended training sessions.

As shown in Figure 17–1, productivity increased substantially during the two-year-change program period, and Weldon's former loss on investment capital (−15 percent) was reversed to +17 percent. During the same period the company's rate of manufacturing defects was reduced by 39 percent and the rate of customer returns declined by 57 percent. Finally, monthly turnover decreased from 10 percent to 4 percent and absenteeism declined from 6 to 3 percent.

Surprisingly, the Weldon change program had little measurable effect upon employee attitudes toward the company; these attitudes shifted from a neutral to a slightly positive position. However, whereas about half of Weldon's employees indicated that they were planning to leave the company when the change program was instituted, most employees indicated that they were planning to stay with the company indefinitely at the time of the post-program assessment.

Weldon's efforts at change appear to have been highly successful.

FIGURE 17–1

Mean Performance at Weldon,
January 1962–March 1964

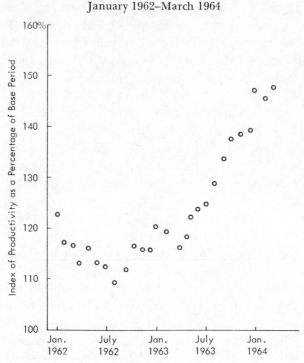

Source: Fig. 13–1. Weldon: Mean weekly operator performance
against standard, 1962–1964. In *Management by participation* by
A. J. Marrow, D. G. Bowers, & S. E. Seashore.

The program of change was planned and implemented well and was
comprehensive in scope. The comprehensiveness of the change program is evident from the fact that it included improvements in work
setup and work flow and new training methods as well as the installation of a participative system of management. This very comprehensiveness makes it impossible, of course, to attribute a specific
proportion of the financial improvement to the psychological
changes as distinct from the mechanical and plant changes. However, Marrow, Bowers, and Seashore (1967) provide some evidence
in support of a *minimum* estimate of 25 percent of the financial
improvement attributable to improved human relationships at the
Weldon plant.

SUMMARY

The theories and research findings of organizational psychologists are ultimately tested by their application to planned organizational change. Although knowledge gaps still exist, much has already been learned about effecting such change. Successful planned change proceeds in an orderly manner and is predicated upon support from top management.

Five illustrative field studies of organizational change are described in this chapter; each represents a different aspect of the change process or a different change strategy.

VI.

Consumer Psychology

You will recall our earlier mention of the fact that psychologists study behavior with a view toward understanding, predicting, and controlling or changing it. The application of these objectives in the realm of consumer behavior is immediately apparent. The purpose of advertising and selling programs is to control or change consumer behavior. The producer, distributor, and advertiser often wish also to predict the way in which potential consumers will respond to various appeals, products, and packages.

The accuracy of such predictions rests in large measure upon an understanding of consumer motivation. This is particularly evident in the American culture wherein masses of consumers have considerable discretion in economic expenditures. In consequence, consumers desire many things today which were hardly known a few years ago. And because of social changes, including those reflecting altered educational levels, income distribution, increased leisure time, more stable

*age patterns, governmental intervention on behalf of the consumer,
and growth of the mass media, it is likely that these felt needs will
continue to proliferate.*

*Part VI considers the psychologist's contribution to the study of
consumer behavior and the understanding of consumer needs; that
is, the research methods and behavior principles germane to consumer psychology. The methods particularly stressed in these chapters are (a) surveys of various kinds, (b) "depth procedures" designed to elicit information about underlying consumer motivation,
and (c) studies of actual consumer behavior. The range of applications of these procedures is extremely broad and includes studies of
the characteristics of consumers and potential consumers, the effectiveness of advertising appeals and alternative distribution channels,
product design, and consumer response to available products and
services. In addition, consumer psychology has increasingly focused
upon the consumer as an organism worthy of study in his own right,
with particular attention to improved health and safety and to an
increased understanding of the factors involved in consumer decisions and choices.*

18. Consumer Research

Two fundamental problems for the producer are: (1) bringing the product to the attention of potential consumers and (2) influencing them to purchase it. Purchase by the consumer involves an element of decision making. The prospective customer must decide on occasion whether or not to buy a product or utilize a service without regard for competing brands. Should he, for example, buy a new car? A new refrigerator? A new coat? He must decide further which of several competing brands or options he ought to select. If he is going to buy a new car, will it be a Chevrolet, Ford, or Pontiac?

Decisions of this kind are not always predicated upon careful consideration of all alternatives. "Impulse buying" results from decisions made precipitously, without much forethought, and in response to factors about which the buyer himself may be quite unaware. Even decisions considered by the consumer to be highly rational may really be based upon irrational factors and unconscious processes.

The complex area of consumer behavior does not fall exclusively within the province of psychology. A comprehensive understanding of consumer behavior must include contributions from such disciplines as sociology, communications, and economics. One of the unique contributions made by the psychologist, however, is the application of rigorous scientific method to consumer research. Psychological methods of inquiry make it possible to replace speculation about consumer behavior with valid and useful information for producers, distributors, and advertisers. Also, because of his knowledge of motivation, perception, decision processes, and learning theory, the psychologist can often interpret the results of a particular study of consumer behavior in a context permitting generalization to other similar consumer problems.

433

SCOPE OF CONSUMER RESEARCH

Consumer studies are often regarded with a high degree of suspicion, particularly when such results are incorporated into an advertising campaign. We have all seen proof of product superiority presented as part of a TV commercial or in a full-page magazine spread. This kind of study does not fall legitimately within the province of consumer research. It often is loaded, either deliberately or unwittingly, in the direction of supporting a predetermined conclusion indicating superiority of the particular product under consideration. By passing out free samples, it would be a simple matter to arrange for 9 out of 10 women on the campus to own a bottle of EFFLUVIUM perfume. However, an advertising campaign based upon the statement that "90 percent of women in a typical midwestern college use EFFLUVIUM" would hardly be using the results of a scientifically conducted investigation.

This kind of unethical practice should not be construed as a condemnation either of advertisers or of consumer research. Although many advertising agencies do in fact employ psychologists to study consumer behavior, the objectives of their investigations are to test hypotheses and answer questions. It is perfectly possible to be as objective in making inquiries about consumer behavior as in studying the behavior of any other group of persons. In addition to advertising agencies, sound studies of consumer behavior are sponsored by certain manufacturing companies, publishers, federal departments, and universities. Other organizations not maintaining a consumer-research unit may avail themselves of the services of market research companies or consultants who specialize in this area of investigation.

Although we will be especially concerned in this chapter with just one area of consumer research—that is, factors influencing consumer choice—it is appropriate here to indicate something of the breadth of inquiry under the broad rubric of such research. For convenience, consumer studies can be grouped into four classifications or areas of application: (1) delineating, defining, and describing the market; (2) reaching the market; (3) product design and testing; and (4) consumer motivation.

Delineating the Market

Delineation of the market is of particular interest to manufacturers, distributors, and advertisers as they attempt to forecast the sales potential of a product. Furthermore, the characteristics of the persons within this market will in large measure determine the way in which the product can be most effectively packaged, displayed, advertised, and sold. Thus, research in this area may include studies of consumer needs, preferences, habits, and attitudes, and the influence upon these of such factors as age, education, income level, marital status, and so on.

The Short-Term Market. Information about the relative strength of the market over a relatively brief period of time may be critical to maintaining satisfactory production schedules, arranging distribution facilities, and timing advertising campaigns. This is particularly apparent in the case of certain products, like pleasure boats, having a seasonal appeal.

Other characteristics of the product may lead to relatively high saturation of the market over the short term and consequent resistance to buying. The consumer is not likely to replace durable goods unless the industry succeeds in convincing him that last year's model is out of date, inferior, or unfashionable. This approach to stimulating short-term markets is obviously successful in the case of the automotive, appliance, and apparel industries.

The Long-Term Market. The fact that an excellent market for a product exists at the present time is no assurance that it will persist in the future. Technological advances may completely outmode a product or heighten the demand for it. If there is evidence for the former, the manufacturer must prepare for economic survival by diversification. Otherwise, he will share the fate of the once prosperous buggy-whip manufacturer who refused to adjust to changing modes of transportation.

The possibility of heightened demand over the long-term must similarly be anticipated. A manufacturer who is unable to fill his orders because he underestimated the demand issues an open invitation to competitors. Persistently increasing consumer demand is dramatically apparent in the case of equipment, gadgets, clothing, and other paraphernalia in the sports and leisure time classifications. Increased demand for other products like children's clothing and school equipment can be anticipated on the basis of projected population growth.

The Potential Consumer. Although projections about the short- and long-term markets establish the number of potential consumers, they do not clarify the characteristics of these persons. It is important to supplement information about *how many* persons will buy the product with information about *who* will buy the product, if it is to be effectively advertised and promoted.

Virtually all products are limited in appeal to certain groups. The limiting factors may include such variables as age, sex, occupation, geographic location, socioeconomic level, educational background, and marital status, to name just a few. Studies of these limiting factors often assist companies in selecting appropriate advertising media, appeals, and distribution facilities. There is not much point, after all, to attempting to sell lawnmowers to apartment-dwellers or horses to Venetians!

Reaching the Market

Once a manufacturer has ascertained the strength of the market and has learned about its composition, he can take steps appropriate to placing the product before the potential consumers. The two primary areas of investigation relative to this problem include studies of advertising and of distribution channels.

Advertising. The ultimate objectives of advertising are to increase consumer awareness of the product and to impel potential consumers to become actual consumers. The various advertising media are not equally effective for all markets. Thus, comparative studies of the relative effectiveness of advertising media (for example, television versus magazines) and between vehicles within a particular medium (for example, *The New Yorker* versus *Esquire*) may provide valuable clues to the most efficient placement of the advertising dollar.

It is important also to study differences in the relative efficiency of various kinds of advertising copy and appeals. The level of vocabulary utilized and the validity of the appeal for the potential consumer are but two of the vital issues in this regard. One could hardly expect ten-year-old youngsters to be effectively reached by an advertisement for a "prestidigitation kit designed to confound your peers." And an advertisement for an expensive encyclopedia had better not begin, "Boy, oh, boy, Mom, every kid in the neighborhood will want to do his homework at your house when you own this set of books!"

Distribution Channels. The development of appropriate channels for distributing the product must parallel effective advertising. Products with a wide potential market should be made widely available; products with a restricted appeal can best be handled by restricted and carefully selected distribution facilities.

Many of the decisions about channels for distribution can be made without recourse to systematic investigation. However, intuition about appropriate distribution facilities may prove to be misleading either because the product is placed before an inappropriate market or because the market once served by a channel has changed. Not long ago the consumer went to a drugstore to buy pharmaceuticals and to a hardware store to buy small appliances and housewares. Now, however, many drugstores have become extremely efficient channels for distributing not only pharmaceuticals and small electric appliances but a potpourri of other products including such unlikely items as lawn furniture, furnace filters, and potato peelers.

Product Design and Testing

A vigorous company cannot afford to maintain an air of complacency about its sales. A once burgeoning market may become progressively diminished by technological advances and products introduced by competitors. Furthermore, consumer needs and desires and their consequent behavior reflect broad social, economic, and educational changes in society generally. Improved educational levels are associated with altered patterns of taste and increased demand for services; improved economic conditions are associated with increased leisure time and a larger amount of discretionary income for entertainment and leisure activities. Psychologists are uniquely qualified to help in designing products and services that will be attractive to special groups, like the aged.

The manufacturer is understandably concerned about the public's reactions to his product. If the product is a new one, he may find it worthwhile to subject it to a consumer appraisal before it is released for distribution to the public. It may be initially distributed in trial areas only, or submitted to consumer tests either in the laboratory or the field. Product features that are clearly satisfactory or appealing to consumers during these trials may be exploited in the subsequently developed advertising campaign. The discovery of unsatisfactory features may indicate a need for modification of the product prior to its release or in extreme cases to its withdrawal from the market.

The utility of product testing is, of course, not limited to new products. Studies of consumer reaction to a well-established product are vital to the maintenance and expansion of the market. A product once regarded by consumers as outstanding may lose ground rapidly in the face of competition. What was good enough 10 years ago, or even last year, may not be good enough for the present market. Consumer's expectations and standards change. It is imperative that the manufacturer be sensitive to these changes.

Consumer Motivation

The matter of sales cannot be reduced simply to considerations of product excellence and appropriateness of advertising media and distribution channels. Human behavior is much more complicated than this. Consumers perceive particular products either as being appropriate or inappropriate to their needs; they purchase need-satisfying products and reject the others.

Studies of the complexities involved in consumer motivation are often subsumed under the heading "motivation research." The intent of such investigation is to discover patterns of underlying consumer needs, both at the conscious and unconscious levels. Such information can provide the manufacturer and advertiser with extremely powerful ammunition for effecting brand changes and reinforcing brand loyalties.

Studies of consumer motivation are not always directed toward the self-interests of particular manufacturers or distributors. There is a growing trend toward research on the consumer as an organism worthy of study in his own right. Such studies focus both on the consumer's welfare (for example, improved health and safety) and on developing a better understanding of the factors involved in his economic decisions.

CONSUMER RESEARCH METHODS

Consumer research entails special applications of the general methods of psychological investigation described in Chapter 2: naturalistic, experimental, and clinical observation. Likewise, the techniques for obtaining data about consumer behavior involve elaborations of such procedures discussed earlier as interviewing, rating, attitude scaling, and testing.

Consumer Surveys

A questionnaire or interview survey is conducted for the purpose of ascertaining consumer opinions and attitudes. It often is desirable to find out how consumers feel about the product, the way in which it is advertised, distributed, and serviced, and the company that manufactures it. Survey findings may indicate, for example, that the product is perceived as one of shoddy construction and poor durability; that the service organization is viewed as unequal to the task of repairing the product and obtaining necessary replacement parts speedily and cheerfully; or that there is considerable consumer resistance to purchasing a product made by a company with a widely publicized history of unsatisfactory labor practices. The identification of such unfavorable attitudes can contribute importantly both to understanding and predicting buying behavior.

One of the assumptions underlying survey procedures is that consumers can verbalize at least some of their attitudes and opinions. Thus, if we wish to discover these feelings, we need only ask respondents to reply to questions contained in some kind of opinionnaire.

The purposes and techniques of consumer surveys are essentially similar to those of political polls. The basic difference between them is that in the former we are generally interested in opinions about products or competing brands, while in the latter we are interested in opinions about political parties or competing candidates.

Sampling. In consumer research, data are collected from a sample of persons and the findings are generalized to the population from which that sample was drawn. The reason for sampling is efficiency. For example, it usually is infeasible to administer a questionnaire to all consumers or potential consumers (the population). This kind of blanket administration generally proves to be too time-consuming and expensive. Instead, the questionnaire is administered to a sample of consumers. The way in which this sample is drawn is of critical importance because we are not after all interested only in the opinions of the specific group of persons included within the sample. Since the survey findings must be generalized from the sample to the population, the ultimate utility of a survey rests heavily upon the adequacy of its underlying sampling procedures.

The importance of adequate sampling in consumer research is not, of course, restricted to identifying persons to whom to administer questionnaires. It is critical to all of the methods of consumer research discussed subsequently in this chapter.

Furthermore, sampling considerations are not unique to *consumer* research. They are important in any kind of research wherein the investigator wishes to generalize from the data at hand to a more general situation; for example, from a sample of job applicants to job applicants in general, from a sample of observed job performances to employee job proficiency, or from a sample of achievement test questions to the respondent's knowledge about the general area in which he is being tested.

The prerequisites for confident generalization from sample to population behavior are (1) sufficient sample size and (2) representativeness of the sample. These two factors, size and representativeness, are independent of each other. It is perfectly possible to have a large but unrepresentative sample. It is also possible to draw a representative sample that is, however, too small to permit accurate generalizations to the universe.

There is no simple answer to the question, "How big must the sample be before it is sufficiently large?" Both statistical and economic considerations are involved in the determination of optimal sample size. Although generalizations based upon large representative samples are less subject to statistical error than those based upon small representative samples, the relationship between sample size and statistical error is not an arithmetic one. Improvements in accuracy obtained by increasing the size of the sample reach a point of diminishing returns. Thus, the increased accuracy gained by surveying a larger sample must be weighed against the additional expense entailed by virtue of the increase. Rather accurate nationwide political polls are conducted with 7,500 respondents or less!

The procedures for insuring sample representativeness generally involve a combination of stratification and random procedures. The population is first stratified, or divided into subgroups, on the basis of characteristics (like economic level, religion, and so on) that are presumed to bear upon the attitudes or opinions under investigation. These characteristics define the parameters of the sample. The persons actually included in the sample are randomly drawn from rosters of some kind to comprise a sample delimited by these parameters.

Administering the Questionnaire. Once the questionnaire has been structured in its final form, it may be administered to a sample of consumers in one of three ways: by mail, telephone interview, or personal interview.

The primary advantages of *mail surveys* are simplicity and economy of administration. Using a mailed questionnaire, it is possible economically to survey the opinions of persons in widely separated geographical locations. In addition, the mail survey eliminates one of the potential sources of bias inherent in the other two methods, that is, the interviewer himself.

In spite of these advantages, most mail surveys are inadequate because of the large proportion of persons in the original mailing who fail to return completed questionnaires. Serious errors can be introduced into the study when generalizations are made from the opinions of the persons who *did* reply to the opinions of those who *did not* reply, and thence to the larger population from which the original sample was drawn. There is evidence that respondents to mail questionnaires are higher both in interest in the topic under consideration and in educational level than are nonrespondents (Franzen & Lazarsfeld, 1945).

In addition to these differences between persons who return and fail to return a mail survey, the number of omitted items on those questionnaires that *are* returned is found to increase with the complexity of the questionnaire and to vary with the type of question and the respondent's age, sex, and occupation (Ferber, 1966). Furthermore, there is some evidence for the conclusion that persons who willingly cooperate with a survey tend to have less traditional or conventional value orientations than do noncooperative persons (Burchinal, 1960).

Thus, it is unsafe to generalize from mail surveys unless the proportion of returns is very high. There are many ways in which to encourage mail questionnaire returns including monetary inducements, simplification of format, preliminary contacts, and skillful follow-ups with persons in the sample (Perloff, 1968). By combining several of these procedures, one investigator reported a rate of completion across 14 surveys (almost 3,000 respondents) of about 74 percent (Francel, 1966). This is an unusually high rate of return, and still one wonders about the characteristics of the 26 percent who were nonrespondents and the possible sampling biases thus incurred.

Surveys conducted by *telephone* rarely need be contaminated by nonrespondents. Perseverance in placing telephone calls to persons in the original sample will usually be rewarded by establishing contacts with almost everyone selected for the survey. Other attractive features of telephone surveys in comparison with direct interviewing include the elimination of travel and the reduction of interview costs (Sudman, 1966).

However, there is a rather obvious source of bias in telephone surveys. The sample thus contacted does not include an adequate representation of segments of the population which for economic or other reasons either do not have telephones or have unlisted telephones. Furthermore, telephone interviewing is unsuitable for lengthy or complex interviews, or for survey problems (like evaluation of advertising copy) requiring subjects to make judgments about materials actually presented to them.

Because of the sampling deficiencies already noted as inherent in mail and telephone surveys, the well-conducted *personal interview* survey tends to produce the most valid findings under most circumstances. However, it must be remembered that the mere fact that personal interviews have been conducted for survey purposes assures neither representativeness of the sample interviewed nor freedom of the replies from bias. For such a survey to succeed, the interviewers must be carefully trained in the techniques of interviewing and in the requirements of representative sampling.

Depth Procedures

The primary value of survey procedures is the accumulation of "head counting" data and expressions of superficial attitudes and feelings. Survey findings tell us *who* bought a product or intends to buy a product. Such data help clarify the present and anticipated market. Depth procedures, on the other hand, are oriented more toward the *why* of consumer behavior. Hence, the application of depth procedures to consumer studies is sometimes referred to as motivation research.

Motivation research seeks to probe beneath the surface of consumer attitudes and to reveal the underlying values, images, and unconscious or hidden feelings influencing consumer behavior. In essence, the approach of the motivation researcher has much in common with that of the clinical psychologist. His tools frequently are similar to those used for clinical diagnosis; they include depth interviews, projective techniques of various kinds, and personality inventories. The fundamental difference between the application of these tools in clinical and consumer psychology is in the intent or objective of the study. The clinical psychologist is patient oriented; his sole concern is with the patient's welfare. The motivation researcher may be similarly consumer oriented, but the producer or advertising agency paying for the research has just one fundamental objective: that is, selling more goods to more people. The consumer psychologist is also consumer oriented and seeks to provide a communication link between the makers and users of goods (Twedt, 1965). However, the producer or advertising agency may in its effort to sell more goods to more people emphasize the "hidden persuader" components of motivation research.

The difference between results obtained from survey and depth procedures is illustrated by a report of the reasons for reading *Time* magazine (Dichter, 1947). Questionnaire responses indicated that *Time* was read for reasons like "It condenses the news for me" or "It is written in brilliant style." When the matter was investigated in greater depth, however, *Time* was found to provide its readers with certain "ego benefits." It conveyed to its readers the feeling that they were busy executives who needed to be well informed. As one reader said in the course of depth study, "When I read *Time* I like myself."

There is obvious merit to considering motivation when seeking to explain behavior. Furthermore, there is ample evidence for the fact that much human motivation is unconscious. The utilization of depth procedures for discovering such hidden determinants of consumer behavior, and the subsequent application of these findings to advertising and selling does, however, raise two important questions. One of these concerns the validity of the findings uncovered by the motivation researcher; the other concerns the ethics of motivation research.

Validity. Since the procedures employed in motivation research are somewhat similar to those used for clinical purposes, they are open to the same criticisms relative to validity. An essential difference between the application of depth procedures in consumer and clinical studies, however, is that the former usually involves a relatively brief time span (for example, a two-hour depth interview or the administration of a single projective instrument) while clinical diagnoses are based upon long-term studies and administration of batteries of instruments.

The effect of misusing instruments that are less than maximally valid to begin with may on occasion lead to distorted or misleading findings. This point is effectively made in an article intriguingly subtitled *Is the Prune a Witch?* The author (Graham, 1953) refers in it to a study, made by Dichter, for the California Prune Advisory Board. This study reported that prunes are symbols of old age, a scapegoat food, and that the prune is a witch. In order to sell more prunes, Dichter advised advertisers to make the pitch that prunes are the black diamonds of the fruit family. Furthermore, he suggested that women be reassured that it is perfectly acceptable to serve prunes, and that they ought not be ashamed because prunes have a cathartic effect. We must agree that there is much about unconscious motivation that is as yet unknown. However, it would seem that characterizing the prune as a witch is carrying things just a bit too far. We cannot dispute the advertiser's right to combat this witch, if he so chooses; he has paid for it! He should, however, exercise a certain amount of judgment in differentiating between witches or windmills and proper targets for combat.

Ethics. It sometimes is argued that motivation research invades the privacy of our thoughts and leads to insidious marketing and advertising practices against which the consumer has no real defense. On the other side of the coin, the suggestion has been made that motivation research applied to consumer behavior may be merely another manifestation of the "genius of our economy." Industrial survival depends upon giving the people what they want, and motivation research may sometimes be necessary to enable industry to discover these wants.

The ethical controversy over motivation research inevitably involves a certain amount of moral judgment. Investigators in this area point out that their subjects are not coerced into cooperating with them, that consumers are not compelled to make a purchase or succumb to an advertising appeal, and that competitive manufacturers are using the methodology of motivation research anyway. The first of these arguments makes sense, but the second begs the question because it is precisely the matter of susceptibility to advertising appeals to unconscious needs that is in question. Ethical justification for motivation research on the ground that competitors are using it is, of course, specious.

Assuming the validity of the information uncovered by depth studies of consumer motivation, what is the investigator's responsibilities both to the consumer and to the manufacturer or advertiser? Consumer psychologists are ethically bound to use their knowledge of human behavior in a socially responsible manner. This means in effect that the proper application of depth studies should benefit both consumer and manufacturer by helping to assure that (*a*) consumers have available the products and services they need, and (*b*) manufacturers are distributing products that are marketable.

Behavioral Studies

We might anticipate a high degree of relationship between what consumers *say* they will do and what they *actually* do. However, there is conflicting evidence regarding this relationship; people do not always do what they say they will do, and do not always feel the way they say they feel. Some of this discrepancy is undoubtedly deliberate; much of it is not. In either case, the surest way to gage consumer behavior is to make controlled observations of the behavior itself. Three kinds of criteria have been employed in behavioral studies: records of actual purchases; expressed preferences for, and identification of, competing brands; psychophysiological indicators.

Field studies of consumer purchases would seem to provide an acid test of the acceptability of a product. However, such studies rarely are productive from a research standpoint. Too many uncontrolled factors may influence the behavior of potential purchasers as they go into a store or market. The sales record may reflect the combined influence of such diverse and relatively inseparable factors as amount and type of advertising, pressures exerted by salesmen and clerks, the relative amount of display space allotted to the product, bonuses or premium stamps offered for the purchase of particular products, and the relative size and attractiveness of the package in which the product is presented.

Psychophysiological measures taken for the consumer or potential consumer are sometimes advocated as means to circumventing some of the difficulties inherent in studying purchasing behavior. It has long been known that emotional arousal evokes such largely involuntary effects of the autonomic nervous system and circulatory system as changes in blood pressure, blood volume, heart rate, and galvanic skin response. In fact, the "lie detector" is simply a device for making simultaneous recordings of several of these psychophysiological indices.

Attempts to use these measures as criteria of emotional arousal in consumer research on advertising and packaging have generally been unsuccessful. There are two major reasons for this: First, such indicators are also sensitive to bodily conditions other than emotional arousal. Second, these indicators fail to reveal anything about the quality of the arousal; that is, whether the emotion is pleasant or unpleasant, favorable or unfavorable.

Another psychophysiological measure, pupil dilation, has shown some promise as an indicator of the interest value of visual stimuli. Whereas small increases in dilation have been noted for interesting content, pupillary contraction is associated with content that lacks the power to interest or arouse the viewer (Hess & Polt, 1960). The superiority of this measure over verbalized opinions for assessing the emotional appeal of advertisements, packages, and products is self-evident provided it can be reliably made and interpreted, is beyond the deliberate control of the respondents, and predicts relevant consumer behavior. Although studies to date offer tentative support for the reliability of the technique (Krugman, 1964) considerably more research is needed on all three of these issues.

FACTORS INFLUENCING CONSUMER CHOICE

As consumers we characteristically exercise two types of choices in spending the money available to us. The first entails a decision about whether or not to buy at a particular time. Assuming this decision is positive, the second choice entails a selection from among competing products or services. Were we to know only a person's income, we would be little aided in predicting either of these choices. Income considered alone determines the ability to buy. Discretionary *demand,* on the other hand, has been demonstrated to be a function both of the ability to buy and the disposition to spend (Katona, Mueller, Schmiedeskamp, & Sonquist, 1967). The latter reflects attitudinal factors not explicable on rational grounds alone, and is the focus of our discussion in this section. We will consider the influence of three factors in the consumer's choice among available products or services: price, consumer personality, and brand preferences and loyalties.

Price

Price is a logical point of entry for this discussion because of the rational appeal of the simplistic (and erroneous) assumption that consumers' decisions reflect their considered evaluation of cost/ benefit ratios. According to this assumption, potential consumers weigh prices against product quality, selecting the particular one offering maximum quality for the money.

One fallacy in this assumption is that it tends to ignore the interaction between price and perceived quality. You are well aware of the tendency to use price as a cue to quality; we tend to regard higher priced products as qualitatively superior to lower priced ones.

In part this association between price and perceived quality rests upon previous experience (Cox & Bauer, 1967). We have all at some time or other purchased cut-rate or discount products which were qualitatively inferior to their higher priced counterparts. Generalizing from such experiences in situations where the consumer is in doubt about the quality of alternatives, he seeks to minimize his risk of obtaining an inferior product by buying insurance, that is, purchasing the higher priced one.

A second basis for the price-perceived quality association is related to equity theory (introduced in Chapter 14 in the context of reward distribution). You will recall that this theory predicts that persons will strive for balance or equity in the ratio of inputs (or effort expended) and outcomes (or benefits derived). Taking price as an index of effort expended to obtain a product, it follows from equity theory that perceived quality (the outcome) will be enhanced for higher priced products and diminished for lower priced products (Cardoza, 1965).

Finally, we cannot discount as a third factor the moderating influence of self-image on the relationship between price and perceived quality. Feelings of self-worth are tied, for many people, to their ability to purchase and display higher rather than lower priced products.

Personality

Granted that the perceived attractiveness or quality of a product is partly evaluated on the basis of its price, we are still left with two unanswered questions: (1) Given the imperfect nature of this correlation, how can we account for the fact that many consumers who can afford a higher priced product (say, a Cadillac) select a lower priced one (perhaps, a Ford)? (2) How can we explain consumer choices among brands of products, like cigarettes or beer, where price is held relatively constant? Studies of the relationships between consumer personality and (*a*) product use or choice and (*b*) perceived product attributes attempt to come to grips with such questions.

Product Use or Choice. Global analyses of the relationship between selected personality characteristics and actual product usage tend to yield only low to moderate correlations. It has been demonstrated, for example, that mouthwash users scored lower on a measure of "responsibility" than those who never or rarely use mouthwash (Tucker & Painter, 1961). Likewise, heavy smokers were found to score higher on the needs—as measured by the Edwards Personal Preference Schedule—for aggression, achievement, and sex and lower on the needs for deference and order than did nonsmokers (Koponen, 1960). Findings of this type permit the inference that certain products may be perceived by the consumer as compatible with his needs or image of himself.

Such an inference undergirds advertising designed to invest products and companies with particular personalities and to formulate an image of the kind of persons for whom the product is appropriate. It is to this matter of the relationship between perceived product attributes and self-image that we will next turn our attention.

Perceived Product Attributes. The image of the appropriate purchaser of a particular product is conveyed by the dominant verbal and pictorial aspects of its underlying advertising appeal. Pepsi-Cola has never tried to capture the old age retirement market! It has a well-established, youthful, lighthearted, gay, sociable image. Similarly, Chrysler Corporation automobiles were perceived for many years as sound, conservative investments in transportation. Prior to the radical change in styling and advertising for the 1957 model, the image of the Plymouth buyer was expressed by such adjectives as "quiet," "careful," "slow," "silent," "moral," "fat," "gentle," and "calm" (Wells, Andriuli, Goi, & Seader, 1957). In 1957, styling changes were accompanied by advertisements peppered with references to *The Forward Look, Three Years Ahead, Flight Sweep Styling,* and the *Fabulous Fury* 301 V-8 *Engine.* The effectiveness of this campaign is evident from the findings in a follow-up study that the Plymouth buyer was subsequently characterized by adjectives like "high-class," "important," "rich," "different," and "particular" (Wells, Goi, & Seader, 1958). This more recent image has persisted to the present.

The impact of the message embodied in any advertisement cannot be considered as independent of the total corporate and/or product image effort. People respond to an advertisement for a particular brand of cigarettes, for example, in terms of their assessment of the tobacco industry and their attitudes toward cigarettes as a product class. In this regard, it is worth noting that even an unknown brand may have an image. This image is derived from the image of the general product class, since the unknown brand is assumed to have the same range of uses and satisfactions common to known brands.

That product images can be established or modified by advertising seems well established. The rationale for attempting to do so is that prospective consumers will select from the available products the one most compatible either with their actual or idealized self-concept. Some support for this contention is provided by depth studies of consumer motivation as illustrated by an ingenious study of attitudes toward instant coffee (Haire, 1950). Instant coffee was available in the stores for a long time before it was accepted by housewives. Women generally indicated on a questionnaire that they did not like its flavor. The investigator decided to use a projective device in order to discover whether some more basic factor might be responsible for unfavorable attitudes toward instant coffee. He devised two shopping lists, identical in all respects except for the fifth item:

List A	*List B*
1½ lb. hamburger	1½ lb. hamburger
2 loaves Wonder bread	2 loaves Wonder bread
Bunch of carrots	Bunch of carrots
1 can Rumford's baking powder	1 can Rumford's baking powder
Nescafe instant coffee	Maxwell House coffee, drip grind
2 cans Del Monte peaches	2 cans Del Monte peaches
5 lb. potatoes	5 lb. potatoes

Samples of housewives were asked to characterize the women who would go to the store with one or the other of these shopping lists. Almost half of the respondents to the list containing *Nescafe* characterized the shopper as lazy and a poor planner, 12 percent indicated that she was a spendthrift, and 16 percent said she was a poor wife. The responses to the *Maxwell House* list were quite different: only 16 percent mentioned laziness or bad planning and none characterized the shopper as a spendthrift or poor wife.

Persuasibility. There are obvious reasons for anticipating a relationship between the consumer's sense of self-confidence and his susceptibility to sales or advertising appeals. Such a relationship has indeed been demonstrated, but with the somewhat surprising and consistent finding that the most easily persuaded consumers tend to score in the mid-range on a scale of self-confidence (Barach, 1967). That highly confident persons should resist attempts to persuade them is self-evident. Persons low in self-confidence may behave with similar resistance as a defensive maneuver.

Brand Preferences and Loyalty

Considerable research on the general subject of brand preference and loyalty supports the contention that consumers establish firm preferences which are reflected in loyalty to particular brands. However, such loyalty is often based on factors other than an ability to distinguish between brands on any objective basis!

A series of studies with cola drinks, for example, demonstrated that (1) respondents could not distinguish between the best-known brands of these beverages solely on the basis of taste; and (2) cola beverages, regardless of brand, were always identified as either Coca-Cola, Pepsi-Cola, or Royal Crown Cola (Pronko & Bowles, 1948 (a), 1948 (b), 1949). Similarly negative findings have been reported for perfumes, cigarettes, and other products. In contrast, studies with some products, like beer (Fleishman, 1951), have indicated that taste and smell panels can indeed express consistent preferences for particular brands.

When consistent preferences are expressed for certain brands by a consumer jury, one may have reason to wonder about the bases upon which such discriminations are made. A certain amount of accumulated evidence seems to indicate that these discriminations are sometimes based upon rather irrelevant considerations. We can assume, for example, that given a choice, consumers would select fresh bread over stale bread. But when loaves of equally fresh bread were wrapped differently for experimental purposes, panels of judges claimed to perceive differences in freshness. Cellophane-wrapped bread felt fresher than bread encased in a wax wrapper (Brown, 1958).

In spite of the questionable ability of most consumers effectively to distinguish between brands of many products solely on the basis of taste, there is little doubt that they *buy* by brand—assuming that the preferred brand is available and price factors are held relatively constant. Furthermore, brand loyalty appears not to be transitory; it has been demonstrated to persist over a period as long as 12 years (Guest, 1955). It has been suggested that one factor underlying the development and persistence of loyalties is the consumers attempt to minimize his perceived risk (Cunningham, 1967). Those consumers who perceive considerable risk in a particular product (for example, headache remedies) are more likely to express distinct brand preferences than those who do not perceive such risk; the known and trusted brand name affords some feeling of security.

SUMMARY

All parties to the manufacture, distribution, and sale of products have a vital interest in understanding, predicting, and controlling consumer behavior. One of the unique contributions of the psychologist in this general area in his application of rigorous scientific methods of inquiry. The scope of consumer research utilizing psychological methodology is exceedingly broad. It may include studies of the size and constituency of markets, the effectiveness of advertising campaigns and distribution facilities, consumer reactions to the product and the company that manufactures it, and the needs and motives underlying consumer behavior. Data for such studies are obtained by (1) surveying consumer opinions, (2) applying depth procedures, and (3) observing consumer behavior.

One of the assumptions underlying *survey* procedures is that people can verbalize many of their attitudes and opinions on a questionnaire. In the interest of economy and ease of administration, the survey is generally conducted with a sample of respondents rather than with the entire population or universe. However, since the survey findings must ultimately be generalized to the larger population, the method whereby the sample is drawn is of considerable importance. The sample must be large enough to insure a high level of statistical accuracy and sufficiently representative of the strata or subgroups within the population to permit for such generalizations.

Depth procedures, including probing interviews and projective techniques, are sometimes used to study the underlying values, images, and unconscious feelings affecting consumer behavior. The conduct of such studies and the subsequent application of the findings from motivation research raises both technical and ethical issues. The misuse of clinical instruments by some motivation researchers may produce findings of dubious validity. Even when validity of studies of the drives underlying consumer behavior can be assumed, the ethics of the approach are open to question. The psychologist participating in such studies must, of course, heed his paramount responsibility to the welfare of society rather than to particular vested interest groups.

Behavioral studies often involve analysis of actual sales records. Although buying behavior may be regarded as the ultimate criterion in consumer research, it must be recognized that sales records sometimes are inaccurately kept and reflect the combined influence of a variety of uncontrolled factors. In order to circumvent these difficulties, many behavioral studies forego analysis of sales records in favor of controlled investigations of such criteria as accuracy of brand identification and expressed brand preferences. Recently, attention has been given also to pupil dilation as a potentially useful psychophysiological indicator of the interest value of visual stimuli.

Three general factors influencing consumer choice were considered in this chapter: product price, consumer personality, and brand loyalty. It is clear that consumer decisions reflect considerations other than a purely rational cost/benefit analysis. Price itself is used as a cue to quality, thereby contaminating the consumer's attempt to evaluate whether the product is worth its cost. The consumer's personality is intimately related to his choice from among available products of the one most compatible either with his actual or idealized self-image. And choices which take the form of brand preferences tend to persist over time, perhaps in an attempt by the consumer to minimize his perceived risk.

19. Advertising and Selling

In terms of the end result sought, advertising and selling have an identical objective. Both aim to persuade potential consumers to purchase products or avail themselves of services. The fundamental difference between advertising and selling inheres in the personal component of the latter. The salesman does not make a blanket appeal to a mass audience. Instead, he seeks to discover the individual buyer's needs and emphasizes product features appropriate to those needs in order to close the sale.

Thus, advertising is a form of preselling. Advertisements make a one-sided pitch in behalf of a particular product, company, or industry. They are disseminated for the express purpose of persuading persons to behave in accord with the desires of a vested interest group. Viewed this way, the functions and techniques of advertising are in many respects similar to those of propaganda.

In this chapter, it is not our purpose to add further to the controversy over the broad social implications of advertising and selling. Instead, we will be concerned with the psychological principles underlying these activities. As we shall see, these principles are more clearly established for advertising than they are for selling.

ADVERTISING

Most potential consumers have a limited amount of money which they spend for commodities they value highly. According to this model of consumer behavior, it should be possible to predict actual purchases from knowledge of (1) the prices of various commodities and (2) the relative preference values attached to those commodities.

To the extent that consumers actually do seek to balance available money against commodity preferences, there are two ways in which sales may be increased: either the cost can be reduced or the preference value attached to a product may be heightened. Advertising seeks to accomplish the latter objective; that is, to enhance the preference value attached to a particular brand of product or to a general class of products.

One feature of our economy is the availability of many different *brands* of the same product all priced competitively. There is little difference indeed between the price of various brands of cigarettes, detergents, beer, or gasoline. Hence, the consumer's decision about particular brand purchases probably reflects greater discrepancies in perceived preference values than in actual cost.

Much advertising is specifically devoted to manipulating subjective preferences for one brand over competitive brands. The impression is conveyed that standardized pricing among competitors does not assure standardization of the satisfactions derived from purchasing competing products. In essence, the consumer is encouraged to prefer the advertised brand to all others within the same product classification.

This may be accomplished in a variety of ways. The advertiser may appeal to rational considerations of product superiority like safety or durability. He may, on the other hand, attempt to reinforce preferences by manipulating feeling tone. The advertisement may suggest that purchase and/or use of the particular brand will make the consumer feel good, like himself better, or be better liked by others. Thus, advertising slogans proclaim *Satisfy Yourself, Feel Really Clean,* and *Be Sociable.*

The consumer's choice between competing brands is often preceded by a choice between *products.* He must decide, for example, to buy a car rather than a boat before he is ready to select from among the automobiles offered within a price bracket by various manufacturers.

Here again, advertising seeks to strengthen preference values in relation to cost. The general approach underlying product advertising is that "you will derive the greatest satisfaction from using your money to buy what we have to sell." On occasion, product advertising (and to a certain extent, brand advertising) is directed toward strengthening relatively weak drives and awakening relatively passive ones. This is particularly true when the market is highly saturated. In order to maintain a high volume of automotive sales, the second car must be regarded as a necessity instead of a luxury.

Although it may not be correct to characterize us as a nation of persons primarily concerned with body odor, our flourishing deodorant industry is some kind of tribute to highly effective advertising. As Americans, we seem to be peculiarly preoccupied with product ownership as symbolic of economic, social, and sexual status. This kind of personalization of the products we own is a reflection of the interactive and mutually enhancing effects of our expanding economy, increased leisure time, and vulnerability to advertising appeals. The latter is not simply a fortuitous circumstance. The analysis and improvement of advertising is the subject of voluminous research. In general, such research revolves about four basic questions (Twedt, 1965) :

1. What shall be said? (message research)
2. How shall it be said? (copy research)
3. Where and when shall it be said? (media research)
4. How effectively was it said? (evaluative research)

Each of these questions is considered separately in the following sections.

The Message

Every advertisement attempts to tell us something. This *message* may be relatively obvious, as in the case of a simple declaration of product superiority. However, it may be quite subtle, suggesting that our virility, status, or likability will be enhanced by using the product in question.

Regardless of the nature of the message, it must ultimately get us to do something or experience particular feelings. To accomplish this, the advertiser typically either promises to satisfy some already existing need or strengthens weak needs to the point where the promise of their satisfaction assumes real importance to the consumer. This point is made rather succinctly by Dichter (1949) as follows:

> No item of merchandise is ever sold unless a psychological need exists which it satisfies. In order words, the actual merchandise is secondary. Advertising's goal has to be the mobilization and manipulation of human needs as they exist in the customer.

For a number of years advertisers sought some kind of magic key to successful appeals by consulting presumably exhaustive compilations of motives, wants, and needs. This tack proved to be relatively fruitless. As discussed in Chapter 15, human motivation is exceedingly complex and therefore defies neat classification and categorization. Even a fundamentally biological drive like hunger, for example, becomes rapidly overlaid with learned preferences and feelings. The food advertiser cannot make a successful appeal to the "need for food." He must appeal, instead, to needs for particular kinds of foods, appetizing in appearance, attractively served, and appropriate to particular circumstances which we have learned to associate with them. Thus, margarine manufacturers learned that they could not compete effectively with butter by emphasizing only the economy and nutritive value of their product. People are reluctant to accept something they can justify solely on the grounds that it is an effective substitute.

Corporate Images.   In addition to developing product images (as discussed in Chapter 18) a considerable amount of advertising is devoted to establishing a favorable attitude toward a company and investing the company with a personality. This advertising approach is particularly useful when the company's products are sold to producers rather than individual consumers (for example, steel, rubber, oil) or when the advertiser sells services like insurance, communications, or travel.

Advertising to develop a corporate image aims to convey to the public that although the company exists for monetary reasons, its concerns extend considerably beyond the balance sheet and the ledger. The company is personalized and humanized. It is transformed by institutional advertising from a huge, impersonal organization controlling the lives of its employees and the tastes of the public to an organization in which employees are partners in an enterprise providing consumers with beneficial goods and services.

Some of the dominant themes of such advertising have been identified as (Pearlin & Rosenberg, 1952) :

1. Elaboration of latent consequences: The company's activities benefit you or some group in which you have a direct and vital interest.
2. Humanization: The company is a warm, friendly, hard-working "individual."
3. Denial and Conversion: Odious charges about big business are

either denied or converted to have socially acceptable implications.

4. Sympathy or Ego-Involvement: Since you have a vital stake in the company, it is in your interest to understand and be sympathetic to the company's problems and to appreciate its solutions.

Public Service. Quite often, institutional advertising takes a less direct approach to developing favorable attitudes. Rather than stressing the company's contribution to your welfare, public service advertising seeks to clarify the company's stake in our society and its role as a "good citizen." The distinction between direct attempts to create a corporate image and the public service approach is a rather fine one. In the latter, the advertisement seeks to establish a rapprochement between the broader interests and welfare of society on the one hand, and the company on the other. It attempts to capitalize upon what has been termed "significant involvement" serving the private interests of the advertiser, the personal interest of the consumer, and the public interest of the nation (Patterson, 1961).

Advertising Copy

The purpose of research on advertising copy is to discover effective means for transmitting messages as a guide to formulating advertisements and evaluating their impact. With respect to the structure of advertising copy, it is important to note that psychologists are not advertising men either by training or, for the most part, by inclination. Developing a good advertisement requires the skills of a number of specialists, including copywriters, artists, layout specialists, and others. The unique contributions of psychologists stem from their fundamental concern with human behavior and familiarity with techniques for investigating changes in behavior.

Copy Format. Advertisements are structured in a manner calculated to attract and maintain attention, spotlight the salient aspects of the message, and encourage retention of the message as well as subsequent action in accord with it. We will briefly review some evidence concerning the effects of several format variables upon the realization of these objectives.

1. Color. The legibility of colored lettering is less dependent upon the specific colors used than upon the brightness differential between the colored letter and the background. In general, the most satisfactory background for colored lettering is grey, and dark colors on a light background are most legible in daylight (Jones & Sumner, 1948).

The value of color in advertising for attracting and maintaining interest is somewhat obscured by such other considerations as the skill with which the color is used, its appropriateness to the product being advertised, and the fundamental purpose of the advertisement. In the latter regard, it has been suggested (Warner & Franzen, 1947) that color is maximally valuable for advertising an established brand and not much superior to black-and-white advertising for promoting a new brand. Furthermore, contrary to belief, it does not necessarily follow that advertisers whose advertisements are in color are perceived as more prestigious than advertisers whose advertisements are in black and white (Guest, 1966).

2. *Movement.*   The fact that a moving object attracts more attention than a stationary one is well known. Youngsters playing hide-and-seek remain as motionless as possible in their hiding place in order to avoid detection. The student who wants desperately to be recognized by his instructor does not merely raise his arm; he often waves his hand rather frantically.

The primary applications of the principle of movement in advertising occur in television and in the outdoor spectacular signs showing bread being sliced, bottles pouring liquid, and water cascading over a dam. In most TV advertising, the movement is real. The viewer watches a skin diver plunging under water to shave, or observes the needle pointer swing revealing the deodorizing power of a mouthwash. The outdoor spectacular signs make use of apparent movement created by lights successively illuminated in sequence with a brief time interval between them. It makes no difference to the observer whether the movement is real or apparent. Movement attracts attention.

3. *Repetition.*   Much advertising is repetitive in nature. The slogan, jingle, or catchy tune repeated over and over again capitalizes upon certain well-established psychological principles. Frequency of presentation both attracts attention and leads to overlearning. Thus, if you let your thoughts wander during a TV commercial, an insistent chant like "Double the flavor, double the fun, with Doublemint, Doublemint, Doublemint gum" is bound to part your intellectual curtain and bring you back to the realities of the world of commercialism. Repetition can, of course, be overdone. Its

value is likely to be greatest when the audience's initial level of interest in the subject material is low (Greenberg & Garfinkle, 1962).

4. Novelty. Things that appear to be new and different contrast markedly with the old and familiar and hence stand out in bold relief. The extent to which product novelty is stressed in magazine advertising is evident from the frequent use of words and phrases like "New!" "No more (messy hands, and so on)," "Revolutionary," "Now! At Last!" "Never before!"

In addition to showing that they have a product that is new or different, many advertisers attempt to advertise in novel ways. There is after all something rather compelling about seeing a miniature butler dispensing paper napkins or omnipotent Mr. Clean springing to life.

Copy Research. The effectiveness of alternative forms of advertising copy often is evaluated before the advertisement is widely disseminated. This can be accomplished either by pretesting the alternative forms with samples of subjects or by actually running limited editions of the alternative advertisements prior to selecting the final form for widespread dissemination.

The assessment of copy may be conducted by interview and/or questionnaire and by behavioral test. It is directed toward determining the relative effectiveness of the copy for (*a*) attracting and maintaining attention and (*b*) evoking the desired feelings and initiating the intended action.

Recall and recognition tests of various kinds are particularly appropriate for assessing attentiveness to advertisements in the printed media. Subscribers to a particular magazine may be asked to recall as many advertisements as they can from a recent issue or to select from a scrapbook (that is, recognize) those advertisements that have actually appeared in the magazine. An interesting finding with reference to the scrapbook technique is that a correction must be made for persons claiming to "recognize" advertisements that have not yet appeared in print! The proportion of such false identifications was found in one study to be as high as 15–20 percent (Lucas & Murphy, 1939).

Even if we were somehow to correct for such false identifications, thereby obtaining a reasonably accurate recall or recognition measure, this measure may have little bearing upon the ultimate criterion of copy effectiveness, that is, subsequent purchasing behavior (Haskins, 1964). It clearly is possible to be aware of an advertisement without being motivated to buy the advertised product.

Behavioral criteria sometimes used to test copy effectiveness include coupon returns and contest entries. Two or more versions of the same basic advertisement are run in alternate copies of a particular publication (*split-run*). Although the contents of these versions are different, all forms of the advertisement contain a coupon to be sent to the company or taken to the dealer, or a suggestion that the reader telephone or write regarding the product. The relative effectiveness of the several versions of the advertisement is determined by comparing the rate of consumer replies evoked by each one.

The Medium

Where advertising is placed (the medium or vehicle) influences the size of the audience and its composition. In the interest of economy, advertisers seek to place their messages before the right prospects, in terms of age, sex, educational level, and so on, and in the right context.

There is a growing body of evidence that the context is particularly important in the case of television advertising. For example, changes in mood during a TV showing of the film "The Nuremburg Trial" were found to be associated with changes in attitude toward products (Axelrod, 1963). In another study (Crane, 1964), it was demonstrated that women may be more susceptible than men to the influence of program context upon attitudes toward commercials. With further research in this direction, we can anticipate the possibility of selecting programs and places within programs which are most suitable for advertising particular products.

Audience Research.   Another kind of media research is directed toward estimating the size and characteristics of the audience exposed to the advertiser's message. This problem can be attacked somewhat more easily for the printed media than for the broadcast media because the number of issues of a particular magazine or newspaper sold can be determined with a fair degree of accuracy.

However, even in the case of printed media, there are certain difficulties in estimating the size of the audience reached by an advertisement. The fact that a particular magazine is purchased does not mean that it is read; conversely, a substantial number of persons read magazines they do not actually purchase. Estimates of audience exposure to printed media are further complicated by the fact that there is a certain amount of duplication between the readership of various magazines carrying the same advertisement. It is likely that simple consideration of the circulation of a particular publication without regard for overlapping publications carrying the same advertisement leads to an overestimate of the size of the advertiser's audience.

The audience reached by the broadcast media (radio and TV) is even more difficult to estimate. The program rating services gather their information in a variety of ways, each with unique shortcomings. The A. C. Nielson Company, for example, compiles its basic data for program ratings from mechanical recorders attached to radio and TV receivers. This device maintains a continuous record of set usage throughout the day for a sample of homes. However, the fact that a receiver is tuned to a particular program is itself no assurance that anyone in the home is actually viewing or listening to the program and its accompanying commercials.

Hooper ratings for radio and Trendex ratings for TV are based upon the "coincidental telephone" survey. Telephone interviews are conducted with a sample of persons while the program under consideration is in progress. In addition to sample bias introduction by limiting the rating to results obtained from telephone-owning homes, this procedure cannot be used for early morning or late evening programs. One just doesn't place telephone calls at 6:00 A.M. or midnight to randomly selected persons inquiring whether they have their TV receiver on and, if so, which program they are watching.

Other rating services conduct coincidental personal (rather than telephone) interviews and use the diary method. In the latter procedure, a sample of respondents is requested to keep a log of all viewing or listening activities. The effect of keeping such a diary upon program selection, and the accuracy of the logs themselves, are both open questions.

Subliminal Advertising. Subliminal perception is a well-established psychological phenomenon. We sometimes respond to stimuli that are below the threshold of awareness. In the tradition of experimental psychology, the *limen,* or threshold of awareness, is defined as a stimulus intensity perceived exactly half the time.

Quite a furor developed about 10 years ago when an apparently successful attempt to capitalize upon subliminal perception for advertising purposes was reported by Vicary (1958). The procedure consisted of flashing the phrases "Eat Popcorn" and "Drink Coca-Cola" at 0.003 second on a movie screen during the showing of a film. According to the report, Coca-Cola sales increased 18 percent and popcorn sales increased 57 percent although the audience did not suspect they were participating in a deliberate attempt to influence their behavior. Thus, the application of subliminal perception in advertising has been aptly termed (Brooks, 1958) "the little ad that isn't there."

Vicary's procedure and findings were never reported in any professional publication. Hence, it is impossible to evaluate the validity of his results. The implications of this technique for presenting advertisements would if it worked be at once startling and frightening. It is repugnant enough to some people to be bombarded by advertisements they can see and hear. But to be victimized by advertising below the threshold of awareness raises such serious moral concerns that it has been banned from both TV and radio.

Both public and professional concern for subliminal advertising have diminished in recent years, largely because of evidence that (*a*) individual differences and variability in the limen make applications of subliminal advertising technically infeasible and (*b*) such advertising is of dubious value for generating needs or changing established behavior patterns.

Evaluating Advertising Effectiveness

It is clear from the foregoing discussion that considerable research using a variation of "attentiveness" as a criterion is often entailed in developing the message, structuring the copy, and selecting an appropriate medium. However, considering all aspects of the advertisement together, the ultimate test of its impact is its effect upon sales.

A difficulty specifically related to the use of sales records for evaluating advertising effectiveness is that the effects of advertising upon sales are delayed. Most sustained advertising does not show significant effects until some time after the campaign has started, and the effects may persist for some time after it has stopped (Meissner, 1961).

This phenomenon has a dual implication (Stewart, 1964). For

the researcher, it means that the sales impact of an advertisement or campaign cannot properly be gaged without attention to long-term sales trends suitably corrected for possible sources of contamination. For the advertiser, it suggests that substantial repetition of an advertisement, involving 15 or more presentations in the case of newspaper advertising, may be required to achieve efficient purchase results.

SELLING

We have attempted throughout this book to develop a feeling for psychology as a science. Psychologists' conclusions about human behavior are based upon careful investigation under controlled circumstances. Casual observation, armchair speculation, and hunches "off the top of the head" may occasionally serve as a starting point for subsequent investigation. They do not, however, constitute a reasonable basis for scientific conclusions without empirical verification. A psychology of anything lacking an experimental literature reflecting a history of careful investigation is not psychology at all; it is common sense. And the wisdom of common sense often is open to question.

A designation like "the psychology of selling" exemplifies a tendency to confuse commonsense analyses of human behavior with a rigorous scientific approach to inquiry. For the present, salesmanship must be regarded pretty much as an art to which psychologists have devoted relatively little attention. The effectiveness of various sales approaches has been demonstrated in the past by experience rather than controlled investigation. This is an area in which there is a serious need for scientific study.

Two Views of Salesmanship

One of the effects of even the sparse amount of attention thus far given by psychologists to the selling process has been to alter the view of the nature of the salesman-prospect interaction. The older, psychologically naive view emphasizes the buyer's passivity and the consequent value of "selling formulas" calculated to manipulate his behavior in the desired direction. The more recent and sophisticated view emphasizes the salesman's role in correctly identifying and satisfying the prospect's needs, desires, and preferences.

The Older View.   Here, the salesman and prospect are regarded as antagonists in a struggle. The salesman is seen as attempting, by virtually any means, to persuade a reluctant prospect to make a purchase. High-pressure tactics, deviousness, and deceitfulness are justified when necessary to force a sale. This view likens the prospect to an almost inanimate and unresponsive recipient of the sales pitch who remains relatively passive while something is *done to* him. Proceeding from the assumption of buyer passivity during the sales interaction, several writers have proposed "selling formulas" designed to lead any prospect through a sequence of steps terminating in his purchase of the product.

One such prescription for salesmanship, proposed before the turn of the century, is the A-I-D-A formula: Attention-Interest-Desire-Action. This formula assumes that all prospects think alike and that the nature of this stream of thought proceeds in orderly fashion through the four stages embodied in the formula. It disregards such important considerations as: the buyer's perceived need for the product (we desire many things we do not buy because we do not need them); his ability to make a purchase (including his authority to buy and the availability of sufficient funds); counterpressures upon him *not* to buy the product in spite of his desire and need for it (including his reactions to the salesperson); conflicting desires for several purchases all of which cannot be simultaneously gratified; and so on. It is naive to assume that the thinking process can be reduced to the uniformly applicable sequential stream hypothesized by the A-I-D-A formula.

Need Satisfaction.   Salesmanship viewed as a process of need-satisfaction focuses more upon the buying process than the selling process. This approach to salesmanship rejects selling formulas as stilted, oversimplified, and unduly concerned with the actions of the seller.

A need-satisfaction point of view is accepted by virtually all sound recent writers on salesmanship. As one author (Pederson & Wright, 1961) states, salesmanship is "the process whereby the seller ascertains and activates the needs or wants of the buyer and satisfies these needs or wants to the mutual, continuous advantage of both the buyer and the seller." Thus, the buyer's needs are regarded as central to the selling process; the salesman's behavior assumes importance only as a vehicle for promising and providing need satisfaction.

There are a number of practical implications of the need-satisfaction approach to salesmanship. Since every prospective buyer is a unique individual with unique needs and perceptions, every sales presentation must be somewhat different. A particular prospect may need assurance that he is getting maximum value for his money; another may need to derive feelings of heightened status by virtue of his dealings with the salesman; yet another may be particularly concerned about the reliability of the company with respect to customer service or its reputation for prompt delivery. The salesman's initial endeavor must be in the direction of discovering the prospect's needs and/or stimulating needs appropriate to whatever he is selling.

Both need discovery and need stimulation require a high degree of sensitivity. The salesman must be a careful listener and an astute observer of the prospect's behavior.

Once the particular buyer's needs are evident, the salesman is in a position to demonstrate and discuss his product or service as a need satisfier. He must be exceedingly flexible, realizing that whatever he is selling can be presented from numerous aspects, each satisfying to particular needs. The salesman attempts to stress those particular satisfactions appropriate to the buyer's needs.

Assuming that the product or service is properly presented, the prospect will want it. He has not been hoodwinked, high-pressured, or embarrassed into making the purchase; he has been convinced that he will benefit from it. It is not surprising, then, that the most effective salesmen tend themselves to be convinced of the value of whatever it is they are selling. A study of variables contributing to success of life insurance salesmen, for example, determined that the amount of life insurance owned by the agent (indicating belief in the value of his product) correlated more significantly with a composite criterion of selling effectiveness than several other factors, including product knowledge and length of service (Baier & Dugan, 1957).

Finally, the salesman's responsibility extends beyond closing the sale to assuring customer satisfaction with his purchase. This is particularly important when repeat sales are desired. Satisfied customers tend to make additional purchases of the product perceived as satisfying. Further, since such customers are favorably disposed to the salesman and the organization he represents, they are an excellent form of word-of-mouth advertising.

The importance of buyer satisfaction was illustrated in an analysis of recordings of the actual selling behavior of expert department store sales personnel. Personal selling of the department store variety is very often a rather routine affair. The customer sees what she likes on the rack, the clerk proffers it for her inspection, shows variations in color, style, and so on, upon request, and ultimately either wraps it and accepts the cash, or replaces it on the rack. Analysis of the recordings of expert salespersons, however, indicated that the most effective personal selling goes an important step beyond facilitating the customer's purchase. The ingredient added by these salespersons is that they help the customer obtain maximum personal satisfaction for the money she spends.

The Selling-Buying Process

We have already indicated that a need-satisfactions approach to salesmanship leads necessarily to a flexible view of selling. Each sales appeal must be individually tailored to the needs of the individual prospect. In this regard it is useful to make a few observations about the reasons for making a purchase and the nature of the sales presentation.

Why People Buy. Here again there is considerable conflict between a commonsense analysis and a psychological analysis of human behavior. It seems just plain good common sense that people buy food to prepare for hunger, new appliances to replace ones that are worn out or defective, and bigger houses to accommodate larger families. Further, assuming the decision has been made, for example, to buy a refrigerator, it is common sense to buy the make and model offering maximum value for the money. Such factors as initial cost, reputation of the manufacturer and retail outlet, and availability of servicing ought to be critical to such a purchase.

Common sense assumes a highly rational basis for buying behavior. However, the point was made in Chapter 18 that buyers often behave rather irrationally by external standards. The reasons given for making a purchase may not be the really operative reasons at all. Thus, although unverbalized as needs, the purchaser may seek to identify with persons whom he respects by buying products endorsed by them. He may seek social approval by purchasing in conformance with certain stereotypes of the well-groomed or masculine man; heightened status by buying expensive or exclusive items; or simply a bargain. Derived (learned) needs for social approval and status rarely are verbalized. Instead, the purchaser prefers to think he is a highly rational buyer basing his decisions upon a careful consideration of the available alternatives. Thus, the salesman must often provide the customer with such *rationalizations* (acceptable reasons) as economy, low upkeep, and once-in-a-lifetime value if he is to close the sale successfully.

The Sales Presentation. Much more research has been devoted to selecting and training salesmen than to the sales presentation itself. The relative lack of research activity in the latter area is attributable to a number of factors. Laboratory studies of the sales interview suffer rather seriously from a sense of artificiality. Field studies, on the other hand, are difficult to conduct because of the enormous range of variation in prospect needs and personalities necessitating a high degree of flexibility in sales presentations. Such flexibility probably increases the number of sales closed but precludes the kinds of control necessary to conduct satisfactory investigations.

Occasionally the sales presentation is atomized for the purpose of study. One investigator (Bauman, 1955), for example, found that department store sales were increased when clerks kept their voices up on the last syllable of the "Good Morning" greeting. Another (Fay & Middleton, 1942) found that superior and inferior sales-clerks could be differentiated on the basis of ratings of voice transcriptions. The recordings of voices of superior clerks were rated higher by a group of college students on "enthusiasm," "convincing-ness," and "sales ability."

Studies like these barely scratch the surface of the sales presentation. At the present time, effective salesmanship must be regarded as an art refined by experience rather than by experimentation, and heavily dependent upon general skills in human relations.

Selecting Salesmen

Three general approaches to selecting personnel, including sales-men, were described in earlier chapters: weighted application blanks, standardized interviews, and psychological tests of various kinds. Rather than review these selection procedures, we will direct our attention to some of the special problems indigenous to selecting salesmen.

Kinds of Salesmen. Salesmanship is not a homogeneous activity. The available classifications of sales occupations generally reflect either the nature of the goods and services sold or the type of employer the salesman represents. Although we need not be concerned with particular classificatory schemes, certain distinctions have important implications for selection.

Manufacturer's salesmen represent the manufacturer to wholesalers, retailers, and others who sell to the ultimate consumer. The manufacturer may be represented in a variety of ways: sales engineers generally assist with improving factory operations; merchandising salesmen engage in sales promotion encouraging greater efforts in selling the company's goods; and so on. *Retail salesmen* sell to customers who come into a store generally committed to the purchase of a product. The retail salesman's primary function is to help the customer make the purchase. The skills and requirements for retail salesmen vary considerably from one store to another. In some, he is essentially a purchase-wrapper and change-maker. In others, particularly where a significant amount of brand competition exists, he must engage in a high level of salesmanship.

These differences in function between salesmen servicing industry and those serving retail customers are reinforced by the self-perceptions of salesmen in these two classifications. Industrial salesmen see their job as placing a heavy emphasis upon ingenuity and inventiveness. Retail salesmen see as prime requirements for success in their job: planning, hard work, and persuading people to their point of view or way of doing things (Dunnette & Kirchner, 1960).

Interesting differences between specialty salesmen, route salesmen, and sales engineers emerged from a comparison of Strong Vocational Interest Blank scores earned by representatives of these three groups (Witkin, 1956). The route salesmen tended to display greater interest than either of the other groups in "business details"; the sales engineers tended to be less interested than either of the other groups in "salesmanship" as measured by two subscales of this inventory. The latter finding is understandable when we recall that sales engineers are technically trained manufacturer's representatives rather than salesmen in the traditional sense.

Results like these support a trend away from the concept of salesmen as a general occupational category and toward the concept of special, more homogeneous, sales occupational groups. In view of the functional differences between various kinds of salesmen, it is unreasonable to expect a single predictor or combination of predictors to be universally applicable for selecting salesmen. Selection procedures must be tailored to the specific requirements and activities of particular sales positions.

Criteria of Sales Success. As of 1945 it was concluded by one reviewer (Cleveland, 1948) that, all claims to the contrary, no one selection technique had emerged as clearly superior to all others. The emphasis in predicting sales personnel success has shifted somewhat during the past 30 years, with considerable attention devoted recently to biographical inventories and personal history blanks. Tests, like those measuring sales comprehension and sales motivation, have also been proposed. However, to the authors' knowledge, the conclusion of 1945 is still applicable today.

Why is it that no one outstanding type of predictor of sales success has been discovered? Part of the answer has already been given in the previous discussion of the heterogeneous nature of positions designated salesman. A related factor is the problem of identifying a satisfactory criterion of job performance for salesmen.

You will recall from Chapter 3 that behavioral predictions are impossible in the absence of suitable criteria against which to validate the predictors. The criterion problem for selecting salesmen may not seem especially formidable at first glance. It would seem that we could use a measure of productivity, like gross sales per unit of time, for evaluating the effectiveness of a particular salesman in comparison with others in a similar position. However, the development of a suitable sales criterion entails certain complexities. Although sales data usually are readily available, they must be corrected for a number of factors in order to make them meaningful as criteria. One such factor is job experience. Salesmen with some experience tend to make more sales per unit of time than inexperienced salesmen, other things being equal. Secondly, it would be necessary to adjust for the potential of the sales territory or outlet. Certain geographical areas, cities, and neighborhoods are more likely to be productive for the salesman than others both because of population density and receptivity to the particular commodity being sold. Third, a correction must be applied for orders that are later rescinded or upon which payment is defaulted. It would probably be wise also to adjust gross sales per unit of time for such factors as repeat orders subsequently placed, and the productivity of a particular territory prior to the time the salesman in question acquired it.

Assuming that a reasonably adequate correction could be devised and applied to a record of gross sales, there is yet the issue of appropriateness of such a criterion. Adjusted sales is only a partial index of success because when considered alone, it neglects the important factor of termination/survival. The effective salesman, defined by adjusted gross sales, who remains with the company for a long period of time is a greater asset to that company than the equally effective salesman who terminates his employment after relatively brief tenure. Predictors of adjusted gross sales may be relatively ineffective for a termination/survival criterion and vice versa.

It is obvious that as the time interval between initial selection and measurement of a performance criterion increases, the criterion itself becomes increasingly contaminated by the factor of voluntary job termination. It has been hypothesized that for studies involving a relatively brief time interval between selection and criterion measurement (that is, when voluntary termination is not a significant factor) successful prediction will depend much more upon measures of *ability* than interest. Conversely, predictions made against a delayed criterion will depend more upon *interest* than ability since the former reflects a desire to stay with a particular company or in a particular position (Ferguson, 1960). Regardless of the merits of this suggestion for improving the accuracy of selecting salesmen, it calls attention to the issue of criterion contamination and the consequence of such contamination for reducing predictive efficiency.

SUMMARY

Advertising and selling are closely related in that both aim to persuade potential buyers to purchase products or avail themselves of services. However, while advertising appeals to the mass market, selling appeals to the individual consumer. Thus, advertising is a form of preselling whereby the buying public is informed about the existence and special features of a product or service. The salesman attempts to personalize the attractive features of the product or service so it is perceived as highly desirable by individual consumers.

Although psychologists are not advertising specialists, they have a fundamental interest in virtually any attempt to influence human behavior. Successful advertisements capitalize upon certain psychological principles related to attentiveness. These relate to such format characteristics as color, movement, repetition, and novelty. Beyond this, the successful advertisement makes an appeal to human needs and motives. If we can project ourselves into the advertisement and perceive ourselves as users of the product, the advertiser has come a long way toward inducing us to make the purchase.

In addition to investigating the effectiveness of advertising copy, the consumer psychologist may study the medium for dissemination of the advertisement, responsiveness to advertising as a function of certain audience characteristics (like age, educational level, and so on), and the impact of advertising upon consumer behavior.

To the present, psychologists have devoted much less research to selling than to advertising. Whatever research has been done on selling has been directed almost exclusively to the matters of selecting and training salesmen. Current thinking about the conduct of sales interviews and the effectiveness of various kinds of sales presentations is based more upon experience than upon the results of carefully controlled investigation.

Early approaches to salesmanship capitalized upon the use of selling formulas. These formulas assumed that buyers are relatively passive and that their thinking proceeded in a uniform and predictable stream through several rather distinct stages.

More recently this rather naive approach to salesmanship has been replaced by one capitalizing upon need satisfaction. The buyer's needs are regarded as central to the selling process. The salesman's behavior assumes importance only as a vehicle for promising and providing need-satisfaction. The fundamental implication of this approach to salesmanship is that since every prospect is a unique individual with unique needs, every sales presentation must be custom-tailored to him.

Two problems of particular significance to selecting effective salesmen are (1) the diversity of duties of and requirements for different kinds of salesmen and (2) the inadequacies of various criteria of selling success. Thus, it is unreasonable to expect a single predictor or combination of predictors to be universally applicable for selecting salesmen. Selection procedures must be tailored to the specific requirements of particular sales positions.

Appendixes

Appendices

A. Statistical Computation

This discussion of computational procedures is not comprehensive. It is limited in scope to certain statistics most frequently encountered by undergraduate students in industrial psychology courses. Furthermore only selected computational formulas are presented, and these without consideration for their derivation. The student who is interested in a more comprehensive discussion of statistical procedures is referred to any one of a number of excellent statistics texts.[1]

RAW DATA

The discussion in this Appendix revolves about the analysis of a single set of raw data. These data were obtained from a personnel testing program wherein a measure of clerical aptitude was administered as a preemployment test to all job applicants. The first 50 applicants were hired regardless of test score. Three months after she was hired, each employee was rated on work proficiency by her supervisor. The supervisor making the proficiency rating had no knowledge about the employee's preemployment test scores. The range of possible test scores extended from a low of 0 to a maximum

---

[1] See, for example, A. L. Edwards. *Statistical methods*. New York: Holt, Rinehart, & Winston, 1967; J. P. Guilford. *Fundamental statistics in psychology and education*. New York: McGraw-Hill, 1965; R. P. Runyan & A. Haber. *Fundamentals of behavioral statistics*. Reading, Mass.: Addison-Wesley, 1971.

TABLE A–1

Preemployment Test Scores and Supervisory Ratings for 50 Employees

Employee	Preemployment Test	Supervisory Rating	Employee	Preemployment Test	Supervisory Rating
A	40	3.0	Z	63	9.0
B	35	6.0	AA	41	8.0
C	49	5.0	BB	50	7.0
D	48	4.0	CC	42	3.0
E	52	6.0	DD	49	5.0
F	46	3.0	EE	48	5.0
G	58	3.0	FF	35	2.0
H	57	7.0	GG	53	2.0
I	53	6.0	HH	45	4.0
J	40	4.0	II	62	9.0
K	56	7.0	JJ	68	9.0
L	60	8.0	KK	44	4.0
M	37	5.0	LL	64	8.0
N	65	7.0	MM	42	2.0
O	55	9.0	NN	54	2.0
P	44	4.0	OO	51	6.0
Q	47	5.0	PP	46	5.0
R	63	8.0	QQ	49	3.0
S	50	6.0	RR	56	7.0
T	49	5.0	SS	38	3.0
U	39	2.0	TT	51	6.0
V	31	1.0	UU	49	5.0
W	50	5.0	VV	32	1.0
X	47	5.0	WW	47	4.0
Y	47	5.0	XX	43	5.0

of 70; the range of possible ratings extended from a low of 1.0 to a maximum of 9.0. The resultant data are summarized in Table A–1.

This table indicates that employee A earned a preemployment test score of 40 and a supervisory rating three months later of 3.0; employee B earned a preemployment test score of 35 and a supervisory rating of 6.0; and so on.

FREQUENCY DISTRIBUTION

We can ask a number of descriptive questions about the data displayed in Table A–1. For example, what were the lowest and highest preemployment test scores earned by persons in this sample? How many persons earned a test score of, say, 49, or a supervisory rating of, say, 5.0? What was the most commonly earned test score?

Although these questions can be answered by examining the raw data, they can be answered more easily by examining a *frequency distribution* prepared from these data. Such a distribution is merely a tabulation of the number of persons (*frequency*) earning each raw score.

Frequency Distributions from Raw Scores

To prepare a frequency distribution, the raw scores are arranged in order, usually from highest to lowest score, with the appropriate frequency indicated for each score. This procedure has been followed in preparing the two frequency distributions (one for preemployment test scores and one for supervisory ratings) shown in Table A–2. Note that a raw score is designated in statistical terminology by a capital letter $(X$ or $Y)$; frequency is designated f.

Now it is apparent at a glance that preemployment test scores ranged between 31 and 68 and that a score of 49 was earned by more people $(f = 5)$ than any other single score. Similarly, the supervisory ratings ranged between 1.0 and 9.0 with 5.0 being the single most frequently assigned rating.

Grouped Data

The frequency distributions in Table A–2 required frequency tallies for each raw score. Although this produced a compact distribution for the supervisory ratings, the distribution for the preemployment test was quite lengthy, involving tabulations for each of 38 separate raw scores.

A distribution with about 15 raw score steps is regarded as optimal for computational convenience. In order to collapse a distribution like the one shown for preemployment scores in Table A–2 into about 15 raw score steps, each step must contain more than one raw score unit. Since every step in a frequency distribution must contain the same number of raw score units as every other step, there are two possibilities for this particular set of data: each step can consist of three raw score units (that is, have an interval of 3); or each step can consist of four raw score units (that is, have an interval of 4). An interval (i) of 3 would generate 16 steps in order to encompass all raw scores from the lowest (31) to the highest (68). An i of 4 would generate 12 steps.

The frequency distribution for preemployment test scores

TABLE A–2

Frequency Distributions for Preemployment Test Scores (X)
and Supervisory Ratings (Y)

Preemployment Test			Supervisory Rating		
X	Tally	f_x	Y	Tally	f_y
68	/	1	9.0	////	4
67		0	8.0	////	4
66		0	7.0	ⅉ	5
65	/	1	6.0	ⅉ /	6
64	/	1	5.0	ⅉ ⅉ //	12
63	//	2	4.0	ⅉ /	6
62	/	1	3.0	ⅉ /	6
61		0	2.0	ⅉ	5
60	/	1	1 0	//	2
59		0			$N = 50$
58	/	1			
57	/	1			
56	//	2			
55	/	1			
54	/	1			
53	//	2			
52	/	1			
51	//	2			
50	///	3			
49	ⅉ	5			
48	//	2			
47	////	4			
46	//	2			
45	/	1			
44	//	2			
43	/	1			
42	//	2			
41	/	1			
40	//	2			
39	/	1			
38	/	1			
37	/	1			
36		0			
35	//	2			
34		0			
33		0			
32	/	1			
31	/	1			
	$N = 50$				

wherein data are grouped with an interval of 3 is shown in Table A–3.

Note that the raw data from which the distributions in Tables A–3 and A–2 were generated are identical. The only difference between these distributions is that in the latter raw scores were used whereas in the former the raw scores were grouped into intervals of three points each.

TABLE A–3

Frequency Distribution for Pre-employment Test Scores When $i = 3$

c.i.	Tally	f
66–68	/	1
63–65	////	4
60–62	//	2
57–59	//	2
54–56	////	4
51–53	///	5
48–50	/// ///	10
45–47	/// //	7
42–44	///	5
39–41	////	4
36–38	//	2
33–35	//	2
30–32	//	2

Certain features of these data are more apparent when they are grouped (Table A–3) than when they are ungrouped (Table A–2). In particular, it is easier to identify by inspection the most "typical" or most "nearly average" scores. The peak frequency is obtained for scores in the *class interval* (c.i.) 48–50.

CENTRAL TENDENCY

The discussion of statistics in Chapter 2 defined three primary measures of central tendency: mean, median, and mode. The ensuing discussion concerns the computation of these measures.

Mean

The mean (X) is defined as the arithmetic average. Thus it is computed by adding (Σ) the raw scores (X) and dividing by the total number of observations (N). The computational formula is written:

$$\bar{X} = \frac{\Sigma X}{N_x} \quad \text{or} \quad \bar{Y} = \frac{\Sigma Y}{N_y} \, .$$

This formula is the "raw score formula" for calculating the mean. The calculation can be made easily from the raw data presented in Table A–1.

For the preemployment test, the sum of the raw scores is 2,440 and the number of observations is 50. Substituting in the formula above,

$$\bar{X} = \frac{2,440}{50} = 48.8 \, .$$

Substituting in similar fashion to calculate the mean supervisory rating, we have

$$\bar{Y} = \frac{253}{50} = 5.0 \, .$$

Using the Frequency Distribution. The work involved in making these calculations can be somewhat simplified by using the appropriate frequency distribution instead of the unorganized listing of raw scores.

Consider the distribution of supervisory ratings in Table A–2. Since each raw score occurs more than once, one need only sum the products of each raw score and its frequency to obtain the same value as ΣY. In other words, since a rating of 9.0 was given to four persons, it contributes 36.0 to the total ΣY. This value can be obtained either by adding 9.0 four times or by multiplying 9.0 by its frequency (4).

Thus the computational formula using data organized in the form of a frequency distribution like the one in Table A–2 for supervisory ratings is

$$\bar{Y} = \frac{\Sigma f Y}{N_y} \quad \text{or} \quad \bar{X} = \frac{\Sigma f X}{N_x} \, .$$

This computation is illustrated for supervisory ratings in Table A–4.

Grouped Data. The procedure just illustrated is quite convenient for ungrouped data. However, how can we compute the mean when data are grouped into class intervals?

TABLE A-4

Calculating the Mean Using a Frequency
Distribution
(Y = supervisory ratings)

Y	f	fY	
9.0	4	36.0	
8.0	4	32.0	
7.0	5	35.0	$\bar{Y} = \dfrac{\Sigma fY}{N_y}$
6.0	6	36.0	
5.0	12	60.0	
4.0	6	24.0	$\bar{Y} = \dfrac{253}{50}$
3.0	6	18.0	
2.0	5	10.0	$\bar{Y} = 5.0$
1.0	2	2.0	
$N_y = 50$		$\Sigma fY = 253.0$	

One approach is to assume that all scores within a class interval
are equally distributed about the midpoint of that interval. Thus
the midpoint can be treated as the "score" to be assigned to all
frequencies in that interval.

To illustrate: Referring to Table A–3, one person earned a score
somewhere between 66 and 68. The best assumption we can make
about that person's score is that it was 67 (the midpoint of the class
interval). If our assumption is incorrect (that is, if he actually
earned a score of 66 or 68), our maximum error cannot exceed one
point. Either of the other possible assumptions (that he earned a
score of 66 or of 68) would open the way for a possible error of two
points.

Now consider the next lower class interval in Table A–3: 63–65.
The best assumption we can make about the four persons in this
interval is that their scores are distributed in balanced fashion with
two above the midpoint of the interval (64) and two below this midpoint. That being the case, all four cases converge upon the midpoint for computational purposes.

Thus when data are grouped into class intervals, the computational formula for the mean is stated as follows:

$$\bar{X} = \frac{\Sigma f \text{ mid.}}{N_x} .$$

TABLE A-5

Calculating the Mean from Grouped Data with $i = 3$
(X = preemployment test scores)

ci.	mid.	f	f mid.	
66–68...........67		1	67	
63–65...........64		4	256	$\bar{X} = \dfrac{\Sigma f \text{ mid.}}{N}$
60–62...........61		2	122	
57–59...........58		2	116	
54–56...........55		4	220	
51–53...........52		5	260	$\bar{X} = \dfrac{2,432}{50}$
48–50...........49		10	490	
45–47...........46		7	322	
42–44...........43		5	215	$\bar{X} = 48.64$
39–41...........40		4	160	
36–38...........37		2	74	
33–35...........34		2	68	
30–32...........31		2	62	
		$N_x = 50$	Σf mid. = 2,432	

The procedure for computing the mean preemployment test score
using the frequency distribution from Table A–3 is shown in Table
A–5.

Note that the arithmetic simplification by this procedure entails
some sacrifice of accuracy. The mean calculated directly from the
raw data is 48.8; from the grouped data it is 48.6. However a loss of
accuracy of this magnitude is usually regarded as unimportant in
view of the convenience of the simplified procedure for hand computation.

Median

The median (*med*) is defined as the middle score in the distribution. It is that score which separates the highest 50 percent of the
scores from the lowest 50 percent of the scores. Thus, when considering a set of raw scores arranged in order from highest to lowest (or
from lowest to highest), the median score is the one earned by the
$N/2$ person. With a set of 50 scores, as in our illustration, arranged
in ascending or descending order, the median score is the one earned
by the 25th person.

If you list the raw preemployment test scores from Table A–1 in
order, you will note that the 25th person earned a score of 49. In the

same way, you can determine that the median supervisory rating is 5.0.

Grouped Data. Clearly, the arrangement of raw scores required to carry out the procedure described above becomes increasingly laborious as the N increases. Therefore, it is usually simpler to calculate the median from data grouped into class intervals than from raw data.

Consider the distribution in Table A–3. By inspection, the median falls somewhere within the interval 48–50. That interval con-

TABLE A–6

Calculating the Median from Grouped Data
(X = Preemployment Test Scores)

Class Interval	f	cf	
66–68	1	50	
63–65	4	49	Median case $= \dfrac{N}{2} = 25$
60–62	2	45	
57–59	2	43	$l = 47.5$
54–56	4	41	$n_m = 3$
51–53	5	37	$f_m = 10$
48–50	10	32	
45–47	7	22	Med $= l + \dfrac{n_m}{f_m}\,(i)$
42–44	5	15	
39–41	4	10	$= 47.5 + \dfrac{3}{10}\,(3)$
36–38	2	6	
33–35	2	4	$= 47.5 + 0.3\,(3)$
30–32	2	2	$= 47.5 + 0.9$
			$= 48.4$

tains the 25th case. But *where* within that interval does the 25th case fall?

Examine the *cumulative frequency (cf)* column of Table A–6. This column simply shows the total frequencies at and below a particular class interval. The *cf* entry for the class interval 45–47 indicates that 22 persons earned test scores of 47 or less. Likewise 32 persons earned test scores of 50 (the upper limit of the class interval 48–50) or less.

Since there are 50 cases in the sample and the median is given by the 25th case, inspection of the cumulative frequency column of Table A–6 confirms that the median is closer to the lower limit of the class interval 48–50 than to the upper limit of that interval. The lower limit lacks three cases of being the median; the upper limit exceeds the median by seven cases.

In order to locate the median within this class interval, we must invoke the assumption about the distribution of cases in a class interval discussed earlier. You will recall that all cases in a class interval are assumed to be distributed equidistantly throughout that interval. Thus, since there are 10 cases in the interval 48–50, that interval is assumed to be divided into tenths as shown below.

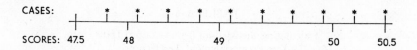

Note that the class interval 48–50 is treated as designating a continuum of scores extending from 0.5 score unit below its lower limit of 48 to 0.5 score unit above its upper limit of 50. The next higher class interval, 51–53, is regarded as extending from 50.5 to 53.5. If this were not done, the score continuum would have gaps between the top of one class interval (for example, 50) and the bottom of the next interval (for example, 51).

The computation of the median as shown in Table A–6 involves the following steps:

1. Identify the median case. This case is given by $N/2 = 50/2 = 25$. Thus the median is that score earned by the 25th person.

2. The lower limit (l) of the class interval containing the median case is 47.5. (The median case falls in the class interval 47.5–50.5.)

3. The number of cases needed from the class interval containing the median (n_m) is 3. Since there are 22 cases below this class interval and the median is given by the 25th case, $25 - 22 = 3$.

4. The number of cases in the class interval containing the median (f_m) is 10.

5. The median $= 48.4$. Since the median case is three tenths of the distance between 47.5 and 50.5 and the total distance of this class interval is three points, the median is located within the class interval at a distance of $3/10$ (3), or 0.9, above the lower limit of the interval.

Related Calculations. The two designations, median and 50th percentile, are synonymous. The median score separates the upper and lower 50 percent of the cases in a distribution; the 50th percentile corresponds to that score and all lower ones earned by 50 percent of the persons in a sample.

Thus the procedure outlined above can be readily used for determining scores corresponding to any percentile. For example, what score corresponds to each 10th percentile (that is, the 10th, 20th, 30th, and so on, percentiles) of the distribution shown in Table A–6?

For the *10th* percentile we will be looking for the case that separates the bottom 10 percent of the cases from the highest 90 percent of the cases. In other words, we will be looking for the fifth case from the bottom of the cumulative frequency distribution (10 percent of $N = N/10 = 50/10 = 5$). For the *20th* percentile, we will be looking for the 10th case from the bottom of the cumulative frequency distribution (20 percent of $N = N/5 = 50/5 = 10$).

These calculations are worked below for each 10th percentile of the distribution shown in Table A–6. The computational formula is identical to that used to calculate the median:

$$\text{Percentile score} = l + \frac{n}{f}(i),$$

where l is the lower limit of the interval containing the desired percentile score; n is the number of cases needed from that interval; f is the frequency in that interval; and i is the size of the interval.

Tenth percentile (5th case) $= 35.5 + \frac{1}{2}(3) = 37.0$
Twentieth percentile (10th case) $= 38.5 + \frac{4}{4}(3) = 41.5$
Thirtieth percentile (15th case) $= 41.5 + \frac{5}{5}(3) = 44.5$
Fortieth percentile (20th case) $= 44.5 + \frac{5}{7}(3) = 46.6$
Fiftieth percentile (median) $= 47.5 + \frac{3}{10}(3) = 48.4$
Sixtieth percentile (30th case) $= 47.5 + \frac{8}{10}(3) = 49.9$
Seventieth percentile (35th case) $= 50.5 + \frac{3}{5}(3) = 52.3$
Eightieth percentile (40th case) $= 53.5 + \frac{3}{4}(3) = 55.8$
Ninetieth percentile (45th case) $= 59.5 + \frac{2}{2}(3) = 62.5$

In similar fashion you can calculate from Table A–6 that the 25th percentile is given by a test score of 43.0 and the 75th percentile by a score of 53.9.

Mode

Since the modal score is the one occurring most frequently, it can be easily identified by inspection. From Table A–2 it is evident that the mode for supervisory ratings is 5.0. In the same table the modal preemployment test score is seen to be 49. However this is somewhat misleading because the distribution does not really have a clear-cut mode; a score of 47 was earned almost as frequently as was 49.

If we were to identify the mode for the preemployment test data grouped as in Table A–6, we would regard the mode as the midpoint of the class interval with the highest frequency, that is, 49.

VARIABILITY

We have already discussed the need for describing a set of data both in terms of its central tendency and its variability (or spread away from the mean). As shown in Chapter 2, distributions may have identical means but differ markedly in their variabilities.

Although there are several statistics of variability, the only one that will concern us here is *standard deviation* (s.d.). The scores defining the range between ± 1 s.d. (one standard deviation either side of the mean) include the middle 68 percent of the cases in a normal distribution.

Computing Standard Deviation from Raw Scores

The raw score formula for standard deviation is

$$\text{s.d.} = \sqrt{\frac{\Sigma D^2}{N}},$$

where D is the difference between each raw score and the mean of the distribution. The following steps are required for this calculation:

1. Calculate the mean $(\overline{X})$ of the scores.
2. Calculate the D for each score $(X - \overline{X})$.
3. Square each D value.
4. Sum the squared D values.
5. Divide this sum by N.
6. Extract the square root.

These steps are illustrated in Table A–7 for the set of raw preemployment test scores listed in Table A–1. This distribution is shown to have a mean of 49 (actually, 48.8) and a standard deviation of 8.6.

TABLE A–7

Standard Deviation Calculated from Raw Scores
(X = preemployment test)

Employee	X	$D=X-\bar{X}$	D^2
A............	40	−9	81
B............	35	−14	196
C............	49	0	0
D............	48	−1	1
E............	52	3	9
F............	46	−3	9
G............	58	9	81
H............	57	8	64
I............	53	4	16
J............	40	−9	81
K............	56	7	49
L............	60	11	121
M............	37	−12	144
N............	65	16	256
O............	55	6	36
P............	44	−5	25
Q............	47	−2	4
R............	63	14	196
S............	50	1	1
T............	49	0	0
U............	39	−10	100
V............	31	−18	324
W............	50	1	1
X............	47	−2	4
Y............	47	−2	4
Z............	63	14	196
AA............	41	−8	64
BB............	50	1	1
CC............	42	−7	49
DD............	49	0	0
EE............	48	−1	1
FF............	35	−14	196
GG............	53	4	16
HH............	45	−4	16
II............	62	13	169
JJ............	68	19	361
KK............	44	−5	25
LL............	64	15	225
MM............	42	−7	49
NN............	54	5	25
OO............	51	2	4
PP............	46	−3	9
QQ............	49	0	0
RR............	56	7	49
SS............	38	−11	121
TT............	51	2	4
UU............	49	0	0
VV............	32	−17	289
WW............	47	−2	4
XX............	43	−6	36
	$\Sigma X = 2{,}440$		$\Sigma D^2 = 3{,}712$

$$\bar{X} = \frac{\Sigma X}{N} = \frac{2{,}440}{50} = 48.8 = 49$$

$$\text{s.d.} = \sqrt{\frac{\Sigma D^2}{N}}$$

$$= \sqrt{\frac{3{,}712}{50}} = \sqrt{74.24}$$

$$= 8.6$$

Computing Standard Deviation from Grouped Data

The laborious calculation for standard deviation described above is considerably simplified when the data are grouped as in Table A–3. The arithmetic operations for such grouped data are shown in Table A–8.

TABLE A–8

Standard Deviation Calculated from Grouped Data
(X = preemployment test score)

ci	f	x	x^2	fx	fx^2
66–68	1	12	144	12	144
63–65	4	11	121	44	484
60–62	2	10	100	20	200
57–59	2	9	81	18	162
54–56	4	8	64	32	256
51–53	5	7	49	35	245
48–50	10	6	36	60	360
45–47	7	5	25	35	175
42–44	5	4	16	20	80
39–41	4	3	9	12	36
36–38	2	2	4	4	8
33–35	2	1	1	2	2
30–32	2	0	0	0	0
	$N = 50$			$\Sigma fx = 294$	$\Sigma fx^2 = 2,152$

$$\text{s.d.} = ci\sqrt{\frac{\Sigma fx^2}{N} - \left(\frac{\Sigma fx}{N}\right)^2}$$

$$= 3\sqrt{\frac{2,152}{50} - \left(\frac{294}{50}\right)^2}$$

$$= 3\sqrt{43.04 - (5.88)^2} = 3\sqrt{43.04 - 34.57} = 3\sqrt{8.47} = 3(2.91)$$

$$= 8.7$$

What have we done to modify the raw score standard deviation formula to the formula shown in Table A–8 for grouped data? You will recall that the raw score formula is

$$\text{s.d.} = \sqrt{\frac{\Sigma D^2}{N}}$$

where $D = (X - \overline{X})$. Thus by substituting $(X - \overline{X})$ for D, this formula can be rewritten

$$\text{s.d.} = \sqrt{\frac{\Sigma(X - \bar{X})^2}{N}} = \sqrt{\frac{\Sigma X^2}{N} - \left(\frac{\Sigma X}{N}\right)^2}$$

As discussed earlier, when calculations are made from raw score frequency distributions, it is easier to sum the fX values than to sum each of the X values. Thus the formula for standard deviation given above may be rewritten as

$$\text{s.d.} = \sqrt{\frac{\Sigma fX^2}{N} - \left(\frac{\Sigma fX}{N}\right)^2}$$

The calculation shown in Table A–8 involves a further simplification of the arithmetic processes. Note particularly that the work sheet in this table codes the class intervals (the x column) in numerical order starting with 0 for the interval 30–32, 1 for the interval 33–35, and so on. We have used the symbol x to represent a coded score, in contrast with X which represents an actual raw score.

When computations are based upon these coded scores rather than raw scores, the formula for standard deviation when the class interval is 1 must be rewritten:

$$\text{s.d.} = \sqrt{\frac{\Sigma fx^2}{N} - \left(\frac{\Sigma fx}{N}\right)^2}$$

One final modification is necessitated by the fact that the scores in Table A–8 are organized into intervals of 3. The above formula would in this case give an estimate of $\frac{1}{3}$ s.d. To make this formula generally applicable regardless of the size of the class interval, requires restatement as follows:

$$\text{s.d.} = ci \sqrt{\frac{\Sigma fx^2}{N} - \left(\frac{\Sigma fx}{N}\right)^2}$$

TRANSFORMATIONS OF RAW SCORES

The discussion of test norming in Chapter 5 clarified the need for transforming raw scores to some sort of common base for comparative purposes. Referring to Table A–1, did person A score "better" on the preemployment test or on the supervisory rating? His raw score on the former was 40; on the latter 3.0. We have already

TABLE A-9

Transformation of Raw Scores to Numerical Ranks

Employee	Preemployment Test X	Rank$_x$	Supervisory Rating Y	Rank$_y$
A	40	42.5	3.0	40.5
B	35	47.5	6.0	16.5
C	49	24.0	5.0	25.5
D	48	27.5	4.0	34.5
E	52	16.0	6.0	16.5
F	46	33.5	3.0	40.5
G	58	8.0	3.0	40.5
H	57	9.0	7.0	11.0
I	53	14.5	6.0	16.5
J	40	42.5	4.0	34.5
K	56	10.5	7.0	11.0
L	60	7.0	8.0	6.5
M	37	46.0	5.0	25.5
N	65	2.0	7.0	11.0
O	55	12.0	9.0	2.5
P	44	36.5	4.0	34.5
Q	47	30.5	5.0	25.5
R	63	4.5	8.0	6.5
S	50	20.0	6.0	16.5
T	49	24.0	5.0	25.5
U	39	44.0	2.0	46.0
V	31	50.0	1.0	49.5
W	50	20.0	5.0	25.5
X	47	30.5	5.0	25.5
Y	47	37.5	5.0	25.5
Z	63	4.5	9.0	2.5
AA	41	41.0	8.0	6.5
BB	50	20.0	7.0	11.0
CC	42	39.5	3.0	40.5
DD	49	24.0	5.0	25.5
EE	48	27.5	5.0	25.5
FF	35	47.5	2.0	46.0
GG	53	14.5	2.0	46.0
HH	45	35.0	4.0	34.5
II	62	6.0	9.0	2.5
JJ	68	1.0	9.0	2.5
KK	44	36.5	4.0	34.5
LL	64	3.0	8.0	6.5
MM	42	39.5	2.0	46.0
NN	54	13.0	2.0	46.0
OO	51	17.5	6.0	16.5
PP	46	33.5	5.0	25.5
QQ	49	24.0	3.0	40.5
RR	56	10.5	7.0	11.0
SS	38	45.0	3.0	40.5
TT	51	17.5	6.0	16.5
UU	49	24.0	5.0	25.5
VV	32	49.0	1.0	49.5
WW	47	30.5	4.0	34.5
XX	43	38.0	5.0	25.5

calculated the mean as 48.8 for the preemployment test and 5.0 for the supervisory rating. Hence, person A scored below the mean on both measures. But how far below each mean were his scores? The difference between his raw test score and its mean (8.8 points) cannot be compared with the difference between his raw rating and *its* mean (2.0 units) without transforming both sets of scores to a common yardstick.

The particular kinds of transformations with which we will here be concerned are numerical rank, percentile rank, and standard score.

Numerical Rank

Raw scores are numerically ranked by arranging them in order from highest to lowest and assigning a rank of *1* to the highest raw score, *2* to the second highest score, and so on. This has been done in Table A–9 for the raw scores listed in Table A–1.

Note the procedure for assigning ranks when two or more persons have the same raw score. Two persons (*R* and *Z*) for example, earned preemployment test scores of 63. Since three persons had scores higher than 63, we had previously assigned the ranks 1, 2, and 3. Therefore a rank of 4.5 (midway between ranks 4 and 5) is assigned to persons *R* and *Z*, and the next lower raw score (62, earned by II) is assigned a rank of 6.

Percentile Rank

A percentile rank states the percent of persons scoring at or below the raw score to which it corresponds. Thus if we are told that a given raw score corresponds to the 72d percentile, we know that 72 percent of the persons taking this test earned scores at or below that raw score. By transforming raw scores from two or more tests to a percentile rank yardstick, it becomes possible to make direct comparisons between a person's performance across these tests.

The easiest method for computing percentile ranks is to begin with a frequency distribution using raw scores rather than class intervals. Cumulative frequencies (*cf*) are next computed for each raw score. The cumulative frequency is the number of persons earning that particular score or lower. These cumulative frequencies are then easily converted to percentile ranks by

$$\%\text{ile rank} = \frac{cf}{N}$$

The procedure is illustrated in Table A–10, taking the frequency distribution from Table A–2. The arrangement of the display in Table A–10 clarifies the usefulness of percentile ranks as raw score transformations. Note, for example, that a raw preemployment test score of 57 carries the same percentile rank as a raw supervisory rating of 7.0. And, returning to our initial question about person A's performance, we note that whereas his preemployment test score ranks at the 18th percentile, his supervisory rating ranks at the 26th percentile.

Standard Score

It is often useful to transform scores in such a way that they can both be directly compared and combined into a single composite score. Whereas percentile ranks permit direct comparisons of raw scores, such ranks cannot be averaged or summed to yield a single composite score. To achieve this end, it is necessary to effect a standard score transformation.

One kind of standard score is the Z score, defined by the formula

$$z_x = \frac{X - \bar{X}}{sd_x} \quad \text{or} \quad z_y = \frac{Y - \bar{Y}}{sd_y}$$

Appropriate Z score transformations of the raw preemployment test and supervisory rating scores are shown in Table A–11. Once again, to clarify the utility of such transformations, the raw scores on both measures are aligned in terms of their Z score equivalents.

CORRELATION

A correlation coefficient indicates both the magnitude and direction of the relationship between two or more sets of scores (see Chapter 2). The discussion in this section is restricted to correlations involving two variables only.

The Scattergram

The meaning of correlation is clarified by plotting a scattergram (or cross-tally) of each person's score on the two variables under

TABLE A–10

Transforming Raw Scores to Percentile Ranks

Preemployment Test				Supervisory Rating			
X	*f*	*cf*	*%ile Rank*	*Y*	*f*	*cf*	*%ile Rank*
68	1	50		9.0	4	50	
67	0	49	98				
66	0	49	98				
65	1	49	98				
64	1	48	96				
63	2	47	94				
62	1	45	90	8.0	4	46	92
61	0	44	88				
60	1	44	88				
59	0	43	86				
58	1	43	86				
57	1	42	84	7.0	5	42	84
56	2	41	82				
55	1	39	78				
54	1	38	76				
53	2	37	74	6.0	6	37	74
52	1	35	70				
51	2	34	68				
50	3	32	64	5.0	12	31	62
49	5	29	58				
48	2	24	48				
47	4	22	44	4.0	6	19	38
46	2	18	36				
45	1	16	32				
44	2	15	30				
43	1	13	26	3.0	6	13	26
42	2	12	24				
41	1	10	20				
40	2	9	18				
39	1	7	14	2.0	5	7	14
38	1	6	12				
37	1	5	10				
36	0	4	8				
35	2	4	8				
34	0	2	4				
33	0	2	4				
32	1	2	4	1.0	2	2	4
31	1	1	2				

TABLE A-11

Z Score Transformations of Raw Scores

	Preemployment Test $(\bar{X} = 49;\ sd_x = 8.7)$		Supervisory Ratings $(\bar{Y} = 5.0;\ sd_y = 2.2)$		
X	$X - \bar{X}$	z_x	Y	$Y - \bar{Y}$	z_y
68	19	2.19			
67	18	2.07			
66	17	1.96			
65	16	1.84	9.0	4	1.82
64	15	1.73			
63	14	1.61			
62	13	1.50			
61	12	1.38	8.0	3	1.37
60	11	1.27			
59	10	1.15			
58	9	1.04			
57	8	0.92	7.0	2	0.91
56	7	0.81			
55	6	0.69			
54	5	0.58			
53	4	0.46	6.0	1	0.46
52	3	0.35			
51	2	0.23			
50	1	0.12			
49	0	0.00	5.0	0	0.00
48	−1	−0.12			
47	−2	−0.23			
46	−3	−0.35			
45	−4	−0.46	4.0	−1	−0.46
44	−5	−0.58			
43	−6	−0.69			
42	−7	−0.81			
41	−8	−0.92	3.0	−2	−0.91
40	−9	−1.04			
39	−10	−1.15			
38	−11	−1.27			
37	−12	−1.38	2.0	−3	−1.37
36	−13	−1.50			
35	−14	−1.61			
34	−15	−1.73			
33	−16	−1.84	1.0	−4	−1.82
32	−17	−1.96			
31	−18	−2.07			

FIGURE A–1

Scattergram Showing the Relationship between Preemployment Test
Scores (X) and Supervisory Ratings (Y)

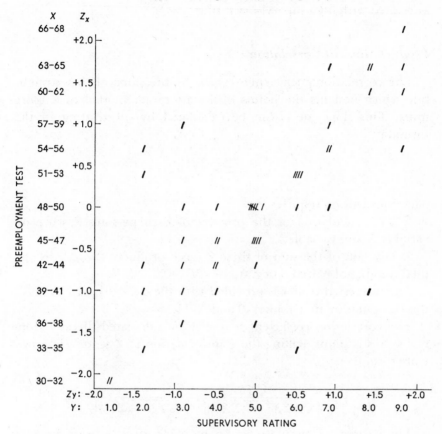

consideration. This has been done in Figure A–1 for the raw score
data taken from Table A–9. Person A's scores ($X = 40$; $Y = 3.0$) are
represented by a tally mark at the intersection of the two appropriate base line intervals (39–41 for X; 3.0 for Y); person B's scores
($X = 35$; $Y = 2.0$) are indicated by a tally at the intersection of the
33–35 interval for X and the 2.0 interval for Y; and so on.

We have already shown, in the previous discussion of standard
scores, that preemployment test raw score units are not equivalent to
supervisory rating raw score units. Therefore the raw scores along
the axes of Figure A–1 are spaced proportionally to their Z score
transformations (as given in Table A–11).

From the discussion in Chapter 2 you will undoubtedly recognize that this particular scattergram provides evidence for a moderately high and positive correlation. High preemployment test scores are associated with high supervisory ratings.

Product-Moment Correlation (r)

The correlation coefficient is given by the slope of that straight line which best fits the points of a scattergram plotted in Z score units. This slope, or r, can be calculated by substituting in the formula

$$r = \frac{\Sigma Z_x Z_y}{N}.$$

Such substitution requires:

1. The calculation of the product of each person's Z score on variable X and variable $Y;$

2. Division of the sum of these Z score products $(\Sigma Z_x Z_y)$ by the total number of paired observations (N).

The interested reader is provided with the data required to make this computation in Tables A–9 and A–11.

The correlation coefficient may also be calculated directly from raw scores without making the transformation to Z scores. The raw score formula is

$$r = \frac{N\Sigma XY - \Sigma X \Sigma Y}{[\sqrt{N\Sigma X^2 - (\Sigma X)^2}][\sqrt{N\Sigma Y^2 - (\Sigma Y)^2}]}$$

The necessary computations can be made directly from the data in Table A–1 by—

1. Adding all X scores $(\Sigma X = 2{,}440)$.
2. Adding all Y scores $(\Sigma Y = 253)$.
3. Adding the products of each pair of X and Y scores $(\Sigma XY = 13{,}001)$.
4. Adding the squares of each X score $(\Sigma X^2 = 122{,}782)$.
5. Adding the squares of each Y score $(\Sigma Y^2 = 1{,}513)$.
6. Squaring the ΣX to obtain $(\Sigma X)^2 = 5{,}953{,}600$.
7. Squaring the ΣY to obtain $(\Sigma Y)^2 = 64{,}009$.
8. Substituting the values above in the raw score formula for r. The resultant value of r is 0.73.

Rank-Difference Correlation

The simplest method for estimating correlation coefficients when the number of paired observations is not too large is the rank-difference method. The formula for this estimate of correlation (ρ:rho) is

$$\rho = 1 - \frac{6\Sigma D^2}{N(N^2 - 1)},$$

where D is the difference in numerical ranks of the two scores comprising each pair. An illustrative computation using the rank data from Table A–9 is given in Table A–12.

THE MEAN DIFFERENCE

The correlation between preemployment test scores and supervisory ratings as in the preceding illustration is a validity coefficient. The value 0.68 tells us that the two measures, one obtained prior to employment (the predictor) and the other three months after employment (the criterion), are related.

Another evidence of this relationship may be obtained by examining the predictor scores of persons judged after three months to perform satisfactorily and unsatisfactorily. Specifically, this procedure involves (a) separating groups of persons eventually earning "high" and "low" criterion ratings and (b) comparing the mean predictor scores for these groups. If the preemployment test were valid, then persons receiving "favorable" supervisory ratings should as a group have earned higher test scores than persons receiving "unfavorable" ratings.

Of the several techniques for interpreting an obtained difference between means, the simplest provides an estimate of the percentage overlap between the two distributions from which the means were calculated. (Another statistic, the t ratio, although commonly used, is beyond the scope of the present discussion.)

In order to apply the percentage overlap procedure to our data, we must first separate the persons in the total sample into "high" and "low" subgroups based upon criterion ratings. Since the supervisory ratings were essentially normally distributed about a mean rating of 5.0 ("average performance"), we can regard ratings be-

TABLE A-12

Calculating the Rank-Difference Correlation between Preemployment
Test Score (X) and Supervisory Rating (Y)

Employee	$Rank_x$	$Rank_y$	D	D^2	Employee	$Rank_x$	$Rank_y$	D	D^2
A........	42.5	40.5	2.0	4.00	Z........	4.5	2.5	2.0	4.00
B........	47.5	16.5	31.0	961.00	AA.......	41.0	6.5	34.5	1,190.25
C........	24.0	25.5	1.5	1.25	BB.......	20.0	11.0	9.0	81.00
D........	27.5	34.5	7.0	49.00	CC.......	39.5	40.5	1.0	1.00
E........	16.0	16.5	0.5	0.25	DD.......	24.0	25.5	1.5	2.25
F........	33.5	40.5	6.5	42.25	EE.......	27.5	25.5	2.0	4.00
G........	8.0	40.5	32.5	1,056.25	FF.......	47.5	46.0	1.5	2.25
H........	9.0	11.0	2.0	4.00	GG.......	14.5	46.0	31.5	992.25
I........	14.5	16.5	*2.0	4.00	HH.......	35.0	34.5	0.5	0.25
J........	42.5	34.5	8.0	64.00	II........	6.0	2.5	3.5	12.25
K........	10.5	11.0	0.5	0.25	JJ........	1.0	2.5	1.5	2.25
L........	7.0	6.5	0.5	0.25	KK.......	36.5	34.5	2.0	4.00
M........	46.0	25.5	21.5	462.25	LL.......	3.0	6.5	3.5	12.25
N........	2.0	11.0	9.0	81.00	MM......	39.5	46.0	6.5	42.25
O........	12.0	2.5	9.5	90.25	NN.......	13.0	46.0	33.0	1,089.00
P........	36.5	34.5	2.0	4.00	OO......	17.5	16.5	1.0	1.00
Q........	30.5	25.5	5.0	25.00	PP.......	33.5	25.5	8.0	64.00
R........	4.5	6.5	2.0	4.00	QQ.......	24.0	40.5	15.5	240.25
S........	20.0	16.5	3.5	12.25	RR.......	10.5	11.0	0.5	0.25
T........	24.0	25.5	1.5	2.25	SS.......	45.0	40.5	4.5	20.25
U........	44.0	46.0	2.0	4.00	TT.......	17.5	16.5	1.0	1.00
V........	50.0	49.5	0.5	0.25	UU	24.0	25.5	1.5	2.25
W........	20.0	25.5	5.5	30.25	VV.......	49.0	49.5	0 5	0.25
X........	30.5	25.5	5.0	25.00	WW......	30.5	34.5	4.0	16.00
Y........	30.5	25.5	5.0	25.00	XX......	38.0	34.5	3.5	12.25

$$\Sigma D^2 = 6,748.75$$

$$= 1 - \frac{6\Sigma D^2}{N(N^2 - 1)}$$

$$= 1 - \frac{6(6,748.75)}{50(2,500 - 1)}$$

$$= 1 - \frac{40,492.5}{124,950.0}$$

$$= 1 - 0.32$$

$$= 0.68$$

tween 6.0–9.0 as "favorable" and those between 1.0–4.0 as "unfavorable."

Having thus defined the high (favorable ratings) and low (unfavorable ratings) criterion subgroups, the next step is to determine the percentage overlap *(0)* in the distributions of preemployment test scores for these subgroups. This requires a reorganization of the raw data originally presented in Table A–1 in the form shown in Table A–13.

TABLE A–13

Calculating the Percentage Overlap

	High Criterion Group (Supervisory Ratings: 6.0–9.0)			Low Criterion Group (Supervisory Ratings: 1.0–4.0)	
Employee	Preemployment Test Score		Employee	Preemployment Test Score	
B	35		A	40	
E	52		D	48	
H	57		F	46	
I	53		G	58	
K	56	$N = 19$	J	40	$N = 19$
L	60	$\bar{X}_h = 55.4$	P	40	$\bar{X}_l = 43.3$
N	65	$sd_h = 7.9$	U	39	$sd_l = 7.1$
O	55		V	31	
R	63		CC	42	
S	50		FF	35	
Z	63		GG	53	
AA	41		HH	45	
BB	50		KK	44	
II	62		MM	42	
JJ	68		NN	54	
LL	64		QQ	49	
OO	51		SS	38	
RR	56		VV	32	
TT	51		WW	47	

$$\bar{X}_h - \bar{X}_l = 55.4 - 43.3 = 12.1$$
$$sd_{av} = \frac{sd_h + sd_l}{2} = \frac{7.9 + 7.1}{2} = 7.5$$
$$\frac{\bar{X}_h - \bar{X}_l}{sd_{av}} = \frac{12.1}{7.5} = 1.61$$

The mean and standard deviation is calculated separately for the high and low criterion subgroups. (Verification of these values as shown in Table A–13 constitutes an easy review exercise.) To estimate the percentage overlap between the two preemployment test distributions, the difference between the two means is divided by the

TABLE A–14

Estimation of Percentage Overlap, 0, between Two Distributions from Means and Standard Deviations

$\dfrac{\bar{X}_h - \bar{X}_l}{sd_{av}.}$*	Percentage Overlap, 0	$\dfrac{\bar{X}_h - \bar{X}_l}{sd_{av}.}$*	Percentage Overlap, 0	$\dfrac{X_h - X_l}{sd_{av}.}$*	Percentage Overlap, 0
0.000	100	0.880	66	1.948	33
0.025	99	0.908	65	1.989	32
0.050	98	0.935	64	2.030	31
0.075	97	0.963	63	2.073	30
0.100	96	0.992	62	2.116	29
0.125	95	1.020	61	2.161	28
0.151	94	1.049	60	2.206	27
0.176	93	1.078	59	2.253	26
0.201	92	1.107	58	2.301	25
0.226	91	1.136	57	2.350	24
0.251	90	1.166	56	2.401	23
0.277	89	1.197	55	2.453	22
0.302	88	1.226	54	2.507	21
0.327	87	1.256	53	2.563	20
0.353	86	1.287	52	2.621	19
0.378	85	1.318	51	2.682	18
0.403	84	1.349	50	2.744	17
0.429	83	1.381	49	2.810	16
0.455	82	1.413	48	2.879	15
0.481	81	1.445	47	2.952	14
0.507	80	1.478	46	3.028	13
0.533	79	1.511	45	3.110	12
0.559	78	1.544	44	3.196	11
0.585	77	1.578	43	3.290	10
0.611	76	1.613	42	3.391	9
0.637	75	1.648	41	3.501	8
0.664	74	1.683	40	3.624	7
0.690	73	1.719	39	3.762	6
0.717	72	1.756	38	3.920	5
0.744	71	1.793	37	4.107	4
0.771	70	1.831	36	4.340	3
0.798	69	1.869	35	4.653	2
0.825	68	1.908	34	5.152	1
0.852	67				

* sd_{av} = average of the standard deviations = $\dfrac{sd_2 + sd_1}{2}$

Source: J. W. Tilton. The measurement of overlapping. *Journal of Educational Psychology*, 1937, 28, 656–662.

average of the two standard deviations and the resultant quotient is entered into Table A–14.[2]

Table A–14 estimates that distributions yielding a quotient of 1.61 overlap 42 percent. In other words, it is estimated that for 42 percent of the cases, the predictor scores will *not* distinguish between satisfactory and unsatisfactory criterion ratings. Conversely, it is estimated that the preemployment test can effectively separate potentially satisfactory from potentially unsatisfactory employees 58 percent of the time.

If a predictor were totally invalid, the estimate of 0 would, of course, be 100 percent. In this case, there would be complete overlapping between the distributions of predictor scores for the two criterion groups. The greater the validity, the lower the 0 until with perfect validity the two distributions of predictor scores are totally independent $(0 = 0.00)$.

---

[2] J. W. Tilton. The measurement of overlapping. *Journal of Educational Psychology*, 1937, **28,** 656–662.

B. Taylor-Russell Tables[1] for Group Prediction[2]

---

[1] H. C. Taylor & J. T. Russell. The relationship of validity coefficients. Pp. 565–578.

[2] Entries are the proportions of employees who will be satisfactory among those selected under specified conditions.

Proportion of Employees Considered Satisfactory = 0.05

	Selection Ratio										
r	*0.05*	*0.10*	*0.20*	*0.30*	*0.40*	*0.50*	*0.60*	*0.70*	*0.80*	*0.90*	*0.95*
0.00	0.05	0.05	0.05	0.05	0.05	0.05	0.05	0.05	0.05	0.05	0.05
0.05	0.06	0.06	0.06	0.06	0.06	0.05	0.05	0.05	0.05	0.05	0.05
0.10	0.07	0.07	0.07	0.06	0.06	0.06	0.06	0.05	0.05	0.05	0.05
0.15	0.09	0.08	0.07	0.07	0.07	0.06	0.06	0.06	0.05	0.05	0.05
0.20	0.11	0.09	0.08	0.08	0.07	0.07	0.06	0.06	0.06	0.05	0.05
0.25	0.12	0.11	0.09	0.08	0.08	0.07	0.07	0.06	0.06	0.05	0.05
0.30	0.14	0.12	0.10	0.09	0.08	0.07	0.07	0.06	0.06	0.05	0.05
0.35	0.17	0.14	0.11	0.10	0.09	0.08	0.07	0.06	0.06	0.05	0.05
0.40	0.19	0.16	0.12	0.10	0.09	0.08	0.07	0.07	0.06	0.05	0.05
0.45	0.22	0.17	0.13	0.11	0.10	0.08	0.08	0.07	0.06	0.06	0.05
0.50	0.24	0.19	0.15	0.12	0.10	0.09	0.08	0.07	0.06	0.06	0.05
0.55	0.28	0.22	0.16	0.13	0.11	0.09	0.08	0.07	0.06	0.06	0.05
0.60	0.31	0.24	0.17	0.13	0.11	0.09	0.08	0.07	0.06	0.06	0.05
0.65	0.35	0.26	0.18	0.14	0.11	0.10	0.08	0.07	0.06	0.06	0.05
0.70	0.39	0.29	0.20	0.15	0.12	0.10	0.08	0.07	0.06	0.06	0.05
0.75	0.44	0.32	0.21	0.15	0.12	0.10	0.08	0.07	0.06	0.06	0.05
0.80	0.50	0.35	0.22	0.16	0.12	0.10	0.08	0.07	0.06	0.06	0.05
0.85	0.56	0.39	0.23	0.16	0.12	0.10	0.08	0.07	0.06	0.06	0.05
0.90	0.64	0.43	0.24	0.17	0.13	0.10	0.08	0.07	0.06	0.06	0.05
0.95	0.73	0.47	0.25	0.17	0.13	0.10	0.08	0.07	0.06	0.06	0.05
1.00	1.00	0.50	0.25	0.17	0.13	0.10	0.08	0.07	0.06	0.06	0.05

Proportion of Employees Considered Satisfactory = 0.10

r	Selection Ratio										
	0.05	0.10	0.20	0.30	0.40	0.50	0.60	0.70	0.80	0.90	0.95
0.00	0.10	0.10	0.10	0.10	0.10	0.10	0.10	0.10	0.10	0.10	0.10
0.05	0.12	0.12	0.11	0.11	0.11	0.11	0.11	0.10	0.10	0.10	0.10
0.10	0.14	0.13	0.13	0.12	0.12	0.11	0.11	0.11	0.11	0.10	0.10
0.15	0.16	0.15	0.14	0.13	0.13	0.12	0.12	0.11	0.11	0.10	0.10
0.20	0.19	0.17	0.15	0.14	0.14	0.13	0.12	0.12	0.11	0.11	0.10
0.25	0.22	0.19	0.17	0.16	0.14	0.13	0.13	0.12	0.11	0.11	0.10
0.30	0.25	0.22	0.19	0.17	0.15	0.14	0.13	0.12	0.12	0.11	0.10
0.35	0.28	0.24	0.20	0.18	0.16	0.15	0.14	0.13	0.12	0.11	0.10
0.40	0.31	0.27	0.22	0.19	0.17	0.16	0.14	0.13	0.12	0.11	0.10
0.45	0.35	0.29	0.24	0.20	0.18	0.16	0.15	0.13	0.12	0.11	0.10
0.50	0.39	0.32	0.26	0.22	0.19	0.17	0.15	0.13	0.12	0.11	0.11
0.55	0.43	0.36	0.28	0.23	0.20	0.17	0.15	0.14	0.12	0.11	0.11
0.60	0.48	0.39	0.30	0.25	0.21	0.18	0.16	0.14	0.12	0.11	0.11
0.65	0.53	0.43	0.32	0.26	0.22	0.18	0.16	0.14	0.12	0.11	0.11
0.70	0.58	0.47	0.35	0.27	0.22	0.19	0.16	0.14	0.12	0.11	0.11
0.75	0.64	0.51	0.37	0.29	0.23	0.19	0.16	0.14	0.12	0.11	0.11
0.80	0.71	0.56	0.40	0.30	0.24	0.20	0.17	0.14	0.12	0.11	0.11
0.85	0.78	0.62	0.43	0.31	0.25	0.20	0.17	0.14	0.12	0.11	0.11
0.90	0.86	0.69	0.46	0.33	0.25	0.20	0.17	0.14	0.12	0.11	0.11
0.95	0.95	0.78	0.49	0.33	0.25	0.20	0.17	0.14	0.12	0.11	0.11
1.00	1.00	1.00	0.50	0.33	0.25	0.20	0.17	0.14	0.13	0.11	0.11

Proportion of Employees Considered Satisfactory = 0.20

	Selection Ratio										
r	0.05	0.10	0.20	0.30	0.40	0.50	0.60	0.70	0.80	0.90	0.95
0.00	0.20	0.20	0.20	0.20	0.20	0.20	0.20	0.20	0.20	0.20	0.20
0.05	0.23	0.23	0.22	0.22	0.21	0.21	0.21	0.21	0.20	0.20	0.20
0.10	0.26	0.25	0.24	0.23	0.23	0.22	0.22	0.21	0.21	0.21	0.20
0.15	0.30	0.28	0.26	0.25	0.24	0.23	0.23	0.22	0.21	0.21	0.20
0.20	0.33	0.31	0.28	0.27	0.26	0.25	0.24	0.23	0.22	0.21	0.21
0.25	0.37	0.34	0.31	0.29	0.27	0.26	0.24	0.23	0.22	0.21	0.21
0.30	0.41	0.37	0.33	0.30	0.28	0.27	0.25	0.24	0.23	0.21	0.21
0.35	0.45	0.41	0.36	0.32	0.30	0.28	0.26	0.24	0.23	0.22	0.21
0.40	0.49	0.44	0.38	0.34	0.31	0.29	0.27	0.25	0.23	0.22	0.21
0.45	0.54	0.48	0.41	0.36	0.33	0.30	0.28	0.26	0.24	0.22	0.21
0.50	0.59	0.52	0.44	0.38	0.35	0.31	0.29	0.26	0.24	0.22	0.21
0.55	0.63	0.56	0.47	0.41	0.36	0.32	0.29	0.27	0.24	0.22	0.21
0.60	0.68	0.60	0.50	0.43	0.38	0.34	0.30	0.27	0.24	0.22	0.21
0.65	0.73	0.64	0.53	0.45	0.39	0.35	0.31	0.27	0.25	0.22	0.21
0.70	0.79	0.69	0.56	0.48	0.41	0.36	0.31	0.28	0.25	0.22	0.21
0.75	0.84	0.74	0.60	0.50	0.43	0.37	0.32	0.28	0.25	0.22	0.21
0.80	0.89	0.79	0.64	0.53	0.45	0.38	0.33	0.28	0.25	0.22	0.21
0.85	0.94	0.85	0.69	0.56	0.47	0.39	0.33	0.28	0.25	0.22	0.21
0.90	0.98	0.91	0.75	0.60	0.48	0.40	0.33	0.29	0.25	0.22	0.21
0.95	1.00	0.97	0.82	0.64	0.50	0.40	0.33	0.29	0.25	0.22	0.21
1.00	1.00	1.00	1.00	0.67	0.50	0.40	0.33	0.29	0.25	0.22	0.21

Proportion of Employees Considered Satisfactory = 0.30

r	0.05	0.10	0.20	0.30	0.40	0.50	0.60	0.70	0.80	0.90	0.95
	Selection Ratio										
0.00	0.30	0.30	0.30	0.30	0.30	0.30	0.30	0.30	0.30	0.30	0.30
0.05	0.34	0.33	0.33	0.32	0.32	0.31	0.31	0.31	0.31	0.30	0.30
0.10	0.38	0.36	0.35	0.34	0.33	0.33	0.32	0.32	0.31	0.31	0.30
0.15	0.42	0.40	0.38	0.36	0.35	0.34	0.33	0.33	0.32	0.31	0.31
0.20	0.46	0.43	0.40	0.38	0.37	0.36	0.34	0.33	0.32	0.31	0.31
0.25	0.50	0.47	0.43	0.41	0.39	0.37	0.36	0.34	0.33	0.32	0.31
0.30	0.54	0.50	0.46	0.43	0.40	0.38	0.37	0.35	0.33	0.32	0.31
0.35	0.58	0.54	0.49	0.45	0.42	0.40	0.38	0.36	0.34	0.32	0.31
0.40	0.63	0.58	0.51	0.47	0.44	0.41	0.39	0.37	0.34	0.32	0.31
0.45	0.67	0.61	0.55	0.50	0.46	0.43	0.40	0.37	0.35	0.32	0.31
0.50	0.72	0.65	0.58	0.52	0.48	0.44	0.41	0.38	0.35	0.33	0.31
0.55	0.76	0.69	0.61	0.55	0.50	0.46	0.42	0.39	0.36	0.33	0.31
0.60	0.81	0.74	0.64	0.58	0.52	0.47	0.43	0.40	0.36	0.33	0.31
0.65	0.85	0.78	0.68	0.60	0.54	0.49	0.44	0.40	0.37	0.33	0.32
0.70	0.89	0.82	0.72	0.63	0.57	0.51	0.46	0.41	0.37	0.33	0.32
0.75	0.93	0.86	0.76	0.67	0.59	0.52	0.47	0.42	0.37	0.33	0.32
0.80	0.96	0.90	0.80	0.70	0.62	0.54	0.48	0.42	0.37	0.33	0.32
0.85	0.99	0.94	0.85	0.74	0.65	0.56	0.49	0.43	0.37	0.33	0.32
0.90	1.00	0.98	0.90	0.79	0.68	0.58	0.49	0.43	0.37	0.33	0.32
0.95	1.00	1.00	0.96	0.85	0.72	0.60	0.50	0.43	0.37	0.33	0.32
1.00	1.00	1.00	1.00	1.00	0.75	0.60	0.50	0.43	0.38	0.33	0.32

Proportion of Employees Considered Satisfactory = 0.40

r	0.05	0.10	0.20	0.30	0.40	0.50	0.60	0.70	0.80	0.90	0.95
						Selection Ratio					
0.00	0.40	0.40	0.40	0.40	0.40	0.40	0.40	0.40	0.40	0.40	0.40
0.05	0.44	0.43	0.43	0.42	0.42	0.42	0.41	0.41	0.41	0.40	0.40
0.10	0.48	0.47	0.46	0.45	0.44	0.43	0.42	0.42	0.41	0.41	0.40
0.15	0.52	0.50	0.48	0.47	0.46	0.45	0.44	0.43	0.42	0.41	0.41
0.20	0.57	0.54	0.51	0.49	0.48	0.46	0.45	0.44	0.43	0.41	0.41
0.25	0.61	0.58	0.54	0.51	0.49	0.48	0.46	0.45	0.43	0.42	0.41
0.30	0.65	0.61	0.57	0.54	0.51	0.49	0.47	0.46	0.44	0.42	0.41
0.35	0.69	0.65	0.60	0.56	0.53	0.51	0.49	0.47	0.45	0.42	0.41
0.40	0.73	0.69	0.63	0.59	0.56	0.53	0.50	0.48	0.45	0.43	0.41
0.45	0.77	0.72	0.66	0.61	0.58	0.54	0.51	0.49	0.46	0.43	0.42
0.50	0.81	0.76	0.69	0.64	0.60	0.56	0.53	0.49	0.46	0.43	0.42
0.55	0.85	0.79	0.72	0.67	0.62	0.58	0.54	0.50	0.47	0.44	0.42
0.60	0.89	0.83	0.75	0.69	0.64	0.60	0.55	0.51	0.48	0.44	0.42
0.65	0.92	0.87	0.79	0.72	0.67	0.62	0.57	0.52	0.48	0.44	0.42
0.70	0.95	0.90	0.82	0.76	0.69	0.64	0.58	0.53	0.49	0.44	0.42
0.75	0.97	0.93	0.86	0.79	0.72	0.66	0.60	0.54	0.49	0.44	0.42
0.80	0.99	0.96	0.89	0.82	0.75	0.68	0.61	0.55	0.49	0.44	0.42
0.85	1.00	0.98	0.93	0.86	0.79	0.71	0.63	0.56	0.50	0.44	0.42
0.90	1.00	1.00	0.97	0.91	0.82	0.74	0.65	0.57	0.50	0.44	0.42
0.95	1.00	1.00	0.99	0.96	0.87	0.77	0.66	0.57	0.50	0.44	0.42
1.00	1.00	1.00	1.00	1.00	1.00	0.80	0.67	0.57	0.50	0.44	0.42

| | Proportion of Employees Considered Satisfactory = 0.50 | | | | | | | | | | |
| | *Selection Ratio* | | | | | | | | | | |
r	0.05	0.10	0.20	0.30	0.40	0.50	0.60	0.70	0.80	0.90	0.95
0.00	0.50	0.50	0.50	0.50	0.50	0.50	0.50	0.50	0.50	0.50	0.50
0.05	0.54	0.54	0.53	0.52	0.52	0.52	0.51	0.51	0.51	0.50	0.50
0.10	0.58	0.57	0.56	0.55	0.54	0.53	0.53	0.52	0.51	0.51	0.50
0.15	0.63	0.61	0.58	0.57	0.56	0.55	0.54	0.53	0.52	0.51	0.51
0.20	0.67	0.64	0.61	0.59	0.58	0.56	0.55	0.54	0.53	0.52	0.51
0.25	0.70	0.67	0.64	0.62	0.60	0.58	0.56	0.55	0.54	0.52	0.51
0.30	0.74	0.71	0.67	0.64	0.62	0.60	0.58	0.56	0.54	0.52	0.51
0.35	0.78	0.74	0.70	0.66	0.64	0.61	0.59	0.57	0.55	0.53	0.51
0.40	0.82	0.78	0.73	0.69	0.66	0.63	0.61	0.58	0.56	0.53	0.52
0.45	0.85	0.81	0.75	0.71	0.68	0.65	0.62	0.59	0.56	0.53	0.52
0.50	0.88	0.84	0.78	0.74	0.70	0.67	0.63	0.60	0.57	0.54	0.52
0.55	0.91	0.87	0.81	0.76	0.72	0.69	0.65	0.61	0.58	0.54	0.52
0.60	0.94	0.90	0.84	0.79	0.75	0.70	0.66	0.62	0.59	0.54	0.52
0.65	0.96	0.92	0.87	0.82	0.77	0.73	0.68	0.64	0.59	0.55	0.52
0.70	0.98	0.95	0.90	0.85	0.80	0.75	0.70	0.65	0.60	0.55	0.53
0.75	0.99	0.97	0.92	0.87	0.82	0.77	0.72	0.66	0.61	0.55	0.53
0.80	1.00	0.99	0.95	0.90	0.85	0.80	0.73	0.67	0.61	0.55	0.53
0.85	1.00	0.99	0.97	0.94	0.88	0.82	0.76	0.69	0.62	0.55	0.53
0.90	1.00	1.00	0.99	0.97	0.92	0.86	0.78	0.70	0.62	0.56	0.53
0.95	1.00	1.00	1.00	0.99	0.96	0.90	0.81	0.71	0.63	0.56	0.53
1.00	1.00	1.00	1.00	1.00	1.00	1.00	0.83	0.71	0.63	0.56	0.53

Proportion of Employees Considered Satisfactory = 0.60

					Selection Ratio						
r	0.05	0.10	0.20	0.30	0.40	0.50	0.60	0.70	0.80	0.90	0.95
0.00	0.60	0.60	0.60	0.60	0.60	0.60	0.60	0.60	0.60	0.60	0.60
0.05	0.64	0.63	0.63	0.62	0.62	0.62	0.61	0.61	0.61	0.60	0.60
0.10	0.68	0.67	0.65	0.64	0.64	0.63	0.63	0.62	0.61	0.61	0.60
0.15	0.71	0.70	0.68	0.67	0.66	0.65	0.64	0.63	0.62	0.61	0.61
0.20	0.75	0.73	0.71	0.69	0.67	0.66	0.65	0.64	0.63	0.62	0.61
0.25	0.78	0.76	0.73	0.71	0.69	0.68	0.66	0.65	0.63	0.62	0.61
0.30	0.82	0.79	0.76	0.73	0.71	0.69	0.68	0.66	0.64	0.62	0.61
0.35	0.85	0.82	0.78	0.75	0.73	0.71	0.69	0.67	0.65	0.63	0.62
0.40	0.88	0.85	0.81	0.78	0.75	0.73	0.70	0.68	0.66	0.63	0.62
0.45	0.90	0.87	0.83	0.80	0.77	0.74	0.72	0.69	0.66	0.64	0.62
0.50	0.93	0.90	0.86	0.82	0.79	0.76	0.73	0.70	0.67	0.64	0.62
0.55	0.95	0.92	0.88	0.84	0.81	0.78	0.75	0.71	0.68	0.64	0.62
0.60	0.96	0.94	0.90	0.87	0.83	0.80	0.76	0.73	0.69	0.65	0.63
0.65	0.98	0.96	0.92	0.89	0.85	0.82	0.78	0.74	0.70	0.65	0.63
0.70	0.99	0.97	0.94	0.91	0.87	0.84	0.80	0.75	0.71	0.66	0.63
0.75	0.99	0.99	0.96	0.93	0.90	0.86	0.81	0.77	0.71	0.66	0.63
0.80	1.00	0.99	0.98	0.95	0.92	0.88	0.83	0.78	0.72	0.66	0.63
0.85	1.00	1.00	0.99	0.97	0.95	0.91	0.86	0.80	0.73	0.66	0.63
0.90	1.00	1.00	1.00	0.99	0.97	0.94	0.88	0.82	0.74	0.67	0.63
0.95	1.00	1.00	1.00	1.00	0.99	0.97	0.92	0.84	0.75	0.67	0.63
1.00	1.00	1.00	1.00	1.00	1.00	1.00	1.00	0.86	0.75	0.67	0.63

Proportion of Employees Considered Satisfactory = 0.70

	Selection Ratio										
r	0.05	0.10	0.20	0.30	0.40	0.50	0.60	0.70	0.80	0.90	0.95
0.00	0.70	0.70	0.70	0.70	0.70	0.70	0.70	0.70	0.70	0.70	0.70
0.05	0.73	0.73	0.72	0.72	0.72	0.71	0.71	0.71	0.71	0.70	0.70
0.10	0.77	0.76	0.75	0.74	0.73	0.73	0.72	0.72	0.71	0.71	0.70
0.15	0.80	0.79	0.77	0.76	0.75	0.74	0.73	0.73	0.72	0.71	0.71
0.20	0.83	0.81	0.79	0.78	0.77	0.76	0.75	0.74	0.73	0.71	0.71
0.25	0.86	0.84	0.81	0.80	0.78	0.77	0.76	0.75	0.73	0.72	0.71
0.30	0.88	0.86	0.84	0.82	0.80	0.78	0.77	0.75	0.74	0.72	0.71
0.35	0.91	0.89	0.86	0.83	0.82	0.80	0.78	0.76	0.75	0.73	0.71
0.40	0.93	0.91	0.88	0.85	0.83	0.81	0.79	0.77	0.75	0.73	0.72
0.45	0.94	0.93	0.90	0.87	0.85	0.83	0.81	0.78	0.76	0.73	0.72
0.50	0.96	0.94	0.91	0.89	0.87	0.84	0.82	0.80	0.77	0.74	0.72
0.55	0.97	0.96	0.93	0.91	0.88	0.86	0.83	0.81	0.78	0.74	0.72
0.60	0.98	0.97	0.95	0.92	0.90	0.87	0.85	0.82	0.79	0.75	0.73
0.65	0.99	0.98	0.96	0.94	0.92	0.89	0.86	0.83	0.80	0.75	0.73
0.70	1.00	0.99	0.97	0.96	0.93	0.91	0.88	0.84	0.80	0.76	0.73
0.75	1.00	1.00	0.98	0.97	0.95	0.92	0.89	0.86	0.81	0.76	0.73
0.80	1.00	1.00	0.99	0.98	0.97	0.94	0.91	0.87	0.82	0.77	0.73
0.85	1.00	1.00	1.00	0.99	0.98	0.96	0.93	0.89	0.84	0.77	0.74
0.90	1.00	1.00	1.00	1.00	0.99	0.98	0.95	0.91	0.85	0.78	0.74
0.95	1.00	1.00	1.00	1.00	1.00	0.99	0.98	0.94	0.86	0.78	0.74
1.00	1.00	1.00	1.00	1.00	1.00	1.00	1.00	1.00	0.88	0.78	0.74

Proportion of Employees Considered Satisfactory = 0.80

	Selection Ratio										
r	0.05	0.10	0.20	0.30	0.40	0.50	0.60	0.70	0.80	0.90	0.95
0.00	0.80	0.80	0.80	0.80	0.80	0.80	0.80	0.80	0.80	0.80	0.80
0.05	0.83	0.82	0.82	0.82	0.81	0.81	0.81	0.81	0.81	0.80	0.80
0.10	0.85	0.85	0.84	0.83	0.83	0.82	0.82	0.81	0.81	0.81	0.80
0.15	0.88	0.87	0.86	0.85	0.84	0.83	0.83	0.82	0.82	0.81	0.81
0.20	0.90	0.89	0.87	0.86	0.85	0.84	0.84	0.83	0.82	0.81	0.81
0.25	0.92	0.91	0.89	0.88	0.87	0.86	0.85	0.84	0.83	0.82	0.81
0.30	0.94	0.92	0.90	0.89	0.88	0.87	0.86	0.84	0.83	0.82	0.81
0.35	0.95	0.94	0.92	0.90	0.89	0.89	0.87	0.85	0.84	0.82	0.81
0.40	0.96	0.95	0.93	0.92	0.90	0.89	0.88	0.86	0.85	0.83	0.82
0.45	0.97	0.96	0.95	0.93	0.92	0.90	0.89	0.87	0.85	0.83	0.82
0.50	0.98	0.97	0.96	0.94	0.93	0.91	0.90	0.88	0.86	0.84	0.82
0.55	0.99	0.98	0.97	0.95	0.94	0.92	0.91	0.89	0.87	0.84	0.82
0.60	0.99	0.99	0.98	0.96	0.95	0.94	0.92	0.90	0.87	0.84	0.83
0.65	1.00	0.99	0.98	0.97	0.96	0.95	0.93	0.91	0.88	0.85	0.83
0.70	1.00	1.00	0.99	0.98	0.97	0.96	0.94	0.92	0.89	0.85	0.83
0.75	1.00	1.00	1.00	0.99	0.98	0.97	0.95	0.93	0.90	0.86	0.83
0.80	1.00	1.00	1.00	1.00	0.99	0.98	0.96	0.94	0.91	0.87	0.84
0.85	1.00	1.00	1.00	1.00	1.00	0.99	0.98	0.96	0.92	0.87	0.84
0.90	1.00	1.00	1.00	1.00	1.00	1.00	0.99	0.97	0.94	0.88	0.84
0.95	1.00	1.00	1.00	1.00	1.00	1.00	1.00	0.99	0.96	0.89	0.84
1.00	1.00	1.00	1.00	1.00	1.00	1.00	1.00	1.00	1.00	0.89	0.84

Proportion of Employees Considered Satisfactory = 0.90

	Selection Ratio										
r	0.05	0.10	0.20	0.30	0.40	0.50	0.60	0.70	0.80	0.90	0.95
0.00	0.90	0.90	0.90	0.90	0.90	0.90	0.90	0.90	0.90	0.90	0.90
0.05	0.92	0.91	0.91	0.91	0.91	0.91	0.91	0.90	0.90	0.90	0.90
0.10	0.93	0.93	0.92	0.92	0.92	0.91	0.91	0.91	0.91	0.90	0.90
0.15	0.95	0.94	0.93	0.93	0.92	0.92	0.92	0.91	0.91	0.91	0.90
0.20	0.96	0.95	0.94	0.94	0.93	0.93	0.92	0.92	0.91	0.91	0.90
0.25	0.97	0.96	0.95	0.95	0.94	0.93	0.93	0.92	0.92	0.91	0.91
0.30	0.98	0.97	0.96	0.95	0.95	0.94	0.94	0.93	0.92	0.91	0.91
0.35	0.98	0.98	0.97	0.96	0.95	0.95	0.94	0.93	0.93	0.92	0.91
0.40	0.99	0.98	0.98	0.97	0.96	0.95	0.95	0.94	0.93	0.92	0.91
0.45	0.99	0.99	0.98	0.98	0.97	0.96	0.95	0.94	0.93	0.92	0.91
0.50	1.00	0.99	0.99	0.98	0.97	0.97	0.96	0.95	0.94	0.92	0.92
0.55	1.00	1.00	0.99	0.99	0.98	0.97	0.97	0.96	0.94	0.93	0.92
0.60	1.00	1.00	0.99	0.99	0.99	0.98	0.97	0.96	0.95	0.93	0.92
0.65	1.00	1.00	1.00	0.99	0.99	0.98	0.98	0.97	0.96	0.94	0.92
0.70	1.00	1.00	1.00	1.00	0.99	0.99	0.98	0.97	0.96	0.94	0.93
0.75	1.00	1.00	1.00	1.00	1.00	0.99	0.99	0.98	0.97	0.95	0.93
0.80	1.00	1.00	1.00	1.00	1.00	1.00	0.99	0.99	0.97	0.95	0.93
0.85	1.00	1.00	1.00	1.00	1.00	1.00	1.00	0.99	0.98	0.96	0.94
0.90	1.00	1.00	1.00	1.00	1.00	1.00	1.00	1.00	0.99	0.97	0.94
0.95	1.00	1.00	1.00	1.00	1.00	1.00	1.00	1.00	1.00	0.98	0.94
1.00	1.00	1.00	1.00	1.00	1.00	1.00	1.00	1.00	1.00	1.00	0.95

C.

Expectancy Tables[1] for Individual Prediction[2]

Percent of Employees Considered Satisfactory = 30%

	Predictor Category				
r	Upper $\frac{1}{5}$	Next $\frac{1}{5}$	Middle $\frac{1}{5}$	Next $\frac{1}{5}$	Bottom $\frac{1}{5}$
0.15	38	32	30	28	22
0.20	40	34	29	26	21
0.25	43	35	29	24	19
0.30	46	35	29	24	16
0.35	49	36	29	22	14
0.40	51	37	28	21	12
0.45	55	38	28	20	10
0.50	58	38	27	18	09
0.55	61	39	27	17	07
0.60	64	40	26	15	05
0.65	68	41	25	13	04
0.70	72	42	23	11	03
0.75	76	43	22	09	02
0.80	80	44	20	06	01
0.85	85	45	17	04	00
0.90	90	46	12	02	00
0.95	96	48	07	00	00

[1] C. H. Lawshe, R. A. Bolda, R. L. Brune, & G. Auclair. Expectancy charts III. Pp. 545–599.

[2] Entries are the probabilities of success of individual employees under specified conditions.

513

Percent of Employees Considered Satisfactory = 40%

r	Upper ⅕	Next ⅕	Middle ⅕	Next ⅕	Bottom ⅕
	Predictor Category				
0.15	48	44	40	36	32
0.20	51	45	40	35	30
0.25	54	44	40	34	28
0.30	57	46	40	33	24
0.35	60	47	39	32	22
0.40	63	48	39	31	19
0.45	66	49	39	29	17
0.50	69	50	39	28	14
0.55	72	53	38	26	12
0.60	75	53	38	24	10
0.65	79	55	37	22	08
0.70	82	58	36	19	06
0.75	86	59	35	17	04
0.80	89	61	34	14	02
0.85	93	64	32	10	01
0.90	97	69	29	06	00
0.95	100	76	23	02	00

Percent of Employees Considered Satisfactory = 50%

r	Upper ⅕	Next ⅕	Middle ⅕	Next ⅕	Bottom ⅕
	Predictor Category				
0.15	58	54	50	46	42
0.20	61	55	50	45	39
0.25	64	56	50	44	36
0.30	67	57	50	43	33
0.35	70	58	50	42	30
0.40	73	59	50	41	28
0.45	75	60	50	40	25
0.50	78	62	50	38	22
0.55	81	64	50	36	19
0.60	84	65	50	35	16
0.65	87	67	50	33	13
0.70	90	70	50	30	10
0.75	92	72	50	28	08
0.80	95	75	50	25	05
0.85	97	80	50	20	03
0.90	99	85	50	15	01
0.95	100	93	50	08	00

Percent of Employees Considered Satisfactory = 60%

	Predictor Category				
	Upper $\frac{1}{5}$	Next $\frac{1}{5}$	Middle $\frac{1}{5}$	Next $\frac{1}{5}$	Bottom $\frac{1}{5}$
r					
0.15	68	64	60	57	52
0.20	71	63	60	56	48
0.25	73	65	60	55	48
0.30	76	66	61	54	44
0.35	78	68	61	53	40
0.40	81	69	61	52	37
0.45	83	71	61	51	34
0.50	86	72	62	50	31
0.55	88	74	62	48	28
0.60	90	76	62	47	25
0.65	92	78	63	45	21
0.70	94	80	64	43	18
0.75	96	83	65	42	14
0.80	98	86	66	39	11
0.85	99	90	68	36	07
0.90	100	94	71	31	03
0.95	100	98	77	24	00

Percent of Employees Considered Satisfactory = 70%

	Predictor Category				
	Upper $\frac{1}{5}$	Next $\frac{1}{5}$	Middle $\frac{1}{5}$	Next $\frac{1}{5}$	Bottom $\frac{1}{5}$
r					
0.15	77	73	69	69	62
0.20	79	75	70	67	59
0.25	81	75	71	65	58
0.30	84	76	71	65	54
0.35	86	78	71	64	52
0.40	88	79	72	63	49
0.45	90	80	72	63	46
0.50	91	82	73	62	42
0.55	93	83	73	61	39
0.60	95	85	74	60	36
0.65	96	87	75	59	32
0.70	97	89	77	58	29
0.75	98	91	78	57	25
0.80	99	94	80	56	20
0.85	100	96	83	55	16
0.90	100	98	88	54	10
0.95	100	100	93	52	04

References

References

Adams, J. S. Inequity in social exchange. In L. Berkowitz (Ed.), *Advances in experimental social psychology*. Vol. 2. New York: Academic Press, 1965.

Adams, J. S., & Rosenbaum, W. B. The relationship of worker productivity to cognitive dissonance about wage inequities. *Journal of Applied Psychology*, 1962, **46**, 161–164.

Adler, A. D. The psychology of repeated accidents in industry. *American Journal of Psychiatry*, 1941, **98**, 99–101.

Albright, L. E., Glennon, J. R., & Smith, W. J. *The use of psychological tests in industry*. Cleveland: Howard Allen, 1963.

American Psychological Association. Bylaws, Article I.1, 1964.

American Psychological Association. Technical recommendations for psychological tests and diagnostic techniques. *Supplement to the Psychological Bulletin*, 1954, **51** (2), pt. 2.

Anderson, L. R., & Fiedler, F. E. The effect of participatory and supervisory leadership on group creativity. *Journal of Applied Psychology*, 1964, **48**, 227–236.

Anonymous. Job description of a bank clerk's wife. *The Dime*, Union Dime Savings Bank. Reprinted in *Personnel Journal*, 1948, **27**, 79–80.

Argyris, C. *Understanding organizational behavior*. Homewood, Ill.: Dorsey Press, 1960.

Ashour, A. S. The contingency model of leadership effectiveness: An evaluation. *Organizational Behavior and Human Performance*, 1973, **9**, 339–355.

Axelrod, J. N. Induced moods and attitudes towards products. *Journal of Advertising Research*, 1963, **3**, 19–24.

Babarik, P. Automobile accidents and driver reaction patterns. *Journal of Applied Psychology*, 1968, **52**, 49–54.

Baier, D. E., & Dugan, R. D. Factors in sales success. *Journal of Applied Psychology*, 1957, **41**, 37–40.

Baker, K. H. Pre-experimental set in distraction experiments. *Journal of General Psychology*, 1937, **16**, 471–486.

Barach, J. A.   Self confidence and reactions to television commercials.   In D. F. Cox (Ed.), *Risk taking and information handling in consumer behavior.* Boston: Division of Research, Harvard University, 1967. Pp. 428–441.

Bartz, A. E.   Attention value as a function of illuminant color change. *Journal of Applied Psychology*, 1957, **41**, 82–84.

Bass, B. M.   Leadership opinions as forecasts of supervisory success: A replication. *Personnel Psychology*, 1958, **11**, 515–518.

Bass, B. M.   *Organizational psychology.* Boston: Allyn & Bacon, 1965.

Bauer, R. W., Cassatt, R. K., Corona, B. M., & Warhurst, F., Jr.   Panel layout for rectilinear instruments. *Human Factors,* 1966, **8**, 493–497.

Bauman, J. N.   How the professional salesman makes his approach. *Sales Management,* 1955, **81**, 58.

Bavelas, A.   Cited in N. R. F. Maier, *Psychology in Industry.* Boston: Houghton Mifflin, 1946. P. 227.

Bavelas, A.   Communication patterns in task oriented groups. *Journal of the Accoustical Society of America,* 1950, **22**, 725–730.

Baxter, B., Taaffe, A. A., & Hughes, J. F.   A training evaluation study. *Personnel Psychology*, 1953, **6**, 403–417.

Belbin, E., & Shimmin, S.   Training the middle aged for inspection work. *Occupational Psychology,* 1964, **38**, 49–57.

Bennett, G. K.   Factors affecting the value of validation studies. *Personnel Psychology,* 1969, **22**, 265–268.

Bennett, G. K., Seashore, H. G., & Wesman, A. G.   *Mechanical reasoning test.* New York: The Psychological Corporation, 1947.

Bentz, V. J.   The Sears experience in the investigation, description, and prediction of executive behavior. In J. A. Myers (Ed.), *Predicting managerial success.* Ann Arbor: Foundation for Research on Human Behavior, 1968. Pp. 59–152.

Bergum, B. O., & Lehr, D. J.   *Vigilance performance as a function of task and environmental variables.* Fort Bliss, Tex.: U.S. Army Air Defense Human Resources Unit, 1962.

Biesheuval, S.   Personnel selection. *Annual Review of Psychology,* 1965, **16**, 295–324.

Bills, M. A.   Relation of mental alertness test score to position and permanency in company. *Journal of Applied Psychology,* 1923, **7**, 154–156.

Bills, M. A.   A tool for selection that has stood the test of time. In L. L. Thurstone (Ed.), *Applications of Psychology.* New York: Harper & Bros., 1952. P. 133.

Blake, R. R., & Mouton, J. S. *The managerial grid.* Houston: Gulf, 1964.

Blake, R. R., Mouton, J. S., Barnes, L. B., & Greiner, L. E. Breakthrough in organization development. *Harvard Business Review,* 1964, **42**, 133–155.

Blum, M. L., & Russ, J. A study of employee attitudes towards various incentives. *Personnel,* 1942, **19**, 438–444.

Bolster, B. I., & Springbett, B. M. The reaction of interviewers to favorable and unfavorable information. *Journal of Applied Psychology,* 1961, **45**, 97–103.

Boring, E. G. *Psychology for the armed forces.* Washington, D.C.: Infantry Journal, 1945. P. 244.

Bray, D. W., & Campbell, R. J. Selection of salesmen by means of an assessment center. *Journal of Applied Psychology,* 1968, **52**, 36–41.

Bray, D. W., & Moses, J. L. Personnel selection. *Annual Review of Psychology,* 1972, **23**, 545–576.

Brayfield, A. H., & Crockett, W. Employee attitudes and employee performance. *Psychological Bulletin,* 1955, **52**, 396–424.

Brayfield, A. H., Wells, R. V., & Strate, M. W. Interrelationships among measures of job satisfaction and general satisfaction. *Journal of Applied Psychology,* 1957, **41**, 201–205.

Broadbent, D. E., & Gregory, M. Division of attention and the division theory of signal detection. *Proceedings of the Royal Society* (London), 1963, 158.

Broadbent, D. E., & Little, E. A. J. Effects of noise reduction in a work situation. *Occupational Psychology,* 1960, **34**, 133–140.

Brogden, H. E., & Taylor, E. K. The dollar criterion—applying the cost accounting concept to criterion construction. *Personnel Psychology,* 1950, **3**, 133–154.

Brooks, J. *Consumer Reports,* 1958, **23**, 7–10.

Brown, P. L., & Berdie, R. P. Driver behavior and scores on the MMPI. *Journal of Applied Psychology,* 1960, **44**, 18–21.

Brown, R. L. Wrapper influence on the perception of freshness of bread. *Journal of Applied Psychology,* 1958, **42**, 257–260.

Bunker, D. R. Individual applications of laboratory training. *Journal of Applied Behavioral Science,* 1965, **1**, 131–148.

Burchinal, L. G. Personality characteristics and sample bias. *Journal of Applied Psychology,* 1960, **44**, 172–174.

Burnett, F. *An experimental investigation into repetitive work.* Industrial Fatigue Research Board Report No. 30. London: H. M. Stationary Office, 1925.

Buros, O. K. (Ed.) *The seventh mental measurements yearbook.* Highland Park, N.J.: Gryphon Press, 1972.

Campbell, J. P. Personnel training and development. *Annual Review of Psychology,* 1971, **22,** 590.

Campbell, J. P., & Dunnette, M. D. Effectiveness of T-group experiences in managerial training and development. *Psychological Bulletin,* 1968, **70,** 73–104.

Campbell, J. P., Dunnette, M. D., Lawler, E. E., & Weick, K. E. *Managerial behavior, performance, and effectiveness.* New York: McGraw-Hill, 1970.

Cardoza, R. N. An experimental study of consumer effort, expectation, and satisfaction. *Journal of Marketing Research,* 1965, **2,** 244–249.

Carroll, S. J. Beauty, bias, and business. *Personnel Administration,* 1969, **32,** 21–25.

Carroll, S. J., Jr., & Taylor, W. H., Jr. A study of the validity of a self-observational central signaling method of work sampling. *Personnel Psychology,* 1968, **21,** 359–364.

Cartwright, D. Risk taking by individuals and groups: An assessment of research employing choice dilemmas. *Journal of Personality and Social Psychology,* 1971, **20,** 361–378.

Catalanello, R. F., & Kirkpatrick, D. L. Evaluating training programs—the state of the art. *Training Development Journal,* 1968, **22,** 2–9.

Chapanis, A. On the allocations of functions between men and machines. *Occupational Psychology,* 1965, **39,** 1–11.

Cleveland, E. A. Sales personnel research, 1935–1945: A review. *Personnel Psychology,* 1948, **1,** 211–255.

Collins, B. E., & Guetzkow, H. *A social psychology of group processes for decision making.* New York: Wiley, 1964.

Colquhoun, W. P., & Baddeley, A. D. Role of pretest expectancy in vigilance decrement. *Journal of Experimental Psychology,* 1964, **68,** 156–160.

Connell, L. The effect of heat upon the performance of men in high speed aircraft: A critical review. USN Special Devices Center Report 151-1-17, 1948.

Conrad, R., & Longman, D. J. A standard typewriter versus chord keyboard—an experimental comparison. *Ergonomics,* 1965, **8,** 77–88.

Costello, T. W., & Zalkind, S. S. *Psychology in administration.* Englewood Cliffs, N.J.: Prentice-Hall, 1963.

Cox, D. F., & Bauer, R. A. Self-confidence and persuasibility. In D. F. Cox (Ed.), *Risk taking and information handling in consumer be-*

havior. Boston: Division of Research, Harvard University, 1967. Pp. 428–441.

Crane, L. E.   How product appeal and program affect attitudes toward commercials. *Journal of Advertising Research*, 1964, **4**, 15–18.

Cunningham, J. W., & McCormick, E. J.   *Worker-oriented job variables: Their factor structure*. Lafayette, Ind.: Occupational Research Center, Purdue University, July 1964.

Cunningham, S. M.   Perceived risk and brand loyalty. In D. F. Cox (Ed.), *Risk taking and information handling in consumer behavior*. Boston: Division of Research, Harvard University, 1967. Pp. 507–523.

Davis, K.   *Human relations at work, the dynamics of organizational behavior*. New York: McGraw-Hill, 1967.

Deese, J.   Changes in visual performance after visual work. USAF, Wright Air Development Center, Technical Report 57–285, 1957.

Dichter, E.   Psychology in market research. *Harvard Business Review*, 1947, **25**, 432–443.

Dichter, E.   A psychological view of advertising effectiveness. *Journal of Marketing*, 1949, **14**, 61–66.

Dill, W. R.   A new environment for training decision-makers—the Carnegie management game. In E. A. Fleishman (Ed.), *Studies in personnel and industrial psychology*. Homewood, Ill.: Dorsey Press, 1967.

Drake, C. A.   Accident proneness: A hypothesis. *Character and Personality*, 1940, **8**, 335–341.

Dubin, R.   Stability of human organizations. In M. Haire (Ed.), *Modern organizational theory*. New York: Wiley, 1959.

Dunnette, M. D.   A modified model for test validation and selection research. *Journal of Applied Psychology*, 1963, **47**, 317–323.

Dunnette, M. D.   A note on the criterion. *Journal of Applied Psychology*, 1963, **47**, 251–254.

Dunnette, M. D.   Personnel selection and job placement of the disadvantaged: Issues, problems, and suggestions. Office of Naval Research Technical Report No. 4001, 1970.

Dunnette, M. D., & Bass, B. M.   Behavioral scientists and personnel management. *Industrial Relations*, 1963, **2**, 115–130.

Dunnette, M. D., Campbell, J., & Hakel, M.   Factors contributing to job satisfaction and job dissatisfaction in six occupational groups. *Organizational Behavior and Human Performance*, 1967, **2**, 143–174.

Dunnette, M. D., & Kirchner, W. K.   Psychological test differences between industrial salesmen and retail salesmen. *Journal of Applied Psychology*, 1960, **44**, 121–125.

Dunnette, M. D., & Maetzold, J.   Use of a weighted application blank in hiring seasonal employees. *Journal of Applied Psychology,* 1955, **39,** 308–310.

Ehrle, R. A.   Quantification of biographical data for predicting vocational rehabilitation success. *Journal of Applied Psychology,* 1964, **48,** 171–174.

Ewell, J. M.   *Safety Bulletin.* Cincinnati: Proctor & Gamble, 1956.

Fay, E. J., & Middleton, W. C.   Relationship between sales ability and rating of transcribed voices of salesmen. *Journal of Applied Psychology,* 1942, **26,** 499–509.

Feinberg, M. R., & Lefkowitz, J.   Image of industrial psychology among corporate executives. *American Psychologist,* 1962, **17,** 109–111.

Ferber, R.   Item nonresponse in a consumer survey. *Public Opinion Quarterly,* 1966, **30,** 399–415.

Ferguson, L. W.   Ability, interest, and aptitude. *Journal of Applied Psychology,* 1960, **44,** 126–131.

Festinger, L.   *A theory of cognitive dissonance.* Evanston: Row, Peterson, 1957.

Fiedler, F. E.   A contingency model of leadership effectiveness. In L. Berkowitz (Ed.), *Advances in experimental social psychology.* New York: Academic Press, 1964.

Fiedler, F. E.   Engineer the job to fit the manager. *Harvard Business Review* 1965, **43,** 115–122.

Fiedler, F. E.   The effect of leadership and cultural heterogeneity on group performance: A test of the contingency model. *Journal of Experimental Social Psychology,* 1966, **2,** 237–264.

Fiedler, F. E.   *A theory of leadership effectiveness.* New York: McGraw-Hill, 1967.

Fiedler, F. E.   Validation and extension of the contingency model of leadership effectiveness: A review of empirical findings. *Psychological Bulletin,* 1971, **76,** 128–148.

Flanagan, J. C.   Critical requirements: A new approach to employee evaluation. *Personnel Psychology,* 1949, **2,** 419–425.

Flanagan, J. C.   Flanagan aptitude classification tests. *Examiner manual.* Chicago: Science Research Associates, 1959.

Fleishman, E. A.   An experimental consumer panel technique. *Journal of Applied Psychology,* 1951, **35,** 133–135.

Fleishman, E. A.   *Leadership climate and supervisory behavior.* Columbus: Personnel Research Board, Ohio State University, 1951.

Fleishman, E. A.   The description of supervisory behavior. *Journal of Applied Psychology,* 1953, **38,** 1–6.

Fleishman, E. A.   Leadership climate, human relations training, and supervisory behavior. *Personnel Psychology,* 1955, **6,** 205–222.

Fleishman, E. A.   Attitude versus skill factors in work group productivity. *Personnel Psychology,* 1965, **17,** 253–266.

Fleishman, E. A., & Berniger, J.   One way to reduce office turnover. *Personnel,* 1960, **37,** 63–69.

Fleishman, E. A., & Harris, E. F.   Patterns of leadership behavior related to employee grievance and turnover. *Personnel Psychology,* 1962, **15,** 43–56.

Fleishman, E. A., Harris, F. F., & Burtt, H. E.   Leadership and supervision in industry. Columbus: Ohio State University, Personnel Relations Board, 1955.

Fletcher, E. D.   *Capacity of special tests to measure driving ability.* State of California, Department of Motor Vehicles, 1949.

Forbes, J. W.   Auditory signals for instrument flying. *Journal of the Aeronautical Sciences,* 1946, **13,** 255–258.

Forehand, G. A., & Gilmer, B. V. H.   Environmental variation in studies of organizational behavior. *Psychological Bulletin,* 1964, **62,** 361–382.

Francel, E. G.   Mail-administered questionnaires: A success story. *Journal of Marketing Research,* 1966, **3,** 89–92.

Franzen, R., & Lazarsfeld, P. L.   Mail questionnaire as a research problem. *Journal of Psychology,* 1945, **20,** 293–310.

Fraser, D. C.   Recent experimental work in the study of fatigue. *Occupational Psychology,* 1958, **32,** 258–263.

Frederickson, N.   Consistency of performance in simulated situations. *Educational Testing Service Research Bulletin* 1961, 61–22.

Frederickson, N.   Factors in in-basket performance. *Psychological Monographs,* 1962, **76** (22, Whole No. 541).

Frederickson, N., Saunders, D. R., & Ward, B.   The in-basket test. *Psychological Monographs,* 1957, **71,** (9, Whole No. 438).

Freedman, J. L., Carlsmith, J. M., & Sears, D. O.   *Social psychology.* Englewood Cliffs, N.J.: Prentice-Hall, 1970.

French, J. R. P., Israel, J., & As, D.   An experiment on participation in a Norwegian factory: Interpersonal dimensions of decision making. *Human Relations,* 1960, **13,** 3–19.

Fried, J., Weitman, M., & Davis, M. K.   Man-machine interaction and absenteeism. *Journal of Applied Psychology,* 1972, **56,** 428–429.

Friedlander, F.   Motivation to work and organizational performance. *Journal of Applied Psychology,* 1966, **50,** 143–152.

Gadel, M. S., & Kriedt, P. H.   Relationships of aptitude, interest, performance, and job satisfaction of IBM operators. *Personnel Psychology,* 1952, **5,** 207–212.

Gassner, S., Gold, J., & Snadowsky, A. M.   Changes in the phenomenal field as a result of human relations training. *Journal of Psychology,* 1964, **58,** 33–41.

General Electric Company.   *Footcandles in Modern Lighting.* Technical Publication LS-119. Nela Park, Cleveland, 1960.

Ghiselli, E. E.   *The measurement of occupational attitude.* Berkeley: University of California Press, 1955.

Ghiselli, E. E.   Managerial talent. *American Psychologist,* 1963, **18,** 631–642. (b)

Ghiselli, E. E.   The validity of management traits related to occupational level. *Personnel Psychology,* 1963, **16,** 109–113.   (a)

Gibb, J. R.   The effects of group size and of threat reduction upon creativity in a problem-solving situation. *American Psychologist,* 1951, **6,** 324.

Giese, W. J., & Ruter, H. W.   An objective analysis of morale. *Journal of Applied Psychology,* 1949, **33,** 421–427.

Gilbreth, F. B.   *Brick laying system.* New York: Clark Publishing Company, 1911.

Gilbreth, F. B., & Gilbreth, L. M.   *Applied motion study.* New York: The Macmillan Co., 1917.

Glaser, R.   Some implications of previous work on learning and individual differences. In R. M. Gagne, (Ed.), *Learning and individual differences.* Columbus: Merrill, 1967.

Goldmark, J., Hopkins, M. D., Florence, P. S., & Lee, F. S.   Studies in industrial physiology: Fatigue in relation to working capacity. No. 1 (Comparison of an 8-hour plant and a 10-hour plant). *Public Health Bulletin No. 106,* U.S. Public Health Service, 1920.

Goldstein, L. G.   *Human variables in traffic accidents: A digest of research and selected bibliography.* Washington, D.C.: National Academy of Sciences, National Research Council, 1962.

Graen, G., Alvares, K. M., Orris, J. B., & Martella, J. A.   Contingency model of leadership effectiveness: Antecedent and evidential results. *Psychological Bulletin,* 1970, **74,** 285–296.

Graham, A.   Adman's nightmare: Is the prune a witch? *Reporter,* 1953, **12,** 27–31.

Grant, D. L.   Relevance of educational to organizational requirements. Proceedings of Western Regional Conference on Testing Problems. Educational Testing Service, 1970.

Greenberg, A., & Garfinkle, N. Delayed recall of magazine articles. *Journal of Advertising Research,* 1962, **3,** 28–31.

Gruenfeld, L. W. A study of motivation of industrial supervisors. *Personnel Psychology,* 1962, **15,** 303–314.

Guest, L. Brand loyalty—twelve years later. *Journal of Applied Psychology,* 1955, **39,** 405–408.

Guest, L. Status enhancement as a function of color in advertising. *Journal of Advertising Research,* 1966, **6,** 40–44.

Guest, R. H. *Organizational change: The effects of successful leadership.* Homewood, Ill.: Irwin, 1962.

Guetzkow, H., & Dill, W. R. Factors in the organizational development of task-oriented groups. *Sociometry,* 1957, **20,** 175–204.

Guetzkow, H., & Kriesberg, M. *Executive use of the administrative conference.* New York: American Management Association, 1950.

Guetzkow, H., & Simon, H. A. The impact of certain communication nets upon organization and performance in task-oriented groups. *Management Science,* 1955, **1,** 233–250.

Guidelines on Employee Selection Procedures. *Federal Register,* 1970, **35,** 12333–12336.

Guilford, J. P. The structure of intellect. *Psychological Bulletin,* 1956, **53,** 267–293.

Guion, R. M. Criterion measurement and personnel judgments. *Personnel Psychology,* 1961, **14,** 141–149.

Guion, R. M. Employment tests and discriminatory hiring. *Industrial Relations,* 1966, **5,** 26.

Guion, R. M. Personnel selection. *Annual Review of Psychology,* 1967, **18,** 105–216.

Haire, M. Projective techniques in market research. *Journal of Marketing,* 1950, **14,** 649.

Haire, M., & Gottsdanker, J. S. Factors influencing industrial morale. *Personnel,* 1951, **27,** 445–454.

Hakel, M. D., & Dunnette, M. D. Interpersonal perception in the employment interview. *Industrial Psychology,* 1968, **5,** 30–38.

Hakel, M., Ohnesorge, J. P., & Dunnette, M. D. Interviewer evaluations of job applicants resumés as a function of the qualifications of the immediately preceding applicants. *Journal of Applied Psychology,* 1970, **54,** 27–30.

Halpin, A. W. The leader behavior and effectiveness of aircraft commanders. In R. M. Stogdell and A. E. Coons (Eds.), *Leader behavior: Its description and measurement.* Columbus: Ohio State University, Bureau of Business Research, Research Monograph No. 88, 1957.

Harmon, F. L.   The effects of noise upon certain psychological and physiological processes. *Archives of Psychology,* 1933, **23,** No. 147.

Haskins, J. B.   Factual recall as a measure of advertising effectiveness. *Journal of Advertising Research,* 1964, **4,** 2–8.

Hayes, J. R.   *Human data processing limits in decision making.* ESD–TDR–62–48. Bedford, Mass.: USAF Electronic Systems Division, 1962.

Hedberg, R., Steffan, H., & Baxter, B.   Insurance fundamentals—a programmed text versus a conventional text. *Personnel Psychology,* 1965, **18,** 165–171.

Hemphill, J. K.   *Dimensions of executive positions.* Columbus: Ohio State University, 1960.

Henry, E. R. (Chm.)   Research conference on the use of autobiographical data as psychological predictors. Greensboro, N.C.: The Richardson Foundation, 1965.

Hersey, R. B.   Emotional factors in accidents. *Personnel Journal,* 1936, **15,** 59–65.

Hersey, R.   Psychology of workers. *Personnel Journal,* 1936, **14,** 291–296.

Herzberg, F.   *Work and the nature of man.* Cleveland: World, 1966.

Herzberg, F.   One more time: How do you motivate employees? *Harvard Business Review,* 1968, **46,** 53–62.

Herzberg, F., Mausner, B., Peterson, R. O., & Capwell, D. F.   *Job attitudes: Review of research and opinion.* Pittsburgh: Psychological Service of Pittsburgh, 1957.

Herzberg, F., Mausner, B., & Snyderman, B. B.   *The motivation to work.* New York: Wiley, 1959.

Heslin, R.   Predicting group task effectiveness from member characteristics. *Psychological Bulletin,* 1964, **62,** 248–256.

Hess, E. H., & Polt, J. M.   Pupil size as related to interest value of visual stimuli. *Science,* 1960, **132,** 349–350.

Hick, W. E.   On the rate of gain of information. *Journal of Experimental Psychology,* 1952, **4,** 11–26.

Hickey, A. E.   Programmed instruction in business and industry. In S. Margulies and L. D. Eigen (Eds.), *Applied programmed instruction.* New York: Wiley, 1961.

Hinrichs, J. R.   Technical selection: How to improve your batting average. *Personnel,* 1960, **37,** 56–60.

Hinrichs, J. R.   Comparisons of "real life" assessments of management potential with situational exercises, paper and pencil ability tests, and personality inventories. *Journal of Applied Psychology,* 1969, **53,** 425–432.

Hinrichs, J. R.   Psychology of men at work. *Annual Review of Psychology,* 1970, **21,** 519–554.

Hodgson, J. D., & Brenner, M. H.   Successful experience: Training hard core unemployed. *Harvard Business Review,* 1968, **46,** 148–156.

Hollingworth, H. L.   *Vocational psychology and character analysis.* New York: D. Appleton & Co., 1923. Pp. 115–119.

Homans, G. C.   *The human group.* New York: Harcourt, Brace & World, 1950.

Hood, P. D., Halpin, A. W., Hanitchak, J. J., Siegel, L., & Hemphill, J. K. Crew member agreement on RB–47 crew operating procedure. Research Report AFPTRC–TN–57–64, ASTIA Document No. 126395. Lackland Air Force Base, Tex.: Air Force Personnel and Training Research Center, 1957.

Hoppock, R.   *Job satisfaction.* New York: Harper & Row, 1935.

Hoppock, R.   Age and job satisfaction. *Psychological Monographs,* 1936, **47,** No. 212.

Hovland, C. I., & Wonderlic, E. F.   Prediction of success from a standardized interview. *Journal of Applied Psychology,* 1939, **33,** 537–546.

Hueting, J. E., & Sarphati, H. R.   Measuring fatigue. *Journal of Applied Psychology,* 1966, **50,** 535–538.

Hulin, C. L.   Job satisfaction and turnover in a female clerical population. *Journal of Applied Psychology,* 1966, **50,** 280–285.

Hulin, C. L., & Blood, M. R.   Job enlargement, individual differences, and worker responses. *Psychological Bulletin,* 1968, **69,** 41–55.

Hull, R. L., & Kolstad, A.   Morale on the job. In W. Goodwin (Ed.), *Civilian Morale.* New York: Reynal & Hitchcock, 1942.

Hummel, C. F., & Schmeidler, G. R.   Driver behavior at dangerous intersections marked by stop signs or by red blinker lights. *Journal of Applied Psychology,* 1955, **39,** 17–19.

Jacques, E.   *The changing culture of a factory.* London: Tavistock, 1951.

Jenkins, W. O.   Tactual discrimination of shapes for coding aircraft-type controls. In P. M. Fitts, *Psychological research on equipment design.* Washington, D.C.: U.S. Government Printing Office, 1947.

Jerison, H. J.   Effects of noise on human performance. *Journal of Applied Psychology,* 1959, **42,** 96–101.

Jones, E. H., & Sumner, F. C.   Relation of brightness differences of colors to their apparent distances. *Journal of Applied Psychology,* 1948, **26,** 25–29.

Jurgensen, C. E.   Report to participants on adjective word sort. Unpublished report, Minneapolis Gas Company, 1966.

Kahn, R. L., & Katz, D. Leadership practices in relation to productivity and morale. In D. Cartwright and A. Zander (Eds.), *Group dynamics.* Evanston, Ill.: Row & Peterson, 1953.

Kalant, H. Marijuana and simulated driving. *Science,* 1969, **166,** 640.

Katona, G., Mueller, E., Schmiedeskamp, J., & Sonquist, J. A. *1966 survey of consumer finances.* Ann Arbor: Survey Research Center, Monograph No. 44, 1967.

Katzell, R. A., Barrett, R. S., Vann, D. H., & Hogan, J. M. Organizational correlates of executive roles. *Journal of Applied Psychology,* 1968, **52,** 22–28.

Kay, E., & Meyer, H. H. The development of a job activity questionnaire for production foremen. *Personnel Psychology,* 1962, **15,** 411–418.

Kelley, T. L. The selection of upper and lower groups for the validation of test items. *Journal of Educational Psychology,* 1939, **30,** 17–24.

Kerr, W. A. Experiments on the effects of music on factory production. *Applied Psychology Monograph,* No. 5., 1945.

Kerr, W. A. Accident proneness of factory departments. *Journal of Applied Psychology,* 1950, **34,** 167–170.

Kerr, W. A. Complementary theories of safety psychology. *Journal of Social Psychology,* 1957, **45,** 3–9.

Kirchner, W. K., & Dunnette, M. D. Identifying the critical factors in salesmanship. *Personnel,* 1957, **34,** 54–59.

Kirkpatrick, J. J., Ewen, R. B., Barrett, R. S., & Katzell, R. A. *Testing and fair employment.* New York University Press, 1968.

Knauft, E. B. Construction and use of weighted check-list rating scales for two industrial situations. *Journal of Applied Psychology,* 1948, **32,** 63–70.

Knight, H. C. A comparison of the reliability of group and individual judgments. Unpublished master's thesis, Columbia University, 1921.

Kogan, N., & Wallach, M. A. Risk taking as a function of the situation, the person, and the group. In G. Mandler, P. Mussen, N. Kogan, & M. A. Wallach (Eds.), *New directions in psychology.* Vol. 3. New York: Holt, Rinehart, & Winston, 1967.

Koponen, A. Personality characteristics of purchasers. *Journal of Advertising Research,* 1960, **1,** 6–12.

Kornhauser, A. *Mental health of the industrial worker.* New York: Wiley, 1965.

Krug, R. E. Some suggested approaches for test development and measurement. *Personnel Psychology,* 1966, **19,** 24–34.

Krugman, H. E. Some applications of pupil measurement. *Journal of Marketing Research,* 1964, **1,** 15–19.

Kuder, G. F. *The preference record.* Chicago: Science Research Associates, 1953.

Kunce, J. T. Vocational interests and accident proneness. *Journal of Applied Psychology,* 1967, **51,** 223–225.

Landry, F. J., & Bates, F. Another look at contrast effects in the employment interview. *Journal of Applied Psychology,* 1973, **58,** 141–144.

Lane, I. M., & Messé, L. A. The distribution of insufficient, sufficient, and over-sufficient rewards: A clarification of equity theory. *Journal of Personality and Social Psychology,* 1972, **21,** 228–233.

Langdale, J. A., & Weitz, J. Estimating the influence of job information on interviewer agreement. *Journal of Applied Psychology,* 1973, **57,** 23–27.

Lawler, E. E. Pay and organizational effectiveness: A psychological view. New York: McGraw-Hill, 1971.

Lawrence, P. The changing of organizational behavior patterns. Boston: Division of Research, Harvard University, 1958.

Lawshe, C. H., Bolda, R. A., Brune, R. L., & Auclair, G. Expectancy charts III: Their theoretical development. *Personnel Psychology,* 1958, **11,** 545–599.

Lawshe, C. H., Jr. Training operative personnel. *Journal of Consulting Psychology,* 1944, **8,** 154–159.

Lawshe, C. H., Jr., Kephart, N. C., & McCormick, E. J. The paired comparisons technique for rating performance of industrial employees. *Journal of Applied Psychology,* 1949, **33,** 69–77.

Leavitt, H. J. Some effects of certain patterns on group performance. *Journal of Abnormal and Social Psychology,* 1951, **46,** 38–50.

Lesieur, F. (Ed.) *The Scanlon plan.* New York: Wiley, 1958.

Lesieur, F., & Puckett, E. S. The Scanlon plan has proved itself. *Harvard Business Review,* 1969, **47,** 109–118.

Lewin, K., Lippitt, R., & White, R. K. Patterns of aggressive behavior in experimentally created social climates. *Journal of Social Psychology,* 1939, **10,** 271–301.

Likert, R. *New patterns of management.* New York: McGraw-Hill, 1961c. Used with permission of McGraw-Hill Book Company.

Likert, R. *The human organization.* New York: McGraw-Hill, 1967c. Used with permission of McGraw-Hill Book Company.

Likert, R. Measuring organizational performance. *Harvard Business Review,* 1968, **36,** 41–50.

Link, H. C. *Employment psychology.* New York: The Macmillan Co., 1920.

Lippitt, R.   An experimental study of the effect of democratic and authoritarian group atmospheres. *University of Iowa Studies,* 1940, **16,** 43–198.

Lippitt, R., Watson, J., & Westley, B.   *The dynamics of planned change.* New York: Harcourt, Brace & World, 1958.

Locke, E. A.   The motivational effect of knowledge of results: Knowledge or goal setting? *Journal of Applied Psychology,* 1967, **51,** 324–329.

Locke, E. A., & Bryan, J. F.   *Goals and intentions as determinants of performance, task choice and attitudes.* Washington, D.C.: American Institute for Research, 1967. (a)

Locke, E. A., & Bryan, J. F.   Performance goals as determinants of level of performance and boredom. *Journal of Applied Psychology,* 1967, **51,** 120–130. (b)

Lopez, F. M.   *The making of a manager.* New York: American Management Association, 1970.

Lorge, I.   The influence of the test upon the nature of mental decline as a function of age. *Journal of Educational Psychology,* 1936, **27,** 100–110.

Lorge, I. D., Fox, D., Davitz, J., & Brenner, M.   A survey of studies contrasting the quality of group performance and individual performance, 1920–1957. *Psychological Bulletin,* 1958, **55,** 337–372.

Lucas, E. B., & Murphy, M. J.   Faults of identification of advertisements in recognition tests. *Journal of Applied Psychology,* 1939, **23,** 264–269.

Mackinney, A. C., & Dunnette, M. D.   The industrial psychologist's job. *Personnel Psychology,* 1964, **17,** 271–280.

Madden, J. M., & Bourdon, R. D.   Effects of variation in rating scale format on judgment. *Journal of Applied Psychology,* 1964, **48,** 147–151.

Maier, N. R. F., & Zerfoss, L. F.   MRP: A technique for training large groups of supervisors and its potential use in social research. *Human Relations,* 1952, **5,** 177–186.

Malo, A. H.   New light on the accident prone. *Personnel,* 1954, **31,** 65.

Mann, F. C., & Hoffman, L. R.   *Automation and the worker: A study of social change in power plants.* New York: Holt, Rinehart & Winston, 1960.

Mann, F. C., Indik, B. P., & Vroom, V. H.   *The productivity of work groups.* Ann Arbor, Mich.: Institute for Social Research, Survey Research Center, 1963.

Mann, R. D.   A review of the relationships between personality and performance in small groups. *Psychological Bulletin,* 1959, **56,** 241–270.

Marquis, D. G.   Industrial responsibility and group decisions involving risk. *Industrial Management Review,* 1962, **3,** 8–23.

Marrow, A., Bowers, D. G., & Seashore, S. E. *Management by participation.* New York: Harper & Row, 1967.

Maslow, A. H. A theory of human motivation. *Psychological Review,* 1943, **50,** 370–396.

Maslow, A. H. *Motivation and personality.* New York: Harper & Row, 1954.

Matthews, J. *Research in the development of valid situational tests, I, survey of the literature.* Pittsburgh: American Institute for Research, 1951.

Mayfield, E. C. The selection interview—a re-evaluation of published research. *Personnel Psychology,* 1964, **17,** 239–260.

McGehee, W. Are we using what we know about training?—Learning theory and training. *Personnel Psychology,* 1958, **11,** 1–12.

McGehee, W., & Owen, E. B. Authorized and unauthorized rest pauses in clerical work. *Journal of Applied Psychology,* 1940, **24,** 604–613.

McGrath, J. E., & Altman, J. E. *Small group research.* New York: Holt, Rinehart & Winston, 1966.

McGregor, D. *The human side of enterprise.* New York: McGraw-Hill, 1960c. Used with permission of McGraw-Hill Book Company.

McLarney, W. J. *Management training: Cases and principles.* Homewood, Ill.: Irwin, 1959.

McMurry, R. N. Validating the patterned interview. *Personnel,* 1947, **23,** 270–271.

McNamara, W. J. Retraining of industrial personnel. *Personnel Psychology,* 1963, **16,** 233–247.

Meissner, F. Sales and advertising of lettuce. *Journal of Advertising Research,* 1961, **1,** 1–10.

Metropolitan Life Insurance Company. *The accident prone employee.* New York, 1930.

Metropolitan Life Insurance Company. *Preventing taxicab accidents.* New York, 1931.

Meyer, H. H. Factors related to success in the human relations aspect of work group leadership. *Psychological Monograph,* 1951, **65,** 1–29.

Milton, O., & West, L. J. *Programmed instruction: What it is and how it works.* New York: Harcourt, Brace & World, 1961.

Minnesota Paper Formboard. (Rev. ed.) New York: The Psychological Corporation, 1941.

Mintz, A., & Blum, M. L. A reexamination of the accident proneness concept. *Journal of Applied Psychology,* 1949, **33,** 196.

Morgan, C. T., Cook, J. S., III, Chapanis, A., & Lund, M. W. *Human engineering guide to equipment design.* New York: McGraw-Hill, 1963. P. 125. Used with permission of McGraw-Hill Book Company.

Morse, N. C.   *Satisfactions in the white collar job.* Ann Arbor, Mich.: Institute for Social Research, University of Michigan,. 1953.

Morse, N. C., & Reimer, E.   The experimental change of a major organizational variable. *Journal of Abnormal and Social Psychology,* 1956, **52,** 120–129.

Morsh, J. E.   Job analysis in the United States Air Force. *Personnel Psychology,* 1962, **37,** 7–17.

Mossin, A. C.   *Selling performance and contentment in relation to school background.* New York: Bureau of Publications, Teachers College, Columbia University, 1949.

Munsterberg, H.   *Psychology and industrial efficiency.* Boston: Houghton Mifflin, 1913.

National Industrial Conference Board.   *Factors affecting employee morale.* Studies in personnel policy, No. 85, 1947.

National Safety Council.   *Accident facts.* Chicago, 1946. P. 17.

Naylor, J. C., & Briggs, G. E.   The effect of task complexity and task organization on the relative efficiency of part and whole training methods. *Journal of Experimental Psychology,* 1963, **65,** 217–224.

Newman, R. I., Jr., Hunt, D. L., & Rhodes, F.   Effects of music on employee attitudes and productivity in a skateboard factory. *Journal of Applied Psychology,* 1966, **50,** 493–496

Nord, W. R., & Costigan, R.   Worker adjustment to the four-day week: A longitudinal study. *Journal of Applied Psychology,* 1973, **58,** 60–66.

Osborn, H. F.   *Applied imagination.* New York: Scribners, 1957.

Otis, A. S.   *Manuals: Gamma, alpha, beta.* New York: Harcourt, Brace & World, 1937, 1939.

Patten, T. H., Jr., & Clark, G., Jr.   Literacy training and job placement of hard core unemployed Negroes in Detroit. *Journal of Human Research,* 1968, **3,** 25–46.

Patterson, W. D.   The power of significant involvement. *Saturday Review,* 1961, **44,** 41–46.

Pearlin, L. I., & Rosenberg, M.   Propaganda techniques in institutional advertising. *Public Opinion Quarterly,* 1952, **16,** 5–26.

Pederson, C. A., & Wright, M. D.   *Salesmanship: Principles and methods.* Homewood, Ill.: Irwin, 1961. Pp. 45–46.

Peres, H.   Performance dimensions of supervisory positions. *Personnel Psychology,* 1962, **15,** 405–410.

Perloff, R.   Consumer analysis. *Annual Review of Psychology,* 1968, **19,** 451.

Pervin, L. A.   Performance and satisfaction as a function of individual environment fit. *Psychological Bulletin,* 1968, **69,** 56–68.

Piper, K.   Motorola's vision program pays off. *Advanced Management,* 1951, **16,** 24–25.

Poffenberger, A. T.   Effects of continuous work on output and feelings. *Journal of Applied Psychology,* 1928, **12,** 459–467.

Poulton, E. C.   Engineering psychology. *Annual Review of Psychology,* 1966, **17,** 184.

Pressey, S. L.   A simple apparatus which gives tests and scores—and teaches. *School and Society,* 1926, **13,** 373–376.

Pronko, N. H., & Bowles, J. W., Jr.   Identification of cola beverages, I. *Journal of Applied Psychology,* 1948, **32,** 304–312. (a)

Pronko, N. H., & Bowles, J. W., Jr.   Identification of cola beverages, II. *Journal of Applied Psychology,* 1948, **32,** 559–564. (b)

Pronko, N. H., & Bowles, J. W., Jr.   Identification of cola beverages, III. *Journal of Applied Psychology,* 1949, **33,** 605–608.

Pruitt, D. G.   Choice shifts in group discussions: An introductory review. *Journal of Personality and Social Psychology,* 1971, **20,** 339–360.

Richardson, M. W., & Kuder, G. F.   Making a rating scale that measures. *Personnel Journal,* 1933, **12,** 36–40

Roby, T. B., Nicol, E. H., & Farrell, F. M.   Group problem solving under two types of executive structure. *Journal of Abnormal and Social Psychology,* 1963, **67,** 530–556.

Roethlisberger, F. W., & Dickson, W. J.   *Management and the worker.* Cambridge, Mass.: Harvard University Press, 1939.

Ronan, W. W., & Prien, E. P.   Towards a criterion theory: A review and analysis of research and opinion. Greensboro, N.C.: The Richardson Foundation, 1966.

Rosen, N. A.   How supervise?—1943–1960. *Personnel Psychology,* 1961, **14,** 87–100.

Rosen, N. A., Williams, L. K., & Foltman, F. F.   Motivational constraints in an industrial retraining program. *Personnel Psychology,* 1965, **18,** 65–79.

Ross, I. C., & Zander, A. F.   Need satisfaction and employee turnover. *Personnel Psychology,* 1957, **10,** 327–338.

Schacter, S.   Deviation, rejection, and communication. *Journal of Abnormal and Social Psychology,* 1951, **46,** 190–207.

Schein, E. H., & Bennis, W. G.   *Personal and organizational changes through group methods: The laboratory approach.* New York: Wiley, 1965.

Schuh, A. J.   The predictability of employee tenure: A review of the literature. *Personnel Psychology,* 1967, **20,** 133–152.

Schwab, D. P., & Cummings, L. L.   Theories of performance and satisfaction: A review. *Industrial Relations,* 1970, **9,** 408–430.

Scollay, R. W.   Personal history data as a predictor of success. *Personnel Psychology,* 1957, **10,** 23–26.

Seashore, H. G.   Women are more predictable than men. Presidential address, Div. 17, American Psychological Association, 1961.

Seashore, S. E.   *Group cohesiveness in the industrial work group.* Ann Arbor, Mich.: Institute for Social Research, 1954.

Selzer, M. L.   Alcoholism, mental illness, and stress in 96 drivers causing fatal accidents. *Behavioral Science,* 1969, **14,** 1–10.

Sharon, A., & Bartlett, C. J.   Effect of instructional conditions in producing leniency on two types of rating scales. *Personnel Psychology,* 1969, **22,** 251–263.

Shaw, M. E.   Comparison of individuals and small groups in the rational solution of complex problems. *American Journal of Psychology,* 1932, **44,** 491–504.

Shaw, M. E., & Blum, J. M.   Effects of leadership style upon group performance as a function of task structure. *Journal of Personality and Social Psychology,* 1966, **3,** 238–242.

Sherif, M.   *The psychology of social norms.* New York: Harper & Bros., 1936.

Siegel, L.   A biographical inventory for students. *Journal of Applied Psychology,* 1956, **40,** 5–10.

Siegel, L., & Siegel, L. C.   A multivariate paradigm for educational research. *Psychological Bulletin,* 1967, **68,** 306–326.

Skinner, B. F.   The science of learning and the art of teaching. *Harvard Educational Review,* 1954, **24,** 86–97.

Smith, H. C.   Music in relation to employee attitudes, work production and industrial accidents. *Applied Psychology Monographs,* No. 14, 1947.

Smith, P. C.   The curve of output as a criterion of boredom. *Journal of Applied Psychology,* 1953, **37,** 69–74.

Smith, P. C.   The prediction of individual differences in susceptibility to industrial monotony. *Journal of Applied Psychology,* 1955, **39,** 322–329.

Snow, C. E.   A discussion of the relation of illumination intensity to production efficiency. *Technical Engineering News,* November 1927.

Stagner, R.   Attitudes of corporate executives regarding psychological methods in personnel work. *American Psychologist,* 1946, **1,** 540–541.

Stagner, R. Psychological aspects of industrial conflict II: Motivation. *Personnel Psychology,* 1950, **3,** 1–16.

Stagner, R. The gullibility of personnel managers. *Personnel Psychology,* 1958, **11,** 347–352.

Stanton, E. S. Company policies and supervisors' attitudes toward supervision. *Journal of Applied Psychology,* 1960, **44,** 22–26.

Stauffer, L. Color punches the time clock. *The Management Review,* 1947, **36,** 452. (After *Popular Science,* June 1947, 124–126.)

Stead, W. H., & Shartle, C. L. *Occupational counseling techniques.* New York: American Book Co., 1940.

Steele, J. L., & Poor, R. Work and leisure: The reactions of people at 4-day firms. In R. Poor (Ed.), *4 days, 40 hours.* Cambridge, Mass.: Burk & Poor, 1970.

Stewart, J. B. *Repetitive advertising in newspapers.* Boston: Harvard Business School, 1964.

Stewart, R. *Managers and their jobs: A study of the similarities and differences in the ways managers spend their time.* London: The Macmillan Co., 1967.

Stockbridge, H. C. W., & Chambers, B. Aiming, transfer of training, and knowledge of results. *Journal of Applied Psychology,* 1958, **42,** 148–153.

Strong, E. K. *Vocational interest inventory.* Stanford, Calif.: Stanford University Press, 1951.

Sudman, S. New uses of telephone methods in survey research. *Journal of Marketing Research,* 1966, **1,** 163–167.

Tannenbaum, P., & Schmidt, W. H. How to choose a leadership pattern. *Harvard Business Review,* 1958, **36,** 95–101.

Tannenbaum, R., Weschler, I. R., & Massarik, F. *Leadership and organization: A behavioral science approach.* New York: McGraw-Hill, 1961. Used with permission of McGraw-Hill Book Company.

Taylor, D. W., Berry, P. C., & Block, C. H. Does group participation when using brainstorming facilitate or inhibit creative thinking? *Administrative Science Quarterly,* 1958, **3,** 23–47.

Taylor, F. W. *The principles of scientific management.* New York: Harper & Bros., 1911.

Taylor, F. W. Psychology and the design of machines. *American Psychologist,* 1957, **12,** 249–256.

Taylor, H. C., & Russell, J. T. The relationship of validity coefficients to the practical effectiveness of tests in selection: Discussion and tables. *Journal of Applied Psychology,* 1939, **23,** 567–578.

Thurstone, L. L. *Primary mental abilities.* Chicago: University of Chicago Press, 1938.

Thurstone, L. L., & Chave, E. J. *The measurement of attitude.* Chicago: University of Chicago Press, 1929.

Tiffin, J., & McCormick, E. J. *Industrial psychology.* Englewood Cliffs, N.J.: Prentice-Hall, 1965. P. 256.

Tinker, M. A. Illumination standards for effective and easy seeing. *Psychological Bulletin,* 1947, **44,** 435–450.

Triandis, H. C. A critique and experimental design for the study of the relationship between productivity and job satisfaction. *Psychological Bulletin,* 1959, **56,** 309–312.

Trist, E. L., & Bamforth, K. W. Some social and psychological consequences of the long wall method of coal getting. *Human Relations,* 1951, **4,** 3–38.

Tucker, W. T., & Painter, J. J. Personality and product use. *Journal of Applied Psychology,* 1961, **45,** 325–329.

Twedt, D. W. Consumer psychology. *Annual Review of Psychology,* 1965, **16,** 277–278.

Uhrbrock, R. S. Music on the job: Its influence on worker morale and production. *Personnel Psychology,* 1961, **14,** 9–38. (a)

Uhrbrock, R. S. 2000 scaled items. *Personnel Psychology,* 1961, **14,** 375–420. (b)

United States Department of Labor, Bureau of Apprenticeship. *Apprenticeship past and present.* Washington, D.C.: U.S. Government Printing Office, 1952.

United States Employment Service. *Dictionary of occupational titles.* Vol. I. *Definition of titles.* Vol. II. *Occupational classification and industry index.* (3d ed.) Washington, D.C.: U.S. Government Printing Office, 1965.

United States Employment Service, Department of Labor. *Training and reference manual for job analysis.* Washington, D.C.: U.S. Government Printing Office, 1944. P. 57.

Utgaard, S. B., & Davis, R. V. The most frequently used training techniques. *Training Development Journal,* 1970, **24,** 40–43.

Valenzi, E., & Andrews, I. R. Individual differences in the decision process of employment interviewers. *Journal of Applied Psychology,* 1973, **58,** 49–53.

Vernon, H. M. *Accidents and their prevention.* Cambridge, Eng.: The University Press, 1936. P. 80.

Vicary, J. M. Memo from Subliminal Projection Co., Inc., to the Federal Communications Commission, January 13, 1958. Cited in R. Wilhelm,

Are subliminal commercials bad? *Michigan Business Review,* 1958, **26.**

Vroom, V. H. Some personality determinants of the effects of participation. *Journal of Abnormal and Social Psychology,* 1959, **59,** 322–327.

Vroom, V. H. *Work and motivation.* New York: Wiley, 1964.

Vroom, V. H., & Mann, F. C. Leader authoritarianism and employee attitudes. *Personnel Psychology,* 1960, **13,** 125–140.

Wanous, J. P., & Lawler, E. E. Measurement and meaning of job satisfaction. *Journal of Applied Psychology,* 1972, **56,** 95–105.

Warner, L., & Franzen, R. Value of color in advertising. *Journal of Applied Psychology,* 1947, **31,** 260–270.

Webster, E. C. Factors pertaining to decision making in the personnel interview. Final Report, Canadian Defense Research Board Grant 9435–9453, 1962.

Wechsler, D. *Wechsler adult intelligence scale.* New York: Psychological Corporation, 1955.

Weick, K. E. The concept of equity in the perception of pay. *Administrative Science Quarterly,* 1966, **11,** 414–439.

Weitz, J. Job expectancy and survival. *Journal of Applied Psychology,* 1956, **40,** 245–247.

Weitz, J. Criteria for criteria. *American Psychologist,* 1961, **16,** 228–231.

Weitz, J., & Nuckols, R. C. Job satisfaction and job survival. *Journal of Applied Psychology,* 1955, **39,** 294–300.

Wells, W. D., Andriuli, F. J., Goi, F. J., & Seader, S. An adjective checklist for the study of product personality. *Journal of Applied Psychology,* 1957, **41,** 317–319.

Wells, W. D., Goi, F. J., & Seader, S. A change in product image. *Journal of Applied Psychology,* 1958, **42,** 120–121.

Welsh, P., Antoinetti, J. A., & Thayer, P. W. An industrywide study of programmed instruction. *Journal of Applied Psychology,* 1965, **49,** 61–73.

Wexley, K., Yukl, G., Kovacs, S., & Sanders, R. Importance of contrast effects in employment interviews. *Journal of Applied Psychology,* 1972, **56,** 45–48.

Wherry, R. J. Criteria and validity. In D. H. Fryer & E. R. Henry (Eds.), *Handbook of applied psychology.* New York: Holt, Rinehart & Winston, 1950. Chap. 27.

White, R. K., & Lippitt, R. Leader behavior and member reaction in three "social climates." In D. Cartwright & A. Zander (Eds.), *Group dynamics.* Evanston. Ill.: Row & Peterson, 1960.

Wilkinson, R. T.   Artificial "signals" as an aid to an inspection task. *Ergonomics,* 1964, **7,** 63–72.

Witkin, A. A.   Differential interest patterns in salesmen. *Journal of Applied Psychology,* 1956, **40,** 338–340.

Wonderlic, E. F.   *Personnel test.* Northfield, Ill., 1945.

Woodson, W. E.   *Human engineering guide for equipment designers.* Berkeley, Calif.: University of California Press, 1954.

Worthy, J. C.   Organizational structure and employee morale. *American Sociological Review,* 1950, **15,** 169–179.

Wright, C. R.   Summary of research on the selection interview since 1964. *Personnel Psychology,* 1969, **22,** 391–413.

Wyatt, S., Langdon, J. N., & Stock, F. G. L.   Fatigue and boredom in repetitive work. *Industrial Health Research Board, Great Britain, Report No. 77,* 1937.

Yonge, K. A.   The value of the interview: An orientation and a pilot study. *Journal of Applied Psychology,* 1956, **40,** 25–31.

Zavala, A.   Development of the forced-choice rating scale technique. *Psychological Bulletin,* 1965, **63,** 117–124.

Indexes

Name Index

Subject Index

A

A. C. Nielson Company, 461
A-I-D-A selling formula, 464
Absenteeism, 71
Accident proneness, 253–56
Accidents
  automobile, 258–60
  causes of
    adjustment-stress hypothesis, 256
    equipment design, 244
    fatigue, 249–51
    goals-freedom-alertness hypothesis,
      256
    illumination, 243–44
    personal adjustment, 251–52
    personal characteristics, 245–51
    work environment, 242–44
  prevention of
    eliminating unsafe practices, 257–58
    personnel selection, 258
    training, 258–62
Achievement tests; see Tests
Adjustment
  and accident frequency, 251–52
  and job satisfaction, 409–10
Advertising
  objectives of, 453–55
  subliminal, 461–62
Advertising copy, 457–60
Advertising medium, 460–61
Advertising message, 455–57
  accidents and, 246–49
  job satisfaction and, 408–9
Alcohol and accidents, 251
Ambiguity
  in questionnaires, 77
  in rating scales, 81
American Board of Professional Psychol-
  ogy, 22
American Psychological Association
  Division of Industrial Psychology, 21–22
  membership in, 21
  purpose of, 21
Apparent movement, 458

B

Application blanks
  rationale, 143
  weighted, 143–45
Aptitude; see Tests
Assessment centers, 345–46
Attitudes
  and accidents, 251 ff.
  and advertising; see Advertising mes-
    sage
  assessing
    by indirect methods; see Motivation
      research
    by scaling, 77–78
Authoritarian leadership; see Leadership,
  authoritarian versus democratic
Automation; see Retraining

B

Behavioral tests
  in consumer research, 445–46
  of leadership, 345–46
Bias
  in interviewing; see Employment inter-
    view, distortions caused, by bias
  in performance rating, 81–82
  sample, 442
Biographical Information Blank, 146–47
Blanks, application, 143–47
Boredom
  alleviation of, 222–25
  factors contributing to
    intelligence, 220–21
    interests, 221
    personality, 221–22
  nature of, 209
Brainstorming, 378–80
Brand, identification and preferences,
  450–51

C

California Prune Advisory Board, 444
Case study, 355–57
Causality, 53; see also Correlation, and
  causality

549

This book has been set in 11 and 10 point Baskerville, leaded 2 points. Part and chapter numbers are in 66 point Weiss Series I; part and chapter titles are in 24 point Goudy Handtooled. The size of the type page is 27 by 45 picas.